AUSTIN-HEALEY
SPRITE Mark I

Workshop Manual

NOTE
Refer to the Section Contents page for the latest instructions when carrying out work on the vehicle.
Additional copies of this publication can only be obtained from an Austin Distributor.
Part No. AKD 4884 should be quoted.

B.M.C. SERVICE LIMITED
Proprietors: The British Motor Corporation Limited
COWLEY, OXFORD, ENGLAND

Telephone: Oxford 77777
Telegrams: BMCSERV, Telex, Oxford
Telex: BMCSERV, Oxford 83145 and 83146
Overseas Cables: BMCSERV, Telex, Oxford, England

Austin-Healey Sprite Mk.I. Issue 6

AUSTIN-HEALEY SPRITE

Introduction

THIS Manual has been compiled for the purpose of assisting Austin Distributors and Dealers to service and maintain the Austin-Healey Sprite Mk.1.

Each assembly of the major components is described in detail. In addition, instructions are given for dismantling, assembling and adjusting these assemblies. Use of the correct Service Tools contributes to an efficient, economic and profitable repair. References have, therefore, been made to such tools throughout the Manual.

When ordering spares it is imperative that operators use the 'Service Parts List' of the appropriate model and not the Manual. It is emphasised that only B.M.C. Genuine Parts should be used as replacements for components found unfit for further service.

AUSTIN-HEALEY SPRITE

CONTENTS

Introduction

General Data

General Information

Maintenance Attention

Engine	Section A
Ignition	,, B
Cooling System	,, C
Fuel System	,, D
Clutch	,, E
Gearbox	,, F
Propeller Shaft	,, G
Rear Axle and Suspension	,, H
Steering	,, J
Front Suspension and Front Hubs	,, K
Brakes	,, L
Electrical System	,, M
Wheels and Tyres	,, N
Bodywork	,, O
Lubrication	,, P
Lubrication Chart	End of Manual

AUSTIN-HEALEY SPRITE

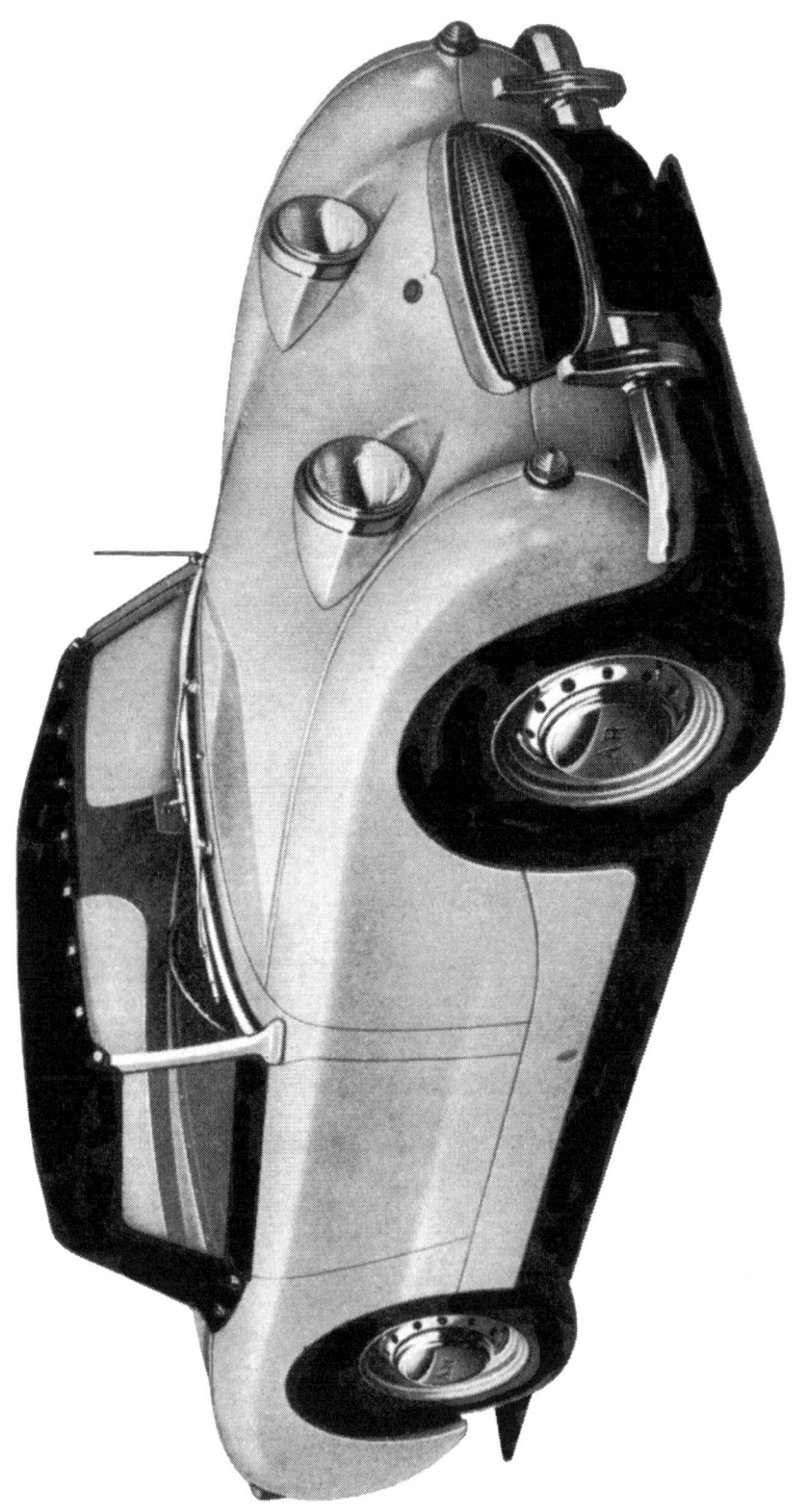

THE AUSTIN-HEALEY SPRITE Mk. 1.

GENERAL DATA

ENGINE

Number of cylinders	Four
Capacity	57·87 cu. ins. (948 cc.)
Weight	245 lbs. (111 kg.)
Torque	52 lbs./ft. at 3,300 r.p.m
Bore	2·478 in. (62·9 mm.)
Stroke	3·00 in. (76·2 mm.)
Compression ratio	8·3 : 1
First oversize bore	·010 in. (·254 mm.)
Second oversize bore	·020 in. (·508 mm.)
Third oversize bore	·030 in. (·762 mm.)
Fourth oversize bore	·040 in. (1·016 mm.)
Firing order	1, 3, 4, 2
Piston type	Aluminium split skirt
Piston clearance at skirt	·001 in. (·025 mm.) to ·0016 in. (·04 mm.)
Piston ring clearance in groove	·0015 in. (·038 mm.) to ·0035 in. (·089 mm.)
Piston ring gap (fitted)	·007 in. (·178 mm.) to ·012 in. (·30 mm.)
Piston rings:	
1st ring (Top)	Plain compression
2nd ring	Taper compression
3rd ring	Taper compression
4th ring (Oil control ring)	Slotted scraper
Width of plain and taper	·069 in. (1·753 mm.) to ·070 in. (1·778 mm.)
Width of oil control ring	·124 (3·15 mm.) to ·125 (3·175 mm.)
Oil capacity, sump	6 pints approx. (fill to dipstick) + 1 pint for filter if changed.
Oil pressure (normal) running	30 to 60 lb./sq. in. (2·1 to 4·22 kg./cm.^{2})
Oil pressure (normal) idling	10 to 25 lb./sq. in. (0·7 to 1·7 kg./cm.^{2})
Oil filter	Full-flow type with renewable element
Gudgeon pin type	Clamped in con. rod
Gudgeon pin diameter	·6244 in. (15·860 mm.) to ·6246 in. (15·865 mm.)
Fit in piston	·0001 in. (·00254 mm.) tight to ·0003 in. (·0076 mm.) slack
Standard crankpin diameter	1·6254 in. (41·285 mm.) to 1·6259 in. (41·298 mm.)
Regrind sizes:	
1st undersize	1·6154 in. (41·031 mm.) to 1·6159 in. (41·044 mm.)
2nd undersize	1·6054 in. (40·777 mm.) to 1·6059 in. (40·790 mm.)
3rd undersize	1·5954 in. (40·523 mm.) to 1·5959 in. (40·536 mm.)
4th undersize	1·5854 in. (40·269 mm.) to 1·5859 in. (40·282 mm.)
Connecting rod length between centres	$5\frac{3}{4}$ in. (146·05 mm.)
Connecting rod—type of bearing	Steel-backed copper—lead (thinwall)
Connecting rod—side clearance	·008 in. (·203 mm.) to ·012 in. (·305 mm.)
Connecting rod—diametral clearance	·001 in. (·025 mm.) to ·0025 in. (·063 mm.)
Number of main bearings	Three
Type	Steel-backed white metal (thinwall)
Standard journal diameter	1·7505 in. (44·463 mm.) to 1·751 in. (44·475 mm.)
Regrind sizes:	
1st undersize	1·7405 in. (44·209 mm.) to 1·741 in. (44·221 mm.)
2nd undersize	1·7305 in. (43·955 mm.) to 1·731 in. (43·967 mm.)
3rd undersize	1·7205 in. (43·701 mm.) to 1·721 in. (43·713 mm.)
4th undersize	1·7105 in. (43·445 mm.) to 1·711 in. (43·459 mm.)
Length of main bearings	$1\frac{3}{16}$ in. (30·16 mm.)

GENERAL DATA

Main bearing running clearance	·001 in. (·025 mm.) to ·0025 in. (·063 mm.)
Crankshaft end thrust taken on	Centre main bearing
Number of camshaft bearings	Three
Camshaft bearing type	Front—steel-backed white metal. Centre and rear—direct in crankcase
Camshaft bearing clearance—front	·001 in. (·0254 mm.) to ·002 in. (·0508 mm.)
Camshaft bearing clearance—centre and rear	·00125 in. (·032 mm.) to ·00275 in. (·07 mm.)
Camshaft end thrust taken on	Front end
Camshaft end float	·003 in. (·0762 mm.) to ·007 in. (·178 mm.)
Camshaft drive type	Single roller chain $\frac{3}{8}$ in. (9·52 mm.) pitch, 52 pitches, endless with synthetic rubber tensioner rings on camshaft gear
Valve timing marking	Adjoining gear teeth are marked

Exhaust valve:

Throat diameter	0·908 in. (23·06 mm.)
Head diameter	1·00 in. (25·4 mm.)
Stem diameter	0·2788 in. (70·81 mm.) to 0·2793 in. (7·094 mm.)

Inlet valve:

Throat diameter	$\frac{31}{32}$ in. (24·6 mm.)
Head diameter	$1\frac{3}{32}$ in. (27·8 mm.)
Stem diameter	0·2793 in. (7·094 mm.) to 0·2798 in. (7·107 mm.)

Valve springs:

Free length	$1\frac{3}{4}$ in. (44·44 mm.)
Fitted length and load	$1\frac{19}{64}$ in. at $52\frac{1}{2}$ lb. (31·925 mm. at 23·81 kg.)
Valve seat angle	45°

Timing:

Inlet valve opens	5° before T.D.C.
Inlet valve closes	45° after B.D.C.
Exhaust valve opens	40° before B.D.C.
Exhaust valve closes	10° after T.D.C.

with 0·019 in. (·48 mm.) valve rocker clearance (for checking purposes only).

Valve clearance for timing	0·019 in. (·48 mm.)
Inlet valve working clearance (cold)	0·012 in. (·3 mm.)
Exhaust valve working clearance (cold)	0·012 in. (·3 mm.)
Valve guides	Removeable and interchangeable
Valve lift	·28 in. (7·14 mm.)

IGNITION

Type	Lucas 12 volt coil
Distributor type	Lucas DM2 PH4
Direction of rotation	Clockwise at rotor arm
Contact breaker gap	0·014 in. (·356 mm.) to 0·016 in. (·406 mm.)
Static timing	5° before T.D.C.
Coil type	Lucas LA12
Sparking plug type	Champion N5
Sparking plug gap	·024 in. to ·026 in. (·6196 mm. to ·6604 mm.)

COOLING SYSTEM

Capacity	10 pints (5·68 litres, 12 U.S. pints)
Circulation	Pump and thermostat

FUEL SYSTEM

Fuel delivery	A.C. Sphinx. 'Y' Type. Mechanical
Carburetter type	Two S.U. H.I. Semi down draught
Needle (normal)	GG

GENERAL DATA

Tank capacity	6 gallons (27·3 litres, 7·2 U.S. gallons)
Air cleaner	Twin 'Pancake'

CLUTCH

Make	Borg and Beck
Type	Single dry plate
Diameter	$6\frac{1}{4}$ in. (16 cm.)
Total frictional area	$15·05 \times 2$ sq. in. ($97·072 \times 2$ cm.^{2})
Thickness of linings	$\frac{1}{8}$ in. (3·175 mm.)
Release bearings	Special carbon graphite or copper carbon graphite
Number of springs	Six
Total axial spring pressure	Earlier power units—540 to 600 lbs. (245 to 272 kg.)
	Later power units—630 to 690 lbs. (286 to 313 kg.)
Thrust plate travel to full release	0·24 in. to 0·27 in. (6·2 to 6·8 mm.)
Pedal free movement	$\frac{5}{32}$ in. (3·969 mm.)

GEARBOX

Type	Synchromesh on 2nd, 3rd and top
Type of gear	Helical constant mesh
Gear ratios:	
First	3·627 : 1
Second	2·374 : 1
Third	1·412 : 1
Top	1·0 : 1
Reverse	4·664 : 1
Layshaft bearing:	
Type	Needle rollers
Length	0·7795 in. (19·8 mm.)
Housing diameter	0·8296 in. to 0·8301 in. (2·1072 to 2·1085 cm.)
Inside diameter	0·6315 in. to 0·6320 in. (1·6040 to 1·6053 cm.)
Number of rollers	23
Diameter of rollers	0·0984 in. (2·5 mm.)
Gearbox bearings:	
Make	R. & M. 2/LJ16—3 dot
Type	Ball journal (light)
Size	$1 \times 2\frac{1}{4} \times \frac{·623 \text{ in.}}{·625 \text{ in}}$
Oil capacity	$2\frac{1}{3}$ pints (1·325 litres, 2·807 U.S. pints)
Weight	35 lbs. (16 kg.)

REAR AXLE

Type	$\frac{3}{4}$ floating
Ratio	9/38
Oil capacity	$1\frac{3}{4}$ pints (1·0 litres, 2·1 U.S. pints)
Weight	83 lbs. (38 kg.)
Final drive	Hypoid
Bearings:	
Pinion Front:	
Make	Timken or Skefco
Type	Taper roller

GENERAL DATA

Size	1 × 2·3125 × ·594 × ·762 in.
Pinion rear:	
Make	Timken or Skefco
Type	Taper roller
Size	1·125 × 2·745 × ·75 × ·745 in
Differential:	
Make	R. & M.
Type	LJT 35—3 dot
Size	35 × 72 × 17 mm.
Hub:	
Make	R. & M.
Type	LJ 35—3 dot
Size	35 × 72 × 17 mm.

REAR SPRINGS

Type	¼ elliptic
Number of leaves	15
Thickness of leaves	5 at $\frac{5}{32}$ in. (3·97 mm.), 10 at $\frac{1}{8}$ in. (3·18 mm.)
Width	$1\frac{3}{4}$ in. (44·45 mm.)
Laden camber	$\frac{21}{32} \pm \frac{1}{8}$ in. (16·67 ± 3·18 mm.) positive
Working load	375 lb. (170 kg.)
Average load rate	97·8 lb. in. (1·13 kg. m.)

Alternative heavy duty type:

Number of leaves	10
Thickness of leaves	$\frac{3}{16}$ in. (4·76 mm.)
Width of leaves	$1\frac{3}{4}$ in. (44·45 mm.)
Laden camber	$\frac{21}{32} \pm \frac{1}{8}$ in. (16·67 ± 3·18 mm.) positive
Working load	375 lb. (170 kg.)
Average load rate	118 lb. in. (1·357 kg. m.)

STEERING

Type	Rack and pinion
Ratio	$2\frac{1}{4}$ turns, lock to lock
Track toe in	0 in. to $\frac{1}{8}$ in. (0 mm. to 3·175 mm.)

FRONT SUSPENSION

Type	Independent by coil springs and wishbones
Spring:	
Free length	9 4 in. (23·8 cm.)
Fitted length	6·625 in. (16·85 cm.) at 750 lbs. (340 kilos) load
Solid length	4·25 in. (10·8 cm.)
Inside diameter of coil	3·125 in. (7·94 cm.)
Number of working coils	7
Diameter of wire	0·5 in. (1·27 cm.)
Spring rate	271 lbs./in. (19 kg./cm.)
Castor Angle	3°
Camber Angle	1°
Swivel pin inclination	$6\frac{1}{2}$°
Shock Absorbers	Lever Hydraulic

BRAKES

Make	Lockheed
Footbrake	Hydraulic
Handbrake	Mechanical on rear wheels only

GENERAL DATA

Drum diameter	7 ins. (17·78 cm.)
Total Friction Area	67·5 sq. in. (435·37 sq. cm.)
Shoe Lining Length	6·75 in. (17·14 cm.)
Shoe Lining Thickness	0·203 to 0·193 in. (5·1562 to 4·9022 mm.)
Shoe Lining Width	1¼ in. (3.175 cm.)
Pedal Free Movement	$\frac{5}{32}$ in. (3·969 mm.)

ELECTRICAL

Battery:
- Type .. BT7A
- Type (export only) .. BTZ7A (dry-charged)
- Voltage .. 12.
- Capacity:
    - 20 hour rate .. 43 amp.hr.
- Initial charging current .. 2·5 amps.
- Normal recharge current .. 4·0 amps.
- Cell electrolyte capacity .. ¾ pint (·43 litre)

Generator:
- Type .. Lucas C39 PV2 with extended drive for tachometer
- Cutting in speed .. 1,050 to 1,200 r.p.m.
- Maximum output .. 13·5 volts 19 amps.
- Field resistance .. 6·1 ohms.

Starting Motor:
- Type .. Lucas M35 G1

Control Box:
- Type .. Lucas RB 106/2
- Regulator setting at:
    - 10°C (50°F) .. 16·1 to 16·7 volts.
    - 20°C (68°F) .. 15·8 to 16·4 volts.
    - 30°C (86°F) .. 15·6 to 16·2 volts.
    - 40°C (104°F) .. 15·3 to 15·9 volts.
- Cut-in voltage .. 12·7 to 13·3 volts.
- Drop off voltage .. 9 to 10 volts.
- Reverse Current .. 3 to 5 amps.

Windscreen wiper:
- Type .. Lucas DR2
- Normal running current .. 2·3 to 3·1 amp. at 12 volts.
- Stall current (Motor hot) .. 8 amp.
- Stall current (Motor cold) .. 14 amp.
- Armature resistance (adjacent commutator segments) ·34 to ·41 ohms.
- Field resistance .. 12·8 to 14·00 ohms.

Fuse Unit
- Type (2 live, 2 spare fuses) .. Lucas SF6

Fuses .. 2×35 amp.

Sidelamps
- Type .. Lucas model 52338A

Headlamps
- Type .. Lucas model F700

Stop Tail Lamps
- Type .. Lucas model 53330

Number Plate Illumination
- Type .. Lucas model 052410

GENERAL DATA

Bulbs

Headlamps, R.H.D. vehicles
- Type .. .. Lucas No. 414 B.M.C. No. BFS414
- Voltage .. .. 12 volts.
- Wattage .. .. 50/40 watts.

L.H.D. Vehicles (not Europe)
- Type .. .. Lucas No. 415 B.M.C. No. BFS415
- Voltage .. .. 12 volts.
- Wattage .. .. 50/40 watts.

L.H.D. Vehicles (France)
- Type (from Car No. 7782) .. .. Lucas No. 411 B.M.C. No. BFS411
- Voltage .. .. 12 volts.
- Wattage .. .. 45/40 watts.

L.H.D. vehicles (Europe except France)
- Type .. .. Lucas No. 370 B.M.C. No. BFS370
- Voltage .. .. 12 volts.
- Wattage .. .. 45/40 watts.
- Type (from Car No. 10489) .. .. .. Lucas No. 410 B.M.C. No. BFS410
- Voltage .. .. 12 volts.
- Wattage .. .. 45/40 watts.

R.H.D. vehicles (Sweden)
- Type (from Car No. 21118) .. .. .. Lucas No. 370 B.M.C. No. BFS410
- Voltage .. .. 12 volts.
- Wattage .. .. 45/40 watts.

Side Lamps and Flasher
- Type .. .. Lucas No. 380 B.M.C. No. BFS380
- Voltage .. .. 12 volts.
- Wattage .. .. 21/6 watts.

Number Plate Illumination
- Type .. .. Lucas No. 989 B.M.C. No. BFS989
- Voltage .. .. 12 volts.
- Wattage .. .. 6 watts.

Rear Flasher
- Type .. .. Lucas No. 382 B.M.C. No. BFS382
- Voltage .. .. 12 volts.
- Wattage .. .. 21 watts.

Stop and Tail Lamp
- Type .. .. Lucas No. 380 B.M.C. No. BFS380
- Voltage .. .. 12 volts.
- Wattage .. .. 21/6 watts.

Headlamp main beam warning lamp
Flashing indicator warning lamp
Instrument illumination lamps
- Type .. .. Lucas No. 987 B.M.C. No. BFS987
- Voltage .. .. 12 volts.
- Wattage .. .. 2·2 watts.

Flashing Indicator Unit (FL5)
- Type .. .. Lucas No. 35010A

GENERAL DATA

TYRE SIZES AND INFLATION PRESSURES

Tyre sizes .. .. 5.20 × 13 Tubeless
Pressures:
    Front .. .. 18 lb./sq. in. (1·27 kg.cm^2)
    Rear .. .. 20 lb./sq. in. (1·41 kg.cm^2)
For sustained speeds in excess of 80 to 85 m.p.h. (129 to 137 k.p.h.) increase pressures to:
    Front .. .. 24 lb./sq. in. (1·69 kg. cm^2)
    Rear .. .. 26 lb./sq. in. (1·83 kg. cm^2)

WHEELS

Type .. .. 13 in. ventilated steel disc with 4 stud fixing

TORQUE SPANNER DATA

Cylinder head stud nuts .. .. 40 lb. ft. (5·5 kg. m.)
Connecting rod big end bolts .. .. 35 lb. ft. (4·8 kg. m.)
Main bearing set screws .. .. 60 lb. ft. (8·3 kg. m.)
Flywheel set screws .. .. 40 lb. ft. (5·5 kg. m.)
Rocker bracket nuts .. .. 25 lb. ft. (3·4 kg. m.)
Gudgeon pin clamp screws .. .. 25 lb. ft. (3·4 kg. m.)
Front hub nuts .. .. 25 to 65 lb. ft. (3·4 to 8·9 kg. m.)
Road wheel nuts .. .. 37 to 39 lb. ft. (5·02 to 5·4 kg. m.)
Steering wheel nut .. .. 25 lb. ft. (3·4 kg. m.)

GENERAL DATA

LEADING DIMENSIONS

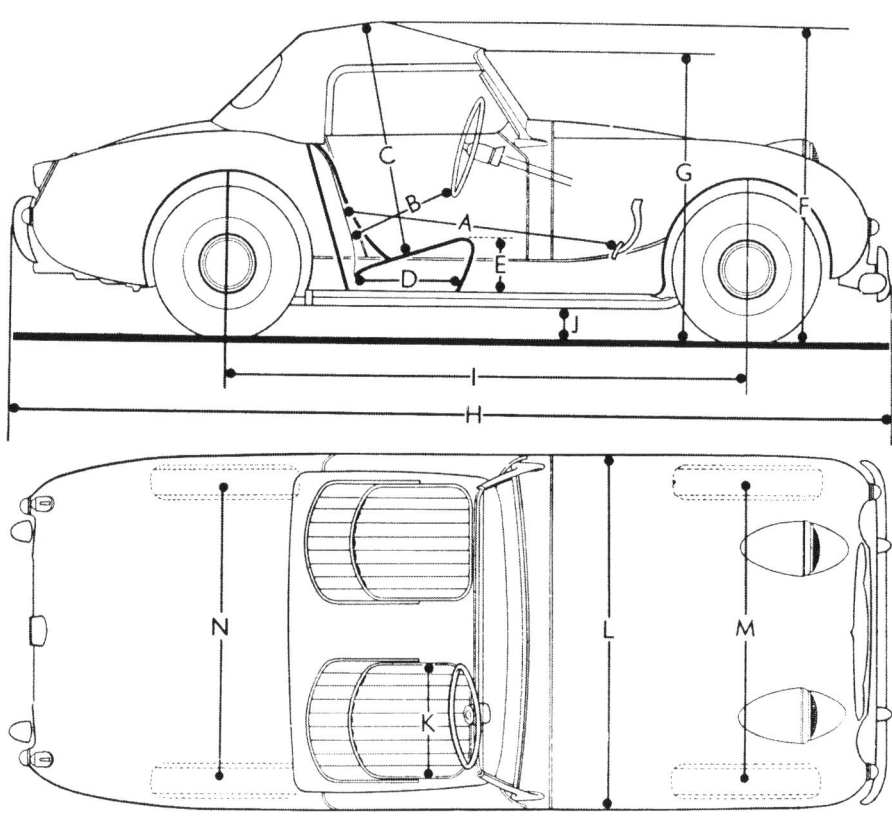

			AS. 52. A
Pedal to seat squab	A	3 ft. 3¼ in.	(1·00 m.)
		3 ft. 7¼ in.	(1·10 m.)
Steering wheel to seat squab	B	1 ft. 2 in.	(0·36 m.)
		1 ft. 5 in.	(0·43 m.)
Height over seat	C	2 ft. 10½ in.	(0·88 m.)
Seat cushion depth	D	1 ft. 7 in.	(0·48 m.)
Seat cushion above floor	E	7¾ in.	(0·20 m.)
Overall height (hood up)	F	4 ft. 1¾ in.	(1·26 m.)
Overall height (hood down)	G	3 ft. 8⅛ in.	(1·12 m.)
Overall length	H	11 ft. 5¼ in.	(3·49 m.)
Wheelbase	I	6 ft. 8 in.	(2·03 m.)
Minimum ground clearance	J	5 in.	(0·13 m.)
Seat cushion width	K	1 ft. 5 in.	(0·43 m.)
Overall width	L	4 ft. 5 in.	(1·35 m.)
Track (front)	M	3 ft. 9¾ in.	(1·16 m.)
Track (rear)	N	3 ft. 8¾ in.	(1·14 m.)
Turning Circle		31 ft. 6 in.	(9·60 m.)
Approximate weight—(Kerbside)		13 cwt. (660 kg.)	

GENERAL INFORMATION

CONTROLS

Gear lever

The gear change lever positions are clearly shown in the diagram.

To engage reverse gear move the lever to the right of the neutral position until resistance is felt, apply side pressure to the lever to overcome resistance, and then pull it backwards to engage the gear.

Synchromesh is provided on second, third, and fourth gears.

Pedals

The left-hand pedal operates the clutch, the centre pedal the brakes, and the right-hand pedal the accelerator.

Do not allow the foot to rest on the clutch pedal while driving or excessive wear of the operating mechanism will result.

Hand brake

The hand brake is applied by pulling upwards on the lever situated between the driver's and passenger's seats. The ratchet mechanism will hold the brake in the 'on' position and will be heard engaging as the lever is pulled. To release the hand brake pull upwards on the lever, depress the button on the end, and push the lever downwards to the 'off' position.

Headlamp dip switch

The foot operated dip switch is mounted on the floor to the left of the clutch pedal. It is of the repeating type, lowering the beams on one application and raising them on the next. The headlamp beam warning light glows when the beams are in the raised position.

Direction indicators and horn

The direction indicator switch is mounted on the fascia above the ignition switch. To operate, move the switch to the left or right according to whichever indicator is required; a warning light flashes green when the indicators are in use.

The horn is operated by pressing the button in the centre of the steering wheel.

Windtone horns (optional extra)

These horns give a soft and loud note.

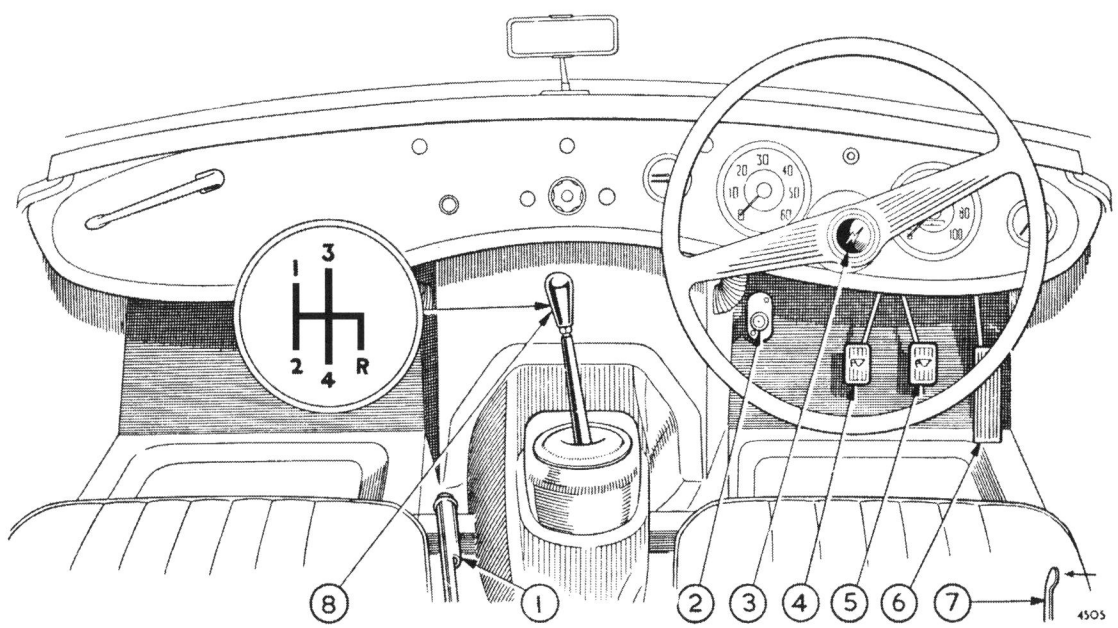

The location of the driving controls.

1. Handbrake.
2. Headlamp dip switch.
3. Horn.
4. Clutch pedal.
5. Brake pedal.
6. Accelerator pedal.
7. Seat adjuster.
8. Gear change lever.

GENERAL INFORMATION

Ignition switch

The switch is situated in the centre of the fascia and is operated by a removable key, which is turned clockwise to switch on the ignition.

Starter switch (marked 'S')

Pull the knob smartly and firmly to operate the starter motor. Release it immediately the engine starts. If the engine fails to start first time wait until the starter motor has come to rest before operating the control again.

Choke or mixture control (marked 'C')

Pull out the control to its limit when starting the engine from cold. Return the control to its normal running position (pushed right in) as soon as possible after starting the engine.

Do not use the control when the engine is warm.

Windshield wiper switch (marked 'W')

Pull the control outwards to set the wipers in motion. The blades are automatically parked when the control is pushed in to the 'off' position.

The windshield wipers will operate only if the ignition is on.

Lamps switch

Turn the central moulding which surrounds the ignition switch clockwise to the first notch for the side and tail lamps, and to the second notch for the head, side and tail lamps.

Panel lamp switch

This is situated on the lower edge of the fascia below the speedometer. No light will be obtained unless the side lamps are in operation.

Windshield washer (optional extra)

To operate the washer press the control knob at the far left-hand side of the fascia. In cold weather it is important to fill the reservoir with a mixture of water and Trico to prevent freezing of the water in the container and on the windshield.

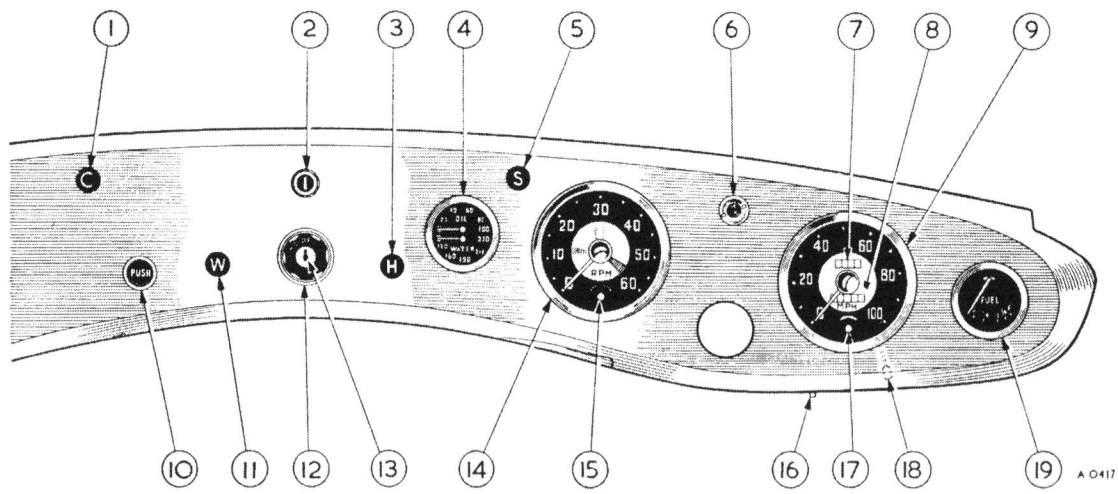

The instruments and switches.

1. Mixture control.
2. Direction indicator switch.
3. Heater switch.
4. Oil pressure and water temperature gauge.
5. Starter.
6. Direction indicator warning lamp.
7. Trip mileage indicator.
8. Total mileage indicator.
9. Speedometer.
10. Windscreen washer knob.
11. Windscreen wiper switch.
12. Lamp switch.
13. Ignition switch.
14. Engine revolution indicator.
15. Main beam warning lamp.
16. Panel lamp switch.
17. Ignition warning lamp.
18. Trip mileage resetting knob.
19. Fuel gauge.

GENERAL INFORMATION

Do not use radiator anti-freeze solution in the windshield washing equipment.

Heating and demisting system (optional extra)

The heating and demisting system is provided for two purposes: (a) heating the interior of the car (b) demisting and defrosting the windshield.

Air for the heater is drawn from a forward-facing intake via an auxiliary blower which should only be needed at speeds below 25 m.p.h. (40 km.p.h.). A shut-off valve is incorporated in the heater intake to prevent fumes from entering the car in traffic. The valve must always be open when heating is required. A water tap is fitted at the rear of the engine. In the summer conditions, this tap may be shut off and the heating system may then be used for cool air ventilation.

The heating and ventilating system is operated by a single control located on the fascia and marked 'H'. For heating and demisting, pull out the knob, and to bring the blower into operation push in the knob and turn in a clockwise direction. Two doors located forward at either side of the gearbox tunnel control distribution of air between screen and car interior. For heating, open the doors; for defrosting and demisting close the doors.

INSTRUMENTS

Speedometer

In addition to showing the car speed this has total distance and trip recorders. The trip recorder can be set to zero by pushing the resetting knob upwards and turning it anti-clockwise.

Engine revolution indicator (optional extra)

The speed of the engine is indicated by this dial which is calibrated in hundreds of revolutions per minute. Normal use of the engine will not require speeds over 5,000 r.p.m.: with care and under favourable conditions between 5,500 and 6,000 r.p.m. may be attained, but this speed must not be exceeded.

Water temperature gauge

The needle registers the coolant temperature only when the ignition is switched on. Should there be a sudden change from the usual running temperature, immediate attention should be given to the cooling system and the cause of the trouble rectified.

Oil pressure gauge

The normal working pressure when the engine is warm is 30 to 60 lb./sq. in. (2.1 to 4.2 kg./cm^2) with a proportionately lower idling pressure. Should the gauge fail to register, stop the engine immediately, investigate and rectify the trouble before starting the engine again.

Fuel gauge

This shows the amount of fuel in the tank and operates only when the ignition is switched on.

Warning lamps

The ignition warning lamp is in the lower half of the speedometer indicator dial. The bright red light will go out as the engine speed is increased; should it glow at all engine speeds the dynamo is not charging the battery, and after ascertaining that the dynamo belt is not broken the circuit should be examined.

In the lower half of the engine revolution indicator is the headlamp main beam warning light. Coloured dark red to avoid dazzle, the warning lamp glows when the headlamps are in the raised position and is extinguished when the beams are dipped for approaching traffic.

The warning lamp immediately above the steering wheel flashes green when the direction indicators are operated.

BODY AND EQUIPMENT

Bonnet

The bonnet lock is situated behind the front number plate. Turn the handle in a clockwise direction to release the bonnet, after which the bonnet will rise about two inches until held by a spring loaded safety catch. Insert the

GENERAL INFORMATION

fingers and lift the catch, and then the bonnet may be lifted right up; it is held open by two telescopic prop rods which automatically lock in the fully extended position.

As a safety measure an extra prop is provided and should always be used to prevent any possibility of an accident. Release the prop from the clip at the side of the radiator and insert the end into the hole provided in the bracket below the heater intake on the underside of the bonnet.

To close the bonnet, release the prop and return it to the securing clip. Raise the bonnet to release the telescopic prop rod locking devices and lower gently. Push downwards on the radiator grille to engage the safety catch and turn the locking handle in an anti-clockwise direction to secure.

Spare wheel and jack

The spare wheel is retained in position horizontally on the floor of the luggage compartment by webbing straps. Access to the spare wheel is gained by tilting forward the seat squabs.

The spare wheel should always be maintained in good repair and inflated to the correct pressure, otherwise its value in an emergency is reduced and tiresome roadside pumping may be involved. It should also be exchanged with the road wheels periodically to ensure even wear on all tyres—every 3,000 miles (5000 km.) is recommended.

The jack is also housed in the luggage compartment. When using the jack, always ensure that the jack lug is properly engaged in the socket below the front doors (normally closed by a rubber plug). Turning the ratchet handle clockwise will raise the car and turning anti-clockwise will lower the car (see Section N.6).

Fuel filler

The fuel filler is located towards the rear on the right-hand side of the body. The tank is sealed by a locking cap which, after unlocking with the key provided, can be turned anti-clockwise for removal.

Filling up with fuel

Considerable loss of fuel can occur as a result of filling the fuel tank until the fuel is visible in the filler tube. If this is done and the vehicle is left in the sun, expansion due to heat will cause leakage, with consequent loss of and danger from exposed fuel. When filling up therefore:
 (1) Avoid filling the tank until the fuel is visible in the filler tube.
 (2) If the tank is inadvertently overfilled, take care to park the vehicle in the shade and with the filler as high as possible.

Hood (first type)

To erect the hood place the hood frame in the body sockets with the hinged rail facing forwards.

Lay the hood over the hood frame and secure the press studs on the two flaps which will hold the hood to the hood frame. Attach the rear hood rail to the two slotted fasteners on the tonneau panel and the hood sides to the body with the turn button and fasteners.

Secure the hood to the windscreen frame with the press stud fasteners.

Removing the hood is a reversal of the above order.

To stow the hood lay it on a flat surface with the lining upwards and roll up from the rear edge carefully avoiding kinking. Withdraw the hood frame and turn it through 180° so that the hinged rail faces rearwards and stow in the sockets provided. Secure the frame in the centre with the strap attached to the underside of the boot. If correctly positioned the frame will follow the contour of the rear edge of the cockpit. Strap the rolled hood to the top of the hood frame with the extreme ends bent round at the seams into the boot. The straps for this purpose will be found in the tool kit.

Hood (second type)—fitted to Car Nos. AN5 5137, 5287, 5288 and 5477 onwards.

To erect the hood place the hood frame in the body sockets with the hinged rail facing forwards, press the main hood frame downwards and rotate the lugs to lock the telescopic ends in the compressed position.

Lay the hood over the hood frame and fit the front rail firmly into the lip of the windshield frame; secure with the two fasteners one at each top corner of the windshield.

GENERAL INFORMATION

Attach the rear hood rail to the two slotted fasteners on the tonneau panel and the hood sides to the body with the turn buttons and fasteners.

Before releasing the two tension springs on the main hood frame make certain that the front hood rail is still firmly secured in the lip of the windshield.

Removing the hood must be a reversal of the above order. Never commence hood removal from the windshield.

To stow the hood proceed as with the first type.

LOCATION OF MAJOR COMPONENT SERIAL NUMBERS

The major components of the vehicle have serial numbers. When in communication with the Company or your Dealer, always quote the car and engine numbers. The registration number is of no assistance and is not required. The car number will be found stamped on the identification plate located on the left-hand inner wheel arch valance under the bonnet. The engine number is stamped on a plate fixed to the right-hand side of the cylinder block. Other major components have their serial numbers stamped upon them and their locations are illustrated below.

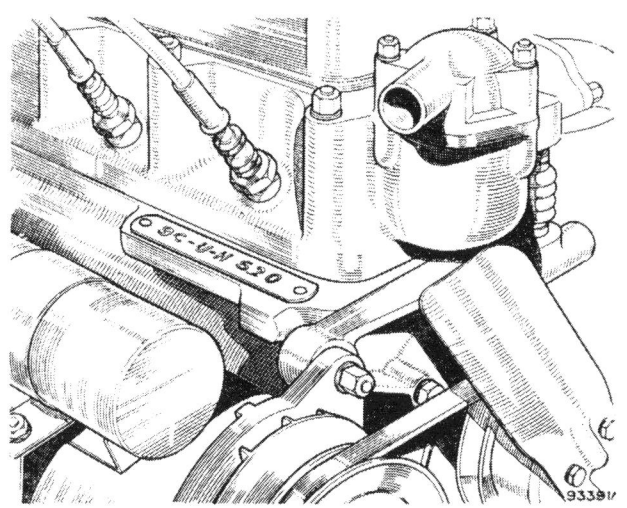

Engine Number. This is stamped on a plate secured to the right-hand side of the cylinder block above the dynamo.

Car (Chassis) Number. This is stamped on a plate mounted on the left-hand inner wheel arch valance under the bonnet.

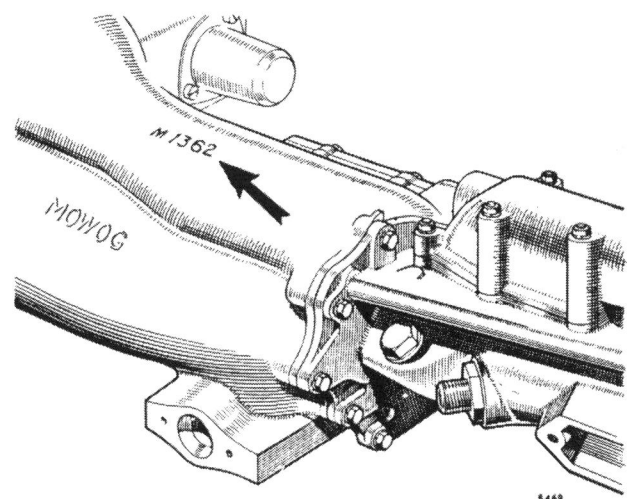

Gearbox Number. This is stamped on the top of the gearbox casting.

Body Number. This is stamped on a plate secured to the left-hand front door pillar.

GENERAL INFORMATION

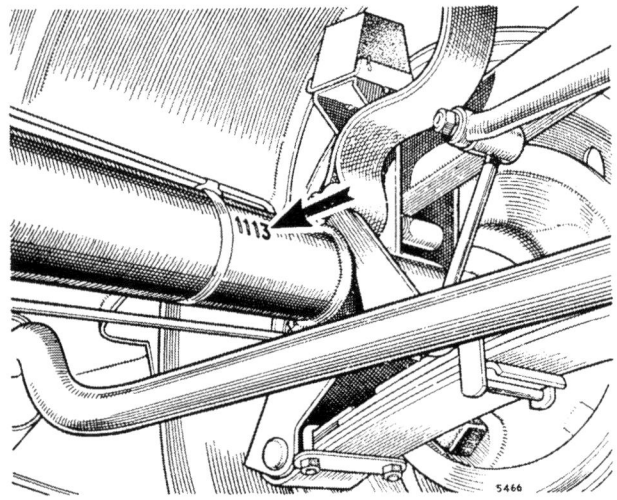

Rear Axle Number. This is stamped on the front of the left-hand rear axle tube adjacent to the spring anchorage.

CLAIMS UNDER WARRANTY

Claims for the replacement of material or parts under Warranty must always be submitted to the supplying Distributor or Dealer, or, when this is not possible, to the nearest Distributor or Dealer, informing them of the Vendor's name and address.

PRESERVATIVE ON EXPORT CARS

To remove the hard film preservative from the external plated parts, a cloth dipped in a solution of equal parts of white spirit and petrol (gasoline) should be used. Take care to keep this solvent from anything other than the plated components.

POWER UNIT SERIAL NUMBER CODING

The engine number comprises a series of letters and numbers, presenting in code the capacity, make, and type of unit, ancillaries fitted, and the type of compression together with the serial number of the unit.

1st PREFIX GROUP—cubic capacity, make, and type

1st Prefix number

8—803 c.c.	22—2200 c.c.
9—950 c.c.	25—2500 c.c.
12—1200 c.c.	26—2600 c.c.
15—1500 c.c.	

1st Prefix letter

B—B.M.C. Industrials	J—Commercial
C—Austin-Healey	M—Morris
G—M.G.	R—Riley
H—Miscellaneous	W—Wolseley

2nd Prefix letter
A—Z used for the variations of engine type.

GENERAL INFORMATION

2nd PREFIX GROUP—Gearbox and ancillaries

A—Automatic gearbox
M—Manumatic clutch
N—Steering column or side gear change gearbox
O—Overdrive (Borg-Warner)
P—Police specification
U—Centre gear change gearbox

3rd GROUP—Compression and serial number

H—High compression
L—Low compression
} and serial number of unit

CODE EXAMPLE

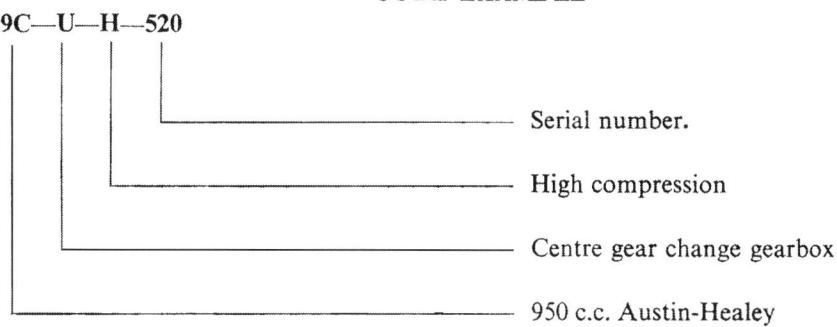

9C—U—H—520

- Serial number.
- High compression
- Centre gear change gearbox
- 950 c.c. Austin-Healey

IDENTIFICATION OF UNIFIED SCREW THREADS

The general standardization of Unified screw threads makes it necessary to identify all nuts, bolts, and set screws with these threads in order to ensure their being matched with correspondingly threaded components and the fitting of correct replacements.

Identification has been standardized and is effected in the following manner:

Nuts. By a circular groove turned on the end face of the nut or by connected circles stamped on one flat of the hexagon.

Bolts and Set Screws. By a circular depression turned on the head or by connected circles stamped on one flat of the hexagon.

Wheel Stud Nuts. By a notch cut in all the corners of the hexagon.

It is of the utmost importance that any nuts, bolts, or set screws marked with the above identifications are used only in conjunction with associated components having Unified threads and that only replacement parts with Unified threads are used, as these are *not* interchangeable with Whitworth, BSF, or Metric threads.

The Unified thread is, however, interchangeable with the American National Fine (ANF) thread for all practical purposes.

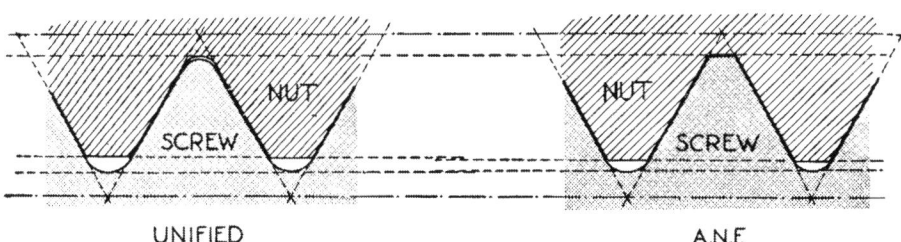

UNIFIED   A.N.F.

GENERAL INFORMATION

The illustration overleaf of the Unified thread and the ANF thread to the same scale indicates their close relationship.

Spanners. It is to be noted that all ANF- and Unified-threaded nuts and hexagon-headed bolts are made to the standard American hexagon sizes and that spanners of the appropriate size must be used when tightening or loosening them.

KEY TO SPANNER SIZES (Nominal widths between jaws)

Diameter of screw thread (inches)	$\frac{1}{4}''$	$\frac{5}{16}''$	$\frac{3}{8}''$	$\frac{7}{16}''$	$\frac{1}{2}''$	$\frac{9}{16}''$	$\frac{5}{8}''$	$\frac{3}{4}''$	$\frac{7}{8}''$	$1''$
For BSF screws and nuts	·448	·529	·604	·705	·825	·925	1·016	1·207	1·309	1·489
For ANF screws and nuts	·440	·504	·566	·629	·755	·880	·944	1·132	1·320	1·508
For Unified screws	·440	·504	·566	**·630**	·755	**·817**	·943	1·132	1·321	1·509
For Unified nuts (normal)	·440	·504	·566	**·692**	·755	**·880**	·943	1·132	1·321	1·509
For Unified nuts (heavy)	—	—	—	—	—	—	1·069	1·258	1·446	—

NOTE.—In the case of some Unified-threaded components the size of the hexagon for the nut is different from that of the bolt. Where this occurs the spanner size is shown in heavy type in the above table.

PART NAME ALTERNATIVES

	Part Name	Alternatives
ENGINE	Gudgeon pin	Piston pin. Small-end pin. Wrist pin.
	Scraper ring	Oil control ring.
	Core plug	Expansion plug. Welch plug. Sealing disc.
	Oil sump	Oil pan. Oil reservoir.
CONTROLS	Mixture control	Choke. Strangler.
GEARBOX	Gear lever	Shift lever.
	Change speed fork	Shift fork. Selector fork.
	First motion shaft	Clutch shaft. First reduction pinion. Main drive pinion. Drive gear.
	Layshaft	Countershaft.
AXLE	Crown wheel	Ring gear. Spiral drive gear.
	Bevel pinion	Small pinion. Spiral drive pinion.
	'U' bolts	Spring clips.
	Axle shaft	Half-shaft. Hub driving shaft. Jack driving shaft.
	Differential gear	Sun wheel.
	Differential pinion	Planet wheel.
STEERING	Swivel pin	Pivot pin. Steering pin. King pin.
	Stub axle	Swivel axle.
	Track-rod	Cross-tube.
	Draglink	Side tube. Steering connecting rod.
ELECTRICAL	Dynamo	Generator.
	Control box	Voltage regulator. Cut-out. Voltage control.
EXHAUST	Silencer	Muffler.
BODY	Bonnet	Hood.
	Wing	Mudguard. Fender.

GENERAL INFORMATION

FROST PRECAUTIONS

Steps must be taken to prevent the water in the cooling system from freezing during frosty weather. Water, when it freezes, expands, with the result that there is a very considerable risk of bursting either the radiator, heater element, or the cylinder block by the pressure generated. Since no provision is made for draining the heater unit, draining the radiator and cylinder block is not a sufficient safeguard.

The cooling system is of the pressurized type and relatively high temperatures are developed in the radiator upper tank. For this reason anti-freeze solutions having an alcohol base are unsuitable owing to their high evaporation rate producing a rapid loss of coolant and a consequent interruption of circulation.

Only anti-freeze of the ethylene glycol type incorporating the correct type of corrosion inhibitor is suitable and owners are recommended to use Bluecol Anti-freeze or any anti-freeze to B.S. 3151/3152.

The recommended quantities of anti-freeze for different degrees of frost are:

Solution	Commences Freezing		Absolute Safe Limit		Amount of Anti-freeze required		
	°C.	°F.	°C.	°F.	Pts.	U.S. Pts.	Litres
20	—9	16	—19	3	2	2·4	1·1
25	—13	9	—26	—15	2½	3·0	1·42
30	—16	3	—33	—28	3	3·6	1·71

Make sure that the cooling system is watertight and examine all joints, renewing any defective rubber hose.

Before adding anti-freeze to the cooling system it is advisable to clean the cooling system thoroughly by swilling out the water passages with a hose inserted in the filler, and with the drain taps open.

Avoid excessive topping up, otherwise there is a risk of losing valuable anti-freeze due to expansion of the solution. Top up only when the system is at its normal running temperature.

Generally speaking, anti-freeze is not injurious to cellulose paint provided it is wiped off in reasonable time.

Radiator anti-freeze must not be used in the windshield washing equipment.

The illustration shows the position of the seat belt when correctly worn

B.M.C. SEAT BELTS

General Description

Seat belts are available from B.M.C. Service Ltd. as an accessory. Attachment points have been incorporated in the body construction.

When in use the long belt passes from the wheel arch downwards across the chest to the sill with the buckle tongue approximately at its centre. The short belt from the tunnel is adjusted so that the buckle is located just in front of the hip, and the tongue on the long belt is pushed into the buckle until it clicks in the locked position. The long belt is then adjusted so that the wearer is held firmly but comfortably in the seat. For quick release it is only necessary to lift up the buckle lever approximately 90°, which immediately frees the wearer.

Take care to stow the long belt in such a way that you are not tripped when getting out of the car.

GENERAL INFORMATION

RUNNING-IN SPEEDS

The treatment given to a new car will have an important bearing on its subsequent life, and engine speeds during this early period must be limited. The following instructions should be strictly adhered to.

During the first 500 miles (800 km.)

DO NOT exceed 45 m.p.h. (72 k.p.h.).

DO NOT operate at full throttle in any gear.

DO NOT allow the engine to labour in any gear

MAINTENANCE ATTENTION

ALL MATERIALS CHARGEABLE TO THE CUSTOMER

3,000 Miles (5000 km.) service

1. *Engine.*
   Top up carburetter piston dampers.
   Lubricate carburetter controls.
   Clean and re-oil air cleaners.
   Check fan belt tension.
   Check water level in radiator and top up if necessary.

2. *Brakes.*
   Check brakes, adjust if necessary.
   Make visual inspection of brake lines and pipes.
   Check level of fluid in the hydraulic brake and clutch master cylinder reservoir and top up if necessary.

3. *Body.*
   Lubricate door hinges, door locks, bonnet lock and operating mechanism and safety catch.
   Lightly smear striker plates with suitable grease.

4. *Electrical.*
   Check battery and top up to correct level.

5. *Lubrication.*
   Change engine oil.
   Top up gearbox and rear axle oil levels.
   Lubricate all grease nipples (except steering rack and pinion).

6. *Wheels and Tyres.*
   Change road wheels round diagonally, including spare to regularise tyre wear.
   Check tyre pressures.

6,000 Miles (10000 km.) service

1. *Engine.*
   Top up carburetter piston dampers.
   Lubricate carburetter controls.
   Clean fuel pump filter.
   Clean and re-oil air cleaners.
   Check fan belt tension.
   Check valve rocker clearances and adjust if necessary.
   Check water level in radiator and top up if necessary.

2. *Ignition.*
   Check functioning of automatic retard and advance mechanism.
   Check and if necessary adjust distributor contact points.
   Clean and adjust sparking plugs.
   Lubricate all distributor parts.

3. *Brakes.*
   Check brakes, adjust if necessary.
   Make visual inspection of brake lines and pipes.
   Check level of fluid in the hydraulic brake and clutch master cylinder reservoir and top up if necessary.

4. *Steering.*
   Check wheel alignment and adjust if necessary.

5. *General.*
   Check rear road spring anchorage bolts.

6. *Body.*
   Lubricate door hinges, door locks, bonnet lock and operating mechanism and safety catch.
   Lightly smear striker plates with suitable grease.

7. *Electrical.*
   Check battery cell specific gravity readings and top up to correct level.
   Lubricate dynamo bearing.
   Check all lamps for correct functioning.

8. *Lubrication.*
   Change oil in engine, gearbox and rear axle.
   Fit new oil filter element.
   Lubricate all grease nipples (except steering rack and pinion).

9. *Wheels and Tyres.*
   Change road wheels round diagonally, including spare, to regularise tyre wear.
   Check tyre pressures.

10. *Test.*
    Road test car and report.

12,000 Miles (20000 km.) service.

1. *Engine.*
   Remove carburetter suction chambers and pistons, clean, reassemble and top up dampers.
   Lubricate carburetter controls.
   Check valve rocker clearances and adjust if necessary.
   Check fan belt tension.
   Lubricate water pump sparingly.
   Clean and re-oil air cleaner.
   Drain, flush out, and refill radiator.

2. *Ignition.*
   Check functioning of automatic retard and advance mechanism.
   Clean and if necessary adjust distributor contact points.
   Fit new sparking plugs.
   Lubricate all parts as necessary.

MAINTENANCE ATTENTION

12,000 Miles (20000 km.) service—*continued.*

3. *Steering.*
   Check steering and suspension moving parts for wear.
   Check wheel alignment and adjust if necessary.

4. *Brakes.*
   Check brakes, adjust if necessary. Make visual inspection of brake lines and pipes. Check level of fluid in the hydraulic brake and clutch master cylinder reservoir and top up if necessary.

5. *General.*
   Check rear road spring anchorage bolts.

6. *Body*
   Lubricate door hinges, door locks, bonnet lock and operating mechanism and safety catch.
   Lightly smear striker plates with suitable grease.

7. *Electrical.*
   Check battery cell specific gravity readings and top up to correct level. Lubricate dynamo bearing.
   Check beam setting and adjust if necessary.
   Check all lamps for correct functioning.

8. *Lubrication.*
   Drain engine, flush out, and refill with fresh oil.
   Change oil in gearbox and rear axle.
   Fit new oil filter element.
   Lubricate all grease nipples.
   Lubricate steering rack and pinion.

9. *Wheels and Tyres.*
   Change road wheels round diagonally, including spare, to regularise tyre wear.
   Check tyre pressures.

10. *Test.*
    Road test car and report.

SECTION A

ENGINE

Section No. A.1	General description
Section No. A.2	Visual inspection
Section No. A.3	Adjustments in the vehicle
Section No. A.4	Engine assembly
Section No. A.5	Lubrication
Section No. A.6	Oil filter
Section No. A.7	Sump and gauze strainer
Section No. A.8	Oil pump
Section No. A.9	Relief valve
Section No. A.10	Adjusting valve clearance
Section No. A.11	Valve rocker shaft
Section No. A.12	Rocker shaft assembly
Section No. A.13	Push rod removal
Section No. A.14	Rocker arm bushes
Section No. A.15	Tappets
Section No. A.16	Renewing valve spring in position
Section No. A.17	Manifold
Section No. A.18	Cylinder head
Section No. A.19	Removing and refitting valves
Section No. A.20	Valve grinding
Section No. A.21	Valve guides
Section No. A.22	Decarbonising
Section No. A.23	Connecting rods and bearings
Section No. A.24	Pistons, rings and gudgeon pins
Section No. A.25	Piston sizes and cylinder bores
Section No. A.26	Timing cover
Section No. A.27	Timing chain and wheels
Section No. A.28	Camshaft and bearings
Section No. A.29	Flywheel and engine rear plate
Section No. A.30	Crankshaft and main bearings
Section No. A.31	Cylinder block
Section No. A.32	Fault diagnosis.
Section No. A.33	Modified valve shrouds and oil seals
Section No. A.34	Modified cylinder head gasket
Section No. A.35	Modified oil pump
Section No. A.36	Fitting flywheel starter rings
Section No. A.37	Fitting valve seat inserts
Section No. A.38	Fitting cylinder liners
End of Section	Service tools

ENGINE A

Section A.1

GENERAL DESCRIPTION

The overhead valve engine has its four cylinders vertically in line and cast integral with the crankcase. The detachable cylinder head is of cast iron and carries the push rod operated valve gear.

Large area water circulating passages and full length water jackets enable the engine to be adequately cooled even under the most arduous operation conditions.

Copper-lead plated bearings are utilised in the connecting-rod big end assemblies, thus necessitating complete and clean lubrication at all times. This is ensured by a rotor type oil pump and the provision of a full flow filter.

The choice of oils is of great importance and those recommended at the end of this manual have been tested under various running conditions and should be used in accordance with the schedule of regular attentions.

Section A.2

VISUAL INSPECTION

Examine the engine for any signs of oil leakage, with particular attention to the sump drain plug, the joint between the oil filter and crankcase, and the rocker cover to cylinder head joint.

The connections to the distributor should be checked occasionally for tightness, and any perished or cracked high tension cables renewed.

Section A.3

ADJUSTMENTS IN THE VEHICLE

The purpose of the following adjustments is to maintain the performance of the engine at its maximum, and consists of a series of cleaning, inspecting and adjusting operations. A compression test of each cylinder should first be made to determine the general condition of the engine before proceeding with any adjustments. If a compression gauge is not available, a simple method to test the compression is to remove all the sparking plugs with the exception of the one in the cylinder being tested, and then rotate the engine with the starting handle through at least two complete revolutions. If the cylinder compression is satisfactory, proceed as detailed below, otherwise the specific fault should be diagnosed by referring to 'Fault Diagnosis', Section A.32.

(1) Clean the engine generally and lubricate as indicated on the lubrication chart.

(2) Adjust the fan belt tension in accordance with the instructions given in Section C.

(3) Remove the valve gear cover and test the cylinder head studs for tightness, using a torque spanner set to the figures quoted under 'General Data'.

(4) Check and adjust the valve and rocker clearances as outlined in Section A.10.

(5) Check for evidence of cracked valve springs or scored or worn stems.

(6) Replace the valve gear cover, using a new gasket if necessary.

(7) Disconnect the high-tension cables and remove the sparking plugs.

(8) Check to make sure that the correct type of sparking plug is being used.

(9) Clean the sparking plugs and examine the insulation for breaks or cracks.

(10) Adjust the sparking plug gaps as specified in Section B.

(11) Test the sparking plugs and renew any found to be unfit for further service.

(12) Refit the sparking plugs, using new copper washers.

(13) Check the high tension cables for wear and deterioration before refitting.

(14) Remove the distributor head cover and clean it inside and out. Examine it for cracks and burned contacts and renew it if necessary.

(15) Inspect the contact breaker points to determine whether new points are needed. Follow the procedure given in Section B to clean and adjust the points.

(16) Check the distributor rotor arm, making sure the carbon brush makes contact. Check the capacitor terminal to make sure it is clean and tight.

(17) Check the ignition timing as outlined in Section B.

(18) Clean the air cleaners in accordance with the instructions in Section D.

(19) Make sure the fuel system is operating properly and clean all filters in the system as detailed in Section D.

(20) Check the carburetter manifold flange gaskets for evidence of leakage.

(21) Adjust the carburetters if necessary, in accordance with the procedure given in Section D.

Section A.4

ENGINE ASSEMBLY

To Remove (without gearbox)

(1) Detach the earth lead from the battery.

(2) Detach the bonnet from the bonnet hinges as described in Section O.2.

ENGINE

(3) Remove the radiator as described in Section C.
(4) Disconnect the heater inlet and outlet hoses at the heater unit (if applicable).
(5) Detach the choke cable and its outer casing at the carburetters.
(6) Detach the throttle cable at the carburetter throttle lever.
(7) Unscrew the oil pressure gauge pipe at its terminal in the cylinder block.
(8) Unscrew the reduction drive (if fitted) complete with tachometer cable from the rear end of the generator.
(9) Release the generator, coil and distributor low tension cables.
(10) Release the high tension cables from their connections at the coil and sparking plugs.
(11) Remove the distributor as detailed in the Ignition Section.

Fig. A.2. Showing the engine being removed at the correct lifting angle.

Note: The bottom right-hand nut and bolt also secures the engine earthing wire.

(17) Remove the four nuts and spring washers securing the engine front mounting bracket to the chassis frame.
(18) Ascertain that the engine mounting bracket is clear of its mounting studs by jacking the gearbox and at the same time lifting the engine.
(19) Hoist and pull the engine forward to disengage the gearbox first motion shaft splines and lift clear of the vehicle (Fig. A.2).

Fig. A.1. Illustrating the position of the rubber mounting and mounting bracket.

(12) Remove the starter as described in the Electrical System.
(13) Disconnect the petrol (gasoline) inlet pipe at the fuel pump union.
(14) Release the clamp attaching the exhaust manifold to the down pipe.
(15) Attach lifting tackle as illustrated in Fig. A.2.
(16) Place a suitable jack beneath the vehicle to support the gearbox and unscrew the nuts, bolts and setpins securing the gearbox bell housing to the engine backplate.

Fig. A.3. Showing the removal of the engine, gearbox and propeller shaft.

ENGINE

To Replace

Replacing the engine is the reverse of the procedure 'To Remove'.

To Remove (with gearbox)

(1) Perform the operations (1) to (14) as detailed previously and then proceed as follows:

(2) Within the car remove the four self tapping screws securing the gear lever aperture cover to the gearbox surround and withdraw the cover.

(3) Unscrew and remove the anti-rattle plunger, spring and cap (accessible within the car) (7, Fig. F.6).

(4) Unscrew the three setscrews attaching the change speed lever retaining plate and remove the change speed lever.

(5) Peel back the carpet surrounding the gearbox cover to expose the two $\frac{5}{16}$ in. gearbox rear mounting setpins, the location of one of the setpins is shown (1) Fig. F. 3, and unscrew the setpins.

(6) Working beneath the vehicle unscrew the speedometer drive cable at its union with the gearbox rear extension.

(7) Detach the slave cylinder from the gearbox bell housing by unscrewing its two mounting setpins and withdrawing the push rod from the rear of the cylinder.

(8) Disconnect the propeller shaft from the rear axle. This operation is performed by removal of the four self-locking nuts.

(9) Unscrew the remaining two gearbox rear mounting setpins. The location of one of the setpins is shown in Fig. F.3 (2).

(10) By means of lifting tackle, similar to that illustrated in Fig. A.2, support the engine.

(11) Remove the four nuts and spring washers securing the engine front mounting bracket to the chassis frame.

(12) Hoist the engine, gearbox and propeller shaft, and at the same time pull the whole assembly forward clear of the vehicle.

Section A.5

LUBRICATION

Description

The oil supply is carried in the sump below the cylinder block, and the filler cap is fitted to the valve rocker cover. The dipstick is on the right-hand side of the engine and is marked to indicate the 'FULL' level.

The eccentric vane non-draining-type oil pump is mounted on the rear end of the crankcase and is driven by the camshaft.

Draining the Sump

The sump on new and reconditioned engines must be drained and filled with new oil after the first 3,000 miles (5000 km.). The hexagon-headed sump drain plug is at the rear on the right-hand side.

The sump should be allowed to drain for at least ten minutes before the drain plug is replaced. The oil will flow more readily if it is drained while the engine is hot. When the sump has been drained, approximately 6 pints (7·2 U.S. pints, 3·41 litres) of oil are required to fill it. The capacity of the filter is approximately 1 pint (1·2 U.S. pints, 0·57 litres), giving a total of 7 pints (8·4 U.S. pints, 3·98 litres). Do not forget to replace the sump drain plug.

Never use petrol or paraffin for flushing purposes. Such cleaning mediums are never completely dispersed from the engine lubricating system, and will remain to contaminate any fresh oil. This may cause premature bearing failure.

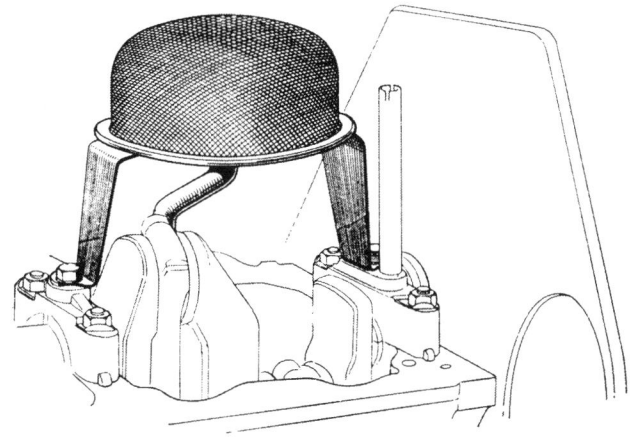

Fig. A.4. Oil Strainer

ENGINE

Every 6,000 miles (10000 km.), a new oil filter element must be fitted after the filter bowl has been carefully cleaned in petrol.

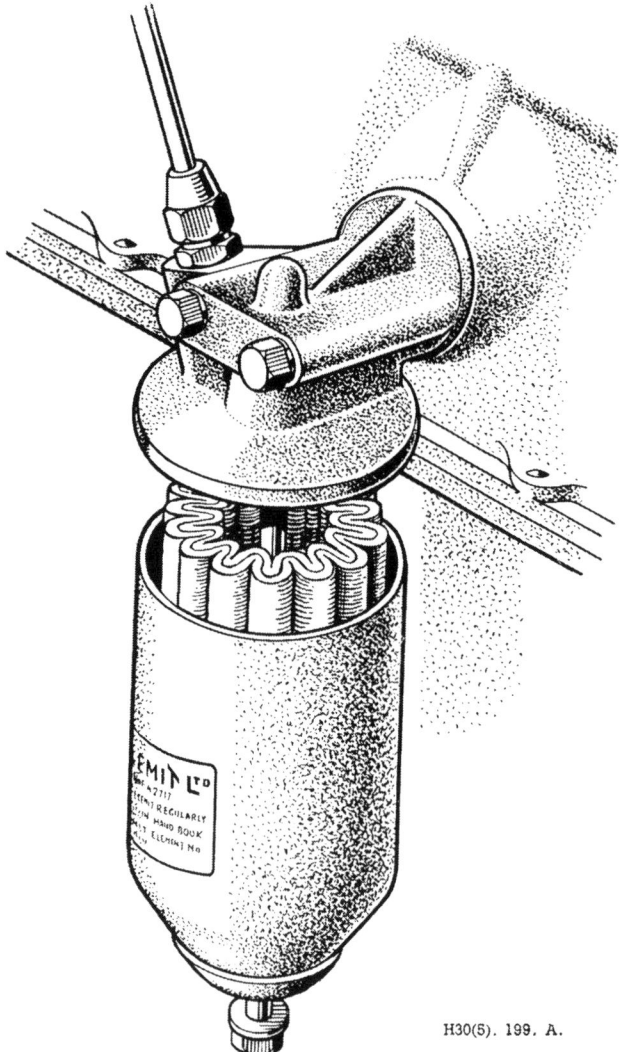

Fig. A.5. Showing the container detached and exposing the filter element.

Refilling

When refilling the sump do not pour the oil in too quickly, as it may overflow from the filler orifice and mislead the operator as to the quantity of lubricant in the engine.

Before testing the level of the oil, ensure that the vehicle is as near level as possible. Always wipe the dipstick clean with a non-fluffy cloth before taking the reading. It must be remembered that time must be allowed for new oil to reach the sump before reading the dipstick. The dipstick location is shown in Fig. A.6.

Oil Pressure

The normal operating pressure is 60 lb./sq. in. (4·2 kg/cm²).

The oil gauge is combined with the thermometer on the instrument panel.

A minimum pressure of 15 lb./sq. in. (1·05 kg/cm²) should be registered when the engine is idling. **If no pressure is registered by the gauge stop the engine at once and investigate the cause.**

Note: The automatic release valve in the lubrication system deals with any excessive oil pressure when starting from cold.

Check for Low Oil Pressure

Check the level of the oil in the sump by means of the dipstick and top up if necessary. Ascertain that the gauze strainer in the sump is clean and not choked with sludge, also that there is no leakage at the strainer union on the suction side of the sump.

In the unlikely event of the oil pump being defective, remove the unit and rectify the fault, see Section A.8. The oil release valve should be examined, see Section A.9.

If the engine bearings are worn the oil pressure will be reduced. A complete bearing overhaul and the fitting of replacement parts is the only remedy, necessitating the removal of the engine from the vehicle.

Section A.6
OIL FILTER

The external oil filter is of the full flow type, thus ensuring that all oil in the lubrication system passes through the filter before reaching the bearings.

The element of the filter is of star formation in which a special quality felt, selected for its filtering properties, is used.

Oil is passed to the filter from the pump at a pressure controlled at 60 lb./sq. in. by the engine oil release valve. This pressure will, of course, be somewhat higher until the oil reaches a working temperature. Some pressure is lost in passing the oil through the filter element, this will only be a pound or two per square inch with a new element, but will increase as the element becomes progressively contaminated by foreign matter removed from the oil.

Should the filter become completely choked due to neglect, a balance valve is provided to ensure that oil will still reach the bearings. This valve, set to open at pressure difference of 15–20 lb./sq. in., is non-adjustable and is located in the filter head casting. When the valve is opened, unfiltered oil can by-pass the filter element and reach the bearings.

To renew the filter element proceed as follows:
(1) Stop the engine, extract the centre fixing bolt, remove the container and drain.
(2) Withdraw the contaminated element and carefully

ENGINE

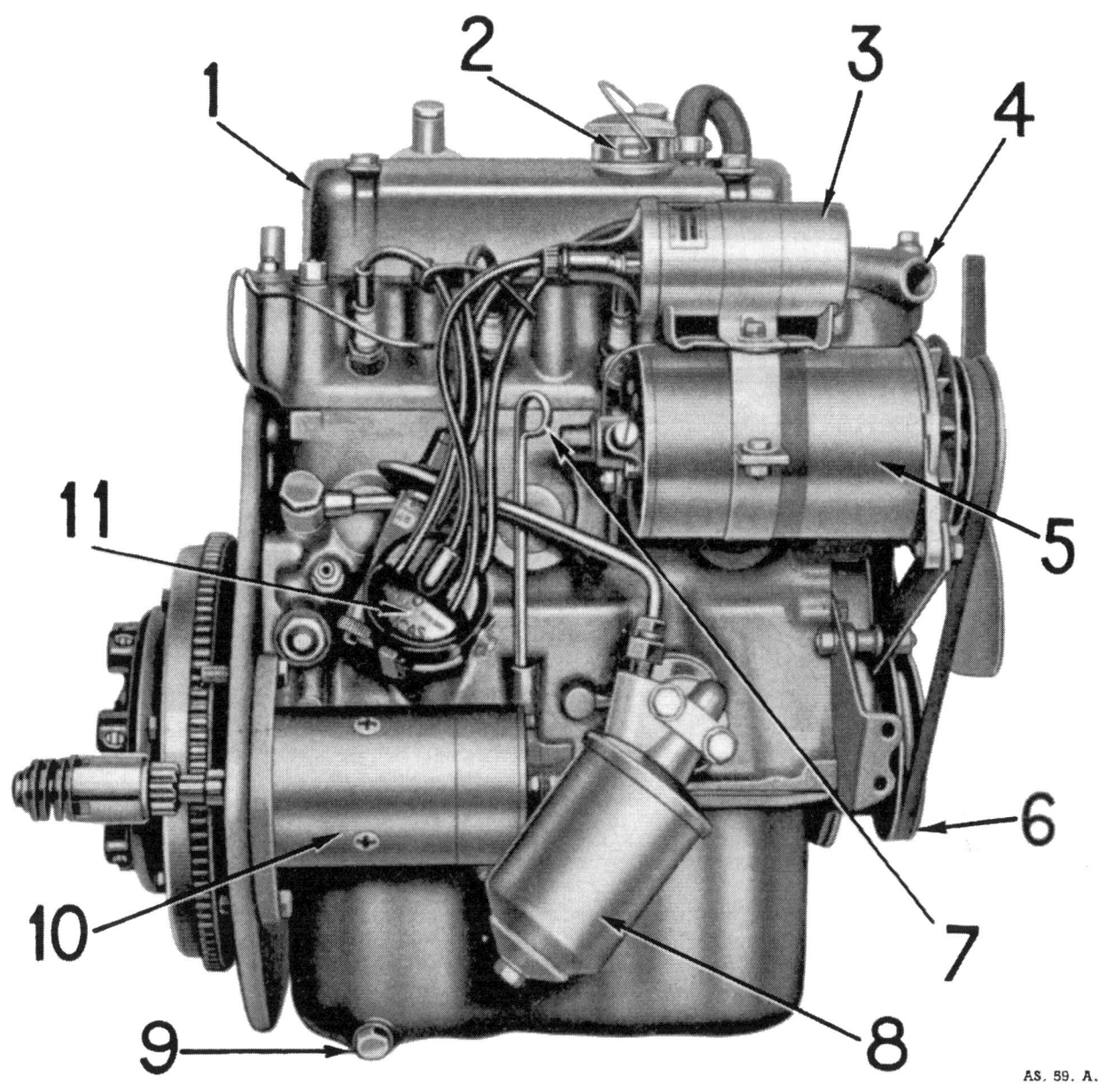

Fig. A.6. *Right-hand view of engine.*

1. Valve rocker cover.
2. Oil filler cap.
3. Ignition coil.
4. Thermostat cover and coolant outlet.
5. Generator.
6. Crankshaft pulley.
7. Oil level dipstick.
8. Full flow oil filter.
9. Oil sump drain plug.
10. Starter motor.
11. Distributor cap.

ENGINE

cleanse the container of all foreign matter that has been trapped.

(3) After ensuring that no fibres from the cleansing operation **have been left in the container,** put in a new element. Care must be taken to ensure that the washers below the element inside the bowl are fitted correctly. The small felt washer must must be positioned between the element pressure plate and the metal washer above the pressure spring. It is essential for correct oil filtration that the felt washer should be in good condition and be a snug fit on the centre-securing bolt. Hold centre bolt firm, prime the filter, and refit to head casting, tightening the centre fixing bolt sufficiently to make an oil-tight joint and then top up the engine with oil.

It is highly recommended that the filter container should not be disturbed other than for cleaning or fitting a new element; to do so invites the hazard of added contamination from accumulated dirt on the outside of the filter entering the container and thus being carried into the bearings on restarting the engine.

Section A.7

SUMP AND GAUZE STRAINER

Removing

(1) Drain off the oil into a suitable container and then extract the setscrews and washers, thus enabling the sump to be removed.
(2) Detach the oil suction pipe at its connection with the crankcase.
(3) Unscrew the two setpins securing the strainer support bracket to the main bearing caps.
(4) The strainer and support bracket may now be removed from the engine.
(5) Swill the strainer in petrol or paraffin and thoroughly dry with a non-fluffy rag.
(6) Inspect the sump joint washers and renew if necessary.

Refitting

(1) Install the strainer and its securing bracket into position, ascertaining that the oil suction pipe is located in its connection to the crankcase.
(2) Tighten the suction pipe connection.
(3) Clean out the sump by washing it in paraffin. Take care to remove any traces of the paraffin before refitting the sump to the engine.

Pay particular attention to the sump and crankcase joint faces, and remove any remainder of old jointing material. Examine the joint washers and renew if necessary. The old joint washers may be used again if they are sound, but it is advisable to fit new ones.

(4) Smear the faces of the joints with grease and fit the joint washers. Lift the sump into position and insert the setscrews into the flange tightening them up evenly.

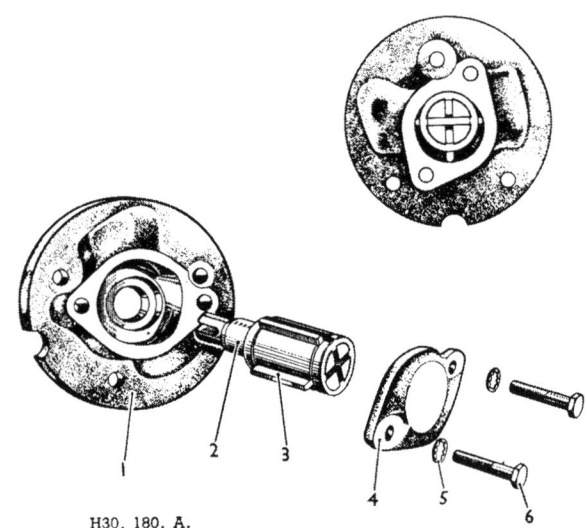

H30. 180. A.

Fig. A.7. Exploded view and plan view of the 'Burman' oil pump.
1. Oil pump flange.
2. Rotor.
3. Vane.
4. Pump cover.
5. Cover bolt washer.
6. Cover bolt.

Section A.8

OIL PUMP

To Remove

(1) The detachment of the oil pump first entails the removal of the engine from the car. Details of this procedure are described in Section A.4.
(2) Remove both flywheel and engine backplate as described in Section A.29 when access is gained to the oil pump.
(3) Tap back the locking washers and remove the three ¼ in. U.N.F. securing setscrews.
(4) Withdraw the pump noting the position of the slot in the driving shaft in order to assist replacement. If the paper joint washer is damaged in any way it must be renewed.

Dismantling

(1) Remove the oil pump cover after unscrewing its two securing setpins.
(2) The oil pump cover, the outer rotor and the combined oil pump shaft and inner rotor are all now removable.

The component parts of the oil pump are shown in Figs. A.7 and A.8. Hobourn Eaton or Burman types are fitted.

Replacing

The replacement of the oil pump is a reversal of the removal procedure; however, the operator must pay

ENGINE

Fig. A.8. Oil pump exploded
1. Pump body
2. Delivery port
3. Outer rotor
4. Inner rotor and driving shaft
5. Setscrew and washer
6. Cover
7. Suction port

particular attention when positioning the paper joint washer to ensure that the intake and delivery ports are not obstructed.

Section A.9
RELIEF VALVE

The oil relief valve (Fig. A.9) is situated at the rear right-hand side of the cylinder block, alongside the distributor. It is non-adjustable and is held in position by a compressed coil spring. This compression is maintained by two fibre washers and a domed screw plug.

The function of the valve is to provide an extra return passage for the oil should the pressure become excessive.

A pre-determined spring rating allows a release pressure of 60 lb./sq. in., and this can be checked by measuring the length of the spring, the correct figure being $2\frac{7}{8}$ in. Fit a new spring if the tension has been lost. Service Tool 18G 69 should be used to grind the valve cup into its seating.

Section A.10
ADJUSTING VALVE CLEARANCE

Lift off the valve cover after removing the two cap nuts. Between the rocker arm and the valve stem there must be a clearance of ·012 in. (·305 mm.) for both inlet and exhaust, clearance being set with the engine hot.

(1) If adjustment is necessary slacken off the locknut (3 Fig. A.13) whilst pressure is applied, with a screwdriver, to the adjusting screw.

(2) Insert a ·012 in. feeler gauge between the valve stem and rocker arm and raise or lower the adjusting screw until the correct clearance is achieved.

(3) Tighten the locknut but re-check the clearance in case the adjustment has been disturbed during the locking process.

(4) When replacing the valve cover, take care that the joint washer (using a new one if necessary) is properly seated to ensure an oil tight joint.

Section A.11
VALVE ROCKER SHAFT

Of hollow construction, the valve rocker shaft is mounted on the cylinder head and secured by means of four pedestal brackets.

It is supplied with oil through a drilling in the foremost pedestal bracket for lubrication to each rocker bearing.

The shaft is plugged at each end, one of the plugs being screwed in order that the shaft may be cleaned internally.

Section A.12
ROCKER SHAFT ASSEMBLY

Removal
(1) Drain the cooling system.

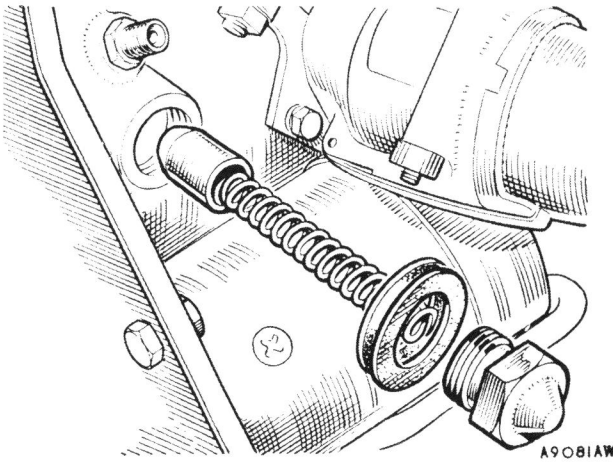

Fig. A.9. Showing the location of the oil relief valve assembly on the right side of the engine

ENGINE

(2) Unscrew the two nuts securing the rocker cover to the cylinder head, taking care not to damage the cork gasket, and remove the rocker cover.

(3) Unscrew the eight rocker shaft bracket fixing nuts and the five external cylinder head securing nuts gradually, a turn at a time, in the order shown in Fig. A.15, until all load has been released.

Note the special locking plate mounted on each rocker bracket.

(4) Completely unscrew the eight rocker shaft bracket nuts and remove the rocker assembly, complete with brackets and rockers.

Dismantling

(1) Remove the grub screw which locates the rocker shaft to the front rocker mounting bracket.

(2) Remove the split pins from each end of the rocker shaft to release thrust washers and double coil springs.

(3) Withdraw rocker, rocker shaft brackets, thrust washers and springs, retaining them in their original order for reassembly.

Reassembly

When reassembling the rocker gear, commence with the front mounting bracket, securing it with the grub screw. Follow up with the remaining brackets and springs. The screwed in end plug of the rocker shaft should be positioned towards the front of the engine.

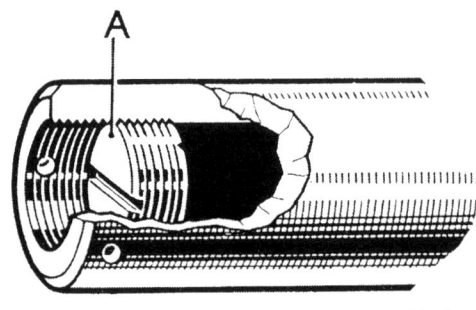

Fig. A.11. Showing a screwed plug 'A' to facilitate internal cleaning of the shaft

All springs, remaining brackets, rockers and locking plates are interchangeable.

Section A.13
PUSH ROD REMOVAL

If the valve rocker assembly has already been removed all that remains is for the push rods to be lifted out. They may on the other hand be taken out without detaching the rocker assembly as described below:

(1) Remove the valve rocker cover as described in Section A.12 and slacken the valve adjustment screw to its full extent.

(2) With the aid of a screwdriver supported under the rocker shaft, depress the valve and slide the rocker sideways free of the push rod.

(3) Withdraw the push rod.

(4) In the case of the rocker at each end, it is necessary to take out the split pins at the end of the shaft.

(5) The above sequence should be reversed when replacing push rods and rockers.

Section A.14
ROCKER ARM BUSHES

(1) While the rocker gear is detached from the head, check for play between the rocker shaft and the rocker arm bushes. If this is excessive new bushes should be fitted. To do this dismantle the rocker assembly as described in Section A.12.

(2) The bush is best removed by using a drift and anvil (Service Tool 18G 148). File and drill out the rivet in the rocker arm oilway.

(3) Drill an oilway through the bush from the top of the rocker using a No. H.7 ·0785 in. diameter drill. A second oilway must be drilled through the bush via the rocker arm using a No. 43 drill ·089 in. diameter.

(4) Plug the oilway in the rocker arm with a rivet and weld its head to the rocker boss. Ream the internal diameter of the bush to suit the shaft.

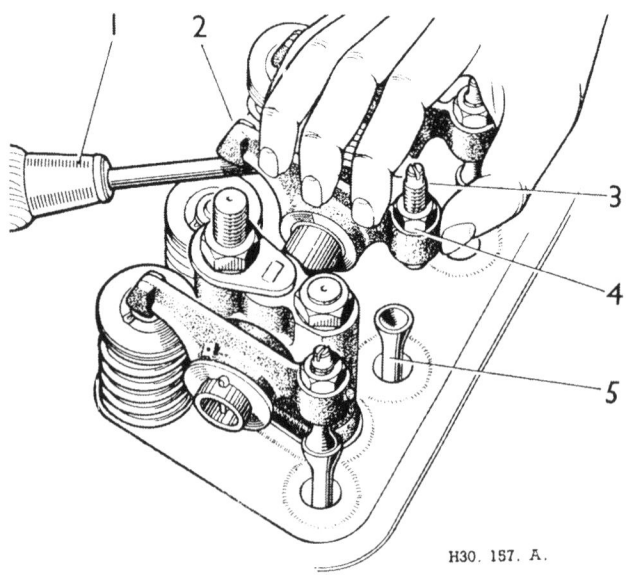

Fig. A.10. Push rod removal
1. Screwdriver
2. Valve rocker
3. Adjusting screw
4. Locknut
5. Push rod

ENGINE

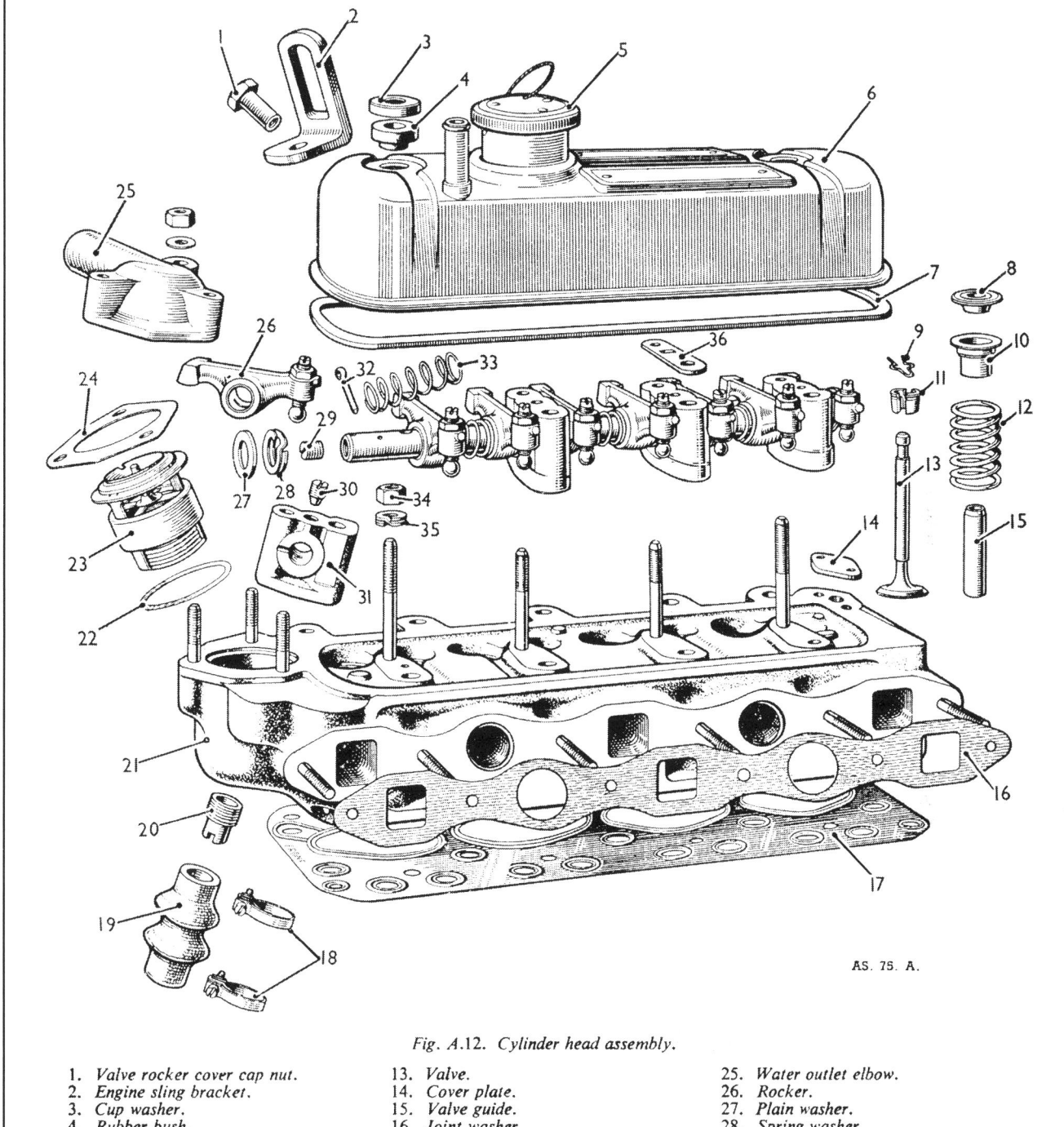

Fig. A.12. Cylinder head assembly.

1. Valve rocker cover cap nut.
2. Engine sling bracket.
3. Cup washer.
4. Rubber bush.
5. Oil filler cap.
6. Valve rocker cover.
7. Rocker cover joint washer.
8. Valve spring cup.
9. Valve cotter circlip.
10. Valve oil seal retainer.
11. Valve cotters.
12. Valve spring.
13. Valve.
14. Cover plate.
15. Valve guide.
16. Joint washer.
17. Gasket.
18. Hose clips.
19. By-pass hose.
20. By-pass tube.
21. Cylinder head.
22. Thermostat joint washer.
23. Thermostat.
24. Water outlet elbow joint washer.
25. Water outlet elbow.
26. Rocker.
27. Plain washer.
28. Spring washer.
29. Rocker shaft plug.
30. Locating grub screw.
31. Rocker shaft pedestal.
32. Split pin.
33. Rocker spacing spring.
34. Rocker bracket nut.
35. Rocker bracket washer.
36. Rocker bracket plate.

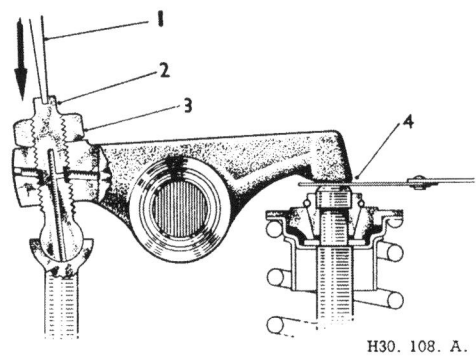

Fig. A.13. Adjusting valve clearance.
1. *Screwdriver.* 2. *Feeler gauge.*

(5) On later type engines, rockers of a pressed steel construction were introduced. This type of rocker can only be supplied complete with bush, and must not be re-bushed. Pressed-steel rockers are interchangeable with the earlier forged type of rocker, but must be fitted in complete sets; forged rockers and pressed steel rockers must not be intermingled.

Section A.15

TAPPETS

Removal

(1) Remove the pushrods after detaching the valve rocker assembly as described in Section A.12.
(2) Release the engine side covers by withdrawing their securing setscrews and fibre washers. The front cover is removed together with its vent pipe.
(3) Lift out the tappets, keeping them in their same respective locations. Inspect the tappet cam contacting surfaces for wear. New tappets should be fitted by selective assembly so that they just fall into their guides under their own weight when lubricated.

Replacement

Assembly is a reversal of the above procedure, but care should be taken to see that the tappet cover joints are oil-tight and that the rockers are adjusted to give the correct valve clearance.

Section A.16

RENEWING VALVE SPRING IN POSITION

(1) In an emergency a new valve spring can be fitted without lifting the cylinder head, but it is advisable first to bring the piston to top dead centre, to ensure that the valve cannot fall into the cylinder during the process.
(2) Remove the sparking plug, and by means of a length of copper tubing or similar tool inserted through the plug hole, the valve can be held on its seat whilst the spring is compressed. The valve rocker shaft can be used as a fulcrum point by an operator using two screwdrivers to bear on the valve spring cap each side of the valve stem, whilst the cotters are removed.

Section A.17

MANIFOLD

Removal and Replacement

(1) Detach the air cleaners from the carburetters by unscrewing the four setpins and releasing the breather pipe attached to the rear air cleaner.
(2) Disconnect the carburetters as described in Section D.
(3) Disconnect the exhaust down pipe by releasing its securing clip.
(4) Disconnect the throttle and choke linkages to the carburetters, together with the vacuum control pipe and petrol feed pipe.
(5) Unscrew and remove the six nuts and washers which secure the exhaust and inlet manifolds to the cylinder head. Four of these nuts bear on special clamping washers. The remaining two secure the end flanges of the exhaust manifold.
(6) The inlet and exhaust manifolds can now be drawn off their studs and lifted clear of the engine.
(7) The inlet and exhaust manifolds are separated by withdrawing the four connecting setscrews, noting the respective positions of the special hot spot and joint washer.
(8) Reassembly is the reverse of the above procedure; always use a new joint washer for the manifolds to ensure a gas-tight joint.

Section A.18

CYLINDER HEAD

Removing

(1) Drain all water from the cooling system, if the water contains anti-freeze mixture, it should be run into a clean container and used again.
(2) Detach the top water hose from the cylinder head.
(3) Disconnect the high tension wires from the sparking plugs.
(4) Detach the inlet and exhaust manifolds, complete with carburetters, as detailed in Section A.17.
(5) Remove rocker cover and breather pipe as described in Section A.12.
(6) Release the suction advance pipe clip from its securing point on the cylinder head. Also slacken the retaining clip and detach the heater inlet hose, if fitted.

ENGINE

(7) Remove the rocker assembly as described in Section A.12.

(8) Withdraw the push rods, keeping them in order of removal taking care not to pull the tappets out of their guides in the block.

(9) Remove the five external cylinder head nuts together with their flat washers and lift off the cylinder head.

(10) If removal of the cylinder head presents difficulty, rotate the engine by means of a spanner applied to the crankshaft pulley nut, when the head should lift off its seating.

Replacing

(1) Replace the cylinder head joint washer with the side marked 'Top' uppermost, it is not necessary to use jointing compound or grease for the gasket.

(2) Having slipped the gasket over the studs, next lower the cylinder head into position and position the cylinder head stud nut washers. Ensure that the suction advance pipe clip is replaced in its original position on the cylinder head.

(3) Insert the push rods, ensuring that the ball ends are correctly located in the tappets.

(4) Replace the rocker gear as described in Section A.12.

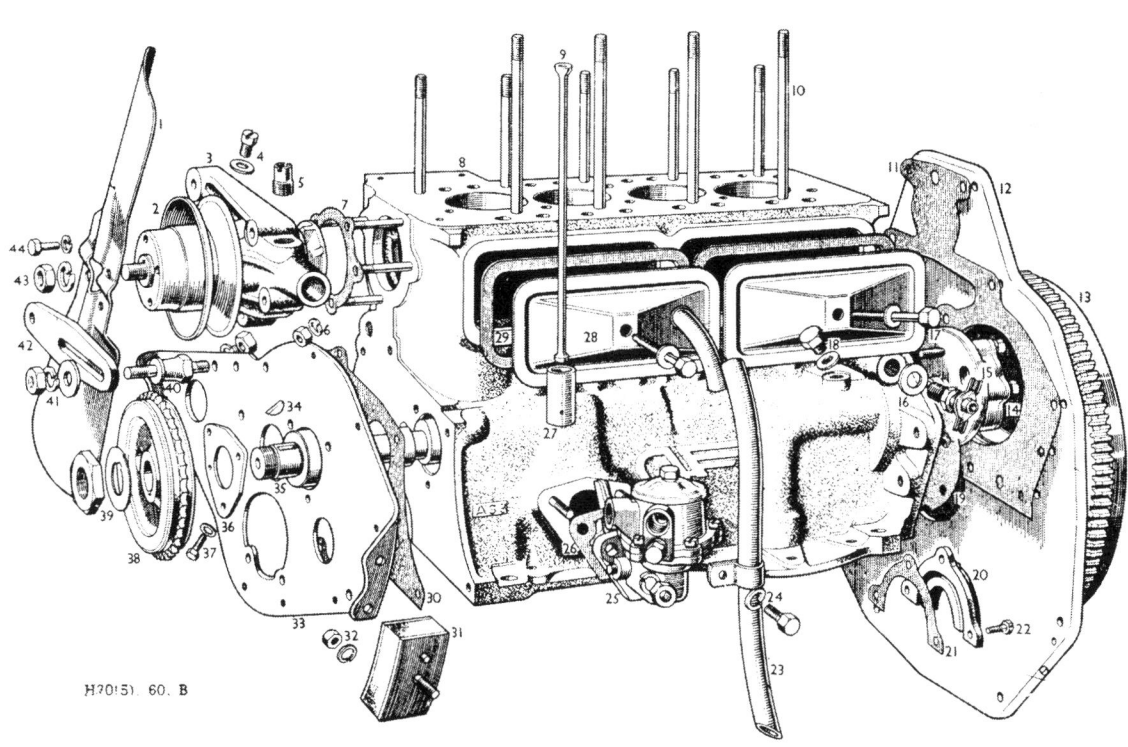

Fig. A.14. An exploded view of the crankcase assembly.

1. Fan blade.
2. Water pump pulley.
3. Water pump.
4. Water pump screwed plug and washer.
5. Water pump by-pass tube.
6. Nut and washer for water pump stud.
7. Water pump joint washer.
8. Cylinder block.
9. Push rod.
10. Cylinder head studs in block.
11. Rear mounting plate joint washer.
12. Rear mounting plate.
13. Flywheel and starter ring.
14. Oil pump.
15. Cylinder block drain tap.
16. Washer for drain tap.
17. Setscrew and washer for side cover.
18. Oil priming plug and joint washer.
19. Oil pump joint washer.
20. Crankcase rear cover.
21. Joint washer for rear cover.
22. Rear cover setscrew.
23. Crankcase vent pipe.
24. Setscrew and washer.
25. Petrol pump.
26. Petrol pump joint washer.
27. Tappet.
28. Cylinder side cover, front.
29. Joint washer for side cover.
30. Front mounting plate joint washer.
31. Rubber mounting.
32. Nut and washer for rubber mounting.
33. Engine front mounting plate.
34. Woodruff key.
35. Camshaft.
36. Camshaft locating plate.
37. Setscrew and shakeproof washer.
38. Camshaft gear and tensioner rings.
39. Nut and lockwasher.
40. Pillar for adjusting link.
41. Nut and washers for link.
42. Dynamo adjusting link.
43. Nut and washer for pulley.
44. Setscrew and washer for fan blade.

ENGINE

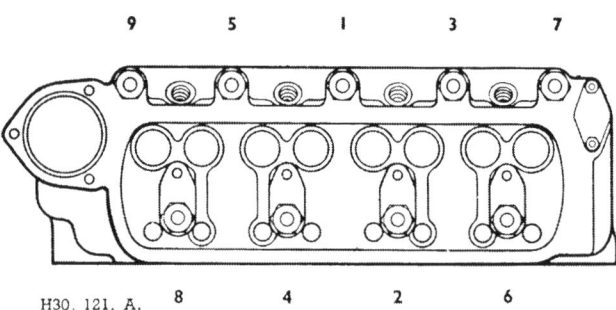

Fig. A.15. *This figure illustrates the order of tightening cylinder head nuts.*

(5) Fit the nuts finger tight and then tighten them a turn at a time, in the order given in Fig. A.15, to the recommended torque spanner readings (see 'General Data.')

(6) Reset the valve clearance, and replace the rocker cover using a new joint washer if the old one is damaged in any way.

(7) Replace the inlet and exhaust manifold and carburetters and connect up the petrol pipe, throttle and choke controls and heater outlet pipe, if fitted. Tighten the manifold nuts evenly ensuring that a good joint is made.

(8) Reconnect heater inlet pipe, water hose from the thermostat housing to the radiator, and breather pipe.

(9) Refill the cooling system, replace the sparking plugs and their washers, and the high tension wires to their respective plugs.

(10) Check the valve clearance again after the vehicle has run about 100 miles (160 km.) as the valves have a tendency to bed down. At the same time it is advisable to test the cylinder head nuts for tightness. Tightening the cylinder head nuts may affect valve clearances, although not usually enough to justify resetting.

Section A.19

REMOVING AND REFITTING VALVES

With the cylinder head removed, a valve lifting tool can be used to compress the springs (Service Tool 18G 45). Take away the circlip, split cotters, and valve stem cap, so releasing the spring and shroud and allowing the valve to be removed.

(1) When removing the valves, place them in a rack, thus enabling them to be paired up with their correct cylinders.

(2) Clean the carbon from the top and bottom of the valve heads, as well as any deposit that may have accumulated on the stems. The valve heads should, if necessary, be refaced at an angle of 45° for both exhaust and inlet valves. If the valve seats show signs of excessive pitting it is advisable to reface these also.

(3) The valves are made without any indentures or slots in the head, this necessitates the use of a rubber suction valve grinding tool.

(4) Reassembly is a reversal of the operations for removal.

Section A.20

VALVE GRINDING

(1) For valve grinding a little grinding paste should be smeared evenly on the valve face, and the valve rotated backwards and forwards against its seat (using Service Tool 18G 29 with suction pad 18G 29B), advancing it a step at short intervals until a clean and unpitted seating is obtained. The cutting action is facilitated by allowing a light spring situated under the valve head, to periodically lift the valve from its seat. This allows the grinding compound to re-penetrate between the two faces after being squeezed out.

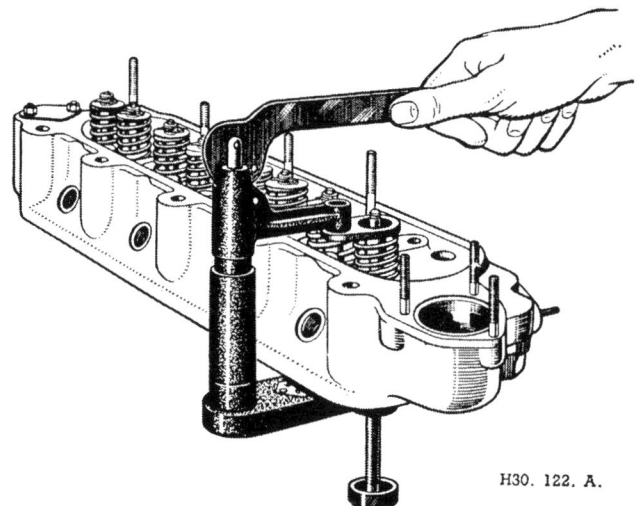

Fig. A.16. *Using Service Tool 18G 45 to compress a valve spring.*

(2) On completion, all traces of compound must be removed from the valve and seating. It is essential that each valve is ground-in and refitted to its own seating.

(3) It is also desirable to clean the valve guides; this can be done by dipping the valve stem in petrol or paraffin, and moving it up and down in the guide until it is free.

ENGINE

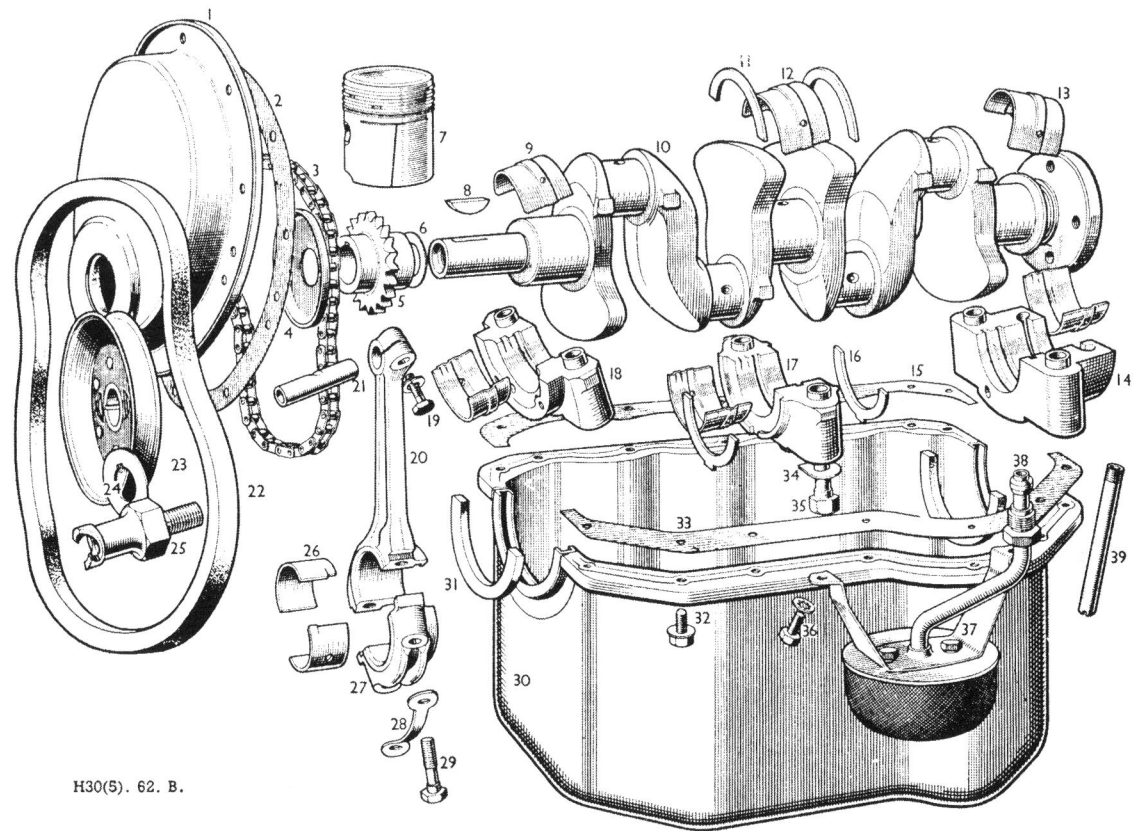

Fig. A.17. *The crankshaft and sump assembly.*

1. Engine front cover.
2. Joint washer for cover.
3. Timing chain.
4. Crankshaft oil thrower.
5. Crankshaft gear.
6. Packing washers.
7. Piston.
8. Woodruff key.
9. Front main half bearing.
10. Crankshaft.
11. Thrust washer, upper.
12. Centre main half bearing.
13. Rear main half bearing.
14. Rear main bearing cap and dowels.
15. Oil sump joint washer, right.
16. Thrust washer, lower.
17. Centre main bearing cap and dowels.
18. Front main bearing cap and dowels.
19. Clamping screw and washer for (20).
20. Connecting rod, less cap.
21. Gudgeon pin.
22. Vee-belt for fan and pulley.
23. Crankshaft pulley.
24. Lockwasher.
25. Starting nut.
26. Connecting rod half bearing.
27. Connecting rod cap.
28. Lockwasher.
29. Setscrew for connecting rod.
30. Oil sump.
31. Cork sealing washer.
32. Set screw and captive washer
33. Oil sump joint washer, left.
34. Main bearing cap lockwasher.
35. Setscrew for main bearing cap.
36. Setscrew and shakeproof washer for strainer bracket.
37. Oil strainer.
38. Suction pipe.
39. Drain pipe for rear main bearing cap

Section A.21

VALVE GUIDES

(1) The valve guides are of a one-piece design. They are pressed into the cylinder head to allow $\frac{19}{32}$ in. (15·0812 mm.) of the guide to protrude above the machined face when fitted.

(2) To position each valve spring on the cylinder head, a stepped pressed steel seating collar is fitted over the part of the guide protruding from the cylinder head.

(3) Valve guides should be tested for wear whenever valves are removed, and if excessive side play is present, a close check should be made of the valve stem and the guide. In the event of wear being noticeable, the defective components should be renewed. If a valve is at fault the wear will be evident on the stem. It should be borne in mind that the valve stem and guide should be a running fit to avoid the possibility of an air leak.

(4) If renewal is necessary due to wear, the valve guide may be driven out after removal of the

ENGINE

valve, as shown in Fig. A.18.

(5) The drift is stepped in order to ensure location and to obviate it slipping off the guide and damaging the port. Knock out the guide in the direction shown.

(6) A new guide should be driven into position in the same direction, that is, inserting it from the top of the cylinder head and knocked downwards.

(7) The final position of the guide is shown in Fig. A.18.

(2) Scrape off all carbon deposit from the cylinder head and ports. Clean the carbon from the piston crowns, care being taken not to damage the pistons, and not to allow dirt or carbon deposit to enter the cylinder barrels or push rod compartment.

When cleaning the top of the pistons do not scrape right to the edge as a little carbon left on the chamfer assists in keeping down oil consumption; with the pistons cleaned right to the edge or new pistons, oil consumption is often slightly though temporarily increased.

(3) Blow out the oil passages and swill out the water passages using a water hose. The gasket contacting surfaces of the head should be checked for flatness with a straight-edge and the surfaces examined for scores. If the cylinder head is found to be badly out of true it should be renewed.

(4) Remove all carbon accumulation from the valves and thoroughly clean them. Inspect the valve bases and seats and if they are slightly pitted or rough, grind them in, as described in Section A.20. If the valves and seats show signs of excessive pitting, or the faces are not flat, the valves and seats should be replaced.

(5) Examine the valve guides, as described in Section A.21.

(6) Broken or weak valve springs should be renewed. The other valve springs should be tested and the results compared with figures given in 'GENERAL DATA'.

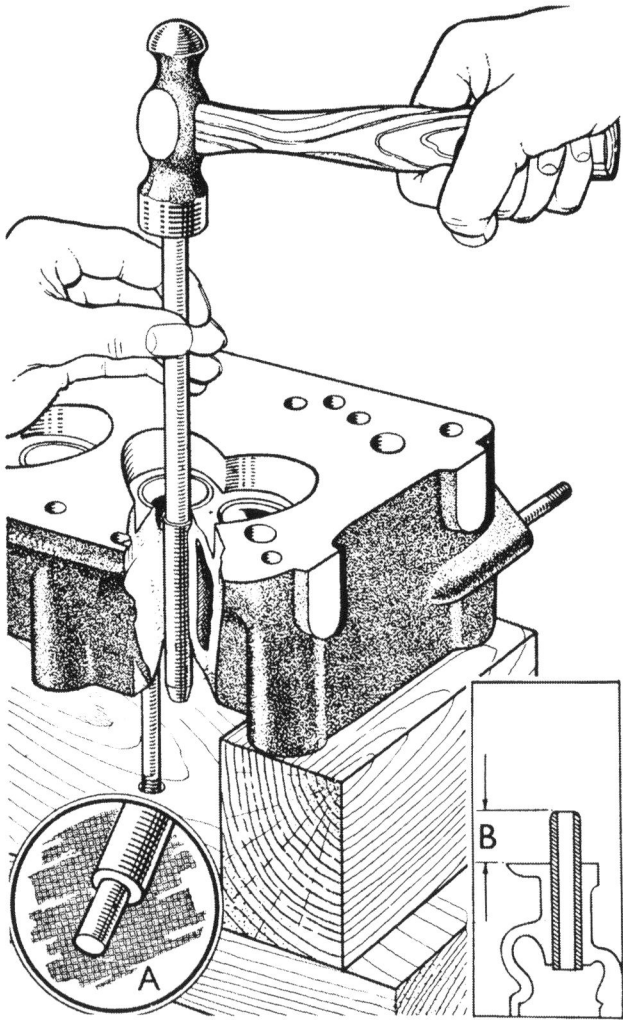

Fig. A.18. *Removing a valve guide.*
The inset 'A' shows the form of the tool.
B. The valve guide should be $\frac{19}{32}$ in. above the cylinder head.

Section A.22

DECARBONISING

(1) Remove the cylinder head as described in Section A.18.

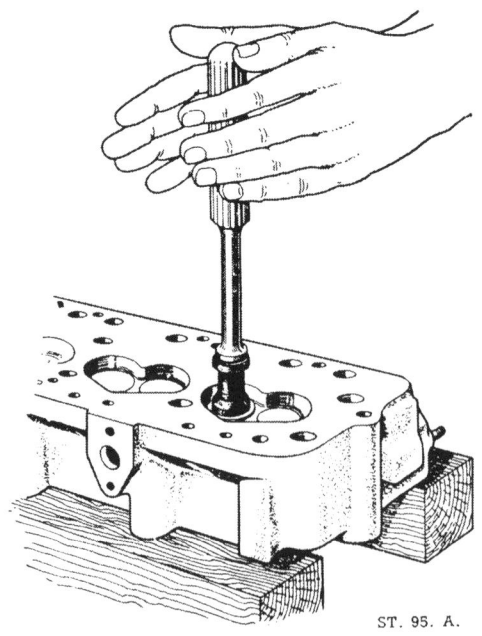

Fig. A.19. *Grinding in a valve.*

ENGINE

(7) Clean the rocker shaft gear and blow out the oil passages as described in Section A.11.

(8) Inspect the rocker shaft, rockers and bushes for wear. Renew any worn rocker bushes as described in Section A.14.

(9) Reassemble and install the cylinder head assembly.

The following operations should be carried out with the engine removed, although in some cases it is possible to perform them with the engine in position.

Before removing or replacing any component it is important to ensure that all surrounding surfaces are perfectly clean, to prevent the entry of foreign matter into the engine. This can best be accomplished by the use of a paraffin bath and brush, and it is also important to note that fluffy rags should never be used, as there is danger of causing obstruction to small oil ways.

Section A.23

CONNECTING RODS AND BEARINGS

Removal

(1) Remove the cylinder head assembly as described in Section A.18.

(2) Drain and remove the sump (see Section A.5).

(3) Unlock and remove the nuts securing the caps and bearings to the connecting rods. Remove the caps and bearings.

(4) Withdraw the pistons and connecting rods upwards through the cylinder bores.

(5) It may be necessary to remove the carbon or ridge from the top of the bores prior to pushing the pistons upwards, to avoid piston-ring fracture.

(6) Remove the pistons from the connecting rods by unscrewing the clamp bolt from the small end of the connecting rod and pushing the gudgeon pin out.

(7) Ensure that each connecting rod, cap and bearing is marked with the cylinder number from which it was removed.

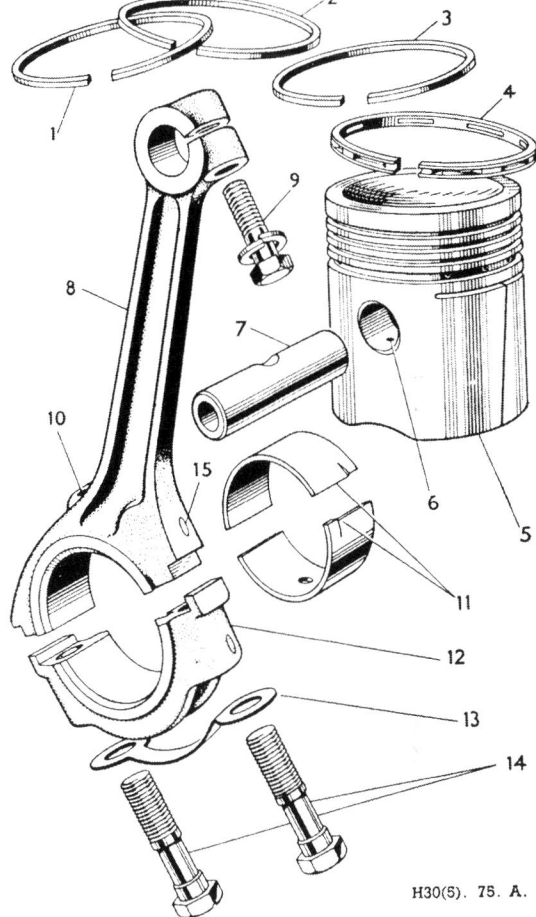

Fig. A.21. *Connecting rod and piston assembly.*

1. Piston ring, parallel.
2. Piston ring, taper.
3. Piston ring, taper.
4. Piston ring, scraper.
5. Piston.
6. Gudgeon pin lubricating hole.
7. Gudgeon pin.
8. Connecting rod, less cap.
9. Clamping screw and washer.
10. Cylinder wall lubricating jet.
11. Connecting rod bearings.
12. Connecting rod cap.
13. Lockwasher.
14. Setscrews.
15. Mark on rod and cap.

(8) The big ends are offset, and rods in numbers 1 and 3 cylinders are offset towards the front, with 2 and 4 cylinders offset towards the rear.

(9) The alignment of the connecting rods should be checked on an alignment fixture. On no account must the rods or caps be filed.

(10) Examine the bearing shells for wear and pits. Renew the bearing shell if necessary. **Bearings**

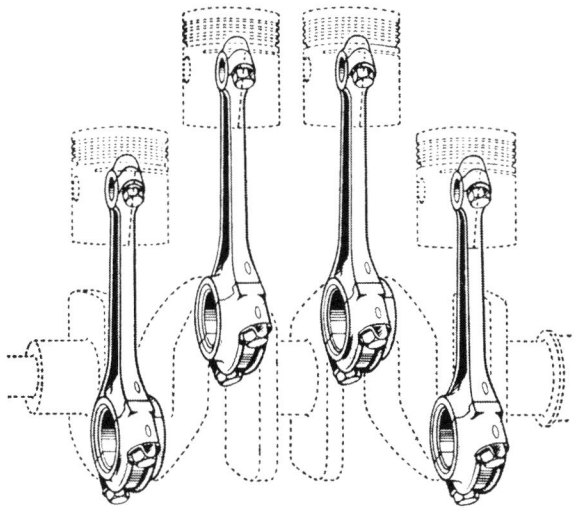

Fig. A.20. *Showing the positions of the offsets and the correct method of assembly.*

ENGINE

are pre-finished with the correct diametral clearance and do not require bedding in.

(11) Check the crankpins with a micrometer, if they are worn oval or are scored, the crankshaft will have to be removed for regrinding, see Section A.30.

Replacing

Before installing the connecting rods and bearings it is assumed that the pistons and rings have been serviced, see Section A.24.

The pistons and connecting rods must be fitted in the same cylinder bores and the same way round as when removed.

(1) Assemble the piston and the connecting rod to the gudgeon pin, so that the split in the piston skirt is adjacent to the split in the top of the connecting rod.

(2) Refit the piston rings very carefully, make quite sure that the pistons and bores are perfectly clean and smear the bores with clean engine oil.

(3) Use a piston ring clamp, Service Tool No. 18G 55A, when replacing the pistons from the top of the bore, and make sure that the split in the piston faces the camshaft.

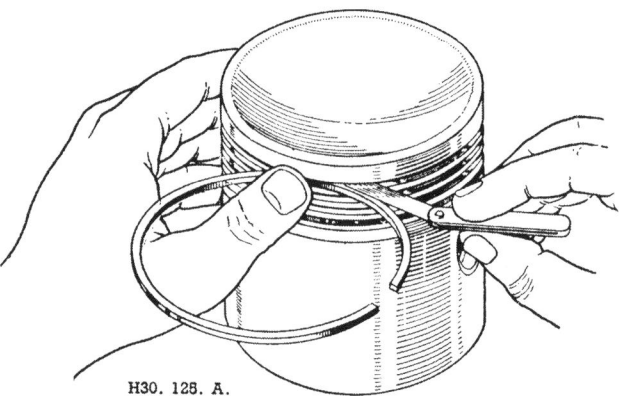

Fig. A.22. *Checking the piston ring groove clearance.*

(4) Clean the crankpins and both sides of the shell bearings, locate the feathered ends in the connecting rod and its cap, and smear the crankpins with engine oil.

(5) Before fitting the cap, check that the number stamped on the rod is the same as that on the cap. Note that the recess in the cap and rod must be on the same side. Tighten and lock the nuts. Turn the crankshaft after fitting each rod, to ensure that the bearing is not binding on the crankpin. Also check the side clearance of each rod, as given under 'General Data'.

(6) Refit the cylinder head assembly, see Section A.18.

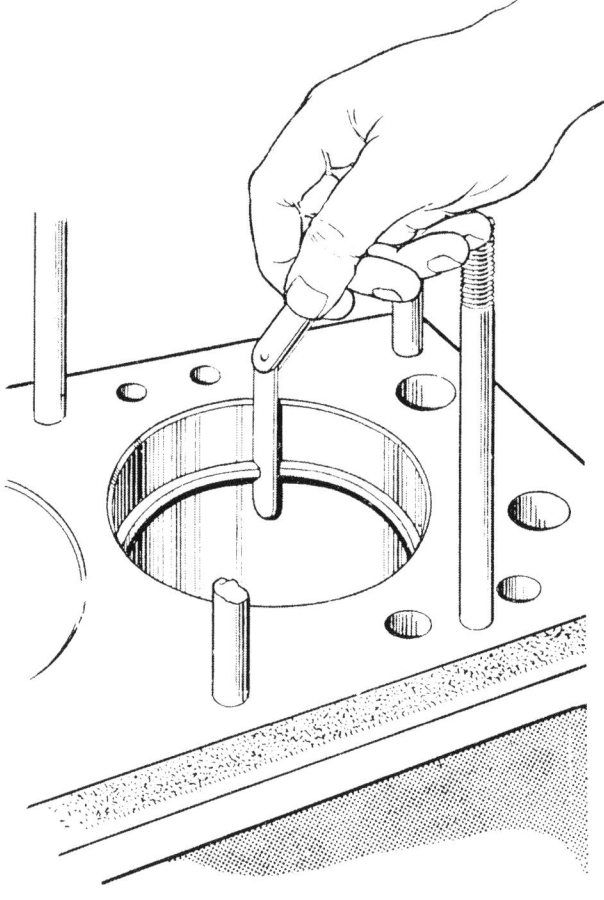

Fig. A.23. *Measuring the piston ring gap.*

(7) Refit the sump and refill with recommended grade of oil, see Section P.

Section A.24

PISTONS, RINGS AND GUDGEON PINS

Removal

The split-skirt pistons are of aluminium alloy material. Four rings are fitted above the gudgeon pin, the bottom ring being of the oil-control type. The pistons are fastened to the connecting rods by gudgeon pins which are clamped rigidly in the small ends of the connecting rods. Bushings are not needed in the gudgeon pin bosses of the pistons because the aluminium alloy material serves as a suitable bearing for the gudgeon pins, the bearing surfaces of which are lubricated by means of splash through the two holes drilled in each boss. To remove the pistons see Section A.23.

To view and overhaul

(1) Remove the rings over the tops of the pistons.

ENGINE

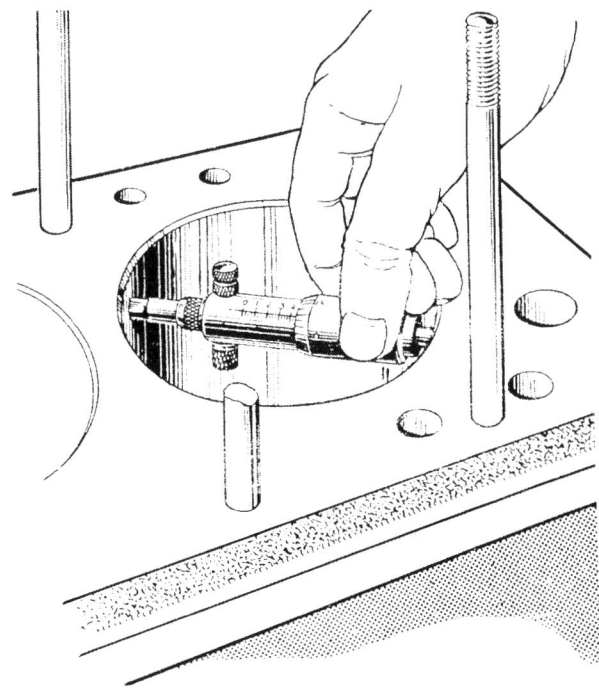

Fig. A.24. Checking the bore for ovality with an internal micrometer

(2) Scrape all accumulation of carbon off the piston heads and, using a piston ring groove-cleaning tool or an old ring section, carefully scrape all carbon out of the ring grooves of the pistons. Clean the carbon out of the oil holes in the piston ring grooves.

(3) Thoroughly clean all the dismantled components in paraffin.

(4) Examine all parts for wear and damage, renew if necessary.

(5) If cylinder reconditioning is required, determine the amount of material to be removed (refer to Section A.25 concerning oversize pistons available).

(6) When fitting new or oversize pistons and rings to reconditioned cylinder bores, the clearances should be controlled within the limits given under 'General Data'.

Selective assembly is necessary, and for this purpose pistons are stamped with distinguishing symbols of grade and oversize.

(7) Piston rings should have a gap clearance (see 'General Data') when installed in the cylinder bores. If new rings are being installed, each ring should be checked in the cylinder bore to determine whether its gap clearance is within the range specified. To do this, use the bottom of a piston to insert the ring part way into the bore. The ring will be squared up in the bore to measure the gap clearance as shown Fig. A.23. To check the ring clearance in the piston grooves, install the rings on the pistons and determine the clearances with a feeler gauge. If the piston ring grooves are worn excessively, as indicated when comparing the actual clearances with those given under 'General Data', renew the rings and pistons.

(8) Gudgeon pins should be a hand-push fit in the pistons. The fit can be checked after the rod has been assembled by holding the piston with the connecting rod in an approximately horizontal position. The weight of the large end of the connecting rod should be just insufficient to turn the gudgeon pin in the piston. On no account must gudgeon pin piston bosses be reamed out as oversize gudgeon pins are not supplied or permitted.

Replacement

See Section A.23.

Section A.25

PISTON SIZES AND CYLINDER BORES

In production pistons are fitted by selective assembly, and to facilitate this the pistons are stamped with identification figures on their crowns.

The number enclosed in a diamond, e.g. a piston stamped with a figure 2, is for a bore bearing a figure 3.

In addition to the standard pistons there is a range of four oversize pistons available for service purposes. Oversize pistons are marked with the actual oversize dimensions enclosed in an ellipse. A piston stamped ·020 is suitable only for a bore ·020 in. (·508 mm.) larger than the standard bore, and similarly, pistons with other markings are suitable only for the oversize bore indicated.

The piston markings indicate the actual bore size to which they must be fitted, the requisite running clearance being allowed for in the machining.

After reboring an engine, or whenever fitting pistons differing in size from those removed during dismantling, ensure that the size of the piston fitted is stamped clearly on the top of the cylinder block alongside the appropriate cylinder bore.

Pistons are supplied in the sizes indicated in the following table.

A

ENGINE

Piston marking	Suitable bore size	Metric equivalent
STANDARD	2·4778 in. to 2·4781 in.	62·935 mm. to 62·940 mm.
OVERSIZE +·010 in. (·254 mm.)	2·4878 in. to 2·4881 in.	63·189 mm. to 63·194 mm.
+·020 in. (·508 mm.)	2·4978 in. to 2·4981 in.	63·443 mm. to 63·448 mm.
+·030 in. (·762 mm.)	2·5078 in. to 2·5081 in.	63·697 mm. to 63·702 mm.
+·040 in. (1·016 mm.)	2·5178 in. to 2·5181 in.	63·951 mm. to 63·956 mm.

Section A.26

TIMING COVER

Removal and Replacement

(1) Drain the cooling system as described in Section C.
(2) Remove the radiator (see Section C.).
(3) Slacken the generator attachment bolts and remove the belt.
(4) Bend back the tab on the crankshaft pulley nut locking washer. Unscrew the nut.
(5) Pull off the crankshaft pulley.
(6) The timing cover is secured by four large setpins and six small ones. Each setpin has a shakeproof washer and a plain washer. Unscrew all ten setpins with their washers and remove the timing cover.
(7) Take care not to damage the timing cover gasket. If it is damaged, clean the face of the cover flange and the engine front mounting plate and fit a new gasket when reassembling.
(8) The oil seal situated in the timing cover should also be renewed if necessary.
   It should be noted that the oil thrower, which is located behind the crankshaft pulley, is fitted with its concave side facing forward.
(9) When the special aligning tool (Service Tool 18G 138) is not available the crankshaft pulley should be assembled to the cover before the cover is refitted to the engine. This will ensure that the timing cover and oil seal are concentric with the crankshaft. Lubricate the hub of the pulley and, with a rotating movement to avoid damage to the oil seal, insert it in the cover. Push the pulley and timing cover on to the crankshaft, lining up the pulley bore keyway with the Woodruff key fitted to the crankshaft. Replace the cover set screws and tighten them up evenly.
(10) Reassembly is now a reversal of the removal procedure.

Section A.27

TIMING CHAIN AND WHEELS

Removal

(1) Remove the timing cover and oil thrower as described in the previous Section.
(2) Unlock and remove the camshaft chain wheel nut and remove the nut and lockwasher. Note that the locating tag on the lockwasher fits into the keyway of the camshaft chain wheel.
(3) Remove the camshaft and crankshaft chain wheels, together with the timing chain, by easing each wheel forward a fraction at a time with suitable small levers. Note the packing washers immediately behind the crankshaft gear wheel.

Replacement

(1) Unless new camshaft or crankshaft components have been fitted, replace the same number of packing washers behind the crankshaft gear wheel. If adjustment is necessary, however, it is required to determine the thickness of packing washers. This is achieved by placing a straight-edge across the sides of the camshaft wheel teeth and measure with a feeler gauge the gap between the straight-edge and the crankshaft gear.

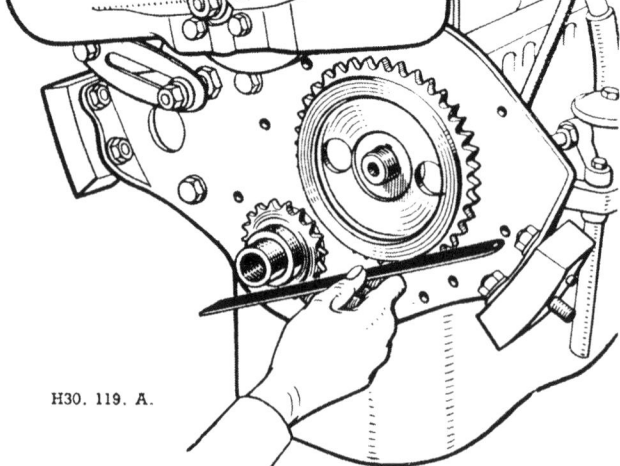

H30. 119. A.

Fig. A.25. Lining up the crankshaft and camshaft gear teeth with a straight-edge.

ENGINE

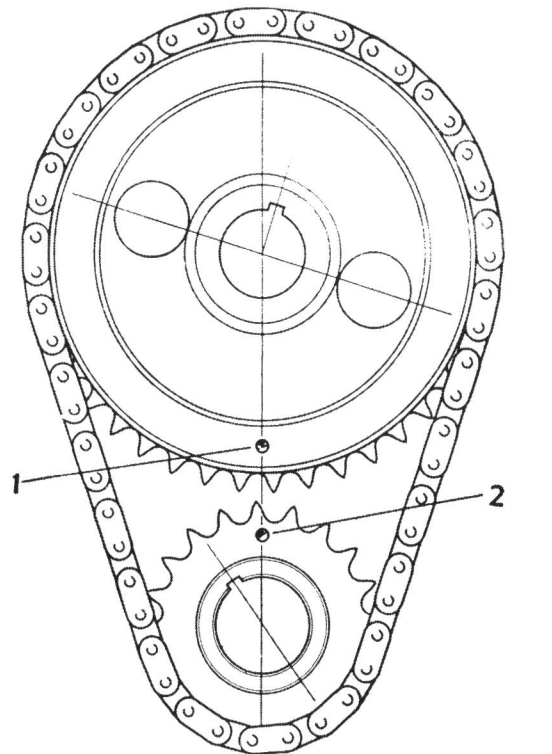 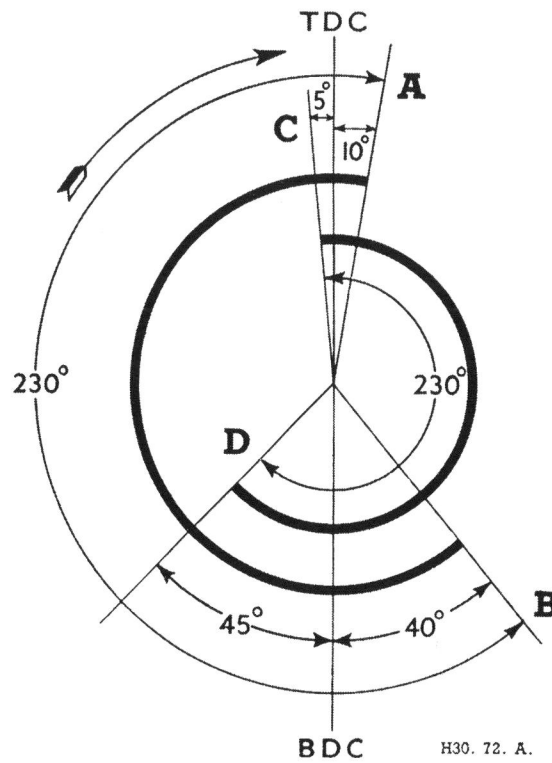

Fig. A.26. Showing timing diagram and position of timing gears. 1 and 2. Timing marks. A. to B. Exhaust open, C. to D. Inlet open, with the valve rocker clearances set at 0·019 in. (for checking purposes only)

(2) Set the crankshaft with its keyway at T.D.C. and the camshaft with its keyway approximately at the one o'clock position when seen from the front.

(3) Assemble the gears into the timing chain with the two marks on the gear wheels opposite each other, Fig. A.26.

(4) Keeping the gears in this position, engage the crankshaft gear keyway with the key on the crankshaft and rotate the camshaft until the camshaft gear keyway and key are aligned.

(5) Push the gears onto the shafts and secure the camshaft gear with the lockwasher and nut.

(6) Replace the oil thrower, concave side forward, and the remaining components as detailed in Section A.26.

Section A.28

CAMSHAFT AND BEARINGS

Removal

(1) Drain the sump and release it from the engine. Remove the rocker assembly.

(2) Remove the push rods and take out the tappets, see Section A.13.

(3) Remove the timing cover, timing chain tensioner, chain and gears, see Sections A.26 and A.27.

(4) Detach the oil pump, see Section A.8.

(5) Remove the distributor and spindle drive, see Section B. Do not slacken the clamping plate bolt or the ignition timing setting will be lost.

(6) Take out the two setscrews which secure the camshaft locating plate to the cylinder block.

(7) Withdraw the camshaft forward, rotating it slowly to assist the withdrawal.

(8) Inspect the camshaft bearing journals and cams for signs of scoring. If the journals are not within the required diameter limits (see under 'General Data'), the camshaft should be renewed.

(9) Examine the camshaft front bearing for scores, pits or evidence of failure. If the bearing has to be renewed it will necessitate the removal of the engine back plate as described in Section A.29.

The old bearing can then be withdrawn and a new one installed, using Service Tool 18G 124A with 18G 124K.

Oil holes must be lined up carefully and the front bearing reamed in line to give ·001 to ·002 in. (·025 to ·051 mm.) clearance, using Service Tool 18G 123A with 18G 123AH.

The centre and rear camshaft bearings are cast in the block and are therefore non-renewable.

ENGINE

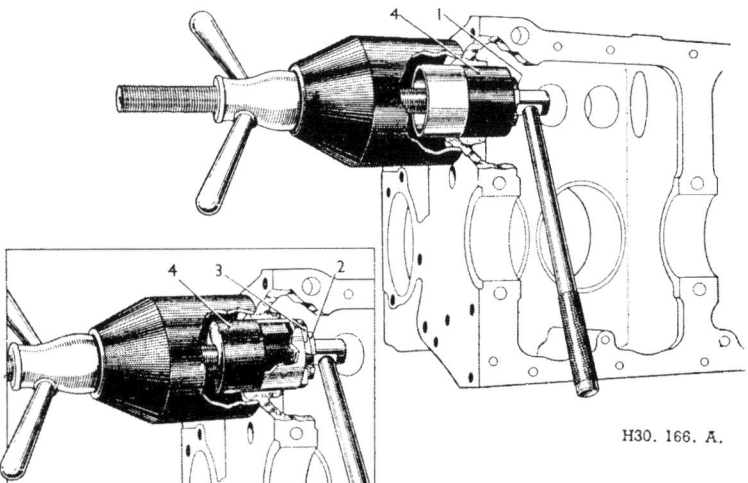

Fig. A.27. Removing a camshaft front bearing using Adaptor 18G 124K in conjunction with Service Tool 18G 124A.

1. 'C' washer.
2. 'C' washer.
3. 'D' washer.
4. Adaptor 18G 124K.

Inset shows the bearing being replaced.

(10) Inspect the tappet cam contacting surfaces for wear. New tappets should be installed wherever evidence of unusual wear is found.

(11) The installation of the camshaft and tappets is a reversal of the procedure **'Removal'**. Lubricate the camshaft journals with engine oil.

Camshaft Liner Removal

When reconditioning cylinder blocks it is usual to renew the camshaft liner. From within the cylinder block place adaptor 18G 124K inside the liner, pass the screw of 18G 124A through the body of the tool and adaptor from in front of the cylinder block.

Position the 'C' washer on the flat at the end of the screw, fit the handle into the hole (to prevent the screw from turning) and screw up the wing nut. Continued tightening of the wing nut will quickly withdraw the liner.

Camshaft Liner Replacement

Place the new liner on the smaller diameter of adaptor 18G 124K and from inside the cylinder block position the adaptor in the camshaft liner bore.

Line up the oil holes in the camshaft liner bore and liner, place the 'D' washer in position behind the liner, pass the screw of Tool 18G 124A through the adaptor, liner and 'D' washer, then fit the 'C' washer and tighten the screw. Secure the handle in the hole in the rear end of the screw to prevent it from turning; tighten the wing nut to draw the liner squarely into position.

Reaming the Liner

Fit the two pilots 18G 123AH into the centre and rear camshaft bores, pass the cutter on to the arbor of Tool 18G 123A and locate it in position '8'. A peg retained in the centre groove of the cutter by means of a spring clip, locates in a hole in the arbor, thus holding the cutter in the desired position.

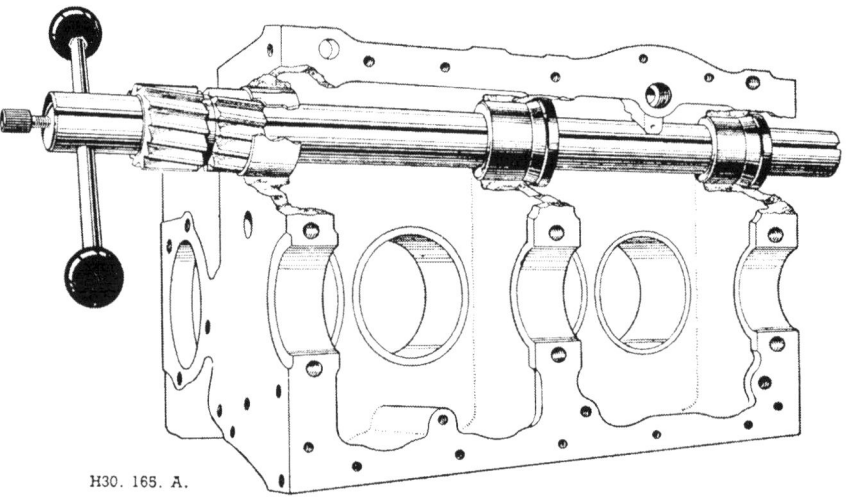

Fig. A.28. Camshaft liner reamer and pilots, 18G 123AH, being used in conjunction with the arbor of 18G 123A to ream the front camshaft bearing shell in line with the centre and rear bearings.

ENGINE

As the tool is made up of roughing and finishing cutters care must be taken to see that it is placed on the arbor with the roughing cutter towards the liner to be reamed.

Carefully pass the arbor through the camshaft bore and two pilots, then when the cutter comes up to the liner, commence to ream, always turning in a clockwise direction. Do not attempt to force the reamer through the liner, but proceed gently. Swarf should be frequently cleared away during the cutting operation.

When the cutter has passed right through the liner, disconnect it from the arbor and hold it inside the cylinder block whilst the arbor is carefully withdrawn.

Note: On no account must the cutter be brought through the reamed hole, on the arbor. Finally, before refitting the camshaft, thoroughly clean the block of all swarf.

Section A.29

FLYWHEEL AND ENGINE REAR PLATE

To Remove

The flywheel complete with starter ring is secured to the flange on the rear of the crankshaft by four set bolts, which are locked in position by two lockplates. The engine rear plate is secured to the crankcase by set bolts and lockwashers. To remove the flywheel and rear plate, after the engine is removed from the vehicle, proceed as follows:

(1) Remove the gearbox from the engine (see Section F).
(2) Remove the clutch (see Section E).
(3) Knock back the tabs of the lockplates, unscrew the bolts and withdraw the flywheel.
(4) Unscrew the set bolts and withdraw the engine rear plate.
(5) Examine the flywheel teeth and friction face for excessive wear. If the teeth on the starter ring are damaged or badly worn, a replacement flywheel and ring should be fitted.

   Note: The fitting of a new starter ring only, requires special workshop equipment for heating the ring evenly to shrink it onto the flywheel. If these facilities are available, heat the ring to a temperature of 1616° to 1652° F. (880° to 900° C.) before fitting.

(6) Examine the engine rear plate for distortion and damage and clean the joint faces of the plate and crankcase and check for scores.

To Install

(1) Refit the engine rear plate to the crankcase, using a new joint washer. Tighten the securing bolts evenly and firmly with a torque wrench to 22 lb. ft. (3·042 kg. m.).

(2) Place the flywheel over the flange and flange bolts of the crankshaft so that the timing mark '1/4' is at T.D.C. when the first throw of the crankshaft is at T.D.C. The joint faces should be perfectly clean. Fit the lockplates and nuts on the bolts and tighten them in diagonal sequence with a torque wrench to 40 lb. ft. (55 kg. m.).

Section A.30

CRANKSHAFT AND MAIN BEARINGS

To Remove

The forged-steel crankshaft is statically and dynamically balanced and is supported in the crankcase by three renewable main bearings of the sintered copper and lead steel-backed type. Crankshaft end float is controlled by thrust washers fitted on both sides of the centre main bearing.

(1) Remove the engine from the vehicle (see Section A.4) and place it upside-down in a dismantling fixture.
(2) Remove the sump and oil strainer (see Section A.7).
(3) Remove the timing chain (see Section A.27).
(4) Remove the flywheel and engine rear plate (see Section A.29).
(5) Check the crankshaft end float to determine whether the renewal of the thrust washers is necessary (Fig. A.29).
(6) Remove the connecting rod bearing caps and shells, keeping the shells with their respective caps for correct replacement, and release the connecting rods from the crankshaft. Remove the sparking plugs from the cylinder head to facilitate the turning of the crankshaft.

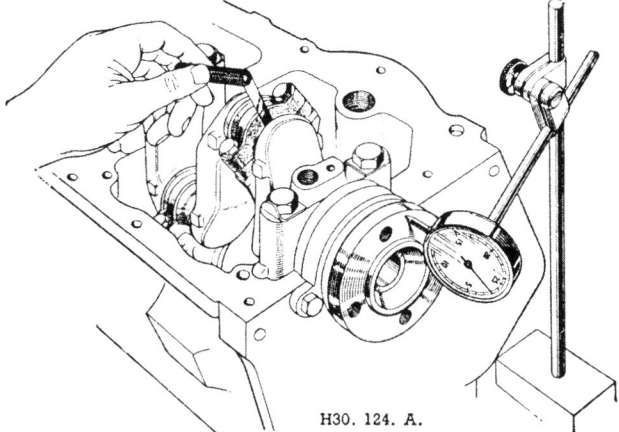

Fig. A.29. A feeler gauge being used to measure connecting rod side clearance and a dial gauge to check crankshaft end float.

ENGINE

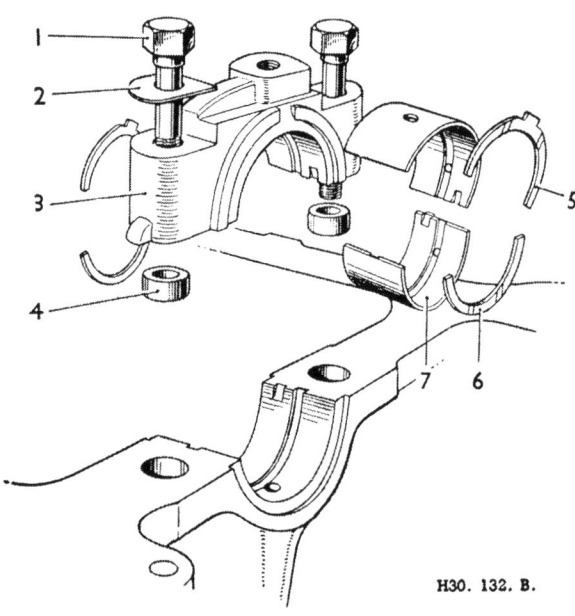

Fig. A.30. Centre main bearing assembly.

1. Main bearing setscrews.
2. Lockwasher.
3. Main bearing cap.
4. Dowels.
5. Thrust washer, lower.
6. Thrust washer, upper.
7. Main bearing shell.

(7) Withdraw the main bearing caps complete with bearing bottom shells. Caps and both bearing half-shells should be kept together. Remove the screwed plug from the rear bearing cap oil return pipe and withdraw the pipe. Note that each main bearing is stamped with a common number, which is also stamped on the centre web of the crankcase near the main bearing. The bottom halves of the two thrust washers will be removed with the centre main bearing cap.

(8) Remove the crankshaft, the two remaining halves of the thrust washers and the top half-shells of the main bearings from the crankcase.

(9) Inspect the crankcase main journals and crankpins for wear, scores, scratches and ovality. If necessary the crankshaft may be re-ground to the minimum limits shown under 'General Data'. Main bearings for re-ground crankshafts are available in sizes to suit.

(10) Clean the crankshaft thoroughly, ensuring that the connecting oilways between the journals and crankpins are perfectly clear. They can be cleaned out by applying a pressure gun containing petrol or paraffin. When clean, inject a thin oil in the same manner.

(11) Thoroughly clean the bearing shells, caps and housings above the crankshaft.

(12) Examine the bearing shells for wear and pitting, and look for evidence of breaking away or picking-up. Renew the shells if necessary.

(13) Bearings are pre-finished with the correct diametral clearance, and do not require bedding in. New bearings should be marked to match up with the marking on the cap, and **on no account should they be filed to take up wear or to reduce running clearance.**

(14) Check the thrust washers for wear on their bearing surfaces, and renew if necessary to obtain the correct end float.

To Install

The installation of the crankshaft and main bearings is a reversal of the procedure 'To Remove', noting the following points:

(1) Ensure that the thrust washers are replaced the correct way round, the oil grooves should face outwards, and locate the bottom half tab in the slot in the bearing cap.

(2) The bearing shells are notched to fit the recesses machined in the housing and cap.

(3) Remember to fit the packing washers behind the crankshaft timing chain wheel.

(4) Lubricate the bearings freely with engine oil.

(5) The rear main bearing cap horizontal joint surfaces should be thoroughly cleaned and lightly covered with WEL-SEAL (manufactured by Messrs. Wellworthy Ltd.) sealing compound before the cap is fitted to the cylinder block. This ensures a perfect oil seal when the cap is bolted down to the block.

(6) Tighten the main bearing nuts, see 'General Data' for torque spanner settings.

Section A.31

CYLINDER BLOCK

To Remove and Dismantle

(1) Remove and dismantle the engine (see Section A.4).
(2) Remove all studs, unions and screwed plugs, etc., if necessary.
(3) If an expansion plug has blown, or leaks, remove the plug by drilling a hole in its centre and lever it out with a screwdriver or other suitable tool.

To View and Overhaul

(1) Scrape as much sediment as possible from the water passages and thoroughly swill out with a water hose.
(2) Clean all gasket surfaces.
(3) Inspect for cracks and scores on gasket surfaces.
(4) It may be advisable to remove the ridge above the ring travel at the top of the cylinder bores before checking the fit of the pistons.

ENGINE A

(5) Wipe the cylinder bores clean and examine them for scores, out-of-round and taper. If the cylinders are found to be out-of-round or excessively tapered when measured with a dial test indicator, they should be reconditioned.

(6) If cylinder reconditioning is required, determine accurately the amount of material to be removed (refer to 'General Data' concerning oversize pistons available).

(7) Make sure that all traces of abrasives are cleaned from all parts of the cylinder block after the cylinder reconditioning operation is completed.

(8) Check the camshaft bearings (see Section A.28).

To Reassemble and Install

(1) Install all studs, unions and screwed plugs, etc.

(2) When installing new expansion plugs, coat the edge of the plug with a sealing compound and insert the plug with the 'bulge' on the outside. A carefully aimed blow at the centre of the plug with a small hammer direct or with a blunt punch will expand the plug sufficiently to make a water-tight joint. If too heavy a blow is used, the plug will be useless and must be replaced by another new one.

(3) Reassemble, install and test the engine (see Section A.4).

Section A.32   FAULT DIAGNOSIS

Symptom	No.	Possible Fault
(a) Will Not Start	1	Defective coil
	2	Faulty condenser
	3	Dirty, pitted, or incorrectly set contact breaker points
	4	Ignition wires loose or leaking
	5	Water on sparking plugs leads
	6	Corrosion of terminals or discharged battery
	7	Faulty starter
	8	Wrongly connected plug leads
	9	Vapour lock in fuel line
	10	Defective fuel pump
	11	Over-choking
	12	Under-choking
	13	Choked petrol filter or jets
	14	Valves leaking
	15	Sticking valves
	16	Valve timing incorrect
	17	Ignition timing incorrect
(b) Engine Stalls		In (a), check 1, 2, 3, 4, 10, 11, 12, 13, 14 and 15
	1	Plugs defective or incorrect gap
	2	Retarded ignition
	3	Mixture too weak
	4	Water in fuel system
	5	Petrol tank breather choked
	6	Incorrect valve clearance
(c) Poor Idling		In (b), check 1 and 6
	1	Air leak at manifold joints
	2	Incorrect slow running adjustment
	3	Air leak in carburetter(s)
	4	Slow running jet choked
	5	Over-rich mixture
	6	Worn piston rings
	7	Worn valve stems or guides
	8	Weak exhaust valve springs

A ENGINE

Symptom	No.	Possible Fault
(d) Misfiring	1	In (a), check 1, 2, 3, 4, 5, 8, 10, 13, 14, 15, 16 and 17 In (b), check 1, 2, 3 and 6 Weak or broken valve springs
(e) Overheating		See Section C
(f) Low Compression	1 2	In (a), check 14 and 15 In (c), check 6 and 7 In (d), check 1 Worn piston ring grooves Scored or worn cylinder bores
(g) Lack of Power	1 2 3	In (a), check 3, 10, 11, 13, 14, 15 and 16 In (b), check 1, 2, 3 and 6 In (c), check 6 and 7 In (d), check 1 Check (e) and (f) Leaking joint washers Fouled sparking plugs Automatic advance not functioning
(h) Burnt Valves or Seats	1	In (a), check 14 and 15 In (b), check 6 In (d), check 1 Check (e) Excessive carbon around valve seat and head
(j) Sticking Valves	1 2 3	In (d), check 1 Bent valve stem Scored valve stem or guide Incorrect valve clearance
(k) Excessive Cylinder Wear	1 2 3 4 5 6	Check 11 in (a) Check (e) Lack of oil Dirty oil Dirty air cleaner Gummed up or broken piston rings Badly fitting piston rings Misalignment of conrods
(l) Excessive Oil Consumption	1 2 3 4 5 6	In (c), check 6 and 7 Check (k) Ring gap too wide Oil return holes in piston choked with carbon Scored cylinders Oil level too high External oil leaks Ineffective valve oil seal

ENGINE

Symptom	No.	Possible Fault
(m) Crankshaft and Connecting Rod Bearing Failure	1 2 3 4 5	In (k), check 1 Restricted oilways Worn journals on crankpins Loose bearing caps Extremely low oil pressure Bent connecting rod
(n) Internal Water Leakage		See Section C.
(o) Poor Circulation		See Section C
(p) Corrosion		See Section C
(q) High Fuel Consumption		See Section D
(r) Engine Vibration	1 2 3 4 5	Loose generator bolts Fan blades out of balance Exhaust pipe mountings too tight

Section A.33

MODIFIED VALVE SHROUDS AND OIL SEALS

From Engine No. 9C/U/H 1397 valve packing rings (Part No. 2A879) of circular cross-section are fitted in place of the valve oil seals previously used. The oil seal retainer has been deleted from the valve guide shroud. The part number of the shroud without the oil seal retainer is 2A545. This modification involves changes in the inlet and exhaust valves and the valve spring caps.

If it is desired to fit the new valve packing rings on earlier engines the modified shrouds (Part No. 2A545), valves (Part Nos. 2A877 [inlet] and 2A878 [exhaust]), and valve spring caps (Part No. 2A880) must be used.

These modifications necessitate certain differences in valve removal and replacement procedure as detailed in Section A.19.

Removal

Remove the valve circlip. Compress the valve spring, using Service Tool 18G 45, and remove the two valve cotters. Release the valve spring and remove the compressor, valve spring cap, shroud, and spring.

Remove the valve packing ring from the cotter groove and withdraw the valve from its guide.

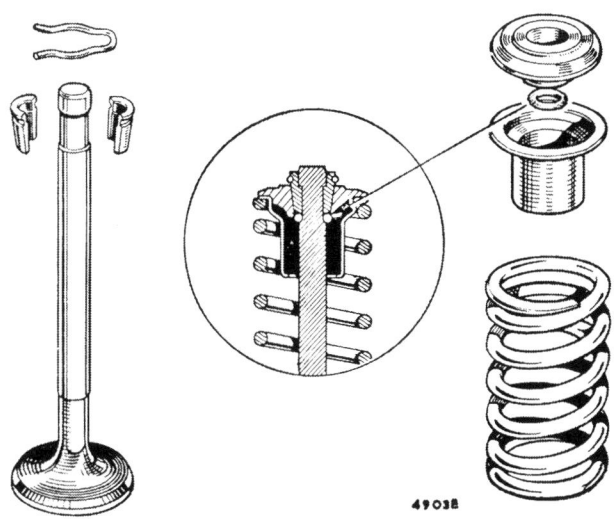

Fig. A.31

Parts of the valve assembly, showing the valve, cotters, circlip, spring, shroud, packing ring, and spring cap. The inset shows the valve packing ring fitted correctly at the bottom of the cotter groove below the cotters.

A ENGINE

Replacement

Place each valve into its guide and fit the springs, shrouds, and caps. Compress the valve spring and push a new synthetic rubber packing ring over the tip of the valve stem down to the bottom of the cotter groove (see Fig. A.31). Refit the two valve cotters and remove the compressor. Replace the valve circlip.

NOTE.—Do not fit old valve packing rings, or oil sealing may suffer. The rings are fitted more easily if they have been soaked in clean engine oil for a short period before use.

Section A.34

MODIFIED CYLINDER HEAD GASKET

From Engine No. 9C/U/H 6733 onwards a modified cylinder head gasket (Part No. 2A971) having ferrules around all the water holes is fitted. The new gasket is interchangeable with that previously used and is introduced to improve water sealing.

Section A.35

MODIFIED OIL PUMP

On later engines the Hobourn Eaton alternative oil pump (Part No. 2A341) is replaced by a Hobourn Eaton pump of modified construction (Part No. 2A962).

The cover and body of the new pump are now dowelled together, being located in the correct position in relation to each other by a $\frac{3}{16}$ in. countersunk screw. The assembly is held securely together by the three cylinder block attachment bolts. The pump cover now embraces the outer rotor and the combined oil pump shaft and inner rotor.

The new oil pump can be identified by the fact that the manufacturer's name and the patent number are cast on the outer flange of the cover instead of appearing around the centre of the cover. It may be interchanged as a unit with the oil pump originally used.

To Dismantle and Assemble

When the pump has been removed from the engine (see Section A.8) the $\frac{3}{16}$ in. countersunk screw can be removed from the engine side of the pump. It will now be possible to pull the body and cover of the pump apart, exposing the inner and outer rotors, which may be removed.

Reassembly is a reversal of the above procedure.

Section A.36

FITTING FLYWHEEL STARTER RINGS

To remove the old starter ring from the flywheel flange split the ring gear with a cold chisel, taking care not to damage the flywheel. Make certain that the bore of the new ring and its mating surface on the flywheel are free from burrs and are perfectly clean.

To fit the new ring it must be heated to a temperature of 300 to 400° C. (575 to 752° F.), indicated by a light-blue surface colour. If this temperature is exceeded the temper of the teeth will be affected. The use of a thermostatically controlled furnace is recommended. Place the heated ring on the flywheel with the lead of the ring teeth towards the flywheel register. The expansion will allow the ring to be fitted without force by pressing or tapping it lightly until the ring is hard against its register.

This operation should be followed by natural cooling, when the 'shrink fit' will be permanently established and no further treatment required.

Section A.37

FITTING VALVE SEAT INSERTS

Should the valve seatings become so badly worn or pitted that the normal workshop cutting and refacing tools cannot restore them to their original standard of efficiency, special valve seat inserts can be fitted.

The seatings in the cylinder head must be machined to the dimension given in Fig. A.32. Each insert should have an interference fit of ·0025 to ·0045 in. (·063 to ·11 mm.) and must be pressed and not driven into the cylinder head.

After fitting, grind or machine the new seating to the dimensions given in Fig. A.32. Normal valve grinding may be necessary to ensure efficient valve seating.

Section A.38

FITTING CYLINDER LINERS

Should the condition of the cylinder bores be such that they cannot be cleaned up to accept standard oversize pistons, dry cylinder liners can be fitted. This operation may be carried out by the use of specialized proprietary equipment or with a power press using pilot adaptors to the dimensions shown in Fig. A.33. The press must be capable of 3 tons (3048 kg.) pressure to fit new liners and 5 to 8 tons (5080 to 8128 kg.) to remove old liners.

Remove the engine from the vehicle as detailed in Section A.4. Dismantle the engine, and remove the

ENGINE

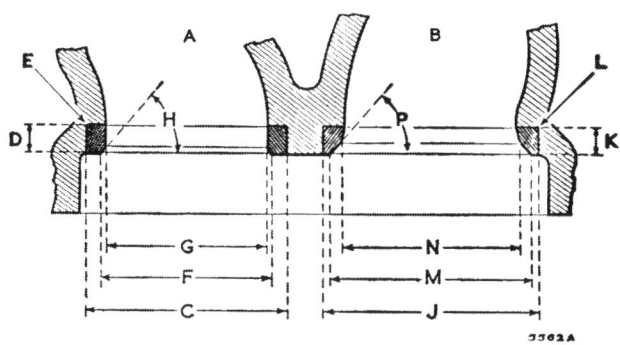

Fig. A.32. Valve seat machining dimensions.

Exhaust (A)		Inlet (B)	
C.	1·124 to 1·125 in. (28·55 to 28·58 mm.).	J.	1·187 to 1·188 in. (30·16 to 30·17 mm.)
D.	·186 to ·188 in. (4·72 to 4·77 mm.).	K.	·186 to ·188 in. (4·72 to 4·77 mm.).
E.	Maximum radius ·015 in. (·38 mm.).	L.	Maximum radius ·015 in. (·38 mm.).
F.	1·0235 to 1·0435 in. (25·99 to 26·50 mm.).	M.	1·0855 to 1·1055 in. (27·58 to 28·07 mm.).
G.	·844 in. (21·43 mm.).	N.	1·000 to 1·006 in. (25·4 to 25·55 mm.).
H.	45°	P.	45°

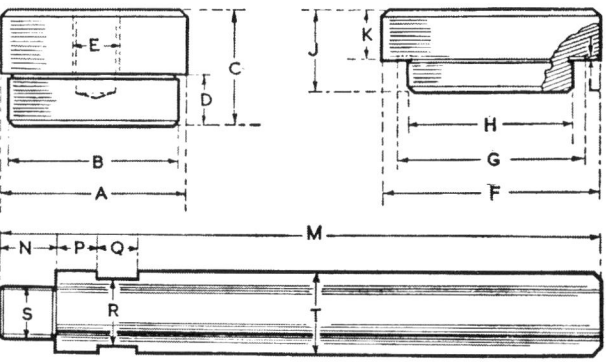

Fig. A.33. Cylinder liner pilots should be made to the above dimensions from 55-ton hardening and tempering steel and hardened in oil at a temperature of 550° C. (1,020° F.).

Pressing-out pilot

- A. $2\frac{37}{64} {}^{+·005}_{-·0}$ in. ($65·48 {}^{+·127}_{-·0}$ mm.).
- B. $2·465 {}^{+·0}_{-·005}$ in. ($62·61 {}^{+·0}_{-·127}$ mm).
- C. $1\frac{1}{4}$ in. (31·75 mm.).
- D. $\frac{3}{4}$ in. (19·05 mm.).
- E. $\frac{3}{4}$ in. BSW thread.

Pressing-in pilot

- F. 3 in. (76·20 mm.).
- G. $2\frac{5}{8}$ in. (66·68 mm.).
- H. $2·455 {}^{+·0}_{-·005}$ in. ($62·35 {}^{+·0}_{-·127}$ mm.).
- J. $1\frac{1}{4}$ in. (31·75 mm.).
- K. $\frac{3}{4}$ in. (19·05 mm.).
- L. ·015 in. (·38 mm.).

Pilot extension

- M. $14\frac{1}{2}$ in. (36·83 cm.).
- N. $\frac{7}{8}$ in. (22·22 mm.).
- P. $\frac{5}{8}$ in. (15·87 mm.).
- Q. $\frac{5}{8}$ in. (15·87 mm.).
- R. 1 in. (25·4 mm.) flats.
- S. $\frac{3}{4}$ in. BSW thread.
- T. $1\frac{1}{4}$ in. (31·75 mm.).

cylinder head studs. If liners have not previously been fitted the bores must be machined and honed to the dimensions given in the table below.

To remove worn liners

Place the cylinder block face downwards on suitable wooden supports on the bed of the press, making sure that there is sufficient space between the block and the bed of the press to allow the worn liner to pass down. Insert the pilot in the bottom of the liner and carefully press the liner from the bore.

To press in new liners

Thoroughly clean the inside of the bores and the outside of the liners. Stand the cylinder block upright on the bed of the press, insert the pilot guide in the top of the liner, and position the liner with its chamfered end in the top of the bore. Make certain that the liner is square with the top of the block and that the ram of the press is over the centre of the pilot. Press the liner fully into the bore.

Each liner must be machined to the dimensions given in the table below after pressing into position.

Engine type	Liner Part No.	Machine bores of cylinder block to this dimension before fitting liner	Outside diameter of liner	Interference fit of liner in cylinder block bore	Machine liner bore to this dimension after fitting
'A' (948 c.c.)	2A784	2·6035 to 2·604 in. (66·128 to 66·14 mm.)	2·606 to 2·60675 in. (66·19 to 66·21 mm.)	·002 to ·00325 in. (·05 to ·08 mm.)	2·477 to 2·4785 in. (62·915 to 62·954 mm.)

ENGINE

SERVICE TOOLS

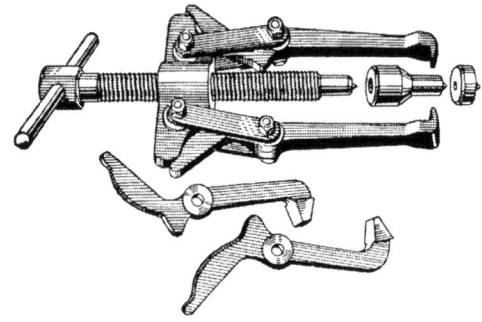

18G2

18G2. Crankshaft Gear, Pulley and Propeller Shaft Flange Remover

A multi-purpose tool, with alternative legs readily interchangeable; one pair with thin flat ends designed for removing crankshaft gears and propeller shaft and bevel pinion flanges; the other pair has tapered ends suitable for fan pulley grooves other than later type models fitted with narrow section fan belts.

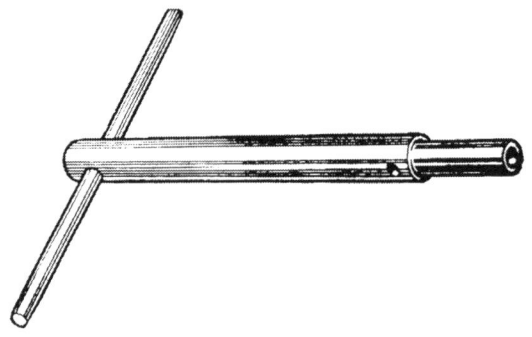

18G27

18G27. Valve Seat Cutter and Pilot Handle

For use with pilot 18G167D, cutters 18G167, 18G167C 18G167B and glaze breaker 18G167A.

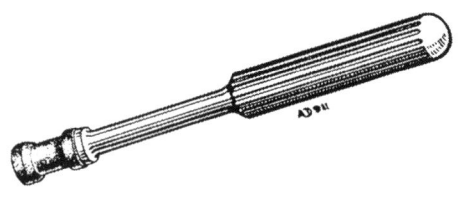

18G29

18G29. Valve Grinding-in Tool

A metal handle complete with a detachable suction pad. For Healey Sprite use alternative suction pad 18G29B.

ENGINE

SERVICE TOOLS

18G45. Valve Spring Compressor

This tool is designed for o.h.v. engines. It has a cam and lever action and screw adjustment. The adaptor ring is shaped to facilitate the fitting of cotters.

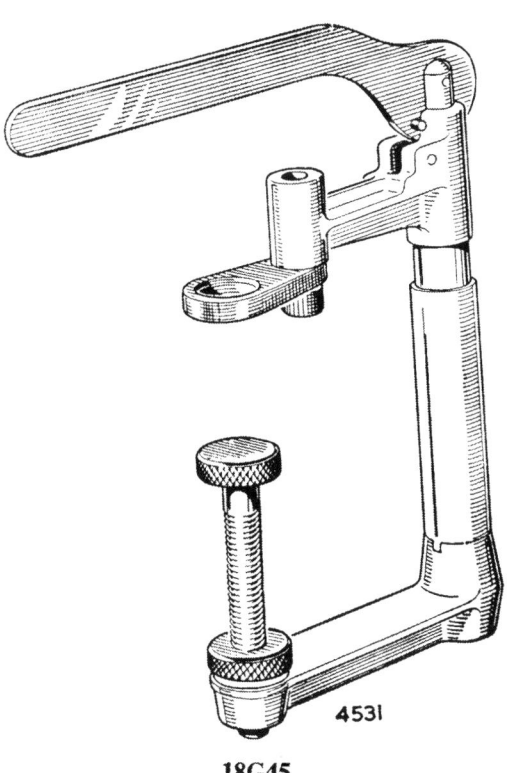

18G55A. Piston Ring Clamp

Designed to cover a wide range of pistons, it is easy to operate and will compress the strongest piston ring, making assembly to the bore a quick and easy operation.

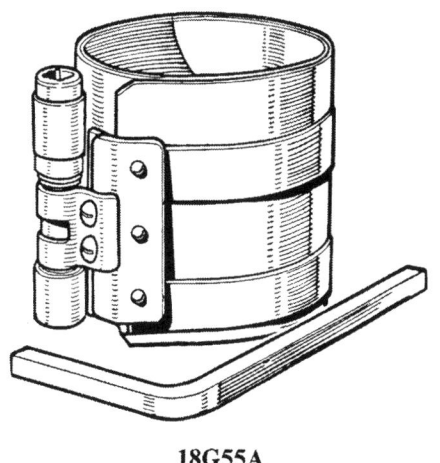

A

ENGINE

SERVICE TOOLS

18G69

18G69. Oil Pump Release Valve Grinding-in-Tool

Designed to facilitate the removal and grinding in of the engine oil release valve. Tightening the set screw expands the rubber plunger, which ensures that the tool is a tight fit when inserted into the hollow oil release valve.

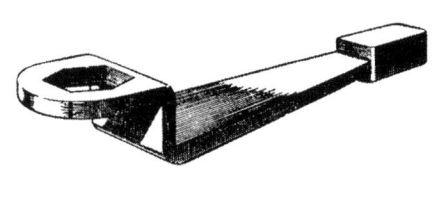

18G98

18G98. Starter Nut Spanner

This shock-type spanner enables the starter nut on Healey Sprite models to be removed without the need for locking the crankshaft with improvised means, which may cause damage to the components.

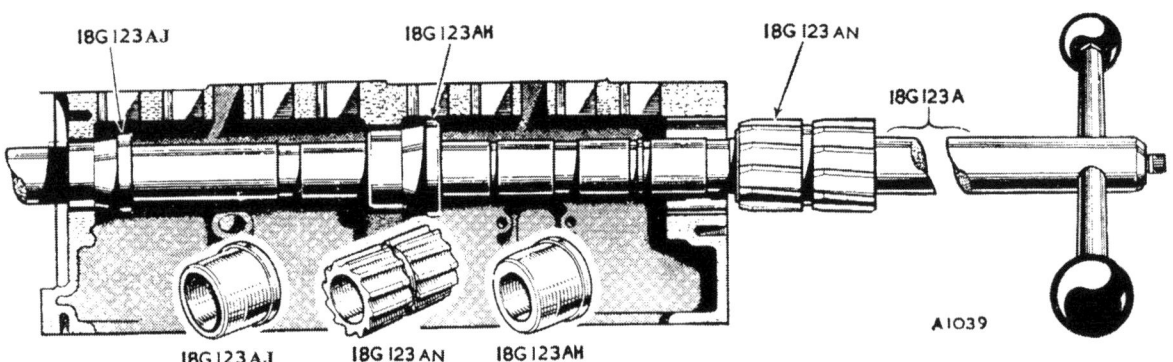

18G123A, 18G123AN, 18G123AH, and 18G123AJ

18G123A, 18G123AN, 18G123AH, and 18G123AJ. Camshaft Liner Reamer

This equipment is essential when reconditioning cylinder blocks on the Healey Sprite, otherwise camshaft liners cannot be reamed in line, and in consequence the clearance between the camshaft journal and liner will be incorrect. This basic tool 18G123A must be used with the cutter 18G123AN and pilots 18G123AH and 18G123AJ. Full instructions for using the equipment will be supplied with each basic tool.

ENGINE

SERVICE TOOLS

18G123AL

A fibre box for the storage of camshaft liner reamer cutters and pilots, and partitioned to protect the edge of the cutters.

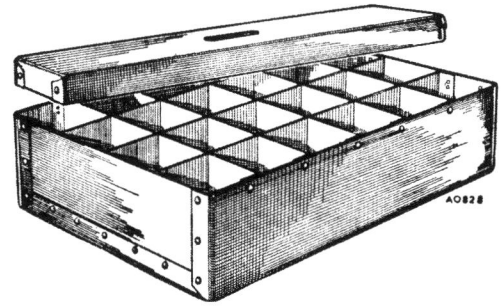

18G123AL

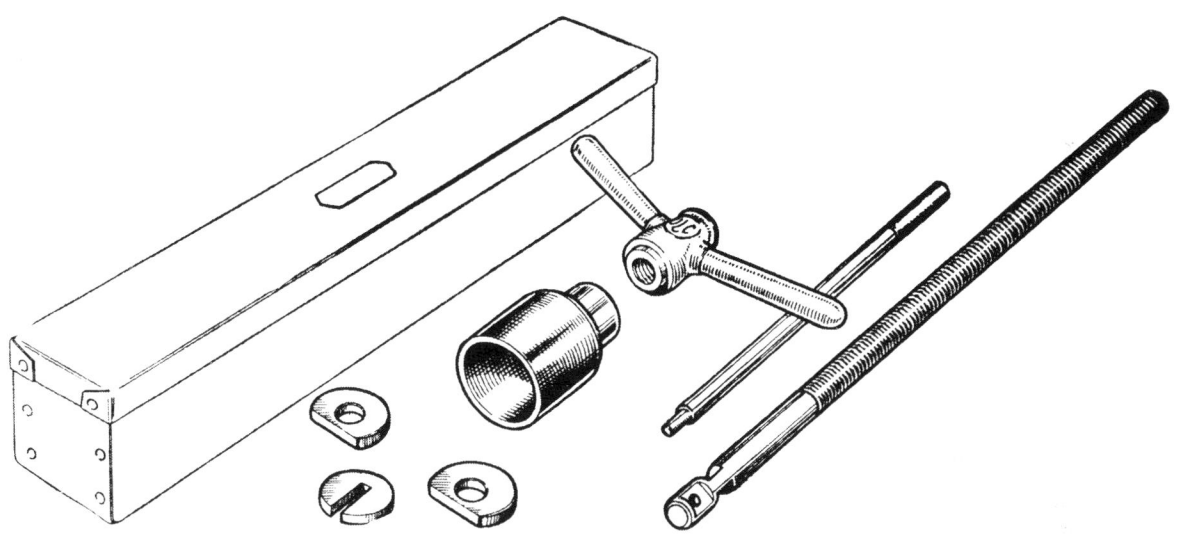

18G124A

18G124A. Camshaft Liner Remover and Replacer (Basic Tool)

The equipment consists of a basic tool 18G124A and various adaptors (supplied separately) for different types of engines, and for this model shown below. Liners can be renewed and replaced without the damage invariably associated with the use of improvised drifts. Full instructions for using the equipment will be supplied with each basic tool.

18G124K Camshaft Liner Remover Adaptor

For use with 18G124A.

18G124K

Austin-Healey Sprite. Issue 1. 28894.

A ENGINE

SERVICE TOOLS

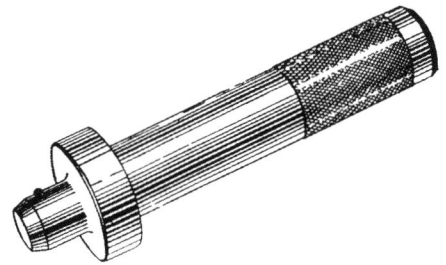

18G134

18G134. Bearing and Oil-Seal Replacer (Basic Tool)

For use with 18G134B, 18G134C, 18G134L and 18G134Q.

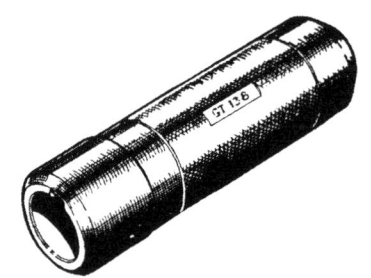

18G138

18G138. Crankshaft Gear, Pulley, and Propeller Shaft Flange Replacer

This tool is used for driving on the crankshaft gear and for lining up the timing cover.

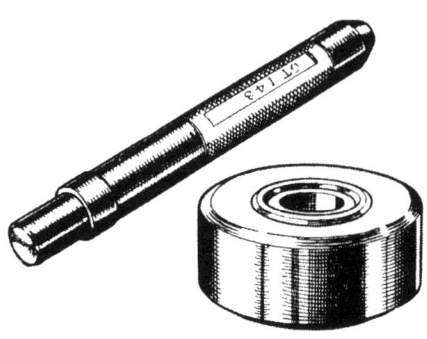

18G148

18G148. Valve Rocker Bush Remover and Replacer

The flange of the driver is recessed to prevent the split bush from opening when being driven into position. The anvil is also recessed to retain the rocker during the operation. Use of a light press is desirable when using this tool, alternatively a vice or copper-faced hammer may be used.

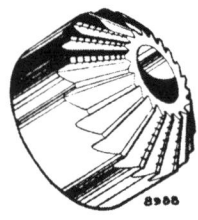

18G167

18G167. Valve Seat Finishing Cutter

Use with pilot 18G375D and handle 18G27.

ENGINE

SERVICE TOOLS

18G167A. Valve Seat Glaze Breaker

Use with pilot 18G167C and handle 18G27.

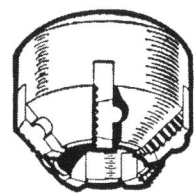

18G167A

18G167B. Valve Seat Narrowing Cutter—Top

Designed to enable seats of the Healey Sprite to be maintained at their original dimensions. Use with pilot 18G375A and handle 18G27A. These cutters must not be used on hardened valve seat inserts—the inserts must be renewed.

18G167B

18G167C. Valve Seat Narrowing Cutter—Bottom

Use with pilot 18G375D and handle 18G27.

18G167C

18G167D. Valve Seat Cutter Pilot

For use with glaze breaker 18G167A, cutters 18G157, 18G167B, 18G167C, and handle 18G27.

18G167D

A

ENGINE

SERVICE TOOLS

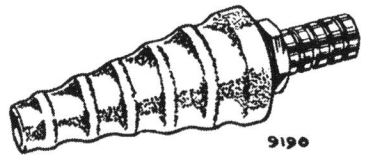

18G187

18G187. Radiator Reverse-flush Adaptors

The adaptors should be used in pairs, one for the radiator inlet hose and one for the outlet hose. The hose connection is 1 in. (25·4 mm.) diameter.

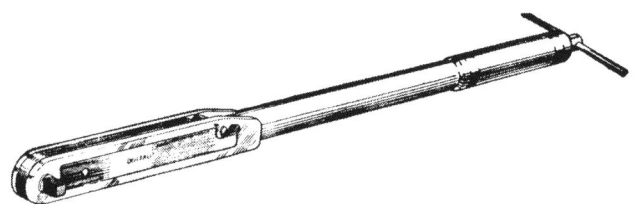

18G372

Tool No. 18G372. Torque Wrench—30–140 lb. ft.

A universal torque spanner for use with standard sockets. This tool is essential if the recommended maximum torque for various studs is not to be exceeded.

18G528. Tool Board Hook—2 in.

A strongly made hook in mild steel with non-corrosive finish used for the display and storage of service tools. Supplied in packs of one dozen.

18G529. Tool Board Hook—3 in.

A larger size of 18G528. Supplied in packs of one dozen.

SECTION B

IGNITION SYSTEM

Section No. B.1	Description
Section No. B.2	Adjustments in the vehicle
Section No. B.3	To test in the vehicle
Section No. B.4	Ignition coil
Section No. B.5	Distributor
Section No. B.6	Distributor driving spindle
Section No. B.7	Sparking plugs
Section No. B.8	High-tension cables
Section No. B.8	Fault diagnosis

IGNITION SYSTEM   B

Section B.1

DESCRIPTION

The ignition system consists of two circuits—primary and secondary. The primary circuit includes the battery, ignition switch, the primary or low-tension circuit of the coil and the distributor contact breaker and capacitor. The secondary circuit includes the secondary or high-tension circuit of the coil, the distributor rotor and cover segments, the high-tension cables and the sparking plugs.

The ignition coil, which is mounted on the right-hand side of the engine, consists of a soft iron core around which is wound the primary and secondary windings. The coil carries at one end a centre high-tension terminal and two low-tension terminals marked (SW) (switch) and (CB) (contact breaker) respectively.

The ends of the primary winding are connected to the (SW) and (CB) terminals and the secondary winding to the (CB) terminal and the high-tension terminal.

The distributor is on the right-hand side of the engine and is driven by a shaft and helical gear from the camshaft. Automatic timing control of the distributor is by a centrifugal mechanism and a vacuum-operated unit each entirely independent of each other. The centrifugal mechanism regulates the ignition advance according to engine speed, while the vacuum control varies the timing according to engine load. The combined effect of the two mechanisms gives added efficiency over the full operating range of the engine. A micrometer adjuster is provided to give a fine timing adjustment.

A keyed moulded rotor with a metal electrode is mounted on top of the cam. Attached to the distributor body above the centrifugal advance mechanism is a contact breaker plate carrying the contact breaker points and a capacitor connected in parallel. A cover is fitted over the distributor body and retained by two spring clips attached to the body.

Inside the cover is a centre electrode and spring-loaded carbon brush which makes contact with the rotor. The brush is of composite construction, the top portion being made of a resistive compound, while the lower portion is made of softer carbon to prevent wear of the rotor electrode. Under no circumstances must a short non-resistive brush be used to replace this long resistive type. A measure of radio interference suppression is given by this brush and to assist this, the sparking plugs are fitted with suppressors. (From Chassis No. 25484, Home market only).

Spaced circumferentially around the centre electrode are the sparking plug high-tension cable segments. The distributor is secured in position on the cylinder block by a clamp plate.

The sparking plugs are located on the right-hand side of the engine and have a 14 mm. thread with a ¾ in. reach.

When the ignition is switched on, the current from the battery flows through the primary circuit, and a magnetic field is built up around the core of the coil. When the contact breaker points are opened the current flow is interrupted, causing a high voltage to be induced in the secondary winding of the coil by sudden collapse and consequent change in the magnetic field. The high-tension current thus generated in the secondary winding of the coil is conveyed by the coil high-tension cable to the centre terminal of the distributor cover. From here the current passes through the carbon brush to the rotor, where the high-tension current passes along the rotor electrode and is distributed to the segments and thence to the sparking plugs via the high-tension cables.

Section B.2

ADJUSTMENTS IN THE VEHICLE

The purpose of the following adjustments is to maintain efficient engine performance and economical running.

(1) Adjust the sparking plugs at the recommended intervals as follows:

The gap of the plug points should be within the limits of ·024 to ·026 in. (·61 to ·66 mm.).

Gap adjustment should be made by bending the side electrode only. Never bend the central electrode. If the plugs are dirty, damaged or excessively burned, see Section B.7.

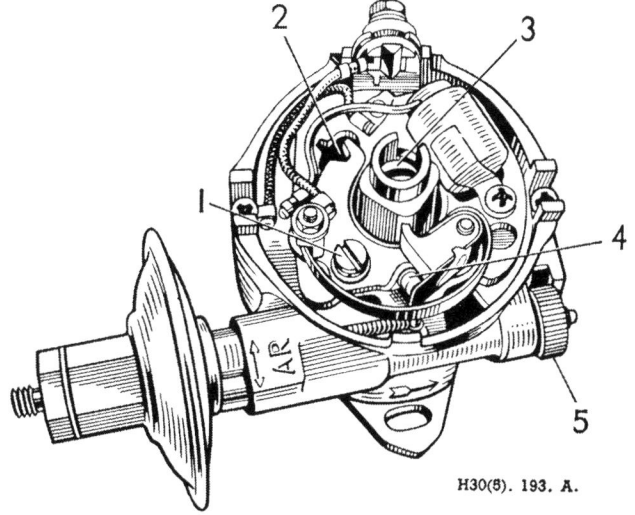

Fig. B.1. *Distributor Platform.*
1. *Contact adjusting screw.*
2. *Contact adjusting slot.*
3. *Cam and drive shaft oiling point.*
4. *Contact points.*
5. *Micrometer adjuster.*

Austin-Healey Spirte Mk. 1. Issue 4. 35471.

IGNITION SYSTEM

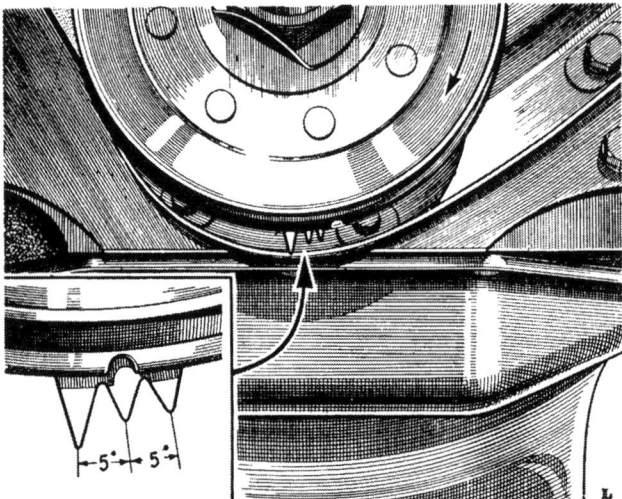

Fig. B.2. The notch in the pulley approaching the T.D.C. positions for pistons 1 and 4. The inset shows the gap of 5° between each timing mark.

(2) Adjust the contact breaker points at the recommended intervals as follows:

Remove the distributor cover and rotor. Turn the engine using a spanner on the crankshaft pulley securing nut until the contacts are fully open. Slacken the fixed contact plate securing screw '1' (Fig. B.1). Insert a screwdriver in the slot '2' and move the plate until the gap gauge is a sliding fit between the contacts (·014 to ·016 in. or ·356 to ·406 mm.) and then fully tighten the securing screw. Recheck the gap. Replace the rotor and cover. If the points are dirty or pitted see Section B.5.

(3) Check the position of the distributor driving spindle (Section B.6) and adjust the ignition timing as follows if the distributor has been disturbed.

Remove the valve rocker cover so that the valve action can be observed. Rotate the engine using a spanner on the crankshaft pulley securing nut until No. 1 Piston is at the top of its compression stroke (i.e. the exhaust valve of No. 4 cylinder is just closing and the inlet valve just opening). Turn the crankshaft until the recess in the crankshaft pulley flange is in line with the largest pointer (TDC) on the timing case cover (Fig. B.2). If the timing cover has been removed, align the timing marks on the camshaft and crankshaft wheels. No. 1 and 4 pistons are now at T.D.C. Set the micrometer adjustment on the distributor in its central position. The crankshaft should now be rotated backwards 5° to obtain its correct position before setting the distributor points, this setting is correct for premium grade fuels only. With the cover removed the distributor body should be rotated until the rotor arm is pointing to the position of No. 1 electrode in the cover. With the contact points just opening, tighten the clamp plate bolt.

To obtain an accurate setting the electrical method should be used in determining the actual position at which the points must break, and the following procedure should be adopted.

Slacken the clamp pinch-bolt and rotate the distributor body in an anti-clockwise direction until the points are fully closed.

With the low-tension lead connected to the distributor turn on the ignition switch, connect a 12 volt lamp in parallel with the contact breaker points (i.e. one lead from the distributor low-tension terminal and the other to earth), and rotate the distributor clockwise until the lamp lights, indicating that the points have just opened. Secure the distributor body in this position by tightening up the clamp plate pinch-bolt.

Finally, check that the rotor arm is opposite the correct segment in the distributor cap for No. 1 cylinder.

Re-connect the vacuum advance pipe and refit the distributor cap and rocker cover. When using a stroboscopic lamp, do not allow the engine r.p.m. to rise high enough to operate the centrifugal advance weights.

If the vacuum advance take-off is direct from the manifold, disconnect it before checking the timing otherwise this will be set retarded.

Finer adjustment can be obtained under road conditions, by means of the micrometer adjustment. **Note:** this adjustment should not be used for initial setting of the ignition; it is only altered if the main setting requires adjustment to meet the characteristics of the grades of petrol being used. There is a considerable amount of latitude for adjustment but only extremely small movements of the adjustment knob should be made at one time.

Replace the distributor cover and cylinder head cover.

Section B.3

TO TEST IN THE VEHICLE

If the ignition system fails, or misfiring occurs, first make sure that the trouble is not due to defects in the engine, carburetter or fuel supply. Faults should be diagnosed by applying the following tests:

(1) Examine the high-tension cables, i.e. the cables from the coil to the distributor, and from the

IGNITION SYSTEM

distributor to the plugs. If the rubber insulation shows signs of deterioration or cracking, the cable should be renewed.

(2) Test the plugs and high-tension cables by removing the plugs in turn and allowing them to rest on the cylinder head or other convenient earthing point, and observing whether a spark occurs at the points when the engine is turned by hand. It should, however, be noted that this is only a rough test, since it is possible that a spark may not take place when the plug is under compression. If necessary, clean and test the plugs, using a plug cleaning and testing machine.

(3) To trace a fault in the low-tension circuit, release the instrument panel from the dash, switch on the ignition, and turn the engine until the distributor contacts are opened. Refer to the wiring diagram, Fig. M.24, and, with the aid of a voltmeter (0 to 20), check the circuit as follows:

(a) **Cable—Battery to starter switch**
Connect the voltmeter between the supply terminal of the starter switch and an earthing point. No reading indicates a faulty cable or loose connection.

(b) **Cable (brown)—Starter switch to two-way fuse unit A.1 terminal**
Connect the voltmeter between the fuse unit A.1 terminal and earth. No reading indicates a faulty cable or loose connection.

(c) **Control box**
Connect the voltmeter between the control box terminal (A.1) and earth. No reading indicates a faulty control box.

(d) **Cable (brown and blue)—Control box to lighting and ignition switch**
Connect the voltmeter between the lighting switch terminal (A) and earth. No reading indicates a faulty cable or loose connection.

(e) **Ignition switch**
Connect the voltmeter between the ignition switch (white cable terminal) and earth. No reading indicates a faulty ignition switch.

(f) **Cable (white)—Ignition switch to fuse unit A.3 terminal**
Connect the voltmeter between the fuse unit A.3 terminal and earth. No reading indicates a faulty cable or loose connection.

(g) **Cable (white)—Fuse unit A.3 terminal to ignition coil**
Connect the voltmeter between the ignition coil terminal (SW) and earth. No reading indicates a faulty cable or loose connection.

(h) **Ignition coil**
Connect the voltmeter between the ignition coil terminal (CB) and earth. No reading indicates a faulty ignition coil.

(i) **Cable (white and black)—Ignition coil to distributor**
Connect the voltmeter between the distributor terminal and earth. No reading indicates a faulty cable or loose connection.

(j) **Distributor**
Connect the voltmeter across the distributor

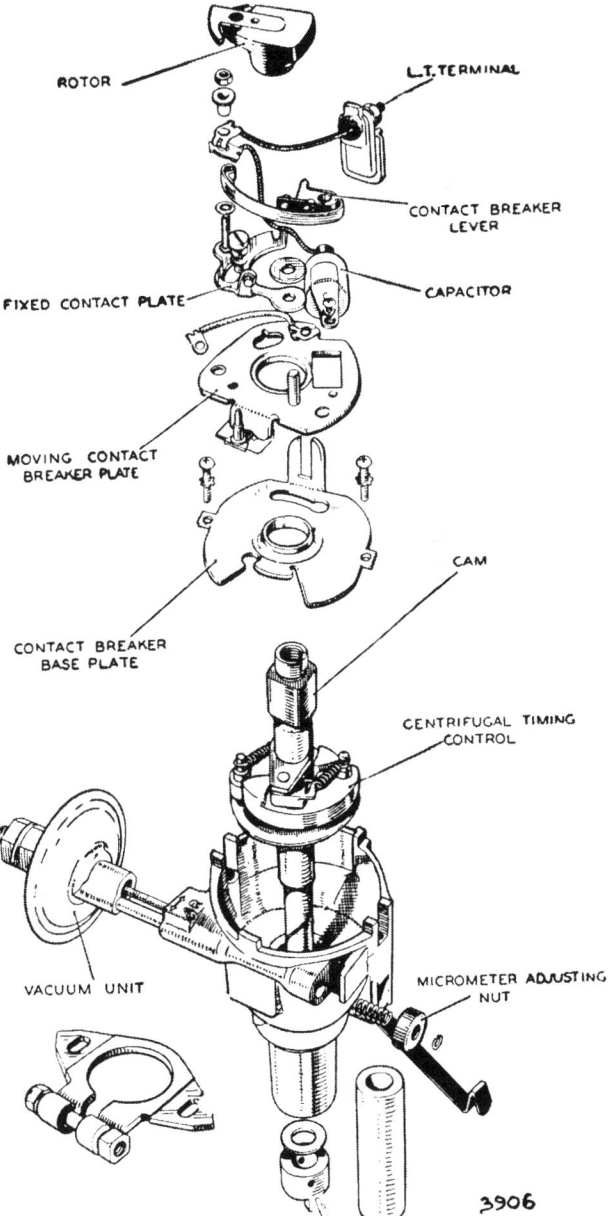

Fig. B.3. The component parts of the DM2 distributor.

Austin-Healey Sprite. Mk.1 Issue 3. 35471.

IGNITION SYSTEM

contacts. If no reading is given, remove the capacitor and test again. If a reading is given, the capacitor is faulty.

(4) If, after carrying out the foregoing tests, the fault has not been located, remove the high-tension cable from the centre terminal of the distributor. Switch on the ignition and crank the engine until the contacts close. Flick the contact breaker lever open while the high-tension cable from the ignition coil is held about $\frac{3}{16}$ in. (5 mm.) away from the cylinder block. If the ignition equipment is in order a strong spark should be obtained. If no spark is given, it indicates a faulty ignition coil.

Section B.4
IGNITION COIL

To remove

(1) Disconnect the high-tension cable from the coil centre terminal.
(2) Disconnect the low-tension cables from the (SW) and (CB) terminals of the coil.
(3) Unscrew the bolts fastening the coil to the generator strap, and remove the coil.

To replace

The installation of the ignition coil is a reversal of the procedure 'To remove'.

Section B.5
DISTRIBUTOR

To remove

(1) The distributor can be removed and replaced without interfering with the ignition timing, provided the clamp plate pinch-bolt is not disturbed.
(2) To facilitate the replacement of the distributor, turn the engine over until the rotor arm is pointing to the segment in the cover for No. 1 cylinder plug lead to provide a datum for replacement. Also, ascertain the approximate position of the vacuum unit in order to facilitate the connection of the vacuum pipe on replacement.
(3) Remove the distributor cover and disconnect the low-tension lead from the terminal on the distributor. Disconnect the suction advance pipe at the union on the distributor.
(4) Unscrew the tachometer drive (if fitted) from its connecting at the rear of the generator.
(5) Extract the two bolts securing the distributor clamp plate to the distributor housing and withdraw the distributor.

To dismantle

The contact breaker plate may be removed as an assembly to give access to the centrifugal weights without completely dismantling the distributor. To do this first remove the rotor arm and then withdraw the slotted nylon low-tension terminal post from the distributor body.

Take out the two screws which secure the plate assembly to the distributor body, ease up the plate and unhook the flexible actuating link connected to the contact breaker plate.

The following procedure is necessary if the distributor is to be completely stripped. Before dismantling, make a careful note of the positions in which the various components are fitted in order that they may be replaced correctly.

(1) Spring back the clips and remove the moulded cap.
(2) Lift the rotor off the top of the spindle. If it is a tight fit it must be levered off carefully with a screwdriver.
(3) Remove the nut and washer from the moving contact anchor pin. Withdraw the insulating sleeve from the capacitor lead and low-tension lead connectors, noting the order in which they are fitted. Lift the moving contact from the pivot pin and remove the large insulating washer from the anchor pin.
(4) Take out the screw, spring and flat washer, securing the fixed contact plate, and remove the plate.
(5) Take out the securing screw and remove the capacitor.
(6) Extract the two screws securing the base-plate to

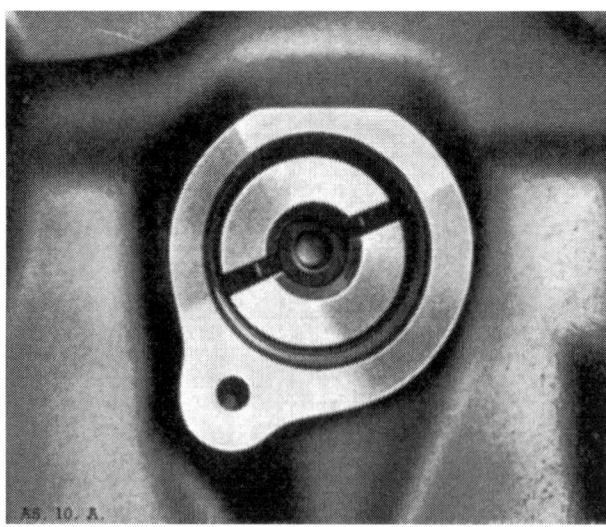

Fig. B.4. Distributor drive, showing the off-set slot in the correct position.

IGNITION SYSTEM   B

the distributor body, noting that one also secures the earthing lead, and lift out the base-plate.

Unhook the flexible actuating link connecting the diaphragm in the vacuum unit with the moving contact breaker plate.

Important.—Note the relative position of the rotor arm drive slot in the cam spindle and the offset drive dog at the driving end of the spindle, to ensure that the timing is not 180° out when the cam spindle is engaged with the centrifugal weights during assembly. (See Fig. B.3.).

(7) Take out the cam retaining screw and remove the cam spindle.

(8) Take out the centrifugal weights. These may be lifted out as two assemblies, each complete with a spring and toggle.

(9) To release the suction advance unit, remove the circlip, adjusting nut and spring. Withdraw the unit. Take care not to lose the adjusting nut lock spring clip.

(10) To release the spindle from the body, drive out the parallel driving pin passing through the collar of the driving tongue member at the lower end of the spindle.

(11) Clean the distributor cover and examine it for signs of cracks and evidence of 'Tracking', i.e. a conducting path may have formed between adjacent segments. This is indicated by a thin black line between the segments, when this has occurred the cover should be renewed.

(12) Ensure that the carbon brush moves freely in the distributor cover.

(13) Examine the attachment of the metal electrode to the rotor moulding. If slack or abnormally burned, renew the rotor.

(14) The contact face of the contact breaker points should present a clean, greyish, frosted appearance. If burned or blackened, renew the contact set or polish the contact face of each point with a fine oil stone, working with a rotary motion. Care should be taken to maintain the faces of the points flat and square, so that when re-assembled full contact is obtained. Clean the points thoroughly in petrol.

(15) Check that the movable contact arm is free on its pivot without slackness.

(16) Check the centrifugal timing control balance weights and pivot pins for wear and renew the cam assembly or weights if necessary.

(17) The cam assembly should be a free sliding fit on the driving shaft. If the clearance is excessive, or the cam face is worn, renew the cam assembly or shaft as necessary.

(18) Check the fit of the shaft in the bushes. If slack, renew the bushes and shaft, as necessary.

Press out the old bushes. The new bushes should be allowed to stand completely immersed in thin engine oil for twenty-four hours, or alternatively for two hours in oil which has been heated to 212°F (100°C), before pressing them into the distributor body.

To reassemble

Reassembly is a direct reversal of the dismantling procedure, although careful attention must be given to the following points:

(1) As they are assembled, the components of the automatic advance mechanism, the distributor shaft, and the portion of the shaft on which the cam fits must be lubricated with thin, clean engine oil.

(2) Turn the vacuum control adjusting nut until it is in the half-way position when replacing the control unit.

(3) When engaging the cam driving pins with the centrifugal weights, make sure that they are in the original position. When seen from above, the small offset of the driving dog must be on the right, and the driving slot for the rotor arm must be in the six o'clock position.

(4) Adjust the contact breaker to give a maximum opening of ·014 to ·016 in. (·36 to ·40 mm.).

To Install

Replacing the distributor is the reverse of the procedure 'To Remove', noting the following points:

(1) Insert the assembled distributor, with its cap removed, into the spindle housing, and turn the rotor arm until the driven dog on the distributor engages with the slot in the housing.

(2) Screw in the two setpins securing the distributor clamp plate to the distributor housing.

(3) Position the distributor so that the vacuum control unit is in the same position as noted before removal.

(4) Check the contact breaker gap and ignition timing as described in Section B.2.

Section B.6

DISTRIBUTOR DRIVING SPINDLE

Removal

(1) Remove the distributor as described in Section B.5

(2) By using a $\frac{5}{16}$ in. U.N.F. bolt approximately 3½ in. long, screwed into the tapped end of the driving spindle, the spindle may be withdrawn.

(3) Examine the drive gear for worn teeth.

B

IGNITION SYSTEM

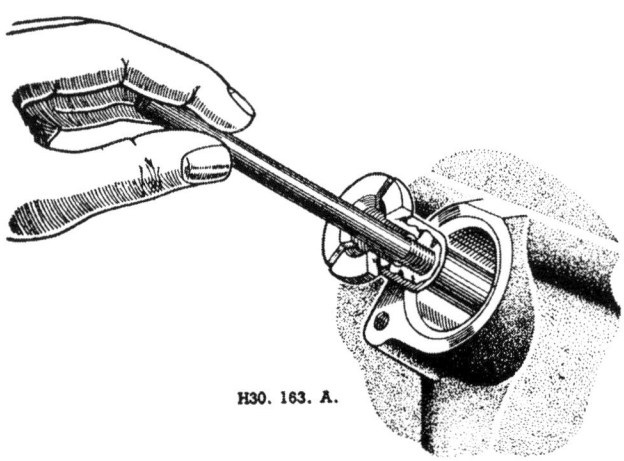

Fig. B.5. Removing the distributor spindle.

To Replace

(1) Remove the valve gear cover (see Section A).
(2) Crank the engine until No. 1 Piston is at the top of its compression stroke (i.e. the exhaust valve of No. 4 cylinder is just closing and the inlet valve just opening).
(3) Turn the crankshaft until the recess in the crankshaft pulley flange is in line with the (T.D.C.) indicating pointer on the timing chain cover (see Fig. B.2).
(4) Screw the $\frac{5}{16}$ in. U.N.F. bolt into the threaded end of the distributor drive and replace the drive into its housing so that the off-set slot takes up the position in Fig. B.4.
(5) Replace the distributor following the instructions given in Section B.5.

Section B.7

SPARKING PLUGS

Inspect, clean, adjust and renew sparking plugs at the recommended mileage intervals (see 'MAINTENANCE ATTENTION').

When sparking plugs are removed from the engine their gaskets should be removed with them and replaced on the plugs, which should be placed in a suitable holder. It is advisable to identify each plug with the number of the cylinder from which it was removed so that any faults revealed on examination can be traced back to the cylinder concerned.

When examining the plugs, place a new plug of the same type beside the others to afford a ready comparison of the relative condition of the used plugs.

Examine for signs of oil fouling. This will be indicated by a wet, shiny, black deposit on the insulator. This is caused by oil pumping due to worn cylinders and pistons or gummed-up or broken rings. Under such conditions, oil from the cylinder walls is forced up past the rings on the suction stroke of the piston, and is eventually deposited on the plugs.

A permanent remedy for this cannot be effected, the only cure being the fitting of a new piston and rings, or, in extreme cases, a rebore may be necessary.

Next examine the plugs for signs of petrol (gasoline) fouling. This is indicated by a dry, fluffy, black deposit which is usually caused by over-rich carburation, although ignition system defects such as a run-down battery, faulty distributor, coil or condenser defects, or a broken or worn-out cable may be additional causes. If the plugs appear to be suitable for further use, proceed to clean and test them.

First remove the plug gaskets and examine them for condition. A large proportion of the heat of the plug is normally dissipated to the cylinder head through the steel gasket between the plug and the head. Plugs not screwed down tightly can thus easily become over-heated so that they operate out of their proper heat range, thus producing pre-ignition, short plug life and 'pinking'. On the other hand, it is unnecessary and unwise to tighten up the plugs too much. What is required is a reasonably good seal between the plug and the cylinder head and the use of a torque wrench is recommended to tighten the plugs to a figure of 30 lb. ft. (4·15 kg. m.).

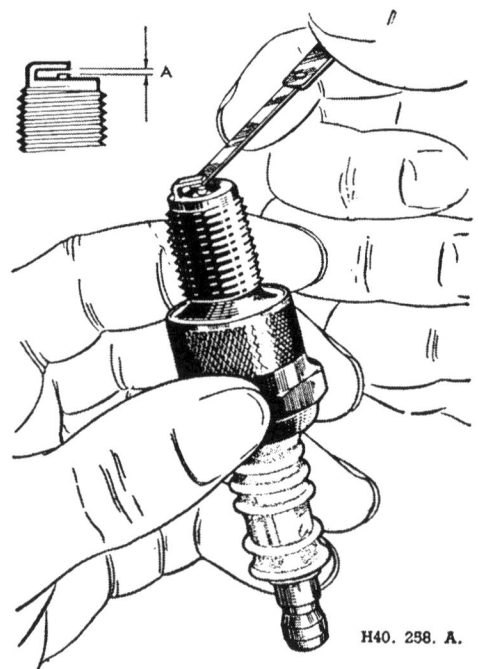

Fig. B.6. Checking sparking plug. Gap 'A' should be ·025in.

IGNITION SYSTEM

If the plugs require cleaning it is preferable to make use of a proper plug cleaner of the type recommended by the plug manufacturers, and the makers' instructions for using the cleaner should be followed carefully.

Occasionally a blistered insulator or a badly burnt electrode may be noticed when examining the plugs.

If the plug is of the type normally recommended for the engine and it was correctly installed (down tightly on the gasket), this condition may have been brought about by a very lean mixture or an overheated engine. There is, however, a possibility that a plug of another type is required, but as a rule the recommended plug should be adhered to.

After cleaning carefully, examine the plugs for cracked insulators and wear of the insulator nose due to excessive previous cleaning. In such cases the plugs have passed their useful life, and new plugs should be installed.

Examine the insulator for deposits underneath the side electrode which have possibly accumulated and which act as a 'hot spot' in service.

After cleaning the plugs in a special cleaner, blow all surplus abrasive out of the body recesses, and off the plug threads, by means of an air-blast. Next examine the threads for carbon. Any deposits can be removed and the threads cleaned with a wire brush. A wire buffing wheel may also be utilized, but reasonable care must be used in both methods in order not to injure the electrodes or the tip of the insulator. The thread section of the plug body is often neglected when cleaning the plugs, owing to the fact that it is not generally realized that, like the gaskets, the threads are a means of heat dissipation and that when they are coated with carbon it retards the flow of the heat from the plug, producing overheating. This simple procedure will also ensure absence of binding on the threads on replacement and also avoid unnecessary use of the plug spanner.

When replacing a plug, always screw it down by hand as far as possible and use the torque wrench for final tightening only. Whenever possible use a socket to avoid possible fracture of the insulator.

Examine the electrodes for the correct gap. (See 'General Data'.) Avoid an incorrect reading in the case of badly pitted electrodes.

Remember that electrode corrosion and the development of oxides at the gap area vitally affects the sparking efficiency. The special cleaner can remove the oxides and deposits from the insulator, but the cleaner stream does not always reach this area with full effect owing to its location, and cannot necessarily deal with corrosion effectively as this sometimes requires too strong a blast for proper removal.

When plugs appear worthy of further use it is good

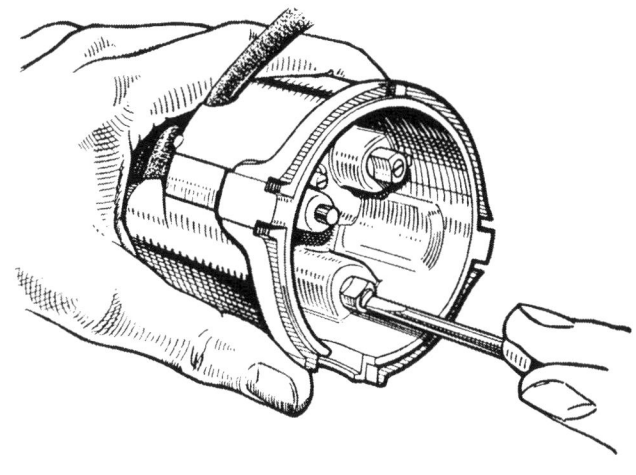

Fig. B.7. Securing the high tension cables to the distributor cap.

practice to dress the gap area on both centre and side electrodes with a small file before resetting them to the correct gap. The intense heat, pressure, explosion shock, and electrical and chemical action to which the plugs are submitted during miles of service are so intense that the molecular structure of the metal points is eventually affected. Plugs then reach a worn-out condition and resetting the points can no longer serve a good purpose. When points are burnt badly, it is indicative that the plug has worn to such an extent that its further use is undesirable and wasteful.

Before replacing the plug in the engine, test it for correct functioning under air pressure in a plug tester, following out the instructions issued by the makers of the plug tester. Generally speaking, a plug may be considered satisfactory for further service if it sparks continuously under a pressure of 100 lb./sq. in. (7 kg./cm.^{2}) with the gap between the points set at ·022 in. (·56 mm.). It is essential that the plug point should be reset to the recommended gap before the plug is refitted to the engine. (See 'General Data'.)

While the plug is under pressure in the tester, it should be inspected for leakage by applying oil round the terminal. Leakage is indicated by the production of air bubbles, the intensity of which will serve to indicate the degree of leakage. The leakage gases have a 'blowtorch' effect when the engine is running which rapidly raises the temperature of the plug, raising it above its designed heat range, thus producing overheating, preignition, and rapid electrode destruction.

The top half of the insulator is frequently responsible for poor plug performance due to the following faults: splashes; accumulation of dirt and dust; cracked insulators, caused by a slipping spanner; overtightness of the terminals.

B IGNITION SYSTEM

Examine for a cracked insulator at the shoulder and the terminal post and remove any accumulations of dirt and dust.

Section B.8

HIGH-TENSION CABLES

To remove

(1) Obtain access to the high-tension cables by raising the bonnet.
(2) Pull the high-tension cables off the sparking plugs.
(3) Unscrew the moulded terminal to release the cable from the coil.
(4) Straighten out the bare strands of cable, remove the brass washer and withdraw the cable from the moulded terminal.
(5) Release the screws, securing the cables in the distributor cap and withdraw the cables.

To renew

(1) Thread a new ignition cable through the moulded coil terminal and brass washer, bend back the bare strands of the cable against the brass washer and screw the moulded terminal onto the coil.
(2) Fill the appropriate hole in the distributor cap with Silicone grease, push the other end of the high tension cable from the coil well home into the distributor cap and secure it with the pointed screw, Fig. *B.7*.
(3) Fill the other four holes in the distributor cap with Silicone grease, cut the remaining cables to length, push them well home into the cap and tighten the securing screws.
(4) In connecting the sparking plugs to their cables, bear in mind that the firing order is 1, 3, 4, 2 and that the distributor rotor rotates anti-clockwise.

Section B.9 FAULT DIAGNOSIS

Symptom	No.	Possible Fault
(a) Engine will not fire	1	Battery discharged
	2	Distributor contact points dirty, pitted or out of adjustment
	3	Distributor cover 'tracked' or cracked
	4	Distributor carbon brush not in contact with rotor
	5	Loose connection in low-tension circuit
	6	Distributor rotor arm cracked
	7	Coil faulty
(b) Engine misfires	1	Distributor contact points dirty, pitted or out of adjustment
	2	Contact breaker spring weak
	3	Distributor cover 'tracked' or cracked
	4	Coil faulty
	5	Loose connection in low-tension circuit
	6	High-tension cables cracked or perished
	7	Sparking plug loose
	8	Sparking plug insulation cracked
	9	Sparking plug gap incorrect
	10	Ignition timing too far advanced

SECTION C

COOLING SYSTEM

Section No. C.1	Description
Section No. C.2	Adjustment in vehicle
Section No. C.3	Radiator
Section No. C.4	Thermostat
Section No. C.5	Temperature gauge
Section No. C.6	Fan and pump assembly
Section No. C.7	Draining and flushing the system
Section No. C.8	Frost precautions
Section No. C.9	Heater unit
Section No. C.10	Modified engine drain tap
Section No. C.11	Fault diagnosis

COOLING SYSTEM

Section C.1

DESCRIPTION

The circulation of the cooling water is effected by a centrifugal pump mounted in front of the cylinder block and driven by a belt from the crankshaft pulley. A thermostat is fitted in the water outlet pipe at the front end of the engine.

When filling or topping-up the radiator, do so when the engine is cold, and if possible use rainwater or clean soft water. Fill up to the filler plug orifice.

The capacity of the system is 10 pints (5·68 litres, 12 U.S. pints.)

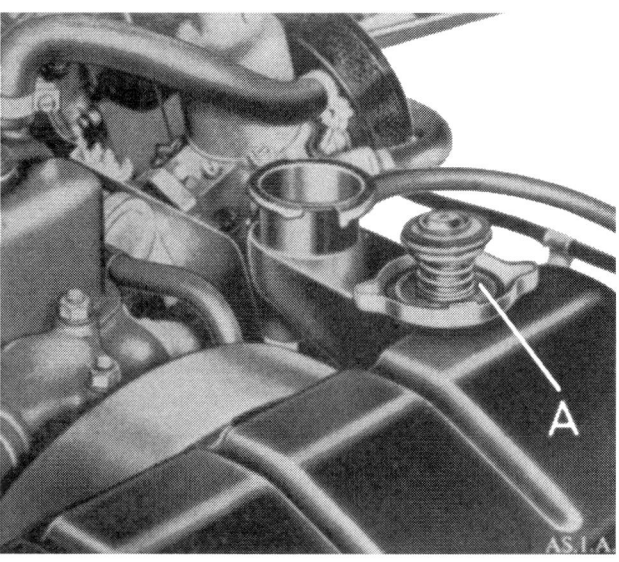

Fig. C.1. Showing the radiator filler with its cap 'A' removed.

Section C.2

ADJUSTMENTS IN VEHICLE

Overheating may be caused by a slack fan belt, excessive carbon deposit in the cylinders, running with the ignition too far retarded, improper carburetter adjustment, a partially chocked radiator causing failure of the water to circulate, or loss of water due to leakage or evaporation.

The belt should be just sufficiently tight to prevent slip yet it should be possible to move it laterally about 1 in. (2·54 cms.). To make an adjustment slacken the bolts 1, 2 and 3, Fig. C.2 which hold the generator in position, then raise or lower the generator until the desired tension of the belt is obtained. Securely lock the generator in position again at securing points 1, 2 and 3, Fig. C.2 when the adjustment has been made.

Section C.3

RADIATOR

To Remove

(1) Drain the cooling system.
(2) Slacken the hose clip, on the upper water hose, at the thermostat housing and with the aid of a screwdriver ease the pipe off the housing extension.
(3) Take off the radiator bottom hose by releasing the clips on the water pump and water outlet pipe if a heater is fitted.
(4) Remove the four nuts (two on each side) which secure the radiator to the mounting flanges and remove the radiator (see Fig. C.3.).
(5) Inspect the radiator core for damage and test it for water leaks. Solder at the points where leakage occurs or renew the core if necessary.
(6) Inspect the drain tap for leaks and renew it if necessary.
(7) Test the filler cap.
(8) Inspect the hose connections for deterioration and renew them if necessary.

Fig. C.2. Fanbelt adjustment.
1 and 3. Generator securing bolts.   2. Swinging link locknut.

To Replace

Installation is a reversal of the procedure 'To remove.'

Section C.4

THERMOSTAT

To Remove

(1) Drain the cooling system (see Section C.7).
(2) Disconnect the outlet hose from the outlet elbow.

Austin-Healey Sprite. Issue 3. 24975.

C COOLING SYSTEM

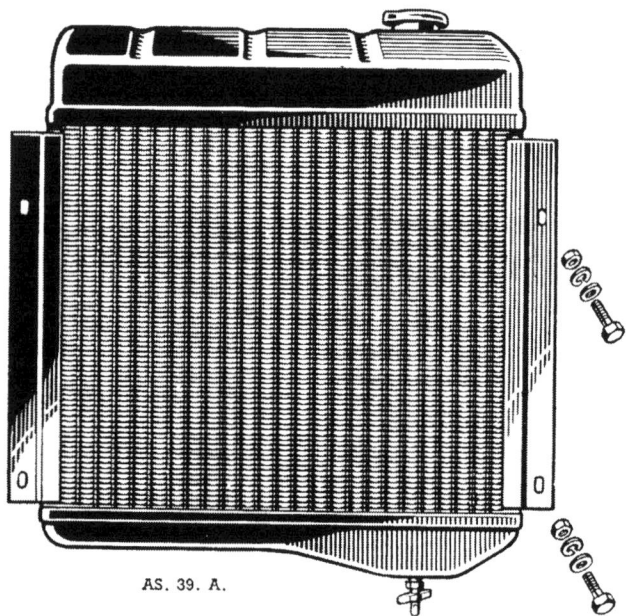

Fig. C.3. Illustrating the positions of the four radiator securing setpins.

(3) Remove the three nuts and spring washers from the thermostat cover and lift the cover off its studs.

(4) Remove the paper joint washer and lift out the thermostat, Fig. C.4.

(5) Test the thermostat opening temperature by immersing it in water at a temperature between 154° and 167°F. (68° and 75°C.). If the thermostat valve does not start to open, or the valve sticks in the fully open position, the thermostat should be renewed. No attempt should be made to repair the thermostat.

(6) Clean the joint faces at the outlet elbow and at the housing in the cylinder head.

To Replace

The installation of the thermostat is a reversal of the procedure 'to remove'. Fit a new paper joint washer between the cover and the cylinder head. In an emergency the engine can be run with the thermostat removed.

Section C.5

TEMPERATURE GAUGE

A temperature gauge unit, consisting of a thermal element and dial indicator is fitted to the vehicle. The thermal element is held in the radiator header tank by a gland nut. The dial indicator is situated in the instrument panel and is connected to the element by a capilliary tube filled with mercury.

Damage to any of the above mentioned parts will necessitate the renewal of the complete temperature gauge unit.

The combined water temperature and oil pressure gauges are of integral construction, and should one of these instruments fail, both will have to be renewed.

Section C.6

FAN AND PUMP ASSEMBLY

To Remove

(1) Remove the radiator (see Section C.3).

(2) Remove the generator (see Section M).

(3) Remove the pump unit from the cylinder block by removing the four securing bolts and spring washers and disconnecting the lower hose, by-pass hose, and interior heater hose if any.

(4) Remove the fan blades if necessary by withdrawing the four set screws from the pulley.

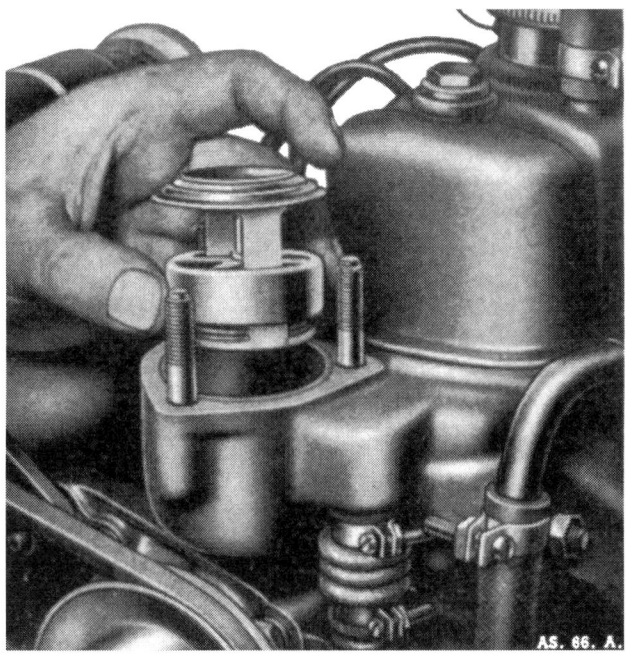

Fig. C.4. Illustrating the removal of the thermostat from its housing

COOLING SYSTEM

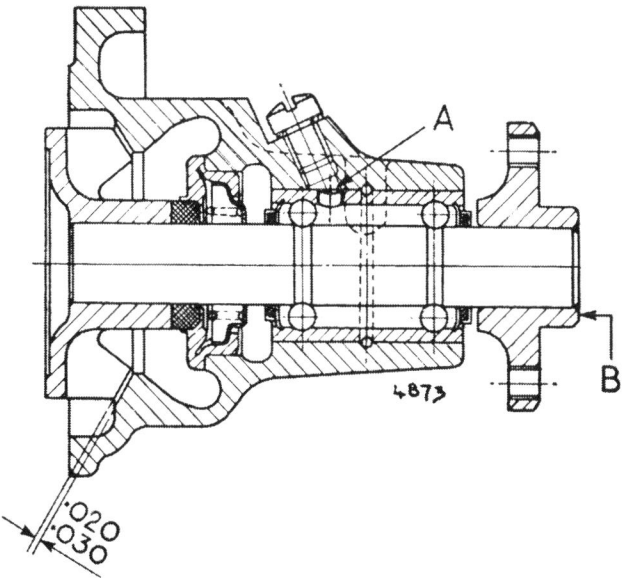

Fig. C.5. A section through the water pump showing the location of the components. When assembled the hole in the bearing must coincide with the lubricating hole in the water pump 'A' and the face of the hub 'B' must be flush with the end of the spindle

To Dismantle

(1) Unscrew the four set bolts which attach the fan and belt pulley to the hub and remove the fan and pulley.

(2) Remove the fan hub with a suitable extractor.

(3) Pull out the bearing locating wire through the hole in the top of the pump body.

(4) Gently tap the pump bearing assembly rearwards out of the pump body. This will release the combined bearing and spindle assembly together with the seal and vane.

(5) Remove the vane from the bearing assembly with a suitable extractor and remove the pump seal assembly.

To Reassemble

Reassembly is a reversal of the procedure 'To dismantle'. Attention should be given to the following points:

(1) Care must be taken to see that the seal assembly is in good condition. If there is any sign of damage the seal should be replaced by a new component.

(2) When the bearing assembly is assembled into the pump the hole in the bearing must coincide with the lubricating hole in the water pump body (see Fig. C.5.).

(3) Remove the water pump greasing plug (A) on the water pump casing and add a small quantity of grease to Ref. C (see Fig. C.6.). The lubricating of the pump must be done sparingly, otherwise grease will seep past the bearings on to the face of the carbon sealing ring and impair its efficiency.

(4) Check to see that the bearings run freely without excessive end play by spinning the fan.

To Replace

The installation of the fan and pump assembly is a reversal of the procedure 'To remove'. Particular note should be made of the following:

(1) Fit a new joint washer between the pump body and the cylinder block.

(2) Inspect the fan belt for uneven wear or frayed fabric, and renew the belt if required.

(3) Adjust the fan belt tension (see Section C.2.).

Fig. C.6. Showing location of greasing plug 'A' on the water pump body

Section C.7

DRAINING AND FLUSHING THE SYSTEM

To Drain the System

When the vehicle is to be stored the entire cooling system should be drained to protect against corrosion, and in certain instances, freezing. To drain the system proceed as follows:

(1) With the vehicle standing on level ground, remove the radiator filler cap.
   Caution—As the system is pressurised, do not remove the radiator filler cap while the engine is running and always wait until the water has cooled.

Austin-Healey Sprite Mk. 1.   Issue 4. 50312

COOLING SYSTEM

Fig. C.7. Showing location of radiator drain tap
1. Radiator drain tap   2. Bonnet safety catch

If it is necessary to remove the filler cap while the engine is hot it is essential to remove it gradually and the filler neck is provided with a shaped cam to enable this to be done.

Unscrew the cap slowly until the retaining tongues are felt to engage the small lobes at end of the filler neck cam, and wait until the pressure in the radiator is fully released before finally removing the cap.

(2) Open the cylinder block and radiator drain taps. If the system contains anti-freeze mixture it should be drained into clean containers, strained and preserved for re-use.

(3) To prevent the possibility of operating the vehicle with the system drained make sure that a suitable notice is placed on the vehicle or other precautions taken.

To Flush the System

Because there are impurities in the water in certain localities, deposits are left in the system. These deposits tend to clog the system and so impair cooling efficiency. It is therefore desirable to flush the radiator and water passages every 12,000 miles (20000 km.).

(1) Remove the filler cap and drain tap and allow the system to be thoroughly cleansed by flushing clean water through the filler orifice.

(2) Remove the radiator from the vehicle (Section C.3) turn it upside down and reverse flush by feeding clean water through the elbow on the bottom tank and allowing waste water to escape through the filler orifice.

(3) Remove and clean the thermostat (Section C.4).

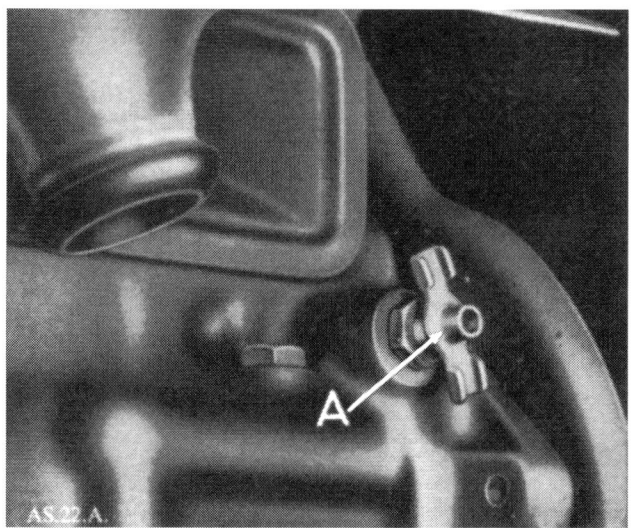

Fig. C.8. Showing cylinder block drain tap 'A' on left side of engine

Section C.8

FROST PRECAUTIONS

Care should be taken to see that the water is drained off completely, for in case of freezing it will do harm by expansion taking place and fracture of the cylinder block may result. There are two drain taps, one of them on to the rear of the engine on the left hand side, and the other at the base of the radiator. Both taps must be opened to drain the system and the vehicle must be on level ground while draining. Freezing may occur first at the bottom of the radiator or in the lower hose connection. Ice in the hose will stop water circulation and may cause boiling.

A muff can be used to advantage but care must be taken not to run with the muff fully closed, or boiling will result.

It must be noted that in the case of a car fitted with a heater no provision is made for draining the heater unit. Draining the radiator and cylinder block is not, therefore, a sufficient safeguard against freezing. An anti-freeze mixture must be used (see GENERAL INFORMATION page 9).

When frost is expected or when the vehicle is to be used in very low temperatures, make sure that the strength of the solution is, in fact, up to the strength recommended by the manufacturers, for conditions likely to be encountered.

COOLING SYSTEM

The strength of the solution must be maintained by topping-up with anti-freeze solution as necessary. Excessive topping-up with water will reduce the degree of protection afforded.

If the cooling system has to be emptied run the mixture into a clean container and use it again.

Section C.9

HEATER UNIT

Description

The Smith's heating and ventilating system is designed to provide heated fresh air to the car interior at floor level and to the windscreen for demisting and defrosting.

Air for the heater is drawn from a forward-facing intake via an auxiliary blower which should only be needed at speeds below about 25 m.p.h. A shut-off valve is incorporated in the heater intake to prevent fumes from entering the car in traffic. The valve must always be open when heating is required. A water tap is fitted at the rear end of the engine. In summer conditions this tap may be shut off and the system may then be used for cool air ventilation.

Fig. C.9. Heater mounting points.
1. *Heater blower bracket mounting setscrews.*
2. *Two of the four heater unit mounting setscrews.*

Controls

The heating and ventilating system is operated by a single control located on the fascia panel. This control takes the form of a knob marked 'Air—Push and Turn'. For heating and demisting, push in the air control knob. The blower may be switched on if required by turning the knob in a clockwise direction. The knob MUST be pushed in before the blower can be switched on. Two doors located forward at either side of the gearbox tunnel control distribution of air between screen and car interior. For heating, open the doors. For defrosting (i.e., boosting flow of hot air to screen) close the doors.

Heater Removal

(1) Drain the cooling system as described in Section C.7.
(2) Disconnect the butterfly valve control wire situated at the right-hand side of the heater unit.
(3) Detach the heater inlet and outlet pipes at their heater connections.
(4) Remove the four setpins securing the heater unit to the engine bulkhead (Fig. C.10).
(5) Withdraw the heater and at the same time slip it off the air intake pipe.

Heater Replacement

Installation of the heater unit is a reversal of the removal procedure.

Section C.10

MODIFIED ENGINE DRAIN TAP

From Engine No. 9C/U/H 6359 a cylinder block drain tap (Part No. 3H576) of improved design is fitted. This tap is introduced to overcome any difficulty of operation and has a plain British Standard Pipe thread in place of the taper thread previously used. A fibre washer must, therefore, be fitted between the cylinder block and the tap.

The new tap is interchangeable with that previously used.

COOLING SYSTEM

Section C.11 — FAULT DIAGNOSIS

Symptom	No.	Possible Fault
(a) Internal Water Leakage	1	Cracked cylinder wall
	2	Loose cylinder head nuts
	3	Cracked cylinder head
	4	Faulty gasket
	5	Cracked tappet chest wall
(b) Poor Circulation	1	Radiator core blockage
	2	Water jacket restriction
	3	Low water level
	4	Loose fan belt
	5	Defective thermostat
	6	Perished or collapsed radiator bottom hose
(c) Corrosion	1	Impurities in water
	2	Infrequent draining and flushing
(d) Overheating		In (b) check 4, 5 and 6
	1	Sludge in crankcase
	2	Faulty ignition timing
	3	Low oil level in sump
	4	Tight engine
	5	Choked exhaust system
	6	Binding brakes
	7	Slipping clutch
	8	Valve timing incorrect
	9	Retarded ignition
	10	Mixture too weak

SECTION D

FUEL SYSTEM

Section D.1.	Fuel tank
Section D.2.	Fuel pump
Section D.3.	Servicing the pump
Section D.4.	Carburetters
Section D.5.	Carburetter adjustment
Section D.6.	Sources of carburetter trouble
Section D.7.	The air cleaners
Section D.8.	Exhaust pipe
Section D.9.	Modified carburetter damper assemblies
Section D.10.	Fault diagnosis

FUEL SYSTEM   D

Section D.1

THE FUEL TANK

To Remove

(1) Remove the drain plug from the tank and drain the petrol into a suitable receptacle.

(2) Remove the filler cap.

(3) Disconnect the fuel outlet pipe at its union with the tank.

(4) Unscrew the six nuts surrounding and securing the tank to the underside of the body.

(5) Lower the tank sufficiently to allow disconnection of the tank unit wire (green with black).

(6) Withdraw the fuel tank from the car.

Section D.2

FUEL PUMP

Description (Fig. D.1).

The fuel pump is an AC-Sphinx 'Y' type mechanical pump operated off an eccentric on the engine camshaft. Fig. D.1 shows a sectional view of the pump.

As the engine camshaft (13) revolves, the eccentric (12) lifts the pump rocker arm (16) which is pivoted at (17). The rocker arm pulls the pull-rod downwards (1) together with the diaphragm (3) against the pressure of the spring (2), thus creating a vacuum in the pump chamber (4). Petrol is drawn from the tank and enters at (6) into the sediment chamber (5), through filter gauze (9), suction valve (11) into the pump chamber (4). On the return stroke the pressure of the spring (2) pushes the diaphragm (3) upwards, forcing petrol from the pump chamber (4) through the delivery valve (7) and port (8) into the carburetter.

When the carburetter bowl is full the float will shut the needle valve, thus preventing any flow of petrol from the pump chamber (4). This will hold the diaphragm (3) downward, against the pressure of the spring (2) and will remain in this position until the carburetter requires further petrol and the needle valve opens. The rocker arm (16), operates the connecting link by making contact at (15) and this construction allows idling movement of the rocker arm when there is no movement of the fuel pump diaphragm.

Spring (14) keeps the rocker arm (16) in constant contact with the pushrod and eccentric (12) to eliminate noise.

Section D.3

SERVICING THE PUMP

To Remove from Engine

Start by disconnecting the pipe unions and then remove the two set screws which hold the petrol pump to the engine crankcase. The fuel pump will now readily come away.

To Dismantle the Pump (Fig. D.2).

(1) Unscrew the set bolt (1) and lift off the cover (3).

(2) Lift off the filter gauze (5) and cork sealing washer (4).

(3) Unscrew the five upper chamber securing screws (23) and separate the two halves of the pump body (6 and 21).

(4) Unscrew the three screws (9) and remove the valve plate (11), inlet and delivery valves (8), valve plate gasket (10) springs (7), and delivery valve spring retainer (12).

(5) Remove the diaphragm and pull rod assembly (25)

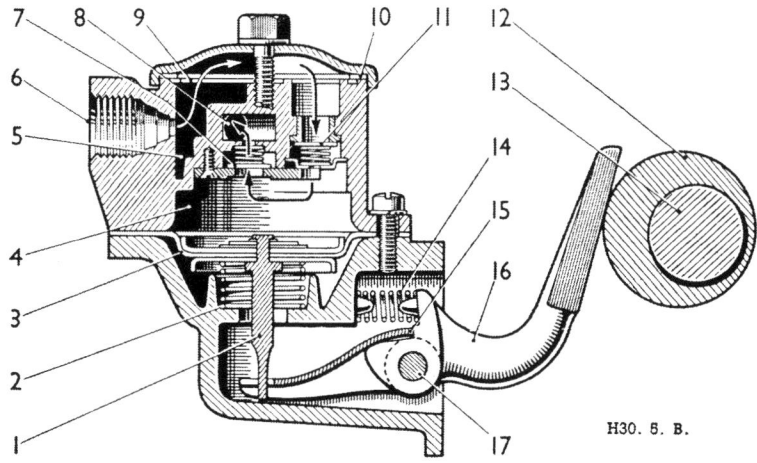

Fig. D.1. Sectioned view of the fuel pump.

1. *Diaphragm pull-rod.*
2. *Diaphragm return spring.*
3. *Diaphragm.*
4. *Pump chamber.*
5. *Sediment chamber.*
6. *Inlet union.*
7. *Delivery valve.*
8. *Delivery port.*
9. *Gauze filter.*
10. *Cork sealing washer.*
11. *Inlet valve.*
12. *Crankshaft eccentric.*
13. *Camshaft.*
14. *Anti-rattle spring.*
15. *Connecting link.*
16. *Rocker arm.*
17. *Rocker arm pivot pin.*

D

FUEL SYSTEM

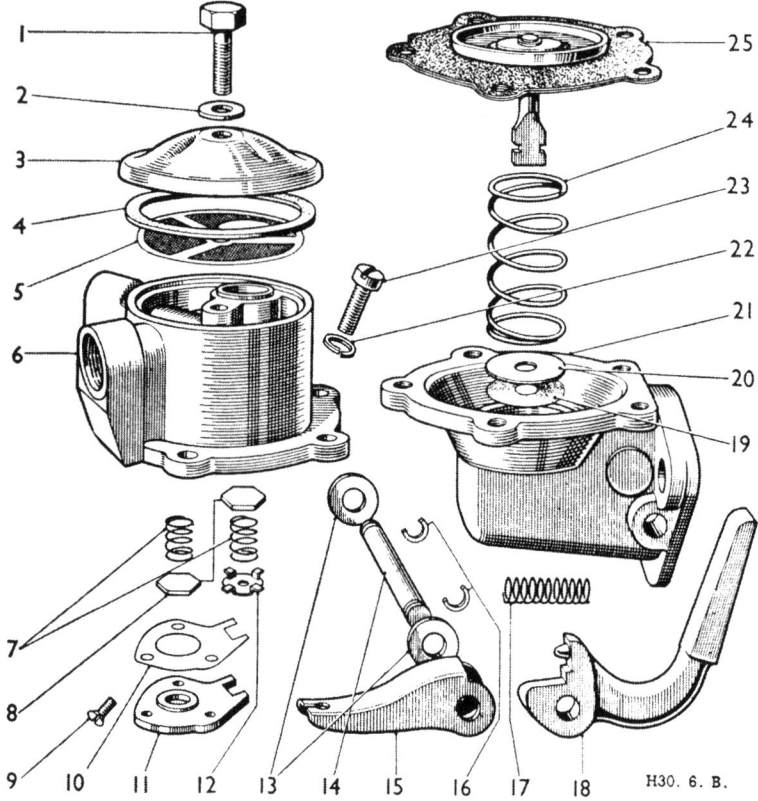

1. Cover retaining screw.
2. Fibre washer.
3. Cover.
4. Cork sealing washer.
5. Gauze filter.
6. Upper casting.
7. Valve springs.
8. Inlet and delivery valves.
9. Valve plate screw.
10. Valve plate gasket.
11. Valve plate.
12. Retainer.
13. Packing washers.
14. Rocker arm pivot pin.
15. Connecting link.
16. Retaining clips.
17. Anti-rattle spring.
18. Rocker arm.
19. Fibre washer.
20. Metal washer.
21. Pump body.
22. Spring washer.
23. Upper chamber securing screws.
24. Diaphragm return spring.
25. Diaphragm assembly.

Fig. D.2. Fuel pump exploded.

by rotating it through 90° and pulling it out. This will release the diaphragm spring (24).

(6) Remove the metal washer (20) and fibre washer (19).

(7) Remove the two retaining circlips (16) and washers (13), push out the rocker arm pivot pin (14) which will release the rocker arm (18), link (15) and spring (17).

Re-assembling the Petrol Pump

The following procedure should be adopted, dealing with the upper portion of the pump first (Fig. D.2).

All valves should be swilled in clean paraffin before re-assembly. Apart from the cleaning effect this improves the sealing between the valve and seat.

(1) Place the delivery valve (8) on its spring (7). Place the inlet valve (8) on the valve seat located in the upper casting.

(2) Put valve spring (7) on the centre of the inlet valve (8).

(3) Position retainer (12) on top of the inlet valve spring (7)—this retainer is a small four-legged pressing which retains the inlet valve spring— taking care not to distort the legs.

(4) Lay valve plate gasket (10) in position.

(5) Locate valve plate (11) in position and secure it with three screws (9).

(6) **Now use a piece of wire to ensure that the valves work freely.**

(7) Place the gauze filter screen (5) in position on top of the casting, making certain that it fits snugly.

(8) Fit the cork sealing washer (4), cover (3), fibre washer (2) and retaining screw (1).

(9) To assemble the lower half proceed as follows: Assemble link (15), packing washers (13), rocker arm (18) and rocker arm spring (17) in the body (21). Insert rocker arm pin (14) through the hole in the body, at the same time engaging the packing washers (13), link and the rocker arm. Then, spring the retaining clips (16) into the grooves on each end of the rocker arm pin. The rocker arm pin should be a tap fit in the body, and if due to wear it is freer than this, the ends of the holes in the body should be burred over slightly.

Note: The fitting of the rocker arm pin can be simplified by first inserting a piece of ·240 in. (6·096 mm.) diameter rod through the pin hole in one side of the body far enough to engage the rocker arm washers and link, then pushing in the rocker arm pin from the opposite side, removing the guide rod as the pin takes up its proper position.

FUEL SYSTEM   D

(10) To fit the **diaphragm** assembly to the pump body: Insert fabric washer (19), metal washer (20) and place the diaphragm spring (24) in position in the pump body.

Place the diaphragm assembly (25) over the spring, the pull rod being downwards, and centre the upper end of the spring in the lower protector washer.

Press downwards on the diaphragm, at the same time turning the assembly to the left in such a manner, that the slots on the pull rod will engage the fork in the link, ultimately turning the assembly a complete quarter turn to the left. This will place the pull rod in the proper working position in the link and at the same time permit the matching up of the holes in the diaphragm with those in the pump body flanges. When first inserting the diaphragm assembly into the pump body, the locating 'tab' on the outside of the diaphragm should be at the 12 o'clock position. After turning the diaphragm assembly a quarter of a turn to the left, the 'tab' should be at the 9 o'clock position. **Note:** Under certain conditions it is possible to insert the diaphragm pull rod too far through the slot in the operating link, with the result that the connecting link instead of engaging the two small slots in the pull rod, rides on the pull rod shoulder.

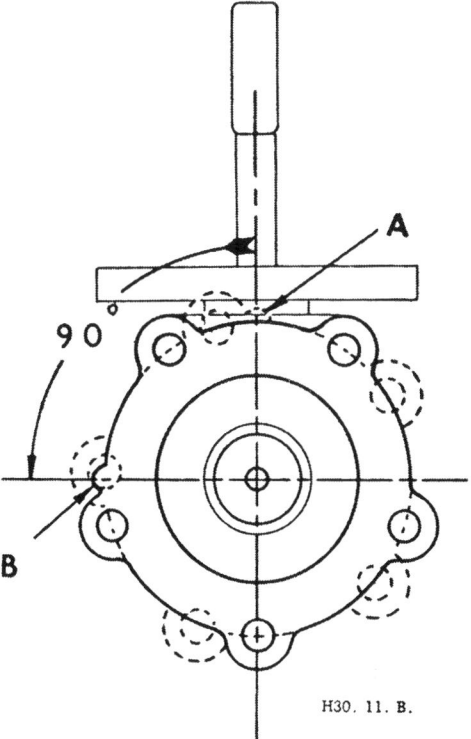

Fig. D.4. *When fitting the diaphragm to the pump body, the locating tab (A) should be in the position shown. Turn the diaphragm to the left, so that the pull rod slots engage in the connecting link fork, until it arrives at position (B).*

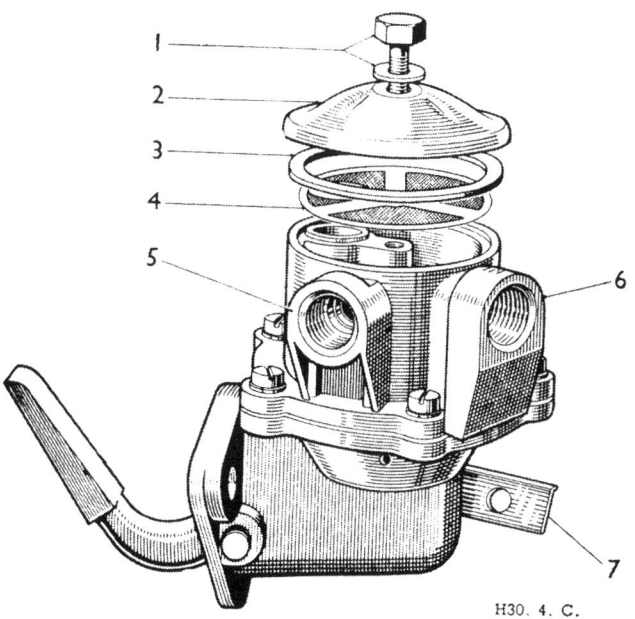

Fig. D.3. *Fuel pump top cover exploded.*

1. Retaining screw.
2. Cover.
3. Cork sealing washer.
4. Gauze filter.
5. Delivery union.
6. Inlet union.
7. Priming lever.

The diaphragm is correctly fitted when the slot in the link engages with the two slots in the diaphragm pull rod after the diaphragm has been turned through 90°.

Correct assembly can be checked by measuring the distance from the top of the pump body to the upper diaphragm protector, when the diaphragm is held at the top of its stroke by the return spring. A measurement of approximately $\frac{9}{16}$-in. (14·29 mm.) indicates correct assembly, whereas one of $\frac{3}{16}$-in. (4·76 mm.) proves that the assembly is unsatisfactory.

(11) The two sub-assemblies of the pump are now ready for fitting together and this is carried out as follows:

Push the rocker arm towards the pump until the diaphragm is level with the body flanges.

Place the upper half of the pump into the proper position, as shown by the mark made on the flanges before dismantling.

Install the cover screws and lockwashers and tighten only until the heads of the screws just engage the washers.

Use a screwdriver to hold the rocker arm at its outward position and while so held, securely tighten the cover screws diagonally.

D

FUEL SYSTEM

Testing the Pump

The best method of testing the pump is by using an AC-Sphinx bench test stand, on which the suction side of the pump is piped to a tin of paraffin at floor level and the outlet side of the pump connected to a stop tap and pressure gauge.

First, flush the pump through to wet the valves and seats, then completely empty it again by continuing to operate the rocker arm by hand with the suction pipe clear of the paraffin. Now, operate the pump again with the suction pipe in the paraffin. Not more than 20 strokes should be necessary to secure delivery of paraffin from the pump outlet.

Using the same apparatus a second test can be made by working the pump with the tap on the delivery side closed, pressure being recorded on the gauge. After ceasing to work the pump it should take several seconds for this pressure to return to zero, thus denoting that the valves are seating properly. Also, while there is pressure, the outer edge of the diaphragm—visible between the two clamping flanges—should be carefully examined for leakage and the retaining screws tightened if necessary. When working the pump by hand a somewhat longer stroke is obtained and the pressure developed is apt to be higher than when fitted to the engine.

When the above apparatus is not available the petrol pump should be tested as follows, using a can of clean paraffin.

Firstly, flush the pump by immersing it in paraffin and working the rocker arm half a dozen times; then, empty the pump by continuing to operate it while held above the bath. With the pump still clear of the paraffin, place a finger over the inlet union (marked 'In') and work the rocker arm several times. Upon removing the finger a distinct suction noise should be heard, denoting that the pump has developed a reasonable degree of suction. Afterwards the finger should be placed over the outlet union and after pressing the rocker arm inwards, the air drawn into the pump chamber should be held under compression of two or three seconds. This should also be done with the pump immersed in paraffin and the clamping flanges of the diaphragm watched for any signs of air leakage.

Refitting to Engine

Reverse the procedure outlined for removal from engine. Ensure that the rocker arm is correctly positioned against the eccentric on the camshaft, as there is a possibility of inadvertently getting the rocker arm under the eccentric or to one side when damage will result on tightening the bolts. After refitting, the engine should be run for a short time and pipe unions and pump examined for the possibility of fuel leakage.

Section D.4

THE CARBURETTERS

The two semi-down-draught S.U. type H.I. carburetters are of the variable-jet type, fitted with twin 'Pancake' air cleaners.

A damper is provided in each carburetter, consisting of a plunger and non-return valve attached to the oil cap nut, and operates in the hollow piston rod which is partly filled with oil. Its function is to give a slightly enriched mixture on acceleration by controlling the rise of the piston and to prevent piston flutter.

Section D.5

CARBURETTER ADJUSTMENT

It is first essential to run the engine until it has attained its normal running temperature before commencing any mixture or slow-running adjustments.

The slow-running is governed by the setting of the jet adjusting screws and the throttle stop screws, all of which must be correctly set and synchronised if satisfactory results are to be obtained.

The carburetter throttles are interconnected by a coupling shaft and spring coupling clips which enable them to be correctly synchronised when adjustments take place.

Before blaming the carburetter settings for bad slow-running make quite sure that it is not due to badly set contact points, faulty plugs, bad valve clearance setting or faulty valves and valve springs.

Good slow-running cannot be obtained if the setting for the jets is incorrect. It is therefore advisable to

Fig. D.5. Lubrication of the carburetter interconnecting linkages. Apply a few drops of oil to each of the enumerated link joints.

FUEL SYSTEM

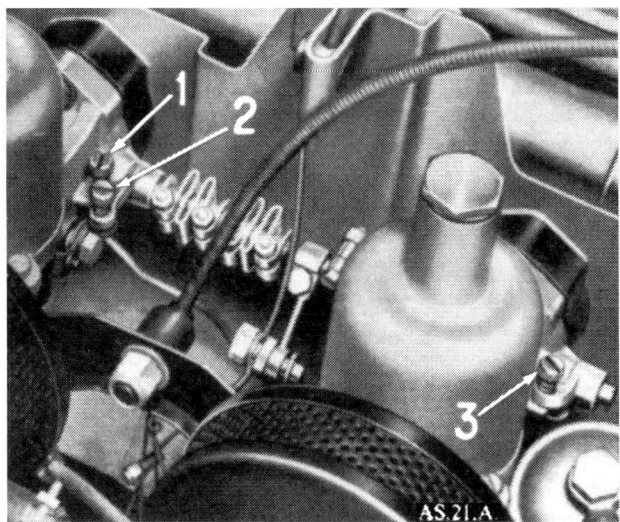

Fig. D.7. 1 & 3. Slow running adjustment screws. 2. Throttle mixture control interconnecting lever adjustor.

commence any adjustments at this point.

In order to adjust the carburetters successfully it is necessary to remove the air cleaners and intake pipe assembly from the carburetters and engine valve cover and make sure the pistons work freely and the jets are properly centred (see below).

Adjusting the Jets

(1) Slacken off the pinch-bolt of one of the spring coupling clips locating the carburetter interconnecting shaft to the carburetter throttle spindles and also release the two screws securing the choke spring to the jet levers, so that each carburetter can be operated independently.

(2) Release the throttle lever adjusting screws until both throttles are completely closed.

(3) Turn the throttle lever adjusting screw for the rear carburetter clockwise until it is just touching the web on the carburetter body and then give it one full turn. This will set the rear carburetter for fast idling and leave the front one out of action. This can be ensured further by lifting the front carburetter piston a matter of $\frac{1}{2}$ in. (13 mm.).

(4) With the engine running, set the jet adjusting screw for the rear carburetter so that a mixture strength is obtained which will give the best running speed for this throttle opening, taking care to see that the jet head is kept in firm contact with the adjusting nut the whole time.

(5) The correctness or otherwise of this setting can be checked by raising the suction piston with a small screwdriver, or similar instrument to the extent of $\frac{1}{32}$ in. (·8 mm). This should cause a very slight momentary increase in the engine speed without impairing the evenness of running in any way.

If this operation has the effect of stopping the engine it is an indication that the mixture setting is too weak.

If an appreciable speed increase occurs and continues to occur when the piston is raised as much as $\frac{1}{4}$ in. (6 mm.) it is an indication that the mixture is too rich.

(6) When the rear carburetter mixture setting has been carried out correctly release its throttle adjusting screw so that it is clear of the stop and the throttle is completely closed, and lift the piston $\frac{1}{2}$ in. (13 mm.) to render it inoperative. Then repeat the jet-adjusting operations on the front carburetter.

(7) When both carburetters are correctly adjusted individually for mixture strength the throttles of each should be set so as to give the required slow-running and synchronisation.

Slow-running and Synchronisation.

Screw each throttle lever adjusting screw so that its end is only just making contact with the web on the carburetter body, then give each screw one full turn exactly.

Start the engine, which will now idle on the fast side.

Unscrew each throttle lever adjusting screw an equal amount, a fraction of a turn at a time until the desired slow-running speed is achieved.

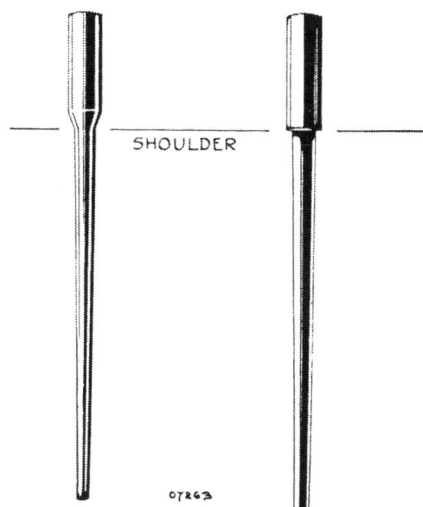

Fig. D.8. The shoulder of the needle should be flush with the underface of the piston. Two types of shoulder are in use and the correct datum point for each is shown.

D

FUEL SYSTEM

THE CARBURETTER COMPONENTS

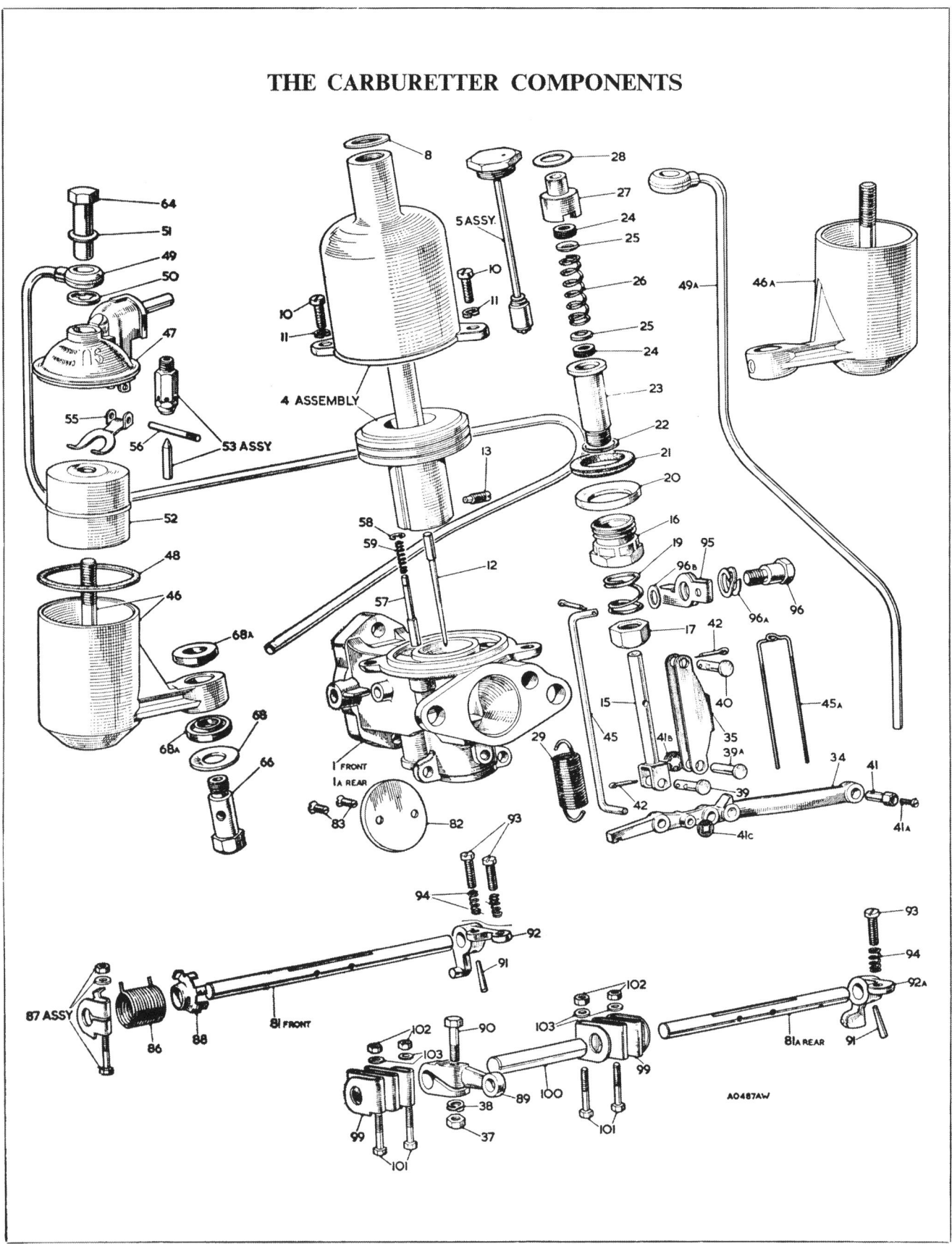

D.6

Austin-Healey Sprite. Issue 2. 21424

FUEL SYSTEM

D

KEY TO THE CARBURETTER COMPONENTS

No.	Description.
1.	Body—bare—front.
1A.	Body—bare—rear.
4.	Suction chamber and piston assembly.
5.	Oil damper assembly.
8.	Fibre washer—oil damper cap.
10.	Securing screw—suction chamber.
11.	Spring washer—D/C—screw.
12.	Jet needle.
13.	Jet needle locking screw.
15.	Jet with head.
16.	Jet sealing nut.
17.	Jet adjusting nut.
19.	Jet adjusting lock spring.
20.	Jet sealing ring—brass.
21.	Jet sealing ring—cork.
22.	Jet bearing copper washer—bottom half bearing.
23.	Jet bearing—bottom half.
24.	Jet gland washer—cork.
25.	Jet gland washer—brass.
26.	Jet gland spring.
27.	Jet bearing—top half.
28.	Jet bearing copper washer—top half bearing.
29.	Jet return spring.
34.	Jet lever.
35.	Jet link.
37.	Nut (2 BA).
38.	Washer.
39.	Pivot pin—short.
39A.	Pivot pin—jet link.
41.	Pivot pin—jet lever to stirrup.
41A.	Screw—cable clamp.
41B.	Starlock washer—jet link.
41C.	Starlock washer—link rod.
42.	Split pin.
45.	Link rod.
45A.	Stirrup—connecting jet lever.
46.	Float-chamber—bare—front.
46A.	Float-chamber—bare—rear.
47.	Float-chamber lid.
48.	Float-chamber lid washer.
49.	Overflow pipe—front.
49A.	Overflow pipe—rear.
50.	Serrated fibre washer—cap nut.
51.	Aluminium packing washer.
52.	Float.
53.	Float needle and seat assembly.
55.	Float hinged lever.
56.	Float hinged lever pin.
64.	Cap nut—float lid.
66.	Holding-up bolt—float—chamber.
68.	Washer—steel—holding-up bolt.
68A.	Rubber grommet—holding-up bolt.
81.	Throttle spindle—front.
81A.	Throttle spindle—rear.
82.	Throttle disc.
83.	Throttle disc screw.
86.	Return spring—throttle—front.
87.	End clip.
88.	Anchor plate.
89.	Throttle lever.
90.	Bolt (2 BA).
91.	Taper pin.
92.	Throttle stop—front.
92A.	Throttle stop—rear.
93.	Adjusting screw.
94.	Lock spring—screw.
95	Rocker lever—front.
96.	Bolt—pivot—front.
96A.	Spring washer—pivot bolt.
96B.	Aluminium washer—cam.
99.	Coupling—folded.
100.	Connecting rod—throttle.
101.	Bolt (4 BA).
102.	Nut (4 BA).
103.	Washer (4 BA).

D FUEL SYSTEM

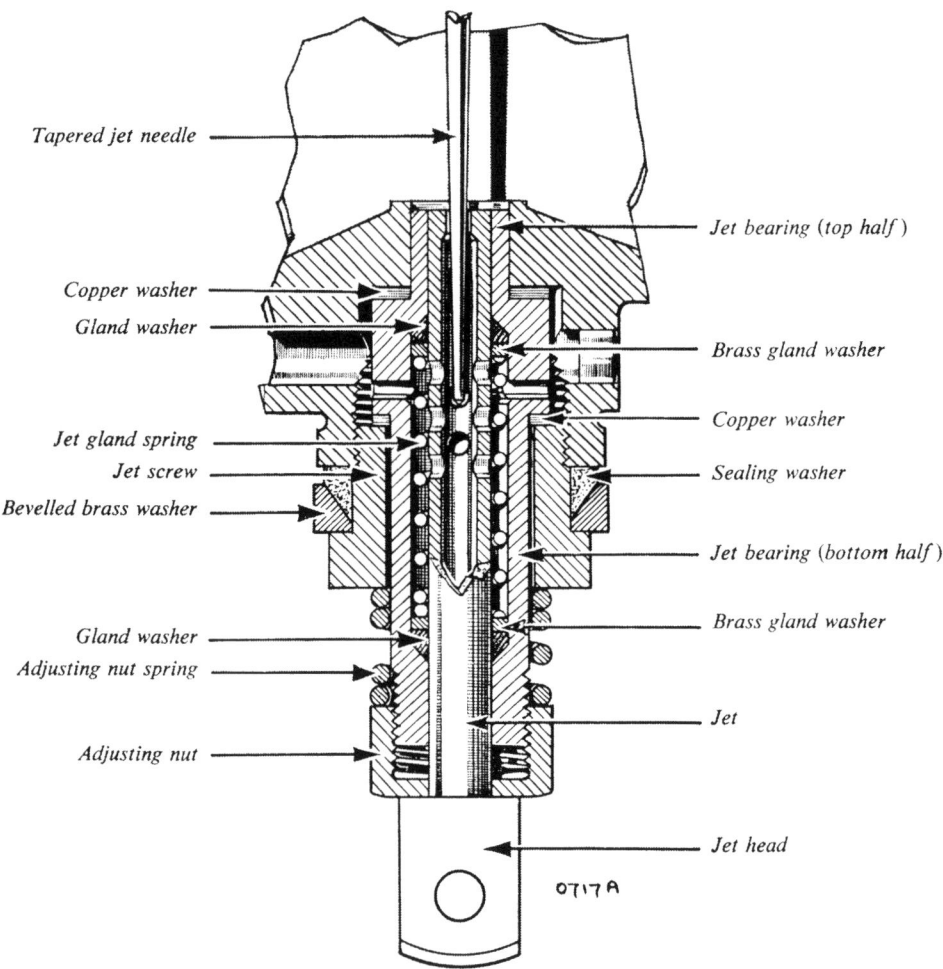

Fig. D.9. Sectioned view of jet assembly.

Correct synchronisation can be checked by listening at each carburetter air intake in turn through a length of rubber tube and notice if the noise produced by the incoming air is the same in both. Any variation in intensity of the sound indicates that one throttle is set more widely open than the other—the louder sound indicates the throttle with the greater opening.

When the same intensity of sound is produced by both carburetters the intercoupling shaft clip should be tightened up firmly to ensure that the throttles work in unison.

Since the delivery characteristics, when both carburetters are operating together, vary somewhat from those existing when each is working separately it will be found necessary to check them again for correctness of mixture strength by lifting the pistons in turn as described in 'Adjusting the jets,' making such adjustments of the jet adjusting nuts as are required to balance the mixture strength and to ensure that it is not too rich.

Fitting New Needles

If the road performance is not satisfactory after the above adjustments have been made, larger or smaller needles may be necessary.

To change the needles, remove the screws and lift off the suction chambers, having marked them to ensure refitting to their respective carburetters. Remove the pistons.

Unscrew the screw at the side of each piston tube and withdraw the needles.

Fit the new needles: a needle should be fitted with its shoulder flush with the face of the piston as shown in Fig. D.8.

The Float-chamber

The position of the forked lever in the float-chamber must be such that the level of the float (and therefore the height of the fuel at the jet) is correct.

This is checked by inserting a $\frac{7}{16}$ in. (11·11 mm.)

FUEL SYSTEM

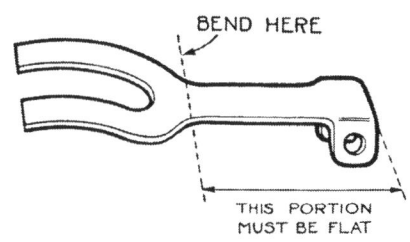

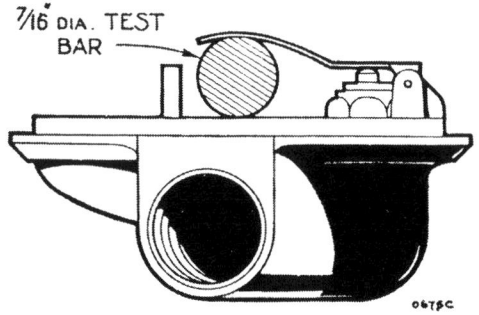

Fig. D.10. The correct method of float lever adjustment

round bar between the forked lever and the machined lip of the float-chamber lid. The prongs of the lever should just rest on the bar (see Fig. D.10) when the needle is on its seating. If this is not so, the lever should be reset at the point where the prongs meet the shank. Care must be taken not to bend the shank which must be perfectly flat and at right angles to the needle when it is on its seating.

Centring a Jet

First remove the clevis pin at the base of the jet which attaches the jet head to the jet operating lever; withdraw the jet completely, and remove the adjusting nut and adjusting nut spring. Replace the adjusting nut without its spring and screw it up to the highest position. Slide the jet into position until the jet head is against the base of the adjusting nut. When this has been done, feel if the piston is perfectly free by lifting it up with the finger with the dashpot piston removed. If it is not, slacken the jet sealing nut and manipulate the lower part of the assembly, including the projecting part of the bottom half jet bearing, adjusting nut and jet head. Make sure that this assembly is now slightly loose. The piston should then rise and fall quite easily as the needle is now able to move the jet into the required central position. The jet sealing nut should now be tightened and a check made to determine that the piston is still quite free. If it is not found to be so, the jet sealing nut should be slackened again and the operation repeated. When complete freedom of the piston is achieved the jet adjusting nut should be replaced. The adjusting nut should now be screwed back to its original position.

Experience shows that a large percentage of carburetters returned for correction have had jets removed and incorrectly centred on replacement.

Section D.6

SOURCES OF CARBURETTER TROUBLE

Piston Sticking

The piston assembly comprises the suction disc and the piston forming the choke into which is inserted the hardened and ground piston rod which engages in a bearing in the centre of the suction chamber and in which is, in turn, inserted the jet needle. The piston rod running in the bearing is the only part which is in actual contact with any other part, the suction disc, piston, and needle all having suitable clearances to prevent sticking. If sticking does occur the whole assembly should be cleaned carefully and the piston rod lubricated with a drop of thin oil. No oil must be applied to any other part except the piston rod. A sticking piston can be ascertained by removing the dashpot piston damper, inserting a finger in the air intake and lifting the piston, which should come up quite freely and fall back smartly onto its seating when released.

Water or Dirt in the Carburetter

When this is suspected lift the piston: the jet can then be seen; flood the carburetter and watch the jet; if fuel does not flow through freely there is a blockage. To remedy this, start the engine, open up the throttle, and block up the air inlet momentarily without shutting the throttle, keep the throttle open until the engine starts to race. This trouble seldom arises with the S.U. carburetter owing to the size of the jet and fuel ways. When it does occur the above method will nearly always clear it. Should it not do so, the only alternative is to remove the jet.

Float-chamber Flooding

This can be seen by fuel flowing over the float-chamber and dripping from the air inlet, and is generally caused by grit between the float chamber needle and its guide. Remove the float chamber top and withdraw the float lever by extracting its pivot pin. The needle valve will now drop out of its seating and can be checked for cleanliness. If there is no grit or foreign matter on the needle or its seating make certain that the needle is not unduly worn. Should this be the case a new needle valve and seating must be fitted.

Float Needle Sticking

If the engine stops, apparently through lack of fuel when there is plenty in the tank and the pump is working properly, the probable cause is a sticking float needle.

D FUEL SYSTEM

An easy test for this is to disconnect the pipe from the fuel pump to the carburetter, turn the engine with the starter motor to check if the fuel is being delivered; if it is starvation it has almost certainly been caused by the float needle sticking to its seating, and the float chamber lid should therefore be removed, the needle and seating cleaned, and refitted. At the same time it will be advisable to clean out the entire fuel system, as this trouble is caused by foreign matter in the fuel, and unless this is removed it is likely to recur. It is of no use whatever renewing any of the component parts of the carburetter, and the only cure is to make sure that the fuel tank and pipe lines are entirely free from any kind of foreign matter or sticky substance capable of causing this trouble.

Section D.7

THE AIR CLEANERS

Remove the units and wash the gauze in fuel every 3,000 miles (5000 km.).

When the gauze is clean and dry, re-oil it with engine oil and allow it to drain before refitting to the engine.

Section D.8

EXHAUST PIPE

To Remove

(1) Disconnect the exhaust down pipe at the manifold by slackening the securing clamp.

(2) Remove the nut and lock nut securing the rear hanging bracket to the underside of the vehicle. This bracket is located on the rear end of the silencer.

(3) Finally release the exhaust pipe from the rubber-mounted hanging bracket situated forward of the silencer. The complete exhaust pipe and silencer assembly may now be withdrawn from the vehicle.

To Install

The installation of the exhaust pipe and silencer is a reversal of the procedure 'To Remove.'

Section D.9

MODIFIED CARBURETTER DAMPER ASSEMBLIES

To allow the carburetter pistons to lift more freely avoiding restriction of performance, new hydraulic damper assemblies have been fitted in production. The damper pistons of the new assemblies have been shortened from ·378 in. (9·596 mm.) to ·308 in. (7·823 mm.).

The new hydraulic damper assemblies (part number AUC8114) are identified by the letter 'O' stamped on the brass hexagon caps. They can be fitted, with advantage, to earlier carburetters in pairs. Alternatively, the original damper pistons may be modified be machining ·070 in. (1·78 mm.) off their lower faces.

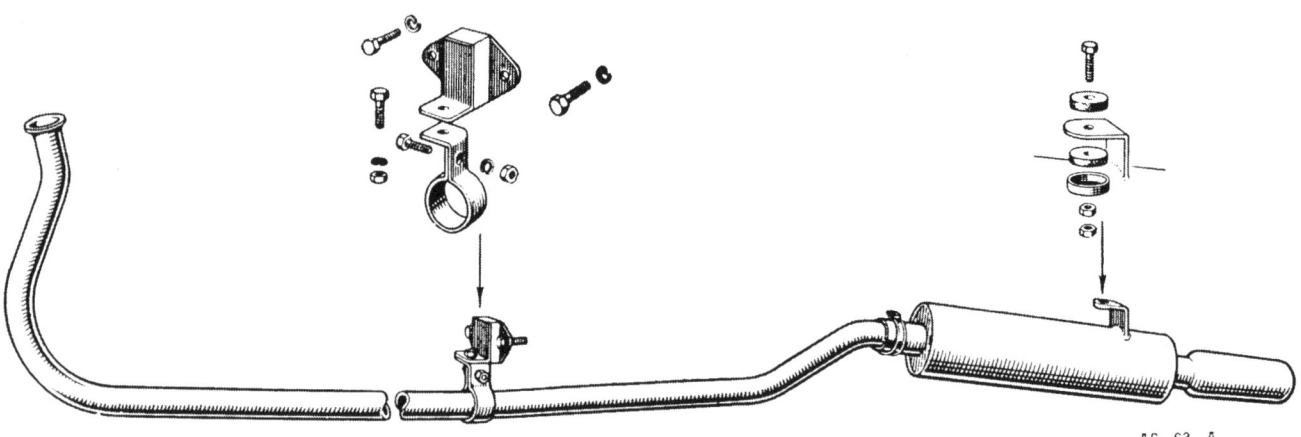

Fig. D.11. The exhaust system exploded

FUEL SYSTEM   D

Section D.10   FAULT DIAGNOSIS

Symptom	No.	Possible Fault
(a) Leakage or insufficient fuel delivery	1 2 3 4 5 6 7 8	Air vent restricted. Pipes restricted or partially clogged. Air leakage at pipe connections. Lift pump or carburetter filter gauze clogged. Lift pump gasket damaged. Lift pump diaphragm damaged. Lift pump valves sticking or seating improperly. Fuel vaporising in pipe.
(b) Excessive fuel consumption	1 2 3 4 5 6 7 8 9	Carburetters out of adjustment. Fuel leakage. Controls sticking. Air cleaners dirty. Excessive engine temperature. Brakes dragging. Under-inflated tyres. Excessive idling. Vehicle overloaded.
(c) Fast idling	1 2 3	Rich fuel mixture. Carburetter controls sticking. Slow-running screws incorrectly adjusted.
(d) Lift pump noise	1 2 3 4	Pump mountings loose. Air leak on suction side. Obstruction in pipe. Filter obstructed.
(e) Air leak on suction side of pump	1 2 3	Suction pipes, pump inlet or pump filter unions loose. Insufficient fuel in the tank. Faulty pipe.

Austin-Healey Sprite. Issue 3. 24975.

SECTION E

CLUTCH

Section No. E.1.	Description
Section No. E.2.	Adjustment in vehicle
Section No. E.3.	Clutch assembly
Section No. E.4.	Clutch pedal
Section No. E.5.	Master cylinder
Section No. E.6.	Slave cylinder
Section No. E.7.	Bleeding the clutch system
Section No. E.8.	Fault diagnosis
End of Section	Service tools

CLUTCH

Section E.1

DESCRIPTION

The clutch is a Borg & Beck single dry-plate-type operated hydraulically. A steel cover bolted to the flywheel encloses the driven plate, the pressure plate, the pressure springs, and the release levers. The driven plate, to which the friction linings are riveted, incorporates springs assembled around the hub to absorb power shocks and torsional vibration. The pressure springs force the pressure plate against the friction linings, gripping the driven plate between the pressure plate and the engine flywheel. When the clutch pedal is depressed, the release bearing is moved forward against the release plate which bears against the three release levers. The outer or shorter ends of the release levers engage the pressure plate lugs; pressure applied by the release bearing causes the pressure plate to be pulled away from the driven plate, compressing the pressure springs which are assembled between the pressure plate and the clutch cover. As the friction linings wear, the pressure plate moves closer to the flywheel face and the outer or shorter ends of the release levers follow. This causes the inner or longer ends of the levers to travel farther towards the gearbox and decreases the clearance between the release lever plate and the release bearing. This is automatically compensated unless the master cylinder has been disturbed.

When the clutch pedal is depressed, fluid pressure is transmitted through the master cylinder to the slave cylinder, which is mounted on the clutch housing, moving the slave cylinder piston, and push rod. As the push-rod is connected to the lower arm of the clutch withdrawal lever, thereby the clutch is released. The push rod is non-adjustable.

Section E.2

ADJUSTMENT IN VEHICLE

A free movement of $\frac{5}{32}$ in. must be maintained at the clutch pedal pad. This clearance is adjusted by means of the hexagon on the master cylinder push rod.

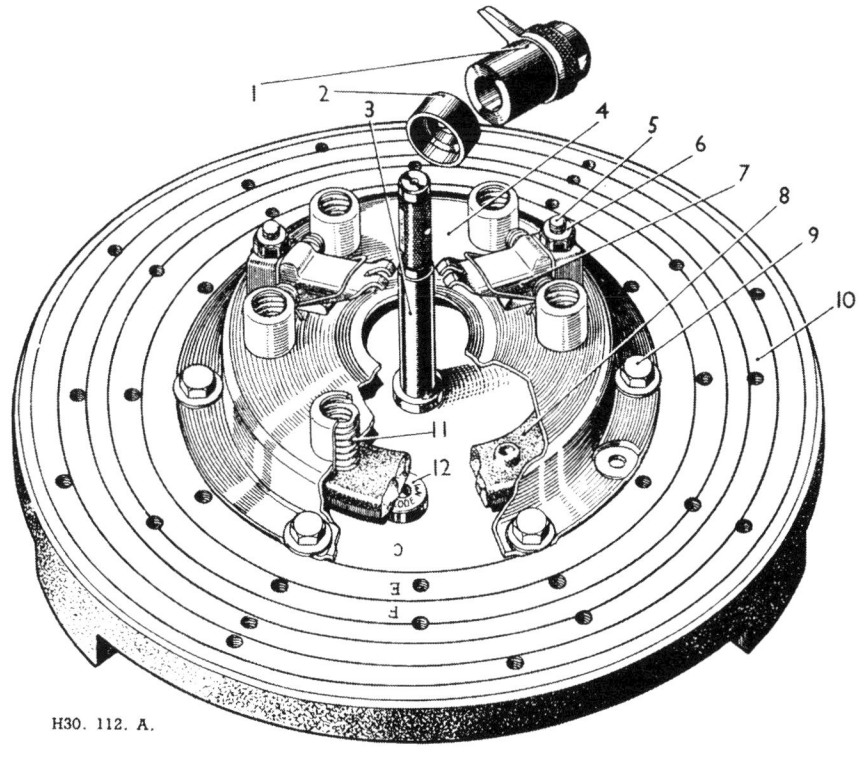

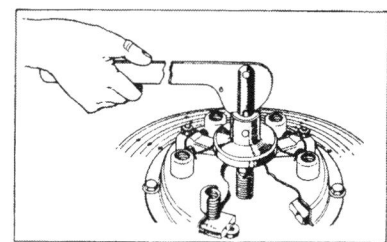

Fig. E.1. *Clutch assembly tool 18G 99A.*

1. *Height finger.*
2. *Distance piece.*
3. *Centre pillar.*
4. *Clutch cover.*
5. *Shoulder stud.*
6. *Adjusting nut.*
7. *Release lever.*
8. *Pressure plate.*
9. *Setpins.*
10. *Base plate.*
11. *Thrust spring.*
12. *Spacing washer.*

Inset shows the clutch actuating mechanism in use.

E CLUTCH

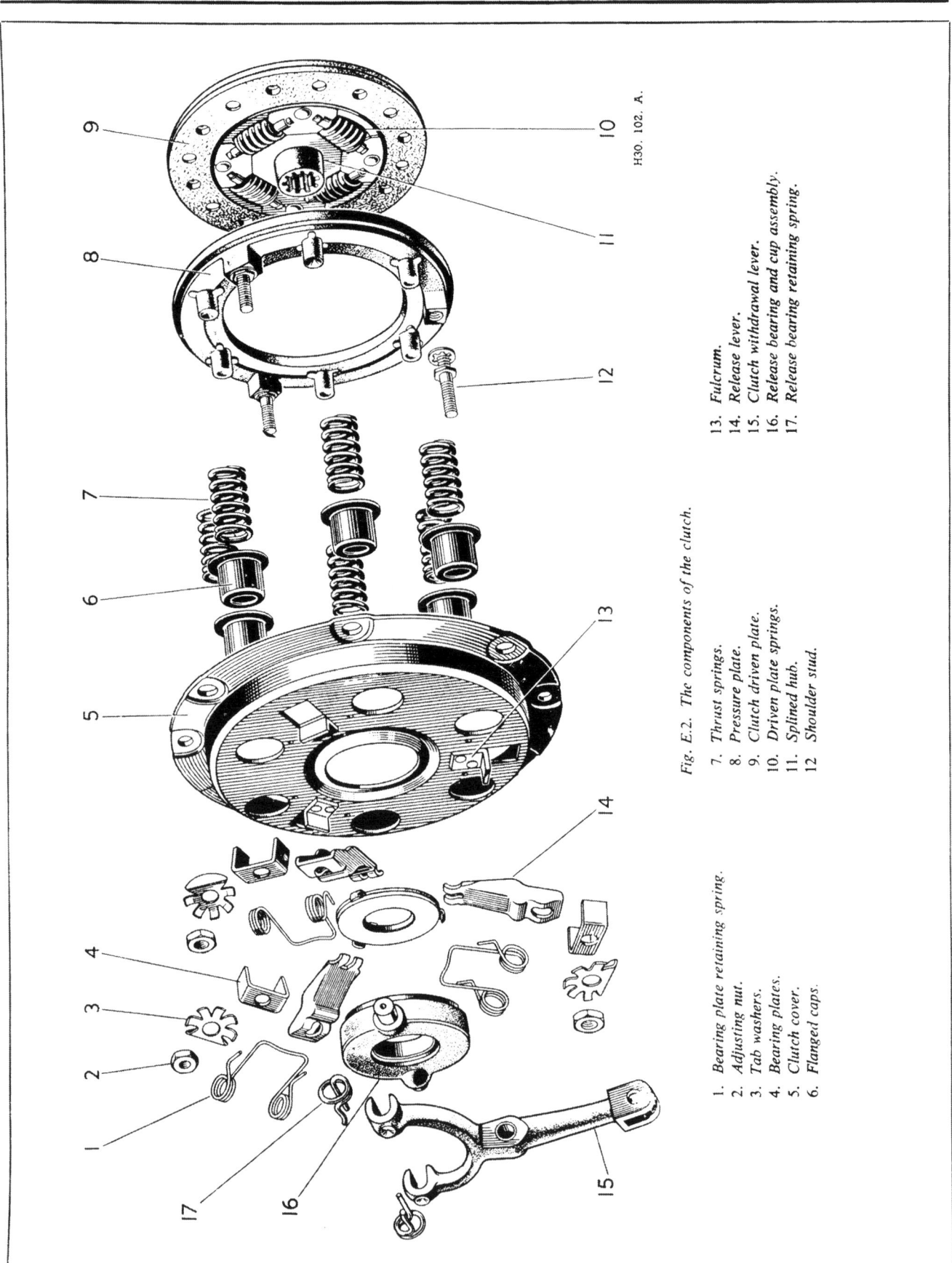

Fig. E.2. *The components of the clutch.*

1. Bearing plate retaining spring.
2. Adjusting nut.
3. Tab washers.
4. Bearing plates.
5. Clutch cover.
6. Flanged caps.
7. Thrust springs.
8. Pressure plate.
9. Clutch driven plate.
10. Driven plate springs.
11. Splined hub.
12. Shoulder stud.
13. Fulcrum.
14. Release lever.
15. Clutch withdrawal lever.
16. Release bearing and cup assembly.
17. Release bearing retaining spring.

CLUTCH

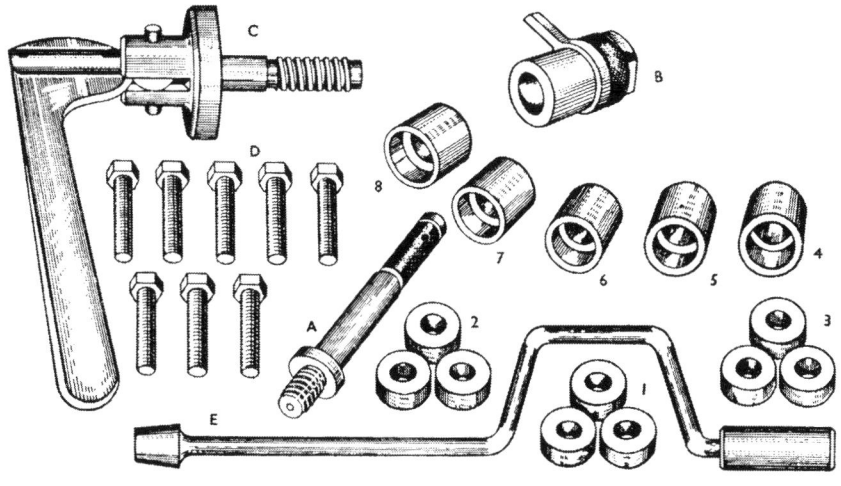

Fig. E.3. *Parts of clutch assembly tool.*

A. Centre pillar.
B. Height finger.
C. Actuating mechanism.
D. Setpins.
E. Speedbrace.
1.
2. } Spacing washers.
3.
4.
5.
6. } Distance pieces.
7.
8.

ST. 132. A.

Section E.3

CLUTCH ASSEMBLY

To Remove

(1) Remove the gearbox as described in Section F.

(2) Slacken the clutch cover screws a turn at a time by diagonal selection until the spring pressure is relieved, when the screws can be taken out and the clutch removed.

To Dismantle

When dismantling the clutch cover assembly the following parts should be suitably marked so that they can be reassembled in exactly the same relative positions to each other to preserve the balance and adjustment—the cover, the lugs on the pressure plate, and the release levers.

The clutch Tool No. 18G 99A provides an efficient and speedy means of dismantling, reassembling and adjusting the clutch with a high degree of accuracy. The tool is universal, and a chart detailing the sizes of spacing washers and distance-pieces for particular types of clutch is provided on the inside of the metal container lid. Proceed as follows:

(1) Detach the retaining springs from the release lever plate and remove the springs and plate.

(2) Rest the tool base plate on a flat surface, ensure that it is clean, and place upon it spacing washers as directed by the chart. For this 6¼ in. (15·88 cm.) clutch select three washers and place them in position 'A' on the base plate.

(3) Position the clutch on the three spacing washers so that the hole in the clutch cover aligns with the tapped holes in the base plate, with the release levers as close to the spring washers as possible.

(4) Insert the tool setscrews, tightening them a little at a time in a diagonal pattern, until the cover is firmly and evenly secured to the base plate. This is most important if the best results are to be achieved.

(5) Knock back the tab washers and remove the shoulder stud adjusting nuts. Lift off the washers, bearing plates and release levers.

(6) Unscrew the setscrews securing the clutch cover to the base plate in a diagonal pattern, releasing the pressure on the clutch springs gradually and evenly. Lift off the cover and remove the pressure springs.

(7) Clean the clutch parts carefully. If the linings are to be used again they should not be allowed to come in contact with cleaning fluids.

(8) Examine the friction linings for wear or loose rivets and check the driven plate for uneven or worn splines, distortion or signs of fatigue cracks. Generally, it is not desirable to fit new friction linings on the original driven plate because refaced driven plates often are distorted or otherwise impaired and produce unsatisfactory clutch action. If renewing old worn linings, the rivets should be drilled out, not punched out.

(9) After refacing, mount the driven plate on a mandrel between centres and check for 'run-out' by means of a dial gauge, set as near to the edge as possible. Where the 'run-out' exceeds 0·15 in. (·38 mm.), true the plate by prising it in the requisite direction after finding the high spots.

(10) Examine the machined face of the pressure plate. if this is badly grooved and rough, the surface may be reground until the grooves disappear.

CLUTCH

(11) Examine the machined surface of the release lever plate. If this is badly grooved, renew the plate. A new plate will also be necessary if the surfaces on the reverse side of the plate, which are in contact with the tips of the release levers, are worn down.

(12) Examine the tips of the release levers which bear on the back of the release lever plate. A small amount of worn flat surface is permissible, but if this is excessive the lever should be renewed. Check for excessive wear in the groove in which the fulcrum bears. If the metal here has worn at all thin, the lever must be renewed as there is a danger of it breaking under load with disastrous results to the whole clutch mechanism.

(13) Examine the release bearing for cracks or bad pitting, also measure the amount of bearing standing proud of the metal cup. If the bearing is cracked or badly pitted, or there is $\frac{1}{16}$ in. (1·6 mm.) or less of bearing standing proud of the cup, the cup and bearing must be renewed.

(14) Examine the pressure springs for weakness or distortion and renew if necessary. Renew in sets only.

(15) Examine the clutch withdrawal shaft for slackness in the bushes. Renew the bushes if necessary.

To Reassemble

Before reassembly note the positions of the marked parts and make sure to replace them in their original locations to preserve balance, unless the parts have been renewed. Using Tool No. 18G 99A, proceed as follows:

(1) Position the pressure plate on the three spacing washers on the base plate as described under 'To dismantle'.

(2) Mount the release levers on the fulcra with their inner ends under the anti-rattle springs, taking care that the levers are correctly seated. Lubricate their bearing surfaces very sparingly with grease.

(3) Place the pressure springs on the bosses on the pressure plate.

(4) Lower the cover over the assembled parts, ensuring that the anti-rattle springs are in position and that the tops of the pressure springs are directly under their seats in the cover. In addition the machined portions of the pressure plate lugs must be directly under the slots in the cover through which they will pass.

(5) Insert the tool setscrews through the cover holes and screw them into the base plate in a diagonal pattern, a little at a time, to prevent distortion. Guide the shoulder studs and pressure plate lugs through the holes in the clutch cover during this gradual tightening down.

(6) Place the bearing plates over the shoulder studs, followed by the tab washers and then screw down the adjusting nuts on the latter.

The clutch must now be adjusted still using the clutch assembly tool. With the clutch bolted to the tool base plate as on completion of assembly, proceed as follows:

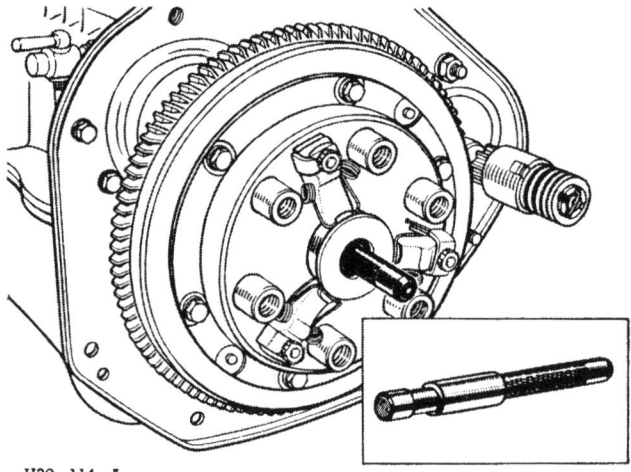

H30. 114. A.

Fig. E.4. Using Service Tool 18G 139 *to centralise the driven plate. Inset shows* 18G 139

(7) Screw the actuator into the base plate and pump the handle a dozen times to settle the clutch mechanism. Remove the actuator.

(8) Screw the tool centre pillar into the base plate and select a distance-piece, as shown on the chart. Place the distance-piece over the centre pillar with its recessed face downwards.

(9) Place the gauge height finger over the centre pillar.

(10) Adjust the height of the release levers by tightening or loosening the adjusting nuts until the height finger, when rotated, just contacts the highest point on the tips of the release levers. Press downwards on the height finger to ensure that it bears squarely on the adaptor while rotating.

(11) Remove the height finger and pillar, and screw in the actuator to the base plate. Operate the clutch several times to enable the components to settle on their knife edges. Remove the actuator and

CLUTCH

replace the centre pillar, distance-piece and height finger. Readjust the release levers if necessary. Repeat the procedure to ensure that the release levers are finally seated, and gauge once more.

(12) Remove the centre pillar, distance-piece and height finger and secure the adjusting nuts with their tab washers.

(13) Fit the release lever plate on the tips of the release levers and secure it by the three retaining springs.

(14) Release the tool setscrews in diagonal sequence a little at a time, relieving pressure slowly and evenly. Remove the clutch assembly from the base plate.

To Replace

Before installing the clutch assembly the engine flywheel should be checked for misalignment (see Section A). To install the clutch proceed as follows:

(1) Hold the clutch cover assembly and driven plate on the flywheel and screw in the cover securing bolts finger-tight. Note that the splines in the hub of the driven plate are chamfered at one end to permit ready entry of the first motion shaft splines. The longer side of the driven plate hub, with the chamfered splines, should be toward the rear.

(2) Insert a pilot shaft or an aligning arbor No. 18G 139, through the clutch cover and driven plate hub so that the pilot enters the spigot bearing in the rear end of the engine crankshaft. This will centralise the driven plate.

(3) Tighten the clutch cover securing bolts a turn at a time in diagonal sequence to avoid distorting the cover.

(4) Remove the pilot shaft or aligning arbor.

(5) Install the gearbox (see Section F.).

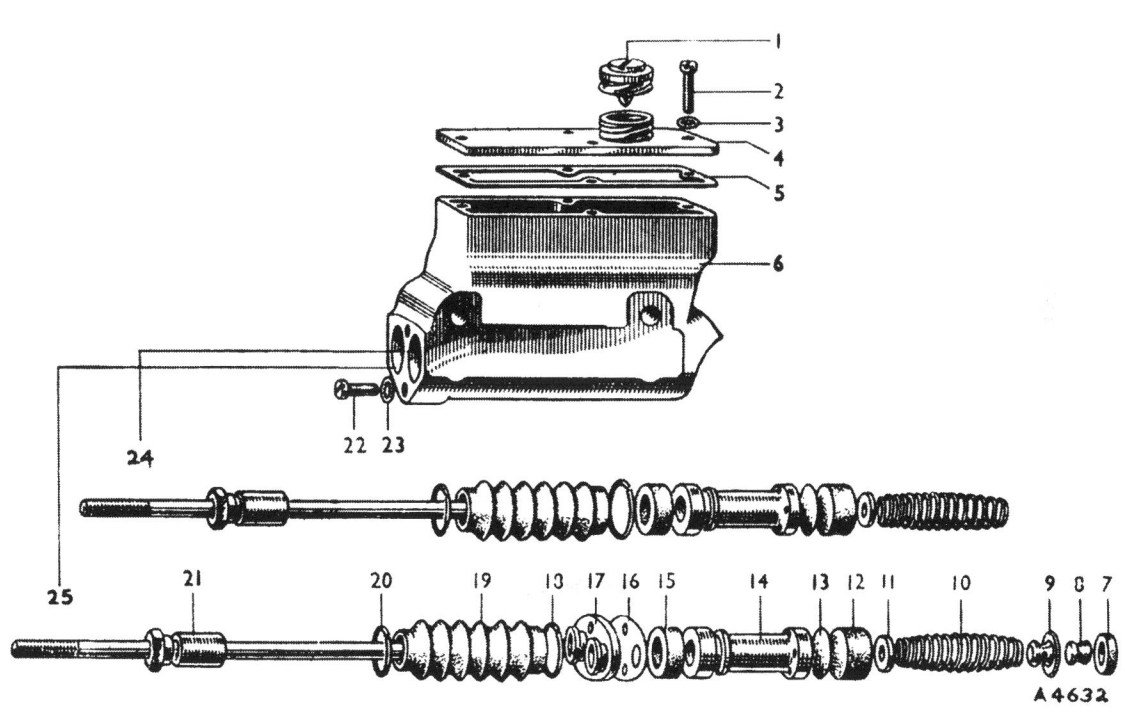

Fig. E.5. Clutch master cylinder exploded.

1. Filler cap.
2. Fixing screw.
3. Shakeproof washer.
4. Tank cover.
5. Tank cover gasket.
6. Cylinder barrel and tank.
7. Valve washer.
8. Valve cup.
9. Valve body.
10. Return spring.
11. Spring retainer.
12. Main cup.
13. Piston washer.
14. Piston.
15. Secondary cup.
16. Gasket.
17. Boot fixing plate.
18. Boot clip.
19. Boot.
20. Boot clip.
21. Push rod.
22. Fixing screw.
23. Shakeproof washer.
24. Clutch bore.
25. Brake bore.

Austin-Healey Sprite Mk. 1. Issue 3. 31628.

E

CLUTCH

Section E.4

CLUTCH PEDAL

To Remove

The removal of the clutch and brake pedal assembly is detailed below.

(1) Working under the bonnet disconnect the clutch and brake pedal levers from the master cylinder pushrods by removing the spring clips and withdrawing the clevis pins.

(2) Within the car remove the nut and spring washer and withdraw the fulcrum pin, noting that a distance piece separates the two pedals.

(3) Remove the pedals downwards.

It is possible, to remove the pedals combined with the clutch and brake master cylinder unit, and this operation is described in both clutch and brake master cylinder sections of this manual.

Section E.5

MASTER CYLINDER

Description

The master cylinder caters for operation of both brake and clutch. It has two bores which are side by side and, except for the fact that one has no check valve, each bore accommodates normal master cylinder parts. The bore with the check valve serves the brakes, the other serves the clutch slave cylinder.

Removal

The following removal procedure involves the withdrawal of the master cylinder unit complete with clutch and brake pedals, as it is not necessary to disconnect the pedals for normal master cylinder maintenance.

Note: Before disconnecting the master cylinder ascertain, for assembly purposes, which bore is communicated with the clutch slave cylinder.

(1) Remove the heater blower unit by first releasing the wire (green and brown) and the earth wire (white) and then unscrewing the two setpins securing the heater blower bracket to the bulkhead.

(2) Unscrew the ten setpins securing the master cylinder mounting plate to the engine bulkhead.

(3) Disconnect the two hydraulic pipes at their unions with the rear of the master cylinder unit.

(4) Withdraw the master cylinder unit upwards and at the same time manipulate the clutch and brake pedals through the aperture in the bulkhead.

(5) Disconnect each pedal from their master cylinder pushrods by removing the spring clips and withdrawing the clevis pins.

(6) The master cylinder unit is attached to its mounting plate by two bolts, nuts and washers, and when these are unscrewed and withdrawn the master cylinder unit is free to be disconnected.

Dismantling the Clutch Cylinder

(1) Unscrew the set screws securing the boot fixing plate to the master cylinder body.

(2) Detach the fixing plate from the master cylinder leaving the boots and push rods attached to the clutch and brake pedals.

(3) Unscrew the common filler cap and drain the fluid into a clean container.

(4) Withdraw the piston (14) Fig. E.5, piston washer (13), main cup (12), spring retainer (11) and return spring (10).

(5) Using only the fingers to prevent damage, remove the secondary cup (15) by stretching it over the end flange of the piston.

(6) Examine all parts, especially the washers, for wear or distortion, and replace with new parts where necessary.

Assembling the Clutch Cylinder

(1) Fit the secondary cup (15) on the piston (14), so that the lip of the cup faces the piston head and gently work the cup round the groove with the fingers to ensure that it is properly seated.

(2) Assemble the retainer (11) on the smaller end of the return spring and insert the assembly into the cylinder.

(3) Install the main cup (12) into the cylinder, lip foremost, taking care not to damage or turn back the lip of the cup.

(4) Follow up with the piston washer, pay particular attention to the illustration showing method of assembly.

(5) Press the piston (14) into the cylinder taking care not to damage or turn back the lip of the secondary cup (15).

(6) Insert the push rod in the piston and manoeuvre the boot fixing plate into position. Secure the plate by its two set screws and then ascertain that the rubber boots are seating correctly. The vent holes in each boot should be at the bottom where the cylinder is mounted on the vehicle.

If the boots are damaged or perished, new ones should be fitted.

CLUTCH

(7) Fill the reservoir with clean Lockheed brake fluid and test the clutch cylinder by pushing the piston inwards and allowing it to return unassisted. After a few applications, fluid should flow from the outlet connection in the cylinder barrel.

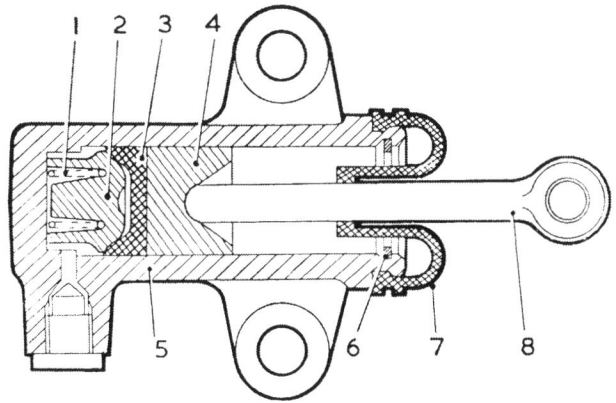

Fig. E.6. Slave cylinder.

1. Spring.
2. Cup filler.
3. Cup.
4. Piston.
5. Body.
6. Circlip.
7. Boot.
8. Push rod.

Replacement

The installation of the master cylinder unit is the reversal of the removal procedure.

If no further maintenance of the clutch is necessary remember to bleed the system.

Section E.6

SLAVE CYLINDER

Description

The cylinder is bolted to the underside of the clutch housing and comprises a piston, rubber cup, cup filler, return spring, push rod and bleeder screw.

To Remove

(1) Place a receptacle to catch the fluid and unscrew the pipe union on the slave cylinder.
(2) Remove the split pin and clevis pin from the clutch withdrawal lever jaw end, thus freeing the slave cylinder push rod.
(3) Remove the two bolts and spring washers securing the cylinder to the clutch housing.

Fig. E.7. Gearbox drain plug (1). Slave cylinder bolts (2).

To Dismantle

(1) Clean all dirt from the outside of the cylinder.
(2) Remove the rubber dust cap from the bleed nipple, attach a bleed tube, open the bleed screw three-quarters of a turn and pump the clutch pedal until all the fluid has been drained into a clean container.
(3) Unscrew the pressure pipe union at the cylinder and remove the bolts from the flange. The slave cylinder can now be removed.
(4) Remove the rubber cover, push rod and circlip, and if an air line is available, blow out the piston and seal. The spring can also be removed.
(5) Clean the slave cylinder components, **using only hydraulic fluid or alcohol.** The main casting may be cleaned with any of the normal cleaning fluids, but all traces of the cleaning fluid must be dried out.
(6) Dry off and examine all rubber components and renew them if they are swollen, distorted or split. If there is any doubt at all as to their condition they must be renewed.
(7) Inspect the piston and cylinder bore for wear and scoring, and renew them as necessary.

Assembling the Slave Cylinder

(1) Place the seal into the stem of the piston, with the back of the seal against the piston.
(2) Replace the springs with the small end on the

CLUTCH

stem, smear well with the recommended fluid and insert into the cylinder. Refit the circlip.

(3) Replace the rubber dust cover and mount the cylinder in position, making sure the push rod enters the hole in the rubber boot.

To Replace

(1) Secure the cylinder to the clutch housing, and screw in the pipe union.
(2) Bleed the clutch hydraulic system as described in Section E.7.

Section E.7

BLEEDING THE CLUTCH SYSTEM

(1) Fill the master cylinder reservoir with brake fluid and keep at least a quarter full throughout the operation, otherwise air will be drawn in, necessitating a fresh start.
(2) Attach a rubber tube to the bleeder screw on the slave cylinder, allowing the free end to be submerged in a little brake fluid in a clean glass jar.

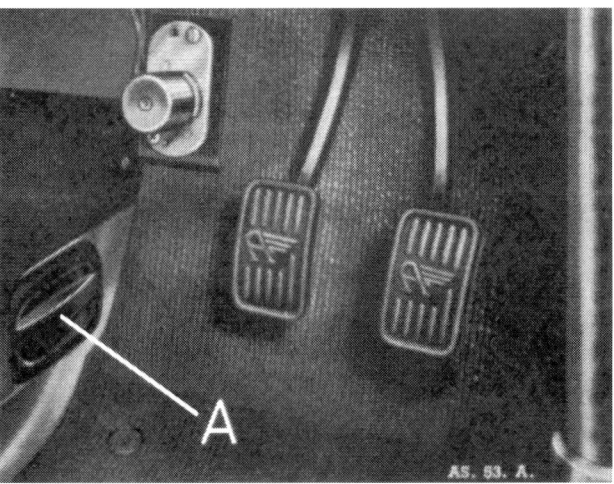

Fig. E.8. Depicting the position of the plug which must be removed in order to gain access to the slave cylinder bleed nipple.

(3) Slacken the bleeder screw and depress the clutch pedal slowly; tighten the screw before the pedal reaches the end of its stroke and allow the pedal to return unassisted.
(4) Repeat (3) until air bubbles cease to appear from the end of the tube in the jar.

CLUTCH

Section E.8   FAULT DIAGNOSIS

Symptom	No.	Possible Fault
(a) Drag or Spin	1	Oil or grease on driven plate linings
	2	Bent engine backplate
	3	Misalignment between engine and first motion shaft
	4	Leaking operating cylinder or pipe line.
	5	Driven plate hub binding on first motion shaft splines
	6	First motion shaft binding on its spigot bush
	7	Distorted clutch plate
	8	Warped or damaged pressure plate or clutch cover
	9	Broken clutch plate linings
	10	Dirt or foreign matter in clutch
	11	Air in clutch hydraulic system
	12	Bad external leak between the clutch master cylinder and slave cylinder
(b) Fierceness or Snatch		Check 1, 2 and 3 in (a)
	1	Check 4 in (a)
	2	Worn clutch linings
(c) Slip		Check 1, 2 and 3 in (a)
		Check 1 in (b)
	1	Weak thrust springs
	2	Weak anti-rattle springs
	3	Seized piston in clutch slave cylinder
(d) Judder		Check 1, 2 and 3 in (a)
	1	Pressure plate out of parallel with flywheel face
	2	Friction facing contact area not evenly distributed
	3	Bent first motion shaft
	4	Buckled driven plate
	5	Faulty engine or gearbox rubber mountings
	6	Worn shackles
	7	Weak rear springs
	8	Propeller shaft bolts loose
	9	Loose rear spring clips
(e) Rattle		Check 3 in (d)
	1	Damaged driven plate, *i.e.* broken springs, etc.
	2	Worn parts of release mechanism
	3	Excessive transmission backlash
	4	Wear in transmission bearings
	5	Release bearing loose on fork
(f) Tick or Knock	1	Worn first motion shaft bush
	2	Badly worn centre plate hub splines
	3	Out of line thrust plate
	4	Faulty bendix drive on starter
	5	Loose flywheel
(g) Driven Plate Fracture		Check 2 and 3 in (a)
	1	Drag and metal fatigue due to hanging gearbox in driven plate

Austin-Healey Sprite. Issue 3. 31628.

E

CLUTCH

SERVICE TOOLS

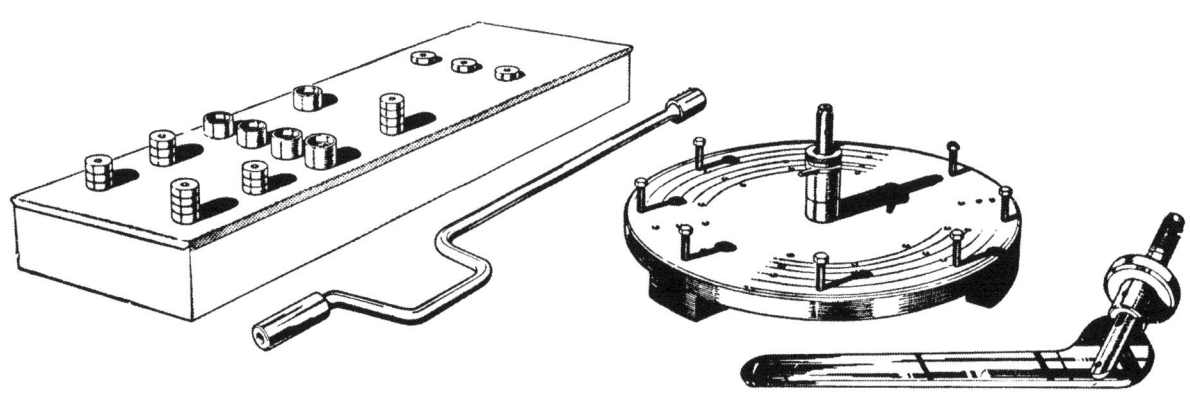

18G99A

Tool No. 18G99A. Clutch Assembly Gauging Fixture

With the use of this tool a clutch assembly can be quickly dismantled, rebuilt, and finally adjusted with a high degree of accuracy. This is a universal tool for clutch assembly from $6\frac{1}{4}$ in. to 11 in. diameter.

18G139. Clutch Centralizer

The driven plate in the Healey Sprite clutch may readily be centralized with the aid of this tool.

18G139

SECTION F

GEARBOX

Section No. F.1	Description
Section No. F.2	Lubrication
Section No. F.3	Removal and replacement
Section No. F.4	Dismantling
Section No. F.5	Dismantling the mainshaft
Section No. F.6	Dismantling the laygear
Section No. F.7	Dismantling first motion shaft
Section No. F.8	Examination for wear
Section No. F.9	Reassembly
Section No. F.10	Fault diagnosis.
End of Section	Service tools

GEARBOX   F

Fig. F.1. Removing the gearbox from the vehicle

Section F.1

DESCRIPTION

The gearbox has four forward speeds and one reverse, and synchromesh is incorporated on second, third and top gears.

Top gear is a direct drive; third and second are in constant mesh; first and reverse are obtained by sliding spur pinions.

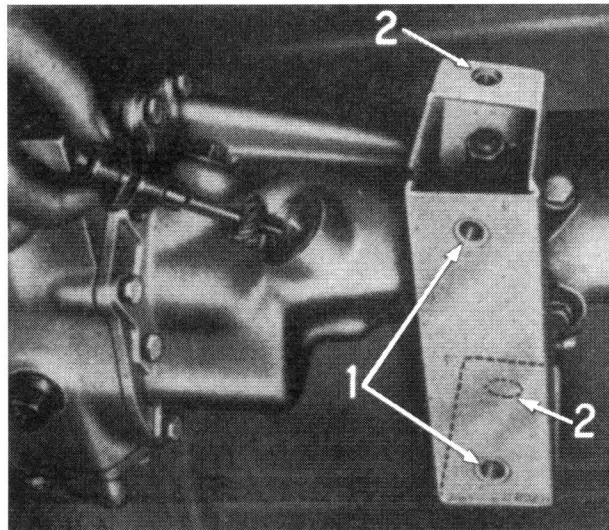

Fig. F.2. The gearbox rear support and position of the speedometer drive gear

1. Location of the $\frac{3}{8}$ in. AF rear mounting setpins
2. Location of the $\frac{5}{16}$ in. AF rear mounting setpins

Section F.2

LUBRICATION

Every 3,000 miles (5000 km.)

Check the oil level and top up if necessary. To gain access remove the rubber plug on the left side of the gearbox covering. The filler plug is then accessible. Remove the plug and fill up to the bottom of the threads. This gives the correct level.

Every 6,000 miles (10000 km.)

Drain after a run when the oil is warm, and refill with new oil. Capacity $2\frac{1}{3}$ imp. pints (1·33 litres, 2·8 U.S. pints).

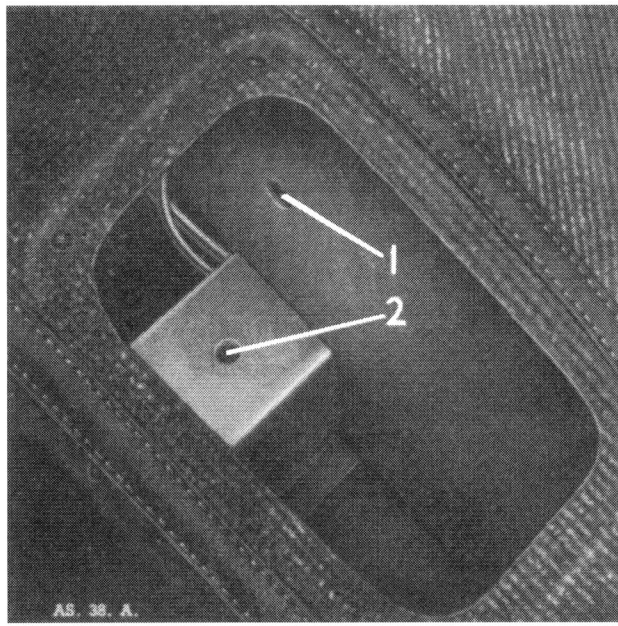

Fig. F.3. View through the gearbox change-speed-lever aperture showing the location of the rear mounting setpins

Section F.3

REMOVAL AND REPLACEMENT

The engine and gearbox may be removed from the vehicle as a complete unit as descibed in Section A.4. Whereupon the gearbox and engine are separated. The alternative method of gearbox removal is first to remove the engine as detailed in Section A.4 and then withdraw the gearbox in the following manner:

(1) Remove the four self tapping screws from the change-speed-lever cover, and withdraw the cover off the lever.

(2) Remove the anti-rattle plunger, spring and cap from the side of the change-speed-lever turret.

(3) Unscrew the three change-speed-lever cover setpins and remove the lever.

Austin-Healey Sprite Mk. 1. Issue 2. 50312

F.1

GEARBOX

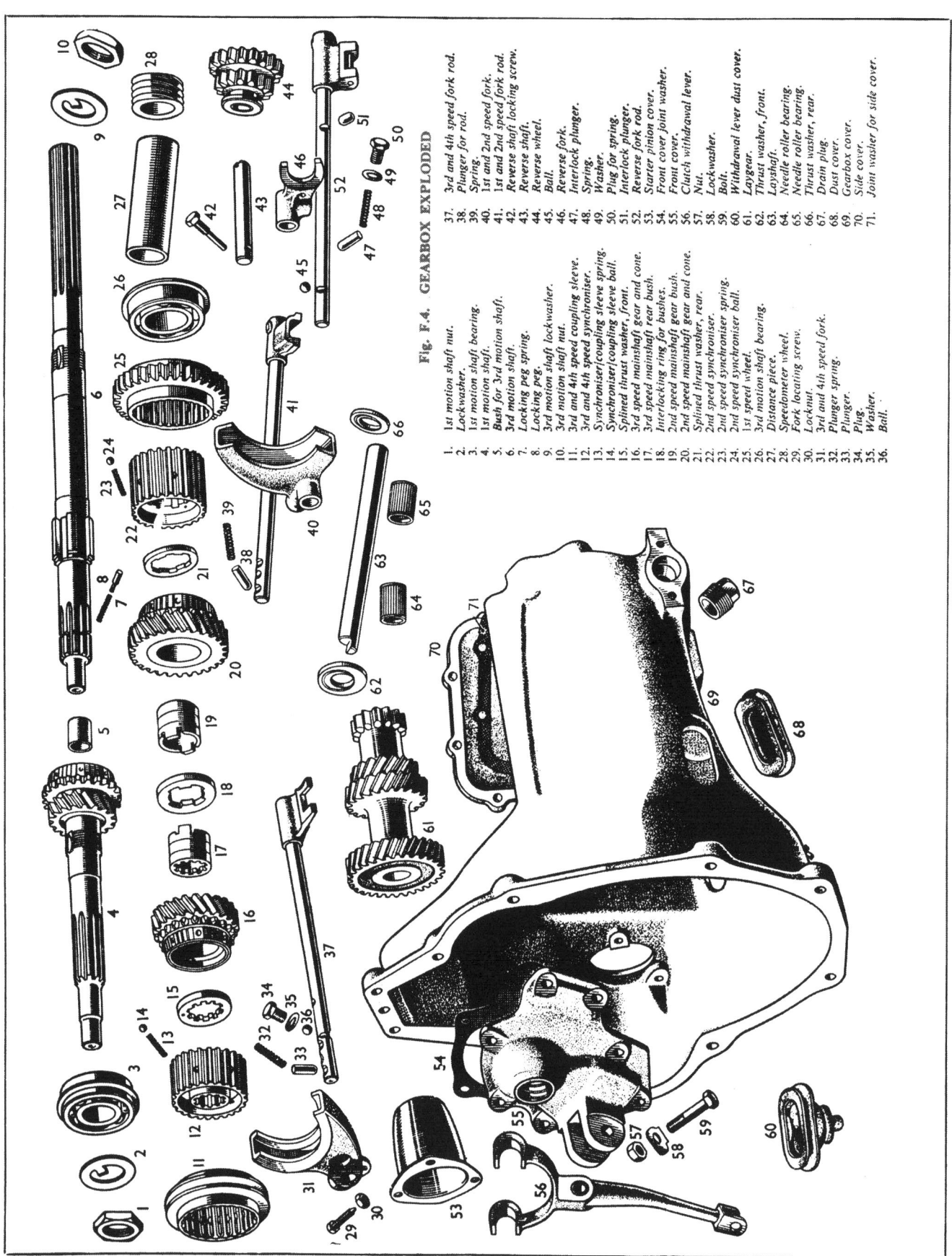

Fig. F.4. GEARBOX EXPLODED

1. 1st motion shaft nut.
2. Lockwasher.
3. 1st motion shaft bearing.
4. 1st motion shaft.
5. Bush for 3rd motion shaft.
6. 3rd motion shaft.
7. Locking peg spring.
8. Locking peg.
9. 3rd motion shaft lockwasher.
10. 3rd motion shaft nut.
11. 3rd and 4th speed coupling sleeve.
12. 3rd and 4th speed synchroniser.
13. Synchroniser/coupling sleeve spring.
14. Synchroniser/coupling sleeve ball.
15. Splined thrust washer, front.
16. 3rd speed mainshaft gear and cone.
17. 3rd speed mainshaft rear bush.
18. Interlocking ring for bushes.
19. 2nd speed mainshaft gear bush.
20. 2nd speed mainshaft gear and cone.
21. Splined thrust washer, rear.
22. 2nd speed synchroniser.
23. 2nd speed synchroniser spring.
24. 2nd speed synchroniser ball.
25. 1st speed wheel.
26. 3rd motion shaft bearing.
27. Distance piece.
28. Speedometer wheel.
29. Fork locating screw.
30. Locknut.
31. 3rd and 4th speed fork.
32. Plunger spring.
33. Plug.
34. Washer.
35. Ball.
36. Ball.
37. 3rd and 4th speed fork rod.
38. Plunger for rod.
39. Spring.
40. 1st and 2nd speed fork.
41. 1st and 2nd speed fork rod.
42. Reverse shaft locking screw.
43. Reverse shaft.
44. Reverse wheel.
45. Ball.
46. Reverse fork.
47. Interlock plunger.
48. Spring.
49. Washer.
50. Plug for spring.
51. Interlock plunger.
52. Reverse fork rod.
53. Starter pinion cover.
54. Front cover.
55. Clutch withdrawal lever.
56. Nut.
57. Lockwasher.
58. Bolt.
59. Withdrawal lever dust cover.
60. Laygear.
61. Thrust washer, front.
62. Layshaft.
63. Needle roller bearing.
64. Needle roller bearing.
65. Thrust washer, rear.
66. Drain plug.
67. Dust cover.
68. Gearbox cover.
69. Side cover.
70. Plug.
71. Joint washer for side cover.

GEARBOX

(4) Peel back the carpet surrounding the gearbox cover to expose the gearbox rear mounting setpins. The location of one of the setpins is shown (1) Fig. F.3. Unscrew both setpins.

(5) Unscrew the speedometer drive cable at its union with the gearbox rear extension.

(6) Detach the clutch slave cylinder from the clutch bell-housing by unscrewing its two mounting setpins and withdrawing the push rod from the rear of the cylinder.

(7) Disconnect the propeller shaft from the rear axle by unscrewing the four self locking nuts.

(8) Unscrew the remaining gearbox rear mounting setpins, one of which is located at (2) Fig. F.3.

(9) Lift the gearbox together with the propeller shaft clear of the vehicle as shown in Fig. F.1.

Reassembly is a reversal of the above procedure. The propeller shaft **must** be connected to the rear end of the gearbox before the gearbox is replaced in the vehicle.

Section F.4

DISMANTLING

(1) Unscrew the filler plug. Drain the oil by removing the plug from the bottom of the gearbox.

(2) Unscrew the speedometer pinion sleeve from the left side of the gearbox rear cover, remove the fibre washer and withdraw the pinion. Commencing at Engine No. 21267, a moulded nylon speedometer pinion sleeve has been introduced. It is essential, when removing or replacing this sleeve that a correctly fitting box spanner, or equivalent, be used to avoid damage to the corners of the hexagon.

(3) Remove the eight nuts securing the remote control housing and lift the housing off the rear cover.

(4) Unscrew the nine set screws and spring washers securing the rear cover to the gearbox.

(5) Pull the rear cover back slightly and turn it in an anti-clockwise direction as viewed from the rear, to enable the control lever to clear the fork rod ends, and then remove the rear cover from the gearbox.

(6) Remove the control shaft locating screw, and screw it into the tapped front end of the control shaft. Slight pressure on the screw will facilitate the removal of the control shaft, which is a push fit in the rear cover. The control lever will slip off the end of the shaft as the shaft is removed.

(7) The two halves of the control lever bush can be lifted out after removal of the circlip. From Gearbox No. 14495, a one-piece interchangeable Nylon bush is used and the circlip is deleted.

(8) Unscrew the four set screws securing the bottom cover to the change-speed-lever tower. Retain the paper joint washer if undamaged.

(9) Unscrew and remove the change-speed-lever locating peg and the two anti-rattle springs. The latter are removed by unscrewing the two caps and then tilting the remote control housing so that the springs and plungers drop out.

(10) Unscrew the three set pins securing the change-speed-lever cover to the top of the change-speed-lever tower and remove the lever care being taken to retain the thrust button and spring.

(11) Release the set screws in the front and rear selector levers, remove the welch plugs at either ends of the remote control housing, and using a suitable drift tap out the remote control shaft. The front and rear selector levers can then be removed.

(12) To remove the reverse selector plunger first unscrew the reverse plunger cap and remove the detent spring and ball, then remove the locating pin.

(13) Remove the clutch release bearing by levering out the two retaining springs.

(14) To remove the clutch withdrawal lever bend back the locking washer and remove the nut and washer. The bolt may then be unscrewed. Do not attempt to knock the bolt out, as it is threaded into the support bracket. To unscrew the bolt remove the rubber dust cover from the hole opposite that which the clutch withdrawal lever passes, and pass a suitable tool through the hole. On left-hand drive cars the clutch withdrawal lever passes through the hole on the left hand side of the bell-housing.

(15) Remove the seven nuts and washers from the front cover, situated within the clutch bell-housing. The front cover may then be withdrawn by gripping the clutch withdrawal lever brackets with the finger and thumb and pulling. Remove the paper joints and packing shim.

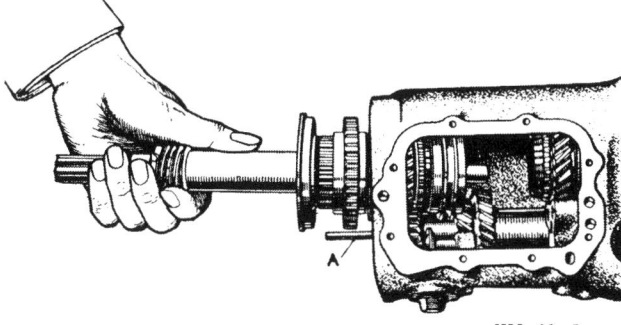

Fig. F.5. Drawing out the third motion shaft assembly after lowering the laygear on to the dummy layshaft 'A.'

GEARBOX

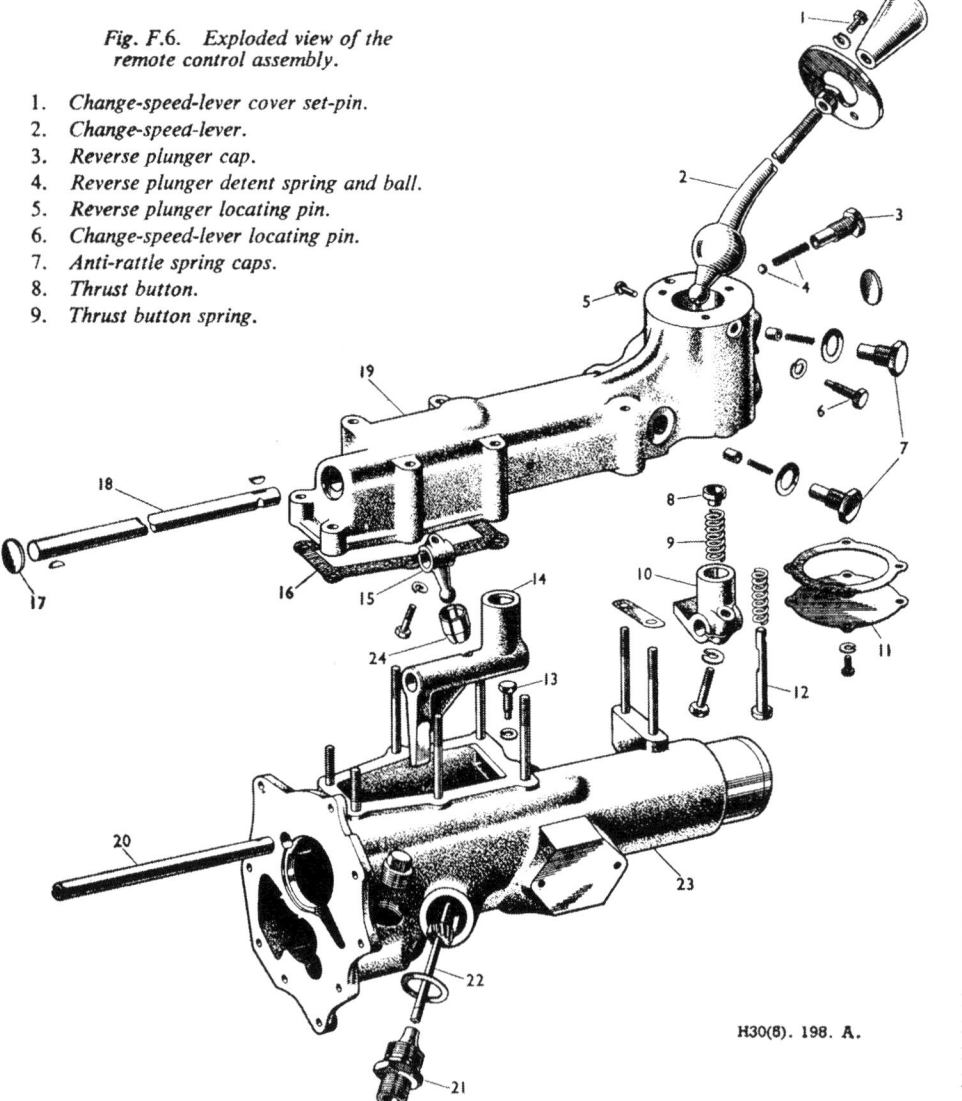

Fig. F.6. Exploded view of the remote control assembly.

1. Change-speed-lever cover set-pin.
2. Change-speed-lever.
3. Reverse plunger cap.
4. Reverse plunger detent spring and ball.
5. Reverse plunger locating pin.
6. Change-speed-lever locating pin.
7. Anti-rattle spring caps.
8. Thrust button.
9. Thrust button spring.
10. Selector lever rear.
11. Bottom cover.
12. Reverse selector plunger.
13. Control shaft locating screw.
14. Control lever.
15. Selector lever front.
16. Joint washer.
17. Welch plug.
18. Remote control shaft.
19. Remote control housing.
20. Control shaft.
21. Speedometer pinion sleeve.
22. Speedometer pinion.
23. Gearbox rear cover.
24. Tapered bush.

(16) Release the eight screws set in the side cover. Remove the side cover and joint washer. Remove the two springs from the front edge of the side cover joining face. Turn the gearbox on its side so that the two plungers fall out of the holes from which the springs were removed.

(17) Remove the two plugs situated near the clutch bell-housing on the side cover side of the gearbox casing. They each have a fibre washer and the lower of the two plugs covers the reverse plunger and spring, which may be removed by tilting the gearbox on its side. The other plug which has a long shank blocks the hole through which the interlock ball between the 1st and 2nd, and 3rd and 4th selector rods is inserted.

(18) Select neutral by aligning the slots in the rear ends of the selector rods. Working on the gearbox, with the side cover facing upwards, unlock and remove the reverse fork locating screw, lock nut and shakeproof washer through the drain plug hole. Similarly remove the locating screw lock nut and shakeproof washer from the 1st and 2nd, and 3rd and 4th speed forks.

(19) Tap the 3rd and 4th speed selector rod from the front end, and draw it out through the back of the gearbox. Similarly remove the 1st and 2nd speed selector rod (nearest side cover) and then the reverse selector rod.

As the selector rods are being drawn out care must be taken to remove the two interlock balls from the front end of gearbox casing. Also the double ended interlock plunger should be removed from the back end of the gearbox casing. The three selector forks may now be lifted out of the gearbox.

GEARBOX

(20) Tap the layshaft out of the front of the gearbox with a bronze drift. On removing the drift the laygear cluster and thrust washers will drop into the bottom of the gearbox.

(21) Draw the main shaft assembly rearwards out of the gearbox case.

(22) Insert a long soft metal drift through the main shaft opening in the rear of the casing and drive the first motion shaft forwards out of the gearbox. The laygear cluster and thrust washers may now be removed.

(23) Remove the reverse shaft locking screw. Place a screwdriver on the slotted end of the reverse shaft and push it into the gearbox with a turning motion. The reverse shaft and gear may now be removed.

Section F.5

DISMANTLING THE MAINSHAFT

(1) Slide off the third and fourth speed synchroniser assembly.

(2) Depress the small spring loaded plunger which locks the splined ring at the front end of the main shaft, and turn the ring so that one of its splines covers the plunger (a peg spanner is useful for turning the splined ring).

(3) Slide the splined ring and 3rd speed gear off the end of the shaft, remove the plunger and spring; slide the 3rd speed bush interlock ring and 2nd speed gear off the end of the shaft. If the 2nd speed gear bush is worn chisel it off and sweat a new bush on.

(4) Draw the splined ring, 1st speed ring and synchroniser off the end of the shaft.

(5) At the other end of the shaft knock back the locking washer and unscrew the securing nut. The speedometer wheel and distance piece may now be removed.

(6) Draw the ball journal bearing off the end of the shaft with its housing, and then drift the bearing out of its housing.

Section F.6

DISMANTLING THE LAYGEAR

Twenty-three needle roller bearings are fitted in each end of the laygear. The needles are held in position by their races (one at each end) and spring rings.

(1) Remove the spring rings from their locating grooves (one at each end of the laygear) and take out the outer race, needle rollers and the inner race.

(2) Remove the inner spring ring from its groove in the large end of the laygear.

(3) Remove the distance piece and spring ring from the small end of the laygear.

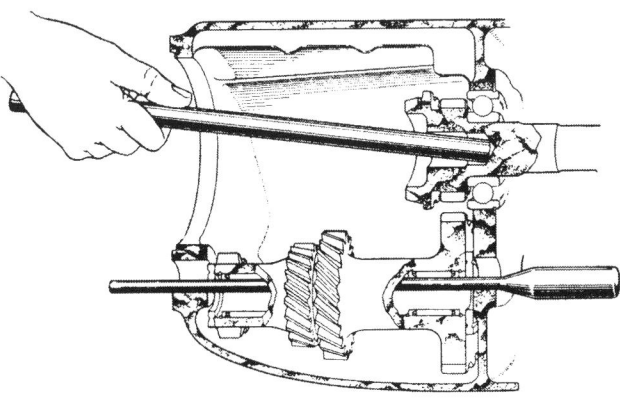

Fig. F.7. Drifting the first motion shaft out of the gearbox casing

Section F.7

DISMANTLING FIRST MOTION SHAFT

(1) Place the 1st motion shaft in a dummy 3rd and 4th speed coupling sleeve, knock back the lock washer and remove the nut.

(2) Remove the bearing with a suitable bearing extractor.

Section F.8

EXAMINATION FOR WEAR

Bearings

The first and third motion shaft bearings become worn after a considerable length of service and should be renewed if there are signs of looseness between the inner and outer races.

Third Motion Shaft Spigot Bush

The bush is fitted to give a clearance of ·002 to ·003 in. (·0508 to ·0762 mm.) with the 3rd motion shaft. Any appreciable wear above this figure, necessitates examination of the bush and shaft and renewal where necessary.

Main Gear Bushes

The 2nd and 3rd speed main shaft gear bushes have an extremely low tolerance of ·00025 to ·0015 in. (·0064 to ·0381 mm.) with the shaft. They should be replaced if

GEARBOX

any appreciable wear occurs between these bushes and the 3rd motion shaft.

Laygear Thrust Washers

These washers are designed to permit a laygear end float of ·001 to ·003-in. (·0254 to ·0762 mm.). If the end float exceeds this amount, the thrust washers must be renewed. The smaller thrust washer, at the rear, is made in varying thicknesses to allow correct end float to be obtained.

Gear Synchronising Cones

These cones are 'shrunk on' to the second, third and fourth speed gears and are normally supplied as a complete unit for spares purposes. Where facilities exist for shrinking on and finally machining the cones, they can be supplied separately. If the gear is to operate satisfactorily, however, care must be taken in fitting them.

The internal machining of the cone is calculated to allow for a shrinkage fit on to the gear, and the cone must be heat expanded before it can be fitted.

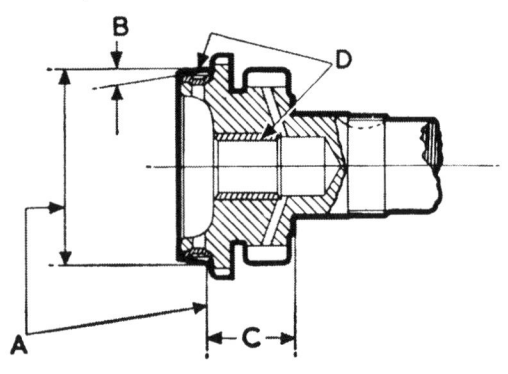

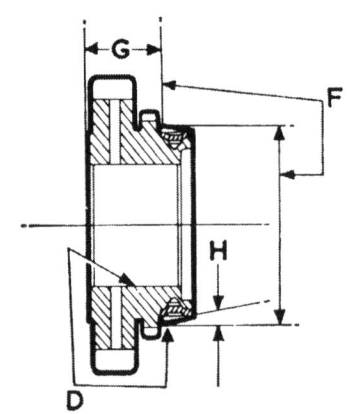

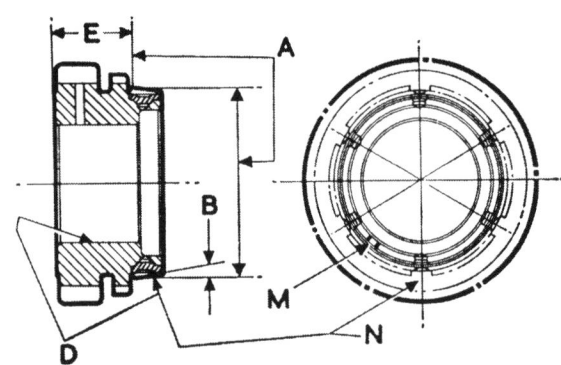

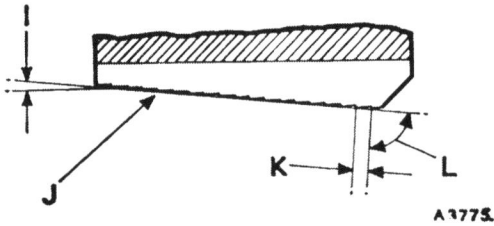

Top left: 1st motion shaft. Bottom left: 3rd speed gear.

Fig. F.8
KEY

Top right: 2nd speed gear. Bottom right: Cone.

A. Taper 1·997 in. (50·72 mm.) dia. at this line to gauge.

B. Taper 10° 10′ to be true and concentric with bore to ·001 in. (·025 mm.).

C. ·909 to ·912 in. (23·09 to 23·16 mm.).

D. Taper to be true and concentric with bore to ·001 in. (·025 mm.).

E. ·862 to ·865 in. (21·8 to 21·9 mm.).

F. Taper 1·966 in. (49·9 mm.) dia. at this line to gauge.

G. ·810 to ·813 in. (20·57 to 20·65 mm.).

H. 8° 20′.

I. 6°.

J. Coarse turning may be either right- or left-hand.

K. ·015 in. (·38 mm.).

L. 90°.

M. One notch to be ground in position shown relative to grooves with indentations.

N. Synchronizing cone to be heated in oil, shrunk on to gear and punched into holes as shown with centre lines of holes and spaces in cone in line.

GEARBOX

When heated in oil to approximately 250° F. (121·1°C.) expansion will allow the cone to be pressed home on to the gear without damage. **Note: The six large recesses on the perimeter of the cone must line up with the holes in the boss of the gear.**

After shrinking on, the unit should be immediately quenched in water to prevent the gear itself being softened. Punch mark the cone in each of the six recesses. This ensures resistance to displacement when changing gear.

When the cone is in position the final machining can be done in accordance with the dimensions given in Fig. F.8. The taper of the cone must be true and concentric with the bore to ·001 in. (·0254 mm.).

Section F.9

REASSEMBLY

Mainshaft

(1) The third motion shaft ball journal bearing outer race is grooved to take a spring ring. This spring ring registers in a recess in the bearing housing.
Press the bearing into the end of the housing with the larger diameter, so that the spring ring end of the bearing is trailing.

(2) Press the bearing and its housing on, from the rear end of the shaft (the end with the long splines) in such a way that the larger diameter of the bearing housing (when fitted) is towards the rear of the shaft. Now fit the distance piece, speedometer drive, lock washer and lock the nut in position.

(3) Fit 1st speed gear and 2nd speed synchroniser assembly onto the shaft with the protruding end of the synchroniser towards the bearing. Place the large internally splined steel thrust washer behind the second speed synchroniser.

(4) Follow the steel thrust washer with the bush for the second speed main shaft gear (largest of the remaining gears), so that its legs are away from the steel thrust washer. Slide the second speed mainshaft gear over the bush with its cone towards the first speed gear and second speed synchroniser assembly. Locate the phosphor-bronze interlocking ring on the legs of the second speed mainshaft gear bush and mate the legs of the third speed mainshaft gear bush in the splines of the interlocking ring.

(5) Place the spring and plunger in their hole; depress the plunger and draw the third speed

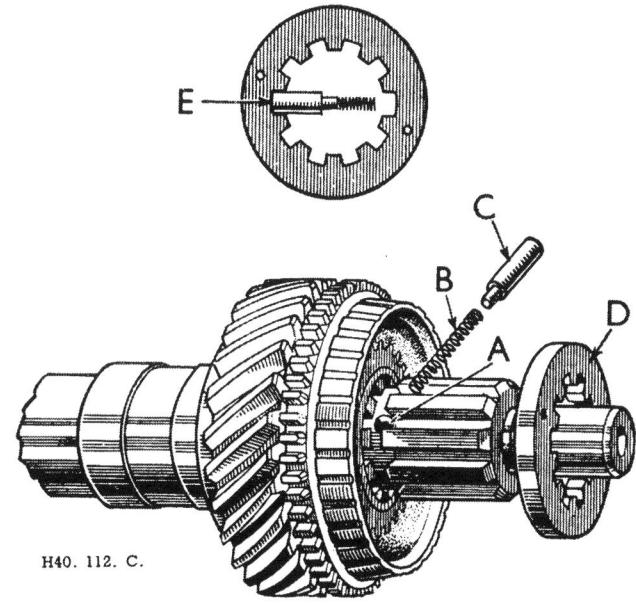

Fig. F.10. Securing the third motion shaft gears.

A. Hole in shaft for locking plunger. B. Spring. C. Locking plunger. D. Locking washer. E. Locking washer with plunger engaged.

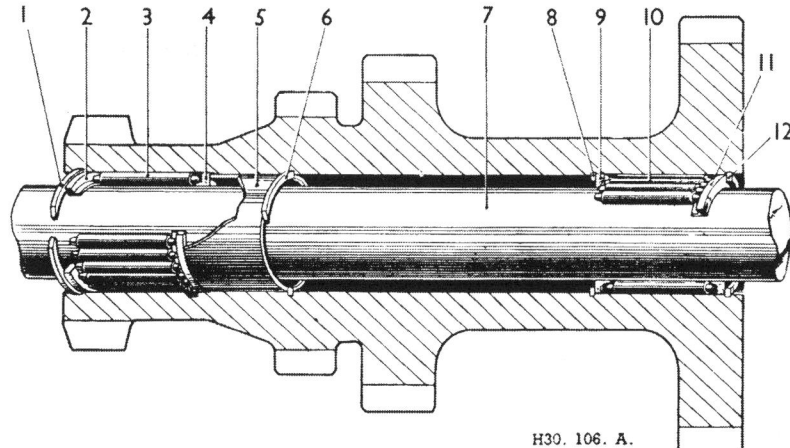

Fig. F.9. Laygear sectioned to show needle roller bearing assembly.

1. Spring ring (outer). ⎫
2. Outer race.
3. Needle rollers. ⎬ Small end.
4. Inner race.
5. Distance piece.
6. Spring ring (inner). ⎭
7. Layshaft.
8. Spring ring (inner). ⎫
9. Inner race.
10. Needle rollers. ⎬ Large end.
11. Outer race.
12. Spring ring (outer). ⎭

Austin-Healey Sprite Mk. 1. Issue 4. 35471.

F

GEARBOX

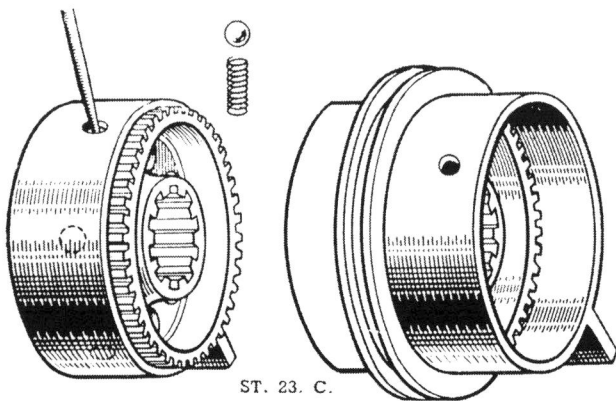

Fig. F.11. Using Service Tool 18G 144 to assemble the spring loaded balls to a coupling sleeve and synchroniser.

mainshaft gear bush slightly forward, to keep the plunger depressed, slide the 3rd speed mainshaft gear onto the bush with its cone away from the interlocking ring.

(6) Put the remaining steel thrust washer behind the 3rd speed main shaft gear and push it as far as it will go.

(7) Slip a tube over the end of the shaft and lightly tap the thrust washer, turn the washer until the plunger is released and locks it.

(8) Slide the 3rd and 4th speed synchroniser onto the shaft, with the boss on the synchroniser hub away from the thrust washer.

First Motion Shaft

(1) Knock the self lubricating bush into the back of the first motion shaft with a drift.

(2) Drift the ball journal bearing onto the shaft with its spring ring away from the geared end.

(3) Position the geared end of the first motion shaft in a dummy 3rd and 4th speed coupling sleeve, put the washer over the bearing, tighten the nut and lock it in position.

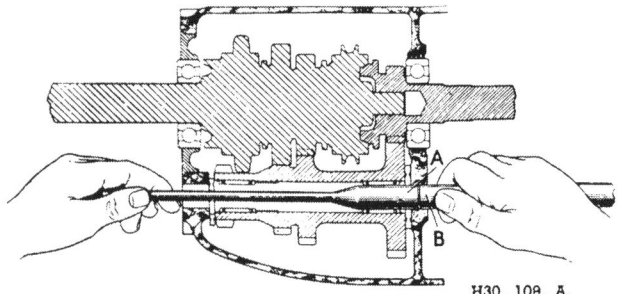

Fig. F.12. A Dummy layshaft Service Tool 18G 471 being used to lift the laygear into position and to insert the layshaft.

Laygear

(1) Locate the spring ring in the inner groove of the small end of the laygear. Drift the distance piece into the small end of the laygear making sure it is right home against the spring ring.

(2) Put the laygear (small end upwards) over a guide shaft if available. Take the needle roller bearing, which is supplied in a cage. Ease the retaining knicks in the one end of the cage. Place the cage over the end of the guide rod, and press the needle rollers out of the cage into position (Service Tool 18G 194).

(3) Take the upper roller race and spring ring out of the cage, place the race over the needle rollers and the spring ring in its groove.

(4) Similarly the needle rollers are assembled into the big end of the laygear.

(5) Insert the thin end of the dummy layshaft (Service Tool 18G 471) from the clutch housing and place the large thrust washer on it, taking care that it does not slip off. Take the laygear,

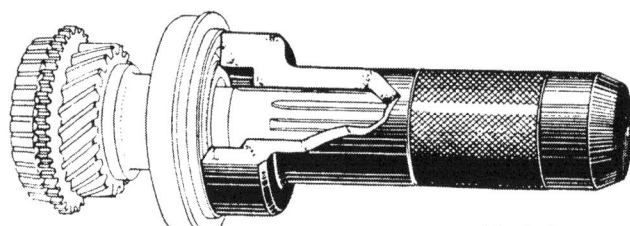

Fig. F.13. Using Service Tool 18G 140 to drift the bearing on to the first motion shaft.

large end first, through the hole in the rear of the gearbox casing and pass the dummy layshaft through it. As the shaft emerges through the small end of the laygear, slip on a suitable small thrust washer to give the laygear an end float of ·001 to ·003 in. (·0254 to ·0762 mm.). Thrust washers for the laygear small end are available in thicknesses of ·123 to ·124 in. (3·124 to 3·150 mm.), ·125 to ·126 in. (3·175 to 3·200 mm.), ·127 to ·128 in. (3·226 to 3·250 mm.) and ·130 to ·131 in. (3·302 to 3·327 mm.), to obtain the required end float. Let the laygear hang on the thin part of the dummy layshaft.

Gearbox

(1) Reassemble the reverse gear on its shaft in the gearbox. Align the hole in the shaft with the hole in the casing and lock the shaft with the locking screw and spring washer.

GEARBOX

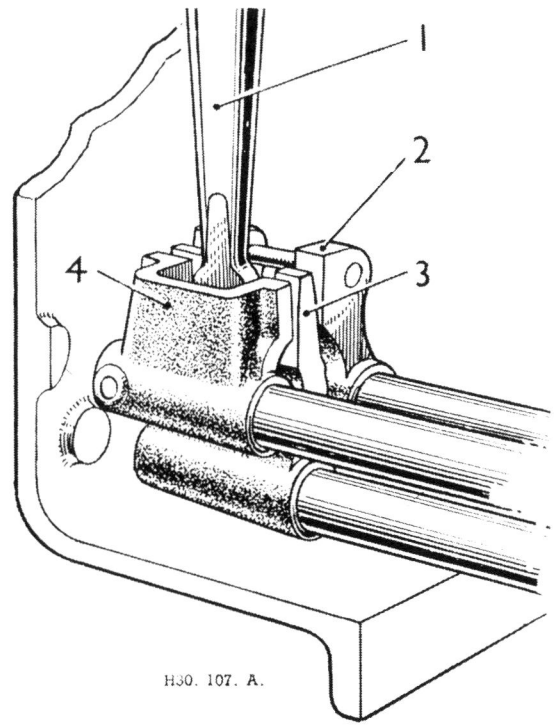

Fig. F.14. Position of selector rods.

1. Change speed lever.
2. Reverse rod.
3. Third and fourth speed rod.
4. First and second speed rod.

that its flange is flush against the recess in the rear of the gearbox casing.

(4) Turn the gearbox casing to ensure that the laygear teeth are clear of the first motion shaft bearing housing. Now drift the first motion shaft into position from the front end (Service Tool 18G140) ensuring that the spring ring registers properly in the recess in the gearbox casing.

(5) By drawing the dummy layshaft rearwards slightly lift the laygears into mesh. Smear the layshaft with oil and follow the dummy.
When the layshaft is being pushed into position maintain contact between it and the dummy layshaft or one of the thrust washers will slip out of position. With the side cover end uppermost, the half-mooned end in the front of the layshaft should be in the U-position with its diameter horizontal.

(6) Place the reverse fork in position with its tapped hole towards the drain plug hole.
Fit the 1st and 2nd speed fork over the first speed wheel, and the 3rd and 4th speed fork over the 3rd and 4th speed coupling sleeve.

(7) With the side cover facing upwards push the reverse fork rod through the lowest hole in the rear of the gearbox casing, through the reverse fork, and through the clearance hole in the 3rd and 4th speed fork. Align the hole in the rod with the tapped hole in the fork, screw in the locking screw and lock it up with the shakeproof washer and nut.

(2) Put the laygear in position in the gearbox complete with its thrust washers, supporting it with the thin part of the dummy layshaft, the thick part being at the front end of the gearbox.

(3) Insert the third motion shaft into the back end of the gearbox and drift the bearing housing so

(8) Drop the double ended plunger through the hole

Fig. F.15. Location of balls and plungers.

1. Hole for interlock plunger between reverse and 1st and 2nd speed fork rods.
2. Hole for ball between reverse and 3rd and 4th speed fork rods.
3. Hole for 1st and 2nd speed fork rod plunger.
4. Hole for 3rd and 4th speed fork rod plunger.
5. Plug for 1st and 2nd, and 3rd and 4th speed ball hole.
6. Plug for reverse plunger hole.

A, B and C are scrap views of sections AA, BB and CC respectively, looking in the direction of the arrows.

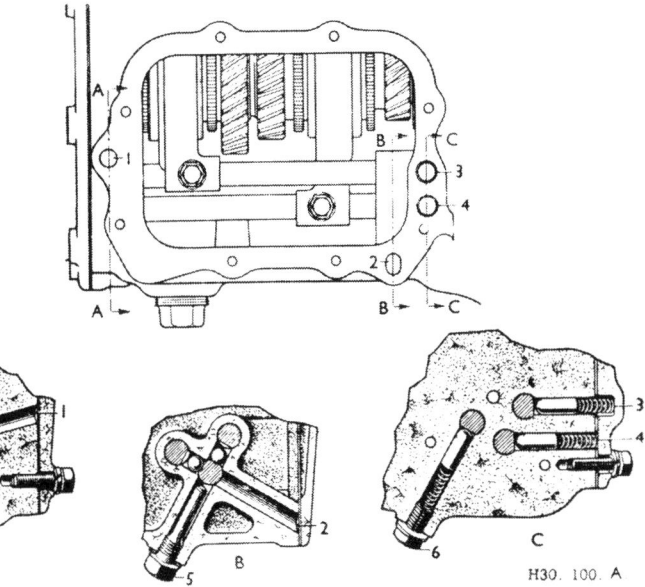

GEARBOX

in the middle of the side cover rear face on the gearbox casing.

(9) Push the first and second speed fork rod through the uppermost selector rod hole in the rear of the gearbox casing, through its fork and into the front of the casing. As before, but through the side cover end of the casing, insert the locating screw and lock it in position.

(10) The third and fourth speed fork rod goes through the hole in the rear of the casing between the other two rods, through the fork and into the front of the gearbox casing.

Push it through till it just enters the hole in the front of the gearbox casing.

Drop a ball down the hole in the edge of the side cover on the drain plug side of the casing and see that it goes between the reverse and third and fourth fork rods. This can be done by looking from the clutch housing end. Place a rod down the same hole and push hard against the ball to centralise the slot in the selector rod. If this is not done the third and fourth fork rod will be damaged in trying to force it into position.

Turn the gearbox so that the drain plug is towards the top and drop a ball in the upper hole (in line with the drain plug hole) and see that it goes between the first and second, and third and fourth fork rods. As before guide a rod up the hole and push hard against the ball to centralise the slot in the rod. Push the third and fourth fork rod home and lock it in position.

Do not knock the selector rods in with a hammer. If any obstruction is felt when pushing the rods through the front of the gearbox casing, it is an indication that the balls are not seating correctly in their slots. Centralise the slots in the rod as previously described, so that the balls do not stand proud of their holes. It will be found that they can now be pushed home quite easily, by hand.

(11) Put the reverse plunger (rounded end first) in the lower hole on the drain plug side, followed by a spring, and fill the hole with its plug and fibre washer. The upper hole is blocked by a long shanked aluminium plug and fibre washer. The two remaining plungers go into the two holes in the front edge of the side cover face of the gearbox casing. Drop one into each hole, rounded end first and follow each plunger with a spring.

(12) Locate the side cover and paper joint washer on the studs, and screw on the eight nuts and spring washers and tighten up evenly by diagonal selection.

(13) Position the front cover joint washer; put the packing shims in the front cover holding it in position with grease; locate the front cover on the studs and secure it with the seven nuts and spring washers.

Although a ·006 in. (·1524 mm.) shim is usually found to be sufficient, use the following method to shim the front and rear covers. Measure the depth of the cover recess and the amount by which the bearing outer race protrudes from the casing, tighten the cover with only the paper joint washer in position to allow it to be compressed. Take off the cover and remove the paper joint washer and measure its thickness. Add the thickness of the joint washer to the depth of the cover recess and subtract the amount by which the bearing protrudes from the casing. The result gives the thickness of shims to be used. Use the least possible number of shims to arrive at the correct thickness. Shims are available in various thicknesses.

(14) Hold the clutch withdrawal lever in position and screw in the pivot bolt.

Place the lockwasher on the bolt and tighten the withdrawal lever from the side opposite the steering. The leg of the clutch withdrawal lever bracket on the steering side of the car is threaded. Screw the bolt through the leg and tighten it sufficiently to take out all play. Lock it in position with the nut and spring washer, and turn the lockwasher over.

Fit the rubber dust cover over the withdrawal lever and plug the other hole with a flat rubber grommet.

(15) Reassembly of the rear cover is effected by reversing the procedure described in Section F.4 Nos. 5 to 15.

Rear Cover

(16) Position the paper joint washer, place a ·006 in. (·1524 mm.) shim in the rear cover bearing recess and fit the rear cover. Shims are also available in thicknesses of ·004 in. (·1016 mm.) and ·010 in. (·254 mm.) Tighten the rear cover (evenly by diametral selection) with the nine long setpins and spring washers. Correct shimming is done in exactly the same way as for the front cover.

(17) Flush the gearbox with flushing oil and replace the drain plug.

GEARBOX

Section F.10 — FAULT DIAGNOSIS

Symptom	No.	Possible Fault
(a) Jumping out of Gear	1	Broken change speed fork rod spring
	2	Excessively worn fork rod groove
	3	Worn coupling dogs
	4	Fork rod securing screw loose
(b) Noisy Gearbox	1	Insufficient oil in gearbox
	2	Excessive end play in laygear
	3	Damaged or worn bearings
	4	Damaged or worn teeth
(c) Difficulty in Engaging Gear	1	Incorrect clutch pedal adjustment
(d) Oil Leaks	1	Damaged joint washers
	2	Damaged or worn oil seals
	3	Front, rear or side covers loose or damaged

SERVICE TOOLS

18G134L. Gearbox Rear Oil Seal Replacer Adaptor

For the replacement of gearbox extension oil seals. Use with handle 18G134.

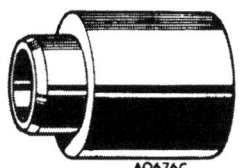

18G134L

F GEARBOX

SERVICE TOOLS

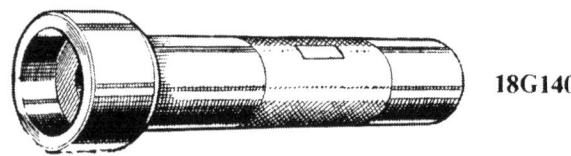
18G140

18G140. First Motion Shaft Assembly Replacer

When threaded over the first motion shaft this tool registers with the outer race of the bearing, which then can be driven home without damage.

18G144

18G144. Synchromesh Assembly Ring

This tool retains the balls and springs in the synchronizer while it is being pushed into the sleeve or first speed wheel.

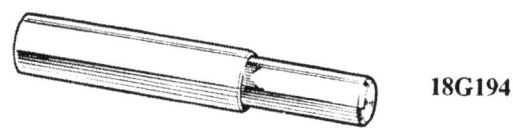
18G194

18G194. Needle-Roller Bearing Replacer

The replacement of needle-roller bearings in the laygear is greatly speeded up by the use of this replacing tool. It can also be used to fit the spring ring after the rollers have been fitted.

18G389

18G389. Gearbox Rear Oil Seal Remover (basic tool)

This basic tool, together with the appropriate adaptor, is essential for removing the gearbox extension oil seal easily and without damage to the extension on the Healey Sprite.

18G389A. Gearbox Rear Oil Seal Remover Adaptor

Use with basic tool 18G389.

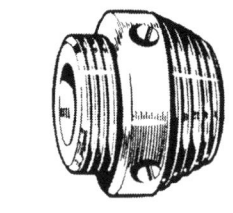

18G389A

18G471. Dummy Layshaft

The fitting of a layshaft to the lay gear on the Healey Sprite is simplified by the use of this tool.

18G471

18G488. Gearbox Oil Seal Clinching Tool

18G488

F.12 Austin-Healey Sprite. Issue 2. 28894.

SECTION G

PROPELLER SHAFT

Section No. G.1. Description

Section No. G.2. Assembly

End of Section Service tools

PROPELLER SHAFT   G

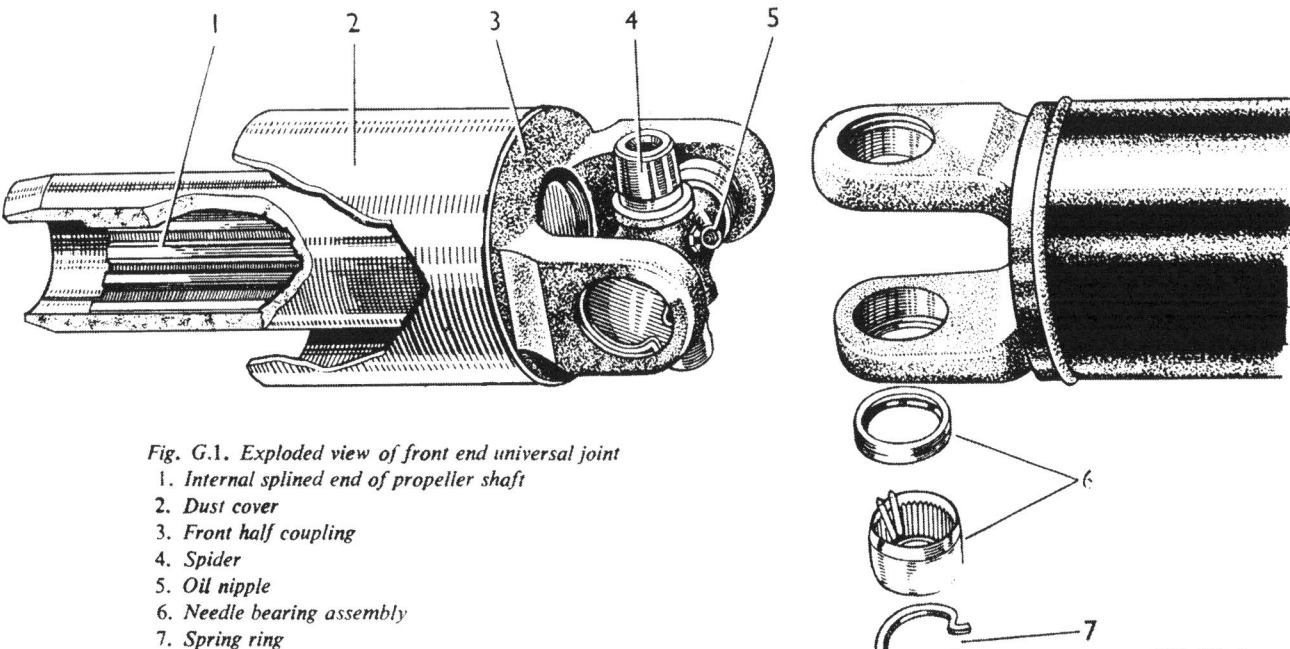

Fig. G.1. Exploded view of front end universal joint
1. Internal splined end of propeller shaft
2. Dust cover
3. Front half coupling
4. Spider
5. Oil nipple
6. Needle bearing assembly
7. Spring ring

Section G.1

DESCRIPTION

The propeller shaft and universal joints (Fig. G.1) are of Hardy Spicer manufacture.

The fore and aft movement of the rear axle and other components is allowed for by a sliding spline between the propeller shaft and gearbox unit. Each universal joint consists of a centre spider, four needle roller bearings and two yokes. Reference to the Lubrication Chart at the rear of this Manual will show the locations of these joints. Oil from the gearbox lubricates the sliding splined joint between the propeller shaft and the gear box.

Section G.2

PROPELLER SHAFT ASSEMBLY

Removing
Disconnect the propeller shaft from the rear axle and remove it over the axle assembly.

Dismantling
The following directions apply to both universal joints of the propeller shaft except for the fact that the front joint can be separated from the shaft, whereas the rear joint has one yoke permanently fixed to the tube.

(1) Clean away the enamel from all the snap rings and bearing faces, to ensure easy extraction of the bearings.

(2) Remove the snap rings by pressing their ends together and prise out with a screwdriver. If the ring does not come out, tap the bearing face lightly to relieve the pressure against the ring.

(3) Hold the splined end of the shaft in one hand and tap the radius of the yoke with a lead or copper hammer (Fig. G.3), when the bearing will begin to emerge. If difficulty is experienced, use a small bar to tap the bearings from the inside, taking

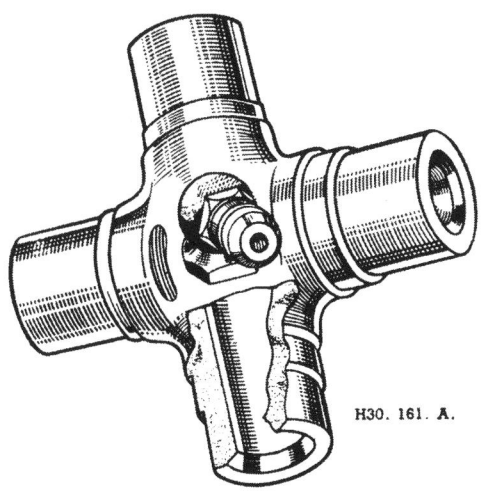

Fig. G.2. Showing the oil channels in the spider

Austin-Healey Sprite Mk. I. Issue 3. 50312

G PROPELLER SHAFT

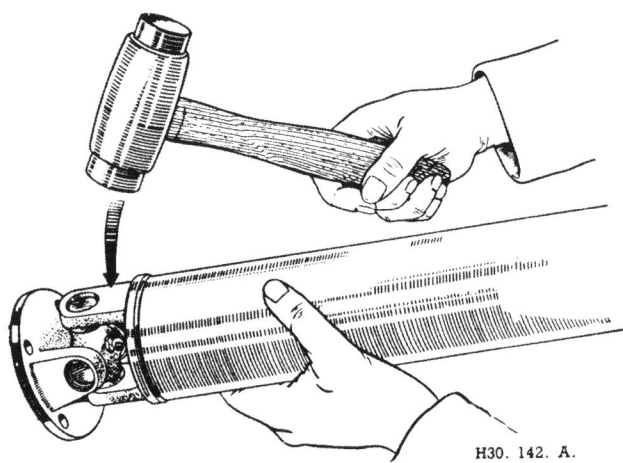

Fig. G.3. Tapping the joint to extract bearing

care not to damage the race itself. Turn the yoke over and extract the bearing with the fingers (Fig. G.4) being careful not to lose any of the needles.

(4) Repeat this operation for the other bearing, and the splined yoke can be removed from the spider.

(5) Using a support and directions as above remove the spider from the other yoke.

Examination and Checking for Wear

When the propeller shaft has been in use for a long time, the parts most likely to show signs of wear are the bearing races and the spider journals.

The complete assembly should be renewed if looseness or stress marks are observed, as no oversize journals or bearings are provided.

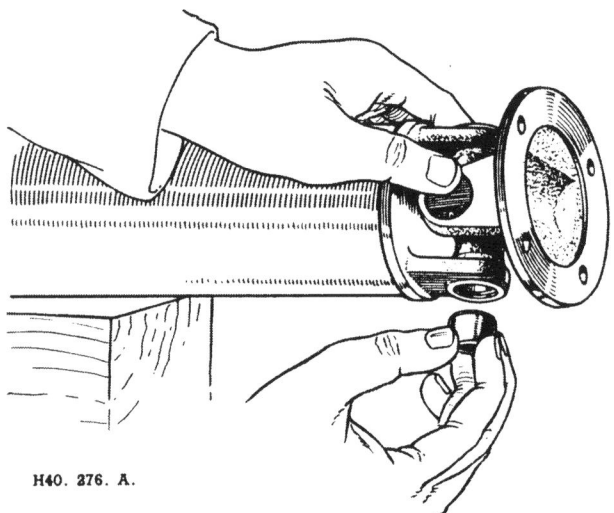

Fig. G.4. Removing a bearing cap complete with needle rollers

It is essential that bearing races are a light drive fit in the yoke trunnions. Any ovality in the trunnion bearing holes, indicates the fitting of new yokes.

Reassembly

(1) See that the drilled holes in the journals of the universal joints are cleaned out and filled with oil.

(2) Assemble the needle rollers in the bearing races and fill with oil. Should difficulty be experienced in assembly, smear the walls of the races with vaseline to retain the needle rollers in place.

(3) Insert the spider in the flange yoke.

(4) Using a soft-nosed drift about $\frac{1}{32}$-in. (·794 mm.) smaller in diameter than the hole in the yoke, tap the bearing in position. It is essential that the bearing races are a light drive in the yoke trunnion.

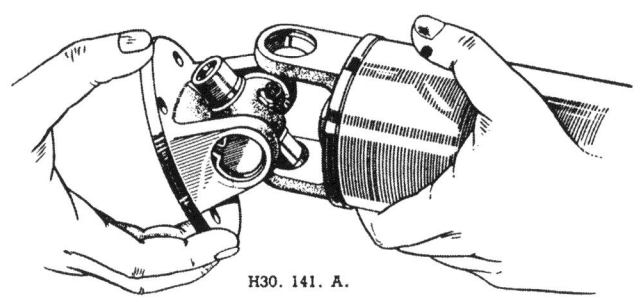

Fig. G.5. Separating the joint

(5) Repeat this operation for the other bearings. The spider journal shoulder should be coated with shellac prior to fitting the retainers to ensure a good seal.

(6) If the joint appears to bind, tap lightly with a wooden mallet which will relieve any pressure of the bearings on the end of the journals. It is advisable to renew cork washers and washer retainers on spider journals, using a tubular drift.

Refitting

Before refitting the propeller shaft to the gearbox smear the splines with oil.

The shaft can be guided into the splines of the third-motion shaft and into the gearbox rear extension with a screwdriver inserted through the front universal joint lubricating hole in the tunnel.

PROPELLER SHAFT

SERVICE TOOLS

18G2. Crankshaft Gear, Pulley, and Propeller Shaft Flange Remover

A multi-purpose tool with alternative legs readily interchangeable: one pair with thin flat ends designed for removing crankshaft gears and propeller shaft and bevel pinion flanges, the other pair has tapered ends suitable for fan pulley grooves other than the later type models fitted with narrow section fan belts.

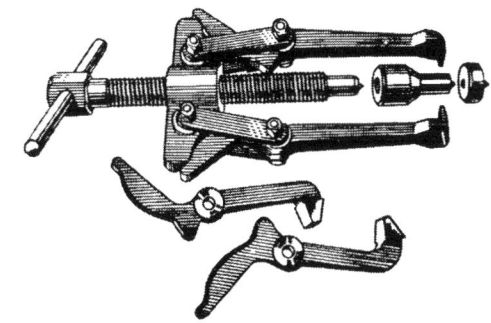

18G2

18G138. Crankshaft Gear and Pulley Replacer

This tool will replace the crankshaft gear and ensure that the engine front cover is correctly located. The felt oil seal and cover must be concentric with the crankshaft, thus safeguarding against oil leaks. The bevel pinion flange can also be replaced with this tool.

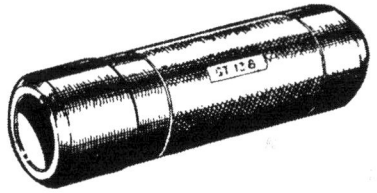

18G138

SECTION H

REAR AXLE AND SUSPENSION

Section No. H.1.	Lubrication
Section No. H.2.	Axle unit
Section No. H.3.	Axle shafts
Section No. H.4.	Hubs
Section No. H.5.	Bevel pinion and differential
Section No. H.6.	Crown wheel and pinion
Section No. H.7.	Spring removal
Section No. H.8.	Dampers
Section No. H.9.	Modified dampers and mountings
End of Section	Service tools

REAR AXLE AND SUSPENSION H

Section H.1

LUBRICATION

For the lubrication of the hypoid axle use lubricants only from approved sources, as tabulated in Section P. Do not, under any circumstances mix various brands of hypoid lubricant. If there is any doubt as to the oil previously used, drain and flush the axle with a little new hypoid oil before finally filling up. Do not use paraffin as a flushing medium. The axle should be drained and refilled every 6,000 miles (10000 km.).

The filler plug is situated on the rear side of the axle, and the drain plug in the bottom of the banjo casing.

Section H.2

AXLE UNIT

To Remove and Replace

(1) Raise up the vehicle by placing a jack under the differential housing. Place supports under the rear spring body anchorage.
(2) The down pipe, silencer and exhaust pipe should be withdrawn from the car as described in Section D.
(3) Keeping the jack in position release the check strap by unscrewing the nut and bolt at its body connection.

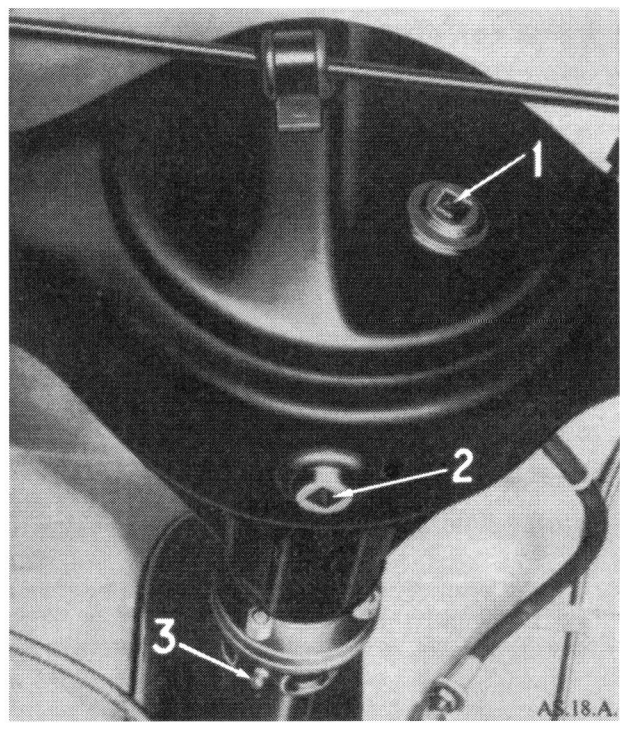

Fig. H.1. Rear axle
1. *Filler plug*   2. *Drain plug*   3. *Propeller shaft universal nipple*

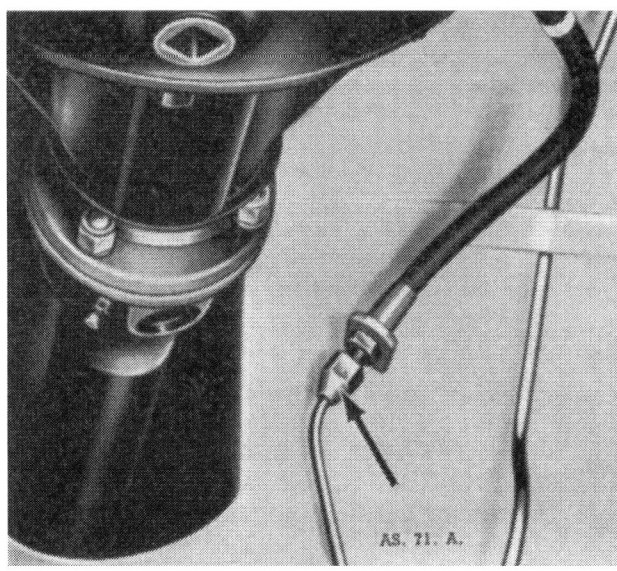

Fig. H.2. Showing the position of the brake hydraulic pipe union which must be disconnected when removing the back axle

(4) Release the damper arm from its connecting linkage.
(5) Disconnect the suspension upper link from the rear axle bracket by unscrewing the nut and bolt and tapping the bolt from its housing.
(6) Disconnect the handbrake cable at the cable adjustment (Fig. L.5).
(7) Working from under the car, unscrew the four self-locking nuts and remove the bolts (U.N.F.) securing the propeller shaft flange to the axle pinion flange.
(8) Disconnect the hydraulic brake pipe at the main union just forward of the differential housing (Fig. H.2).
(9) After ascertaining that the weight of the axle is fully on the jack, unscrew and remove the shackle pins.
(10) Lower the axle and withdraw it from the car.

The replacement of the rear axle is a reversal of the removal procedure with attention to the following:

> If, for any reason, it has been necessary to remove the suspension upper link and at the same time the rear axle has been withdrawn from the car, do not tighten the shackle pins until the upper link is mounted in position.

Section H.3

AXLE SHAFTS

To Remove and Replace

(1) Loosen the wheel nuts of the wheel concerned before jacking up the car.

Austin-Healey Sprite Mk. 1. Issue 4. 50312

REAR AXLE AND SUSPENSION

(2) Remove the wheels after further unscrewing the wheel nuts.

(3) Take out the drum locating screw, using a screwdriver.

(4) The drum can be tapped off the hub and brake linings, provided the handbrake is released and the brake shoes are not adjusted so closely as to bind on the drum.

Should the brake linings hold the drum when the handbrake is released, it will be found necessary to slacken the brake shoe adjuster a few notches.

(5) Remove the axle shaft retaining screw and draw out the axle shaft by gripping the flange outside the hub. It should slide easily but if it is tight on the studs it may need gently prising with a screwdriver inserted between the flange and the hub. Should the paper washer be damaged it must be renewed when reassembling.

(6) Replacement is a reversal of the above operations.

Section H.4

HUBS

To Remove and Replace

(1) Remove the drum and axle shaft as described above.

(2) Knock back the tab of the locking washer and unscrew the nut with Service Tool 18G 152.

(3) Tilt the lock washer to disengage the key from the slot in the threaded portion of the axle casing; remove the washer.

(4) The hub can then be withdrawn with a suitable extractor such as Service Tool 18G 146.

The bearing and oil seal will be withdrawn with the hub. (Fig. H.4).

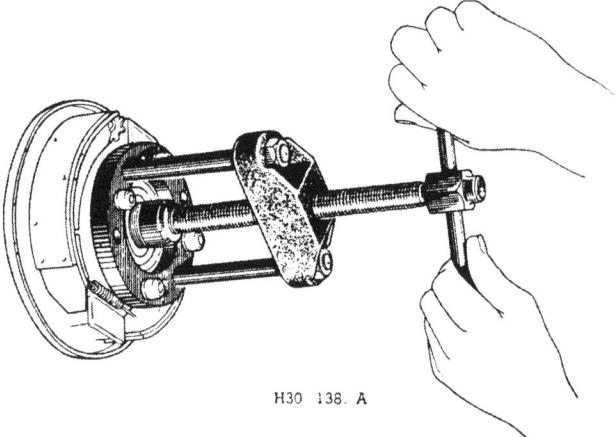

Fig. H.3. *Withdrawing the rear hub using tool* 18G 146

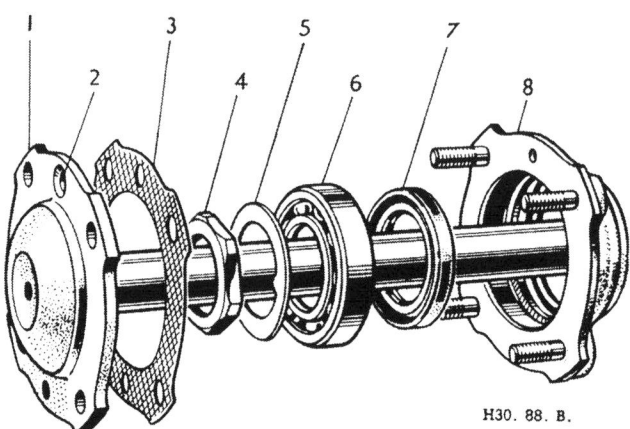

Fig. H.4. *Rear hub assembly exploded*
1. Axle shaft flange
2. Fixing screw countersunk hole
3. Joint washer
4. Hub securing nut
5. Lockwasher
6. Hub bearing
7. Oil seal
8. Hub casing

Hub Assembly

The hub bearing is non-adjustable and is replaceable in one operation, by pressing it into place.

It is essential when fitting the axle shaft that the paper joint washer between its flange and the hub is compressed before the abutment shoulder of the shaft pulls up against the bearing races. If, in an emergency, a paper joint washer is hand made, ensure that it is about ·010 in. (·254 mm.) thick. An oil leak will invariably result if this washer is too thin.

If the oil seal has been removed, it must be drifted into position with Tool 18G 134 and adaptor 18G 134Q (lip towards the bearing) before the bearing is inserted.

The hub is then drifted on to the axle casing with Service Tool 18G 134 and adaptor 18G 134Q followed by a new lockwasher, whose peg must register in its location, and nut.

When the nut has been tightened, bend the lockwasher against one of its flats so locking it.

Assemble the axle shaft, brake drum and wheel as previously described (Section H.3).

Section H.5

BEVEL PINION AND DIFFERENTIAL

Removing and Refitting Bevel Pinion Oil Seal

(1) Mark the propeller shaft and the pinion driving flanges so that they may be replaced in the same relative position. Disconnect the propeller shaft.

(2) Unscrew the nut in the centre of the driving flange with Service Tool 18G 34A to prevent the flange from turning. Remove the nut and washer and withdraw the flange and pressed-on end cover from the pinion shaft.

REAR AXLE AND SUSPENSION

(3) Extract the oil seal from the casing.
(4) Press a new oil seal into the casing with the edge of the sealing ring facing inwards.
(5) Replace the driving flange end cover, taking care not to damage the edge of the oil seal. Tighten the nut with a torque wrench to a reading of 140 lb. ft. (19·36 kg. m.).
(6) Reconnect the propeller shaft, taking care to fit the two flanges with the locating marks in alignment.

Removing and Replacing the Differential Pinions
(1) Drain the oil from the axle casing, and remove the axle shafts.
(2) Mark the propeller shaft and pinion shaft driving flanges so that they may be replaced in the same relative positions; unscrew the nuts and bolts and separate the joint.
(3) Unscrew the nuts securing the bevel pinion and gear carrier casing to the axle banjo; withdraw the casing complete with the pinion shaft and differential assembly.
(4) Make sure that the differential bearing housing caps are marked so that they can be replaced in their original positions, then remove the four nuts and spring washers. Withdraw the bearing caps and differential assembly.
(5) Tap out the dowel pin locating the differential pinion shaft. The diameter of the pin is ⅛ in. (3·17 mm.). The pinions and thrust washers can then be removed from the cage.
(6) Examine the pinions and thrust washers and renew as required.
(7) Replace the pinions, thrust washers and pinion shaft in the differential cage and insert the dowel pin. Peen over the entry hole.
(8) Refill the axle with oil to Ref. B (page P.1).

Removing the Differential Bearings and the Crown Wheel
(1) Remove the differential bearings from the differential cage using Service Tool 18G 47C and adaptors 18G 47M. Note that the word 'Thrust' is stamped on the thrust face of each bearing and that shims are fitted between the inner ring of each bearing and the differential cage.
(2) Knock back the tabs of the locking washers, unscrew the nuts from the bolts securing the crown wheel to the differential, and remove the crown wheel.
(3) Examine the crown wheel teeth. **If a new crown wheel is needed, a mated pair—pinion and crown wheel—must be fitted (see Section H.6).**

Removing the Pinion
(1) Remove the differential assembly. Unscrew the nut; remove the spring washer, the driving flange and the pressed end cover.

(2) Drive the pinion shaft towards the rear; it will carry with it the inner race and the rollers of the rear bearing, leaving the outer race and the complete front bearing in position.
(3) The inner race of the front bearing may be removed with the fingers after removal of the oil seal, and the outer races may be withdrawn with Service Tool 18G 264 with adaptors 18G 264D and 18G 264E.
(4) Slide off the pinion sleeve and shims; withdraw the rear bearing inner race from the pinion shaft, using Service Tool 18G 285, noting the spacing washer against the pinion head.

NOTE.—**If it proves necessary to fit a new crown wheel and pinion or new bearings, the axle assembly must be set up as detailed in Section H.6.**

Section H.6
CROWN WHEEL AND PINION

Replacing Crown Wheel and Pinion
Fitting a new crown wheel and pinion involves four distinct operations:
(1) Setting the position of the pinion.
(2) Adjusting the pinion bearing pre-load.
(3) Adjusting the differential bearing pre-load.
(4) Adjusting the backlash between the gears.

To carry out these operations correctly, four special tools are required; the bevel pinion and differential setting gauge, Service Tool 18G 191 and 18G 191A, the pinion bearing outer race remover and replacer, Service Tool 18G 264 with adaptors 18G 264D and 18G 264E, the pinion inner race remover and replacer, Service Tool 18G 285 and the pre-load checking tool, Service Tool 18G 207.

Setting the Pinion Position
(1) Fit the bearing outer races to the gear carrier.
(2) Smooth off the pinion head with an oil stone, but do not erase the markings that are etched on the pinion head.
(3) Fit a washer of known thickness to the pinion

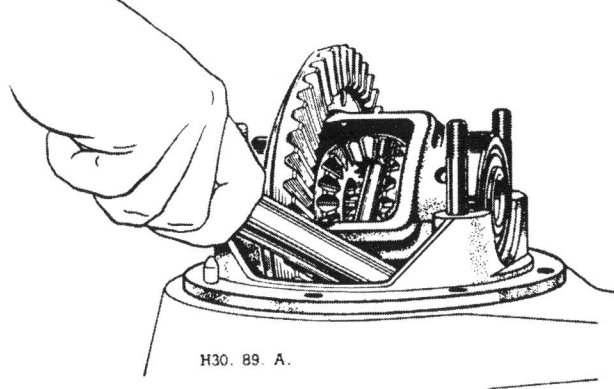

Fig. H.5. Showing the method of levering out the differential unit

H REAR AXLE AND SUSPENSION

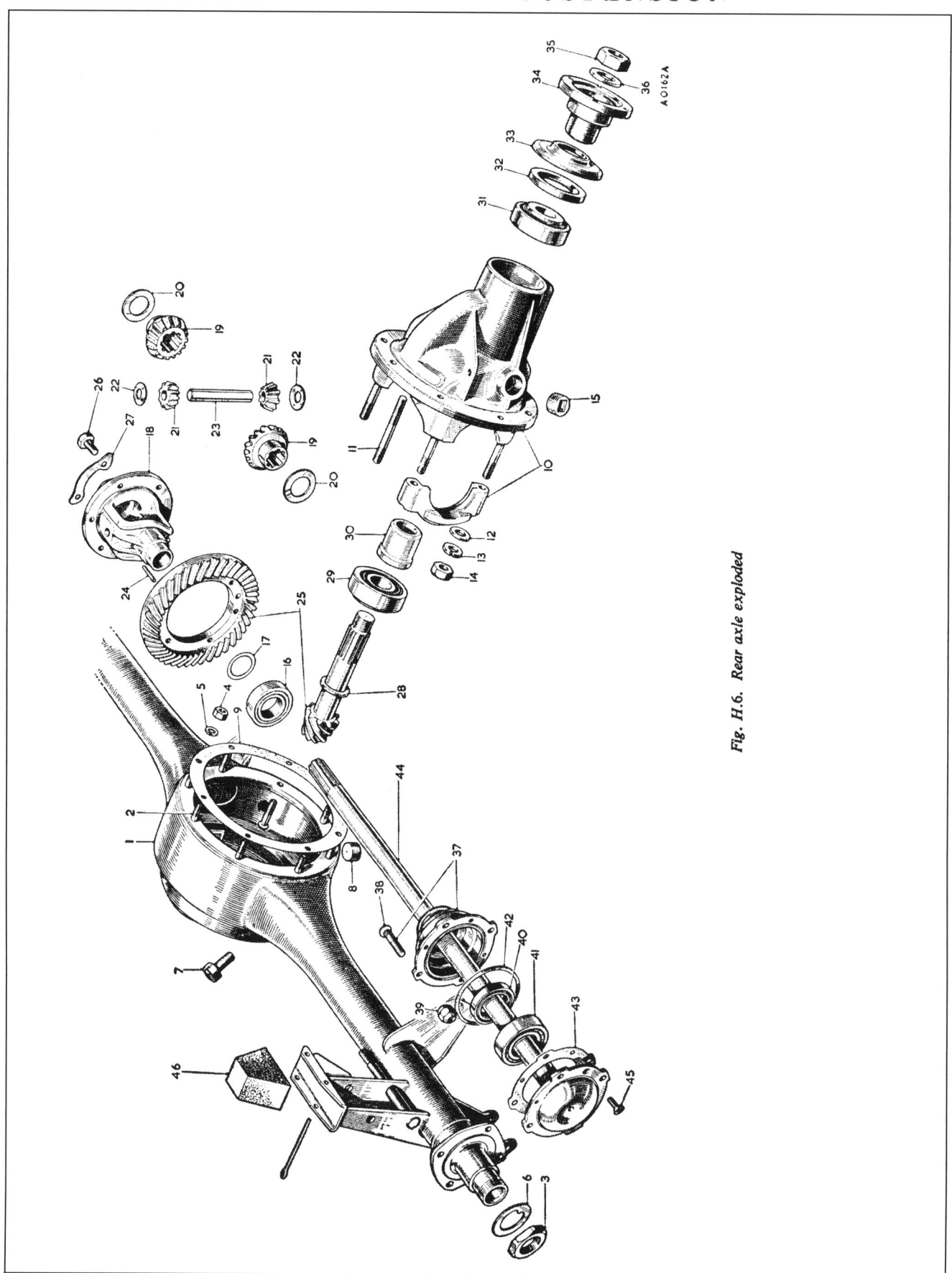

Fig. H.6. *Rear axle exploded*

KEY TO THE REAR AXLE COMPONENTS

No.	Description	No.	Description
1.	Case assembly.	17.	Bearing packing washer.
2.	Gear carrier stud.	18.	Differential cage.
3.	Bearing retaining nut.	19.	Differential wheel.
4.	Gear carrier to axle case nut.	20.	Thrust washer.
5.	Spring washer.	21.	Differential pinion.
6.	Washer.	22.	Thrust washer.
7.	Breather assembly.	23.	Pinion pin.
8.	Drain plug.	24.	Pinion peg.
9.	Gear carrier joint.	25.	Crown wheel and pinion.
10.	Carrier assembly.	26.	Bolt.
11.	Bearing cap stud.	27.	Lock washer.
12.	Plain washer.	28.	Pinion thrust washer.
13.	Spring washer.	29.	Inner pinion bearing.
14.	Stud.	30.	Bearing spacer.
15.	Filler plug.	31.	Pinion outer bearing.
16.	Differential bearing.		

No.	Description
32.	Oil seal.
33.	Dust cover.
34.	Universal joint flange.
35.	Pinion nut.
36.	Spring washer.
37.	Hub assembly.
38.	Wheel stud.
39.	Nut.
40.	Oil seal.
41.	Hub bearing.
42.	Oil seal ring.
43.	Hub shaft joint.
44.	Axle shaft.
45.	Screw.
46.	Bump rubber.

head. If the original washer is damaged or not available, select a washer from the middle of the range of thicknesses.

(4) Fit the inner race of the rear bearing to the pinion shaft using Service Tool 18G 285 and position the pinion in the gear carrier without the distance tube and oil seal. Fit the inner race of the front bearing.

(5) Refit the universal joint driving flange and tighten the nut gradually until a pre-load figure of 8 to 10 lb. in. (·092 to ·115 kg. m.) is obtained.

(6) Adjust the dial indicator to zero on the machined step 'A' of the setting block (Service Tool 18G 191).

(7) Remove the keep disc from the base of the magnet; clean the pinion head and place the magnet and dial indicator in position. Move the indicator arm until the foot of the gauge rests on the centre of the differential bearing bore at one side and tighten the knurled locking screw. Obtain the maximum depth reading and note any variation from the zero setting. Repeat the check in the opposite bearing bore. Add the two variations together and divide by two to obtain a mean reading.

(8) Take into account any variation in pinion head thickness. This will be shown as an unbracketed figure etched on the pinion head and will always be minus (—). If no unbracketed figure is shown, the pinion head is of nominal thickness.

Using the mean clock gauge reading obtained and the unbracketed pinion head figure (if any), the following calculation can be made:

(a) **If the clock reading is minus** add the clock reading to the pinion head marking, the resulting sum being minus. **Reduce** the washer thickness by this amount.

Example: Clock reading .. .. −·002 in.
Pinion marking .. .. −·005 in.
Variation from nominal .. −·007 in.

Reduce the washer thickness by this amount.

(b) **If the clock reading is plus and numerically less** than the pinion head marking **reduce** the washer thickness by the difference.

Example: Pinion marking .. .. −·005 in.
Clock reading .. .. +·003 in.
Variation from nominal .. −·002 in.

Reduce the washer thickness by this amount.

(c) **If the clock reading is plus and numerically greater** than the pinion head marking, **increase** the washer thickness by the difference.

Example: Clock reading .. .. +·008 in.
Pinion marking .. .. −·003 in.
Variation from nominal .. +·005 in.

Increase the washer thickness by this amount.

Fig. H.7. Checking differential bearing width with Service Tool 18G 191 and 18G 191A

The only cases where no alterations are required to the washer thickness are when the clock reading is **plus** and **numerically equal** to the unbracketed pinion head marking, or when the clock reading is zero and there is no unbracketed marking on the pinion head.

(9) Allowance must finally be made for the mounting distance marked on the pinion head in a rectangular bracket. Proceed as follows:

If the marking is a **plus** figure, **reduce** the washer thickness by an equal amount.

If the marking is a **minus** figure, **increase** the washer thickness by an equal amount.

A tolerance of ·001 in. is allowed in the thickness of the washer finally fitted.

REAR AXLE AND SUSPENSION

Pinion Bearing Preload

A washer of the thickness indicated by the use of the tool and calculations should now be fitted under the pinion head and the pinion assembled with bearings, pinion bearing distance piece, oil seal, and universal joint flange.

The pinion bearing distance piece is of the collapsible type. That is to say, when the pinion nut is tightened to the correct torque spanner reading of 135 to 140 lb. ft. (18·69 to 19·4 kg. m.) the distance piece collapses to give the correct bearing preload of 11 to 13 lb. in. (·126 to ·149 kg. m.). It will only perform this function once. Thus when the pinion is reassembled a new distance piece must be fitted.

Prevent the universal joint flange from turning and tighten the pinion nut gradually to a torque spanner reading of 140 lb. ft. (19·4 kg. m.). Checks should be made during the tightening, using service tool 18G207 to ensure the pinion bearing preload does not exceed 13 lb. in. (·149 kg. m.). When the nut is correctly tightened it should provide a pinion bearing preload of 11 to 13 lb. in. (·126 to ·149 kg. m.). When the correct preload is obtained no further attention is needed so far as the pinion is concerned.

Adjusting the Differential Bearing Preload

The differential bearings must be preloaded and this is done by 'pinching' them to the extent of ·002 in. on each bearing, the 'pinch' being obtained by varying the thickness of the shims fitted between each bearing inner ring and the differential cage. The shim thickness is calculated as shown below.

In making the necessary calculations, machining tolerances and variations in bearing width must be taken into account. Machining variations are stamped on the component: bearing width variations must be measured.

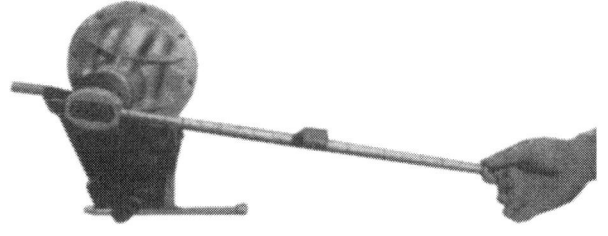

Fig. H.8. Checking the bevel pinion bearing pre-load (Service Tool 18G207).

B. 137. A.

Fig. H.9. Illustrating the machining variations for the differential bearing housings as marked by the factory inspector.

The dimensions involved in pre-loading the differential bearings are illustrated in Fig. H.11, and it is emphasised that it is the variation from nominal on each dimension which is important and referred to in the formula used.

The dimensions are:

(1) From the centre line of the differential to the bearing register on the left-hand side of the gear carrier.
Variation: stamped on the carrier.

(2) From the centre line of the differential to the bearing register on the right-hand side of the carrier.
Variation: stamped on the carrier.

(3) From the bearing register on one side of the differential cage to the register on the opposite side.
Variation: stamped on the cage.

(4) From the rear face of the crown wheel to the bearing register on the opposite side.
Variation: stamped on the cage.

To calculate the shim thickness:

Left-hand side:

Formula: $A + D - C + ·002$ in. (·05 mm.)

Substitute the dimensional variations for the letters in the formula. The result is the thickness of the shims required at the left-hand side to compensate for machining variations and to give the necessary pinch, with bearings of standard width. The width of the bearing must now be checked and any variation from standard added to or subtracted from the shim thickness. If the bearing width is under standard, that amount must be added to the shim thickness, and *vice versa*.

REAR AXLE AND SUSPENSION

To Check Bearing Width

(1) Rest the bearing on the small surface plate of Tool 18G 191A, with the inner race over the recess and the thrust face downwards.

(2) Place the magnet on the surface plate and set the dial indicator to zero on the step marked 'A' of the small gauge block; this is the width of a standard bearing. Transfer the indicator to the plain surface of the bearing inner race and, holding the race down against the balls, note the reading on the dial. A **negative** reading shows the additional thickness to be **added** to the shims at this side; a **positive** reading, the thickness to be **subtracted**.

Right-hand side:

Formula: B—D+·006 in. (·15 mm.)

The procedure is the same as that for the left-hand side.

When a framed number is marked on the back of the crown wheel, e.g. +2, it must be taken into account before assembling the shims and bearings to the differential cage. This mark assists in relating the crown wheel with the pinion.

If, for example, the mark is +2, then shims to the value of ·002 in. (·05 mm.) must be transferred from the left-hand side (the crown wheel side) to the right-hand

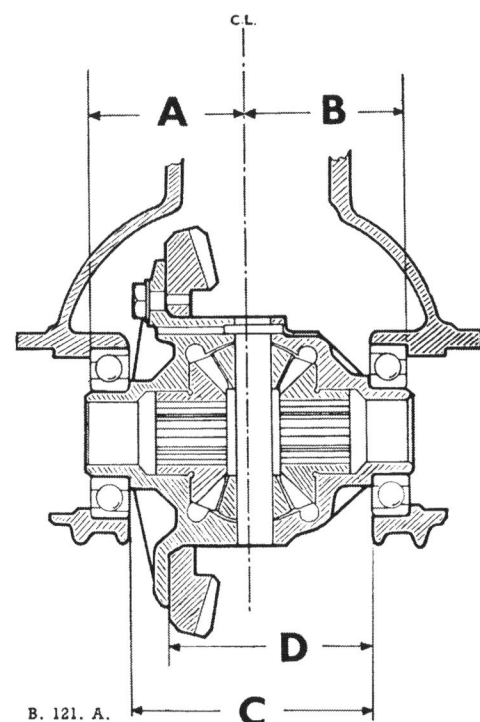

Fig. H.11. Illustrates the points from which the calculations must be made to determine the shim thickness for the bearings on each side of the carrier.

side. If the marking is —2, then shims to the value of ·002 in. (·05 mm.) must be moved from the right-hand side to the left-hand side.

Adjusting Backlash

(1) Assemble the bearings (thrust faces outwards) and shims of calculated thickness to the differential cage.

(2) Bolt the crown wheel to the differential cage, but do not knock over the locating tabs. Tighten the nuts to a torque wrench reading of 60 lb. ft. (8·3 kg. m.).

(3) Mount the assembly on two 'V' blocks and check the amount of run out of the crown wheel as it is rotated, by means of a suitably mounted dial indicator.

(4) The maximum permissible run out is ·002 in. (·05 mm.) and any greater irregularity must be corrected. Detach the crown wheel and examine the joint faces on the flange of the differential case and crown wheel for any particles of dirt.

(5) When the parts are thoroughly cleaned the crown wheel should run true.

(6) Tighten the bolts to the correct torque wrench reading and knock over the locking tabs.

(7) Refit the differential to the gear carrier. Tighten the bearing cap nuts to a torque wrench reading of 65 lb. ft. (8·99 kg. m.).

Fig. H.10. Checking crown wheel to pinion backlash (Service Tool 18G 191 and 18G 191A).

REAR AXLE AND SUSPENSION

(8) Mount the dial indicator on the magnet bracket so that an accurate measurement of the backlash can be taken. The recommended backlash is etched on the crown wheel.

(9) Vary the backlash by decreasing the thickness of the shims at one side and increasing the thickness of the shims at the other side by the same amount, thus moving the crown wheel into or out of mesh as required. The total thickness of the shims must not be changed.

(10) The minimum backlash allowed in any circumstances is ·005 in. (·127 mm.) and the maximum is ·011 in. (·279 mm.).

(11) A movement of ·002 in. (·05 mm.) shim thickness from one side of the differential to the other will produce a variation in backlash of approximately ·002 in. (·05 mm.). Thus it should be possible to set up the differential, even though the backlash is incorrect, by removing the bearings on one occasion only.

Section H.7

SPRING REMOVAL

To remove a rear spring proceed as detailed under 'Axle Unit' Section H.2 items 1 to 10.

The spring can now be removed simply by extracting the two set bolts which pass upwards at the forward end of the spring into caged nuts on the upper leaf. The 'U' bolt must also be removed when the spring can be pulled out of its mounting.

Section H.8

DAMPERS

General Description

The dampers are of the hydraulic double acting piston type. All the working parts are submerged in oil. They are carefully set before dispatch and cannot be adjusted without special equipment. Any attempt to dismantle them will seriously affect their operation and performance. Should adjustment or repair be necessary, they must be returned to their makers.

Maintenance

The maintenance of the hydraulic dampers should include a periodical examination of their anchorages to the body frame and axle brackets. The fixing bolts and nuts must be tightened as necessary.

The cheese-headed screws securing the cover-plates must be kept fully tightened to prevent leakage of the fluid.

Fig. H.12. Rear spring mounting.
1. *Spring securing set bolts.* 2. *Damper nuts.*
3. *'U' bolt nuts.*

When checking the fluid level every 6,000 miles (10000 km.) all road dirt must be carefully cleared away from the vicinity of the filler plugs before the plugs are removed. This is most important as it is absolutely vital that no dirt or foreign matter should enter the operating chamber.

The correct fluid level is just below the filler plug threads.

The use of Armstrong Super (thin) Shock Absorber Oil is recommended. When this is not available any good quality mineral oil to Specification S.A.E. 20/20 W is acceptable. This alternative is not suitable for low temperature operation and is deficient in various other ways.

Removing Dampers

Remove the nut and spring washer that secures the damper lever to the link arm between lever and axle. Withdraw the two fixing bolts from the damper body and body frame, then remove the damper, threading the lever over the link arm bolt.

Refitting Dampers

Dampers may be replaced by simply reversing the removal procedure. However, when handling dampers that have been removed from their mountings, it is important to keep the assemblies upright as far as possible, otherwise air may enter the working chamber and cause erratic resistance.

Damper Arm Rubber Bushes

The rubber bushes integral with both ends of the damper to axle connecting links cannot be renewed. When these bushes are worn renew the arm.

REAR AXLE AND SUSPENSION

Section H.9

MODIFIED DAMPERS AND MOUNTINGS

From Car No. AN5/4333 intermittent to 4507 (a mark of red paint on the damper mounting brackets identifies the first 200 modified cars) and 4508 onwards modified dampers (Part Nos. AHA5311-2) and body mounting brackets (Part Nos. AHA5305-6) are fitted. The mounting brackets, which previously supported only the forward ends of the upper suspension arms, now also accommodate the damper fixing bolts. The dampers are positioned at a different angle from the horizontal, having shorter arms and longer links. This has involved changes to the damper link attachment brackets welded on to the axle casing. The Part Number of the axle casing is now ATA7419.

These modified components are **not** interchangeable with those previously used.

Fig. H.13. Modified suspension body mounting bracket.

SERVICE TOOLS

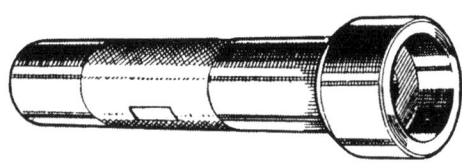

18G4

18G4. Rear Hub Bearing Replacer

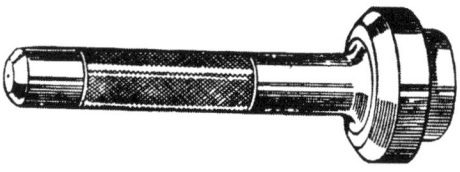

18G14

18G14. Bevel Pinion and Rear Hub Oil Seal Replacer

This replacer is contoured to the exact shape of the oil seal, and bevelled at its leading edge to facilitate insertion of the seal, and fitting without damage.

REAR AXLE AND SUSPENSION

SERVICE TOOLS

18G34A. Bevel Pinion Flange Wrench

The two sets of tapered pins on this tool ensure that it will hold the propeller shaft flange against rotation while the flange nut is released or tightened on semi-floating or three-quarter-floating axles.

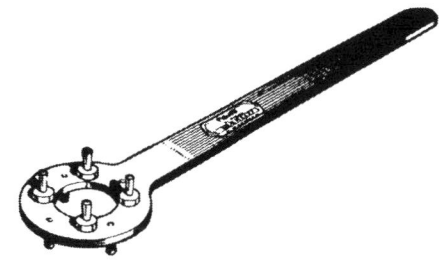

18G34A

18G47C. Differential Bearing Remover (basic tool)

A standardised basic tool; with various adaptors it will cover several models.

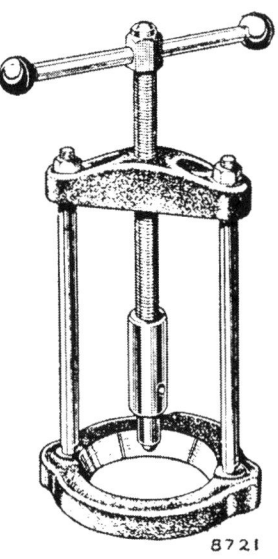

18G47C

18G47M. Differential Bearing Remover Adaptor

For use with 18G47C.

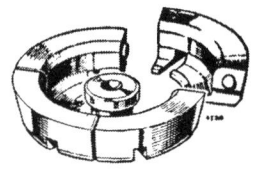

18G47M

REAR AXLE AND SUSPENSION

SERVICE TOOLS

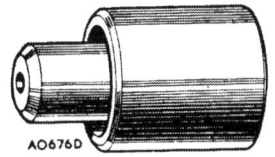

18G134Q

18G134Q. Rear Hub Replacer and Adaptor

Use with handle 18G134.

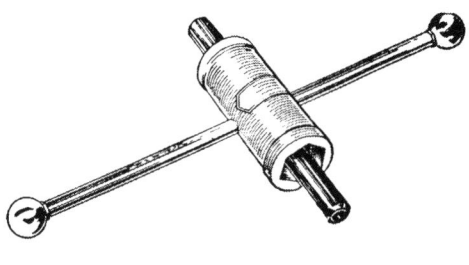

18G152

18G152. Rear Hub Nut Spanner

A reinforced tubular spanner complete with tommy-bar, designed to pilot in the axle tube with the axle shaft withdrawn.

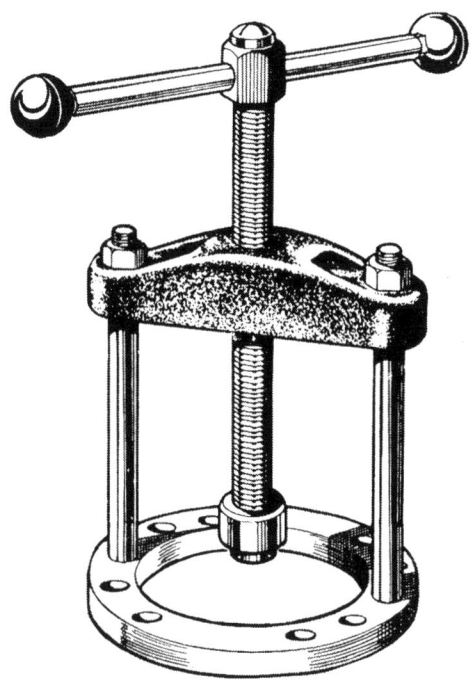

18G146

8G146. Front and Rear Hub Remover

The thrust pad supplied with the tool is for use only when removing the rear hubs.

REAR AXLE AND SUSPENSION

SERVICE TOOLS

18G191. Bevel Pinion Setting Gauge

A gauge block and dial indicator is essential to obtain accurate location of the pinion in the axle case.

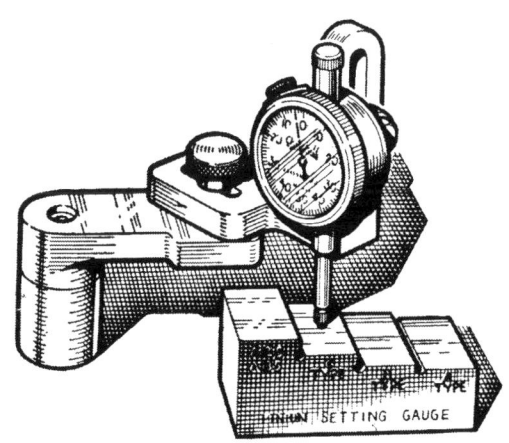

18G191

18G191A. Differential Bearing Gauge

This gauge used with the component parts of 18G191 is designed to check the bearing width. It can also be used to mount the clock gauge on the gear carrier to check crown wheel and bevel pinion backlash.

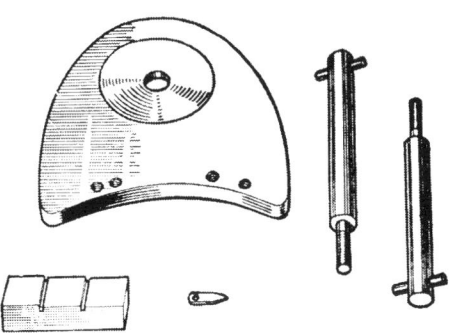

18G191A

18G207. Bevel Pinion Bearing Preload Gauge

The movable arms of the tool are located in opposite holes of the bevel pinion flange and the weight moved along the rod to the poundage required.

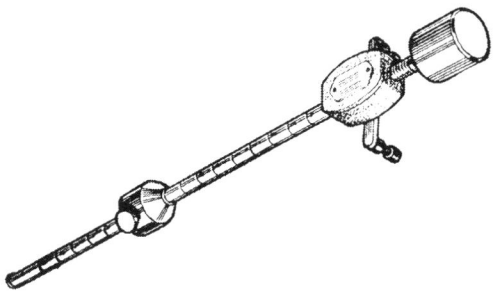

18G207

REAR AXLE AND SUSPENSION

SERVICE TOOLS

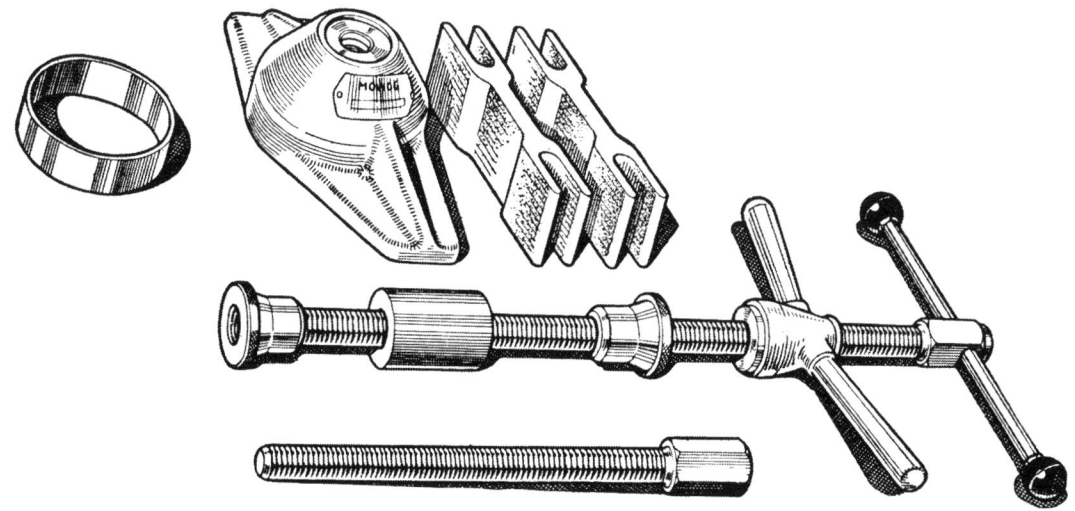

18G264. Bevel Pinion Bearing Outer Race Remover (basic tool)

Comprising a body, centre screw with extension and tommy bar, wing nut, guide cone, and two distance pieces. A plain ring is also included to serve as a pilot when the rear bearing outer races are being replaced. Use with adaptors 18G264D, 18G264E.

18G264

18G264D

18G264D. Bevel Pinion Bearing Outer Race Remover Adaptor

Use with 18G264.

18G264E

18G264E. Bevel Pinion Bearing Outer Race Remover Adaptor

For use with basic tool 18G264.

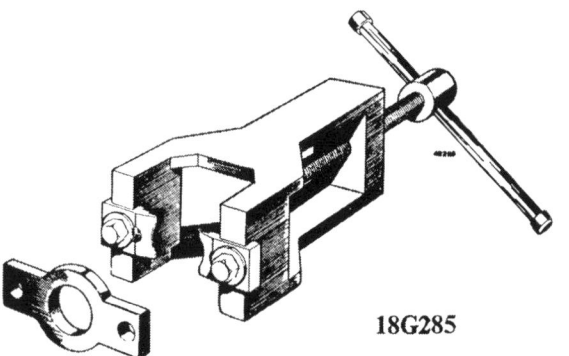

18G285. Bevel Pinion Bearing Inner Race Remover and Replacer

A tool which is essential when withdrawing or replacing the inner bearing race of the pinion shaft.

SECTION J

STEERING

Section No. J.1	Description
Section No. J.2	Maintenance
Section No. J.3	Adjustments in the vehicle
Section No. J.4	Steering column assembly
Section No. J.5	Steering rack assembly
Section No. J.6.	Fault diagnosis
End of Section	Service tools

STEERING   J

Section J.1

DESCRIPTION

The steering gear is of the rack and pinion type and is secured above the front frame cross member immediately behind the radiator. Tie-rods, operating the swivel arms, are attached to each end of the steering rack by ball joints enclosed in rubber gaiters.

The steering column engages the splined end of a helical-toothed pinion to which it is secured by a clamp bolt.

End play of the pinion is eliminated by adjustment of the shims fitted beneath the pinion tail end bearing. A damper pad inserted in the steering rack controls the backlash between the pinion and the rack.

Section J.2

MAINTENANCE

Provision has been made to replenish the rack housing with hypoid oil every 12,000 miles (20000 km.). The oil nipple is situated on the left side (right side for L.H.D. vehicles) of the rack housing and is positioned to enable the lubricant to be injected from above. Avoid overfilling the rack housing and keep the clips on the rubber gaiters fully tightened to prevent the oil escaping.

Apply the lubricating gun to the nipple on each tie-rod ball joint every 3,000 miles (5000 km.).

Section J.3

ADJUSTMENTS IN THE VEHICLE

The following adjustments maintain the performance of the steering at its maximum, and consists of aligning the front wheels and taking up backlash in the steering gear. Proceed as detailed below:

(1) Front wheel alignment is governed by four factors—camber, castor, swivel pin inclination and

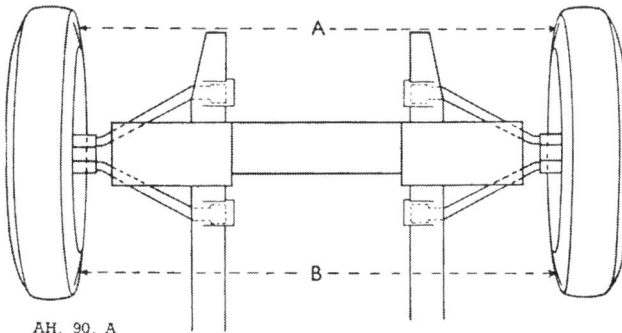

Fig. J.1. *The toe-in must be adjusted so that 'A' is $\frac{1}{16}$" to $\frac{1}{8}$" less than 'B.'*

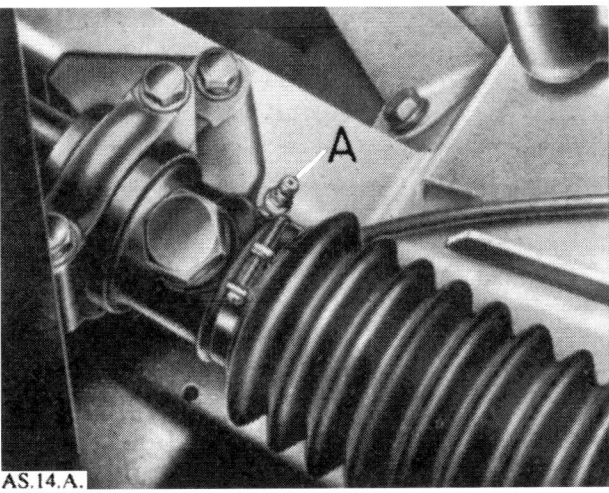

Fig. J.2. *Oil nipple provided for lubrication of the steering rack and pinion.*

wheel toe-in. The correct camber and swivel pin angles are built into the front suspension and will change only if the suspension is distorted by accidental damage. It is most important that the front wheels should toe-in $\frac{1}{16}$ in. (1·58 mm.) to $\frac{1}{8}$ in. (3 mm.) and this is governed by the length of the tie-rods. Adjustments are provided so that the tie-rods may be lengthened or shortened to maintain the correct alignment.

Should adjustment be necessary, slacken the locknut of each tie-rod ball joint and the clips securing the rubber gaiters to the tie-rods, then rotate each tie-rod equally in the necessary direction. Both tie-rods have right-hand threads and should be rotated with a spanner applied to the flats provided.

When making adjustments remember that they are double, that is to say, adjustments of the rim in one direction makes a similar increase of the opposite portion of the rim in the other direction.

The track is best adjusted by means of a Dunlop Optical Alignment Gauge, particulars of which can be obtained from the Dunlop Rubber Co. Ltd., Fort Dunlop, Erdington, Birmingham, England.

When adjustment are completed make sure to re-tighten the locknuts and rubber gaiter clips and particularly that the bottom surfaces of the ball joints are in the correct plane.

When the track is correctly adjusted and the wheels are in the straight-ahead position the tie-rods should be adjusted to equal lengths. This can be checked by measuring the distance from the spanner flats to the ball joint locknuts.

J STEERING

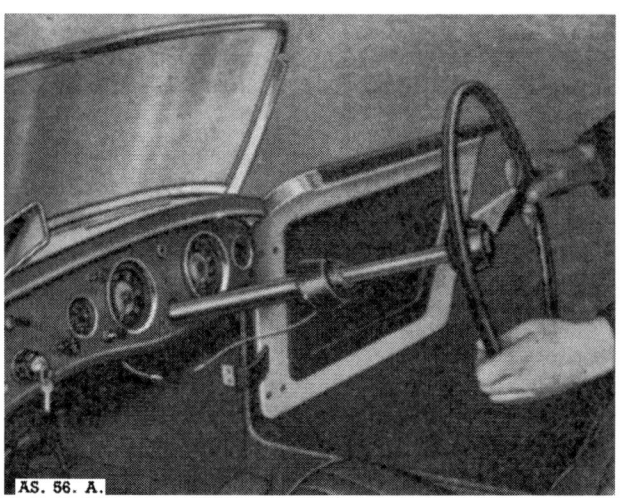

Fig. J.3. *Showing the removal of the steering column.*

When adjusting the track the following precautions should be observed:

(a) The car should have come to rest from a forward movement. This ensures, as far as possible, that the wheels are in their natural running position.

(b) It is preferable for alignment to be checked with the car laden and the tyres inflated to the standard pressure of 18 lb./sq. in. (1·27 kg./cm²).

(c) With conventional base-bar type alignment gauges measurements in front of and behind the wheel centres should be taken at the same points on the tyres or rim flanges. This is achieved by marking the tyres where the first reading is taken and moving the car forwards approximately half a road wheel revolution before taking the second reading at the same points.

With the Dunlop Optical Gauge two or three readings should be taken with the car moved forwards to different positions—180° road wheel turn for two readings and 120° for three readings. The average figure should then be calculated.

Wheels and tyres vary laterally within their

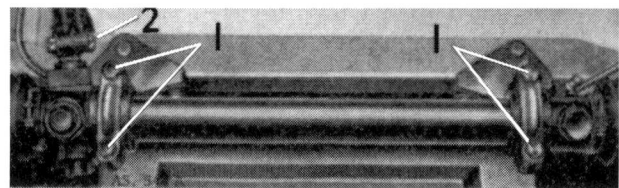

Fig. J.4. *Showing the mounting points '1' of the steering rack and '2' being the steering column clamp bolt.*

manufacturing tolerances, or as the result of service, and alignment figures obtained without moving the car are unreliable.

(2) Adjustment is provided between the rack damper cap and the rack body. This is to eliminate back-lash between the pinion and the rack.
To adjust the damper cap proceed as follows:

(a) Disconnect the tie-rods from their respective swivel arms in order to free the gear of all loads.

(b) Unscrew the steering column clamp bolt and withdraw the column from the pinion shaft splines.

(c) Unscrew the damper cap and remove its shims and plunger spring. Position the plunger in the cap and replace the cap. Then screw down the cap until it is just possible to rotate the pinion shaft by drawing the rack through its housing.

(d) A feeler gauge is then used to measure the clearance between the hexagon of the damper cap and its seating in the rack housing (Fig. J.5). To this figure must be added a clearance of ·002 to ·005 in. (·05 to ·127 mm.) to arrive at the correct thickness of shims which must be placed beneath the damper cap. The shims are available in thicknesses of ·003 and ·010 in. (·076 and 0·254 mm.).

(e) Remove the damper cap and plunger, Insert the spring beneath the plunger and replace and tighten the assembly with the requisite number of shims fitted as defined in the previous paragraph.

(f) Refit both steering column and swivel arms to the steering rack assembly.

(3) Excessive end play of the pinion is rectified by the fitting of shims of pre-determined thicknesses and is performed in the following manner:

(a) Disconnect the tie-rod(s) from the swivel arm(s) to free the gear of all loads.

(b) Unscrew the steering column clamp bolt, 2 Fig. J.4, and withdraw the column from the pinion and shaft splines.

(c) By means of a dial gauge placed at the splined end of the pinion shaft, check the end play of the shaft which should be between ·002 in. and ·005 in. (·05 and ·13 mm.). If necessary the shims must be adjusted to give this end play.

(d) Refit both steering column and swivel arms to the steering rack assembly.

(4) The ball joints linking the tie rods to the rack

STEERING

must be a reasonably tight sliding fit without play. If by examination this is not correct then the following procedure should be adopted:

(a) Disconnect the tie-rod(s) from the swivel arm(s).

(b) Place a suitable receptacle under the ball joint concerned and release the gaiter clips from the rack housing and tie-rod(s) and remove the rubber gaiter(s).

(c) Tap back the washer locking the ball housing. Unscrew the ball joint caps with Service Tool 18G 313 and remove the lockwasher.

(d) Fit a new ball housing lockwasher. Replace the shims and ball seat and, after inserting the ball into its mating socket screw up the ball housing until it is quite tight.

(e) The ball must be a reasonably tight sliding fit without play. Any adjustment required is carried out by varying the thickness of shims fitted beneath the ball joint cap seating. The shims are available in thicknesses of ·005, ·008 and ·010 in. (·127, ·20 and ·254 mm.).

(f) When correctly adjusted the ball housing must be locked in three places with the flange of the lock washer.

(g) Replace the rubber gaiter(s) and clips and replenish the rack housing with hypoid oil. (See Section J.2.)

(h) Refit the tie-rod(s) to the swivel arm(s).

Section J.4

STEERING COLUMN ASSEMBLY

To Remove

(1) Remove the connector from the negative battery terminal.

(2) Unscrew and remove the clamp nut bolt from the splined lower end of the steering column.

(3) Disconnect the horn wire (brown with black) at its snap connection beneath the facia.

(4) Remove the steering column surround, situated between the facia panel and the steering wheel, after unscrewing its three securing setscrews located behind the facia.

(5) Slacken the two bolts securing the column bracket beneath the facia panel.

(6) As illustrated in Fig. J.3, the steering column complete may now be withdrawn rearwards from the facia panel.

To Dismantle

The inner and outer columns can be separated once the steering wheel motif, steering wheel securing nut and steering wheel have been removed. To avoid damage to the ebonite horn switch contact, use Service Tool 18G562 to loosen the nut.

To Replace

The installation of the steering column assembly is the reversal of the procedure to remove. Tighten the steering wheel nut to the figure given in 'GENERAL DATA', using service Tool 18G562, on successive hexagons so that the cutaway on the socket clears the horn switch contact.

Section J.5

STEERING RACK ASSEMBLY

To Remove

(1) Remove the radiator as described in Section C.3.

(2) Remove the clamp nut and bolt from the splined lower end of the steering column and disengage the column from the splines.

(3) Detach the tie-rod ball joint from the swivel arm

Fig. J.5. Checking the adjustment of the damper cap.

by first removing the split pins and then unscrewing the castellated nuts from the ball pins. Service Tool 18G 313 will facilitate the separation of the tie-rod from the swivel arm.

(4) Extract the four setpins and washers securing the two steering rack clamps to the mounting brackets. The rack assembly complete with tie-rods may now be withdrawn from the car.

To Dismantle

(1) Measure and record the distance from the spanner flats on the tie-rods to each of the ball joint locknuts; this will be of great assistance when reassembling.

(2) Slacken the ball joint locknuts and unscrew the ball joint assemblies.

(3) Position the rack housing over a receptacle to catch the oil and release the gaiter clips from the rack housing and tie-rods and remove the rubber gaiters.

(4) Unscrew the hexagonal cap which is adjacent to the oil nipple on the housing and withdraw it complete with sealing washer, pressure pad and spring.

(5) Unscrew the damper pad housing fitted at the pinion end of the rack housing and withdraw it complete with plunger, spring and shims.

(6) Extract the two bolts securing the pinion shaft tail bearing and remove the bearing and shims. Withdraw the pinion complete with the bottom thrust washer. The top thrust washer (the thickest one) is trapped behind the rack teeth and may be removed after the rack is withdrawn.

(7) Secure the rack housing between suitable clamps in a vice and tap back the washers locking the tie-rod ball housings. Unscrew the ball joint caps with the special tie-rod C-spanner, Service Tool 18G 313. **Note:** In some cases the latter operation releases the ball seat housing from the ball joint cap, in this case difficulty will be experienced in removing the ball housing from the rack. It is therefore essential that the ball housing is released from the rack before the ball seat housing and joint cap are separated.

(8) Remove the lock washers. The steering rack may be withdrawn from the housing.

(9) Screw the ball seat housing from the ball joint caps using the C-spanner previously mentioned together with the tie-rod pin spanner 18G 312. The shims and ball seats are now free to be removed; ensure that the shims are kept to their respective sides.

(10) Thoroughly clean and examine for wear all parts of the pinion housing, shaft and teeth. If badly worn, the pinion or housing, or both, should be renewed.
Fractures or hollows, or any roughness on the surface of the teeth, will render the rack or pinion unserviceable.
Clean off and examine the rubber gaiters. If they are damaged, new ones **must** be fitted.
Remove the grease nipple from the rack housing and the two on the ball joints. Check them by forcing oil through them with the oil gun to ensure that they are not blocked.
If the tie-rod inner ball housings or seats are badly worn they must be renewed and then adjusted as detailed in (4) Section J.3.

The outer ball joint is not adjustable and if worn must be replaced by a new assembly.

To Reassemble

(1) Fit a new lock washer to one end of the steering rack, then replace and tighten the ball seat housing. Replace the shims and ball seat and, after inserting the ball end of the tie-rod, screw up the ball housing until it is quite tight.

(2) Adjust the ball joint, if necessary, as detailed in (4) Section J.3.

(3) Insert the rack in the housing and refit and adjust the other ball seat in a similar manner.

(4) Draw the rack through its housing until the centre tooth (number 12 from either end) is in the centre of the pinion housing.

(5) Place the thickest of the pinion thrust washers in position in the rack housing with its chamfered edge towards the rack. Replace the smaller thrust washer on the plain end of the pinion shaft with the chamfered edge towards the pinion teeth.

(6) Replace the pinion, ensuring that the centre tooth on the rack is in line with the mark on the splined end of the pinion shaft. Correct engagement of the rack and pinion is essential if the steering wheel position is not to be affected.

(7) Replace the shims and tail end bearing. Adjust the end play of the pinion as detailed in (3) Section J.3.

(8) Refit the rubber gaiters and clips.

(9) Replace the ball joint locknuts and joint assemblies in approximately their original positions, referring to the figures recorded when the rack was dismantled.

(10) Replace and adjust the steering rack damper as described in (2) Section J.3.

(11) Replace the secondary damper, pressure pad, sealing washer and spring.

(12) Fit a new pinion shaft oil seal, and pump 10 fluid ounces (0·28 litre approx.) of hypoid oil into the rack housing through the nipple provided.

To Replace

Replacement of the steering rack is a reversal of the procedure 'to remove' except that the bolts securing the housing to its mounting brackets should not be fully tightened until the steering column assembly (if removed) has been fitted and secured to the column support bracket. This method of assembly will ensure that the steering rack pinion is in correct alignment with the column. Do not forget to finally tighten the rack housing bolts.

STEERING

Section J.6 — FAULT DIAGNOSIS

Symptom	No.	Possible Fault
(a) Wheel Wobble	1	Unbalanced wheels and tyres
	2	Slack steering connections
	3	Incorrect steering geometry
	4	Excessive play in steering gear
	5	Broken or weak front springs
	6	Worn hub bearings
	7	Loose or broken shackles
(b) Wander		Check 2, 3 and 4 in (a)
	1	Broken spring clips
	2	Front suspension and rear axle mounting points out of alignment
	3	Uneven tyre pressures
	4	Uneven tyre wear
	5	Weak dampers or springs
(c) Heavy Steering		Check 3 in (a)
	1	Excessively low tyre pressures
	2	Insufficient lubricant in steering rack
	3	'Dry' steering connections
	4	Out of track
	5	Incorrectly adjusted steering gear
	6	Misaligned steering column
(d) Tyre Squeal		Check 3 in (a)
		Check 1 in (c)

J STEERING

SERVICE TOOLS

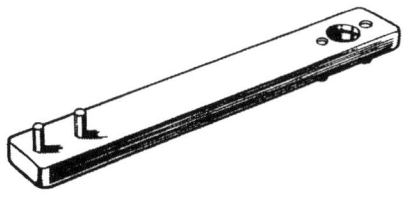

18G312

18G312. Steering Tie-rod Pin Spanner

This tool is designed for use with the special C-spanner 18G313 for dismantling the steering tie-rod ball housing. In use it is clamped in a vice and the pins of the spanner are engaged with the holes in the housing. Use the spanner 18G313 to unscrew the housing cap.

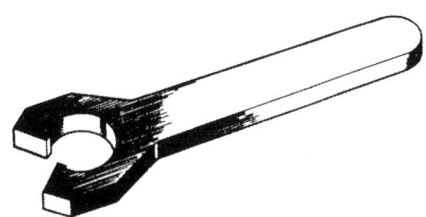

18G313

18G313. Steering Tie-rod C-Spanner

Designed to engage the shallow splines of the steering rack ball housing cap and remove it without damage.

18G562

18G562. Steering Wheel Nut Spanner

Designed to enable the steering wheel nut to be tightened without damage to the ebonite horn switch contact.

SECTION K

FRONT SUSPENSION AND FRONT HUBS

Section No. K.1. Independent front suspension.

Section No. K.2. Coil springs.

Section No K.3. Front suspension

Section No. K.4. Examination for wear

Section No. K.5. Reassembling front suspension

Section No. K.6. Castor and camber angles and swivel pin inclination

Section No. K.7. Front hubs

Section No. K.8. Dampers

Section No. K.9. Lower link mountings

Section No. K.10. Fault diagnosis

End of Section   Service tools

FRONT SUSPENSION AND FRONT HUBS K

Section K.1

INDEPENDENT FRONT SUSPENSION

Description

The independent suspension is of the 'wishbone' type. It consists of a single armed Armstrong double-acting damper, bolted to its support bracket, at its upper end. The single arm is towards the front of the car and is secured to the swivel pin trunnion link by a fulcrum pin and metalastik rubber bushes. The bottom end of the swivel pin is secured to the outer end of the lower links by a fulcrum which is cottered in position.

The inner arms of the lower links are fixed to brackets by metalastik rubber bushes and fulcrum pins.

A rebound buffer is fitted to the bottom of the coil spring top bracket and a smaller rebound buffer under the damper arm.

A spring seat is secured to the lower links by four bolts, flat washers and self-locking nuts, thus keeping the spring compressed.

Checking for wear

The following tests should be made to check for wear in various components of the suspension unit.

(1) Wear of the swivel pin, its bushes, or both, may be checked by jacking up the car until the front wheels are clear of the ground. Grip two parts of the tyre diametrically opposite in a vertical plane and endeavour to rock the wheel in that plane. If any movement is felt at the wheel, the swivel pin, its bushes, or both are worn.

(2) Vertical or horizontal movement of the damper cross shaft relative to its body, denotes wear in the damper bearings, and can only be remedied by fitting a new damper. These bearings are best checked with the suspension dismantled, when with some freedom of movement it is possible to move the damper arm which is attached to the cross shaft.

(3) The metalastik fulcrum pin bushes slowly deteriorate due to wear and weather conditions. They must therefore be renewed if softening of the rubber or side movement is evident.

(4) The threaded bushes of the screwed trunnion fulcrum pin in the lower links may develop excessive play due to wear. Dismantle the assembly, check and renew as necessary. The threaded bushes are not renewable by themselves, but only by changing the lower links.

Section K.2

COIL SPRINGS

To remove

(1) Place a hard wood or metal block ($1\frac{1}{8}$ in. i.e. 2·86 cms. long) under the damper arm to keep the arm off its rubber rebound buffer when the car is jacked up.

(2) Jack up the car on the side concerned and use Service Tool 18G 153 to screw up the spring seat after two diametrically opposite spring seat securing bolts have been withdrawn. Remove the nuts and washers, then screw back the centre bolt of the service tool to allow the spring to expand.

(3) When the spring has fully expanded lift off the tool and take out the spring, its seat and the bolts. In the absence of Service Tool 18G 153 two high tensile bolts about $4\frac{1}{2}$-ins. (11·43 cms). long, threaded their entire length, will be required to allow the spring to expand.

Take out two diametrically opposite bolts in the spring seat, replace them with the long slave bolts which should be screwed up tight, release the two other bolts and nuts, and slacken the nuts on the slave bolts, a little at a time, until the spring is fully expanded. Now the nuts and slave bolts can be taken out and the spring removed.

Fig. K.1. *Front suspension lubrication.*
1. *Damper filler plug.*
2. *Swivel axle pin top bush.*
3. *Swivel axle pin bottom bush.*
4. *Tie rod end.*
5. *Lower link outer bushes.*

Austin-Healey Sprite Mk. 1. Issue 3. 35471.

K FRONT SUSPENSION AND FRONT HUBS

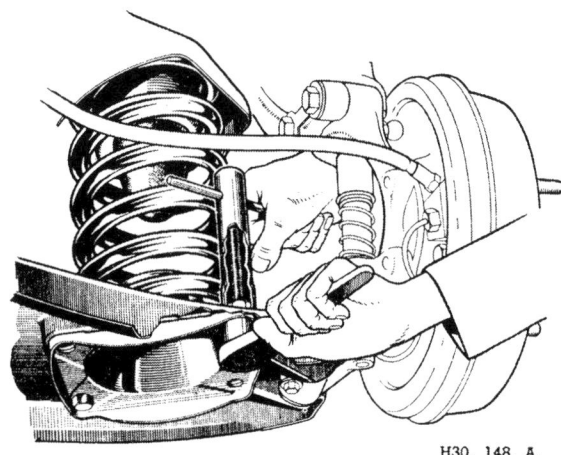

Fig. K.2. Using a pair of slave bolts to remove or replace a coil spring.

If the spring is cracked, weakened, broken or in any way differs from its specifications, it should be renewed.

To replace

(1) Offer the spring and seat into position, fit the spring compressor, put two guide rods in diametrically opposite holes to bring the spring seat and wishbone lower links into line and compress the spring by turning the centre bolt.

(2) When the spring has been compressed insert and tighten two of the bolts with their washers and nuts, withdraw the two guide rods and spring compressor, insert and finally tighten the two remaining bolts with their nuts and washers. Go over the four nuts to see that they have been fully tightened down.

Section K.3

FRONT SUSPENSION

To Remove

(1) Jack up the car and remove the wheel and coil spring as already described in Section K.2.

(2) Disconnect the steering side-tube from the steering arm by withdrawing the split pin and unscrewing the castellated nut. If the ball pin shank is tight in the steering arm slacken the nut but do not take it off, sharply tap the steering arm at the side tube end with a hammer, when it will be found to come away quite easily on removing the nut.

(3) Disconnect the flexible brake hose.

(4) Withdraw the split pins, undo the nuts, tap the fulcrum pins through the lower link inner ends and take away the two rubber bushes at the outer ends of the lower link inner brackets. The lower end of the suspension is now free.

(5) At the upper end remove the clamp bolt and shake-proof washer in the damper arm, withdraw the split pin and release the castellated nut on the fulcrum pin. Tap the fulcrum pin off, and retrieve the rubber bushes. The suspension unit is now free and can be lifted away.

To Dismantle

(1) Secure the suspension by clamping the web of the lower links between a dummy baseplate at the bottom and a solid metal disc and bolt at the top.

(2) Take out the drum securing screw and withdraw the brake drum.

(3) Draw off the hub as described in Section K.7.

(4) Detach the backplate by removing its four bolts and shakeproof washers.

(5) Knock back the lockwasher and remove the two setscrews to release the steering lever.

(6) Extract the split pin and undo the castellated nut at the top of the swivel axle pin. Take off the trunnion and preserve the shims for use during assembly. Lift off the phosphor bronze oilite thrust washer and the swivel axle along with the dust excluder tubes and their spring, and the bevelled cork sealing ring at the bottom of the swivel axle pin.

Caption to Fig. K.3.

1. Lubricator.
2. Swivel axle bush (top).
3. Steering side tube arm.
4. Lockwasher.
5. Setscrew.
6. Trunnion bush (bearing).
7. Trunnion link.
8. Trunnion fulcrum pin.
9. Oilite thrust washer.
10. Adjustment washer (shim).
11. Clamp bolt.
12. Rebound buffer.
13. Damper.
14. Setscrews.
15. Rebound rubber bumper.
16. Coil spring.
17. Spring seat.
18. Bolts.
19. Simmonds nut.
20. Fulcrum pin.
21. Rubber bush (bearings).
22. Lower link bush (inner).
23. Rubber bush (bearing).
24. Special washer.
25. Lower link.
26. Welch plug.
27. Fulcrum pin (outer).
28. Screwed plug.
29. Lubricator.
30. Cork rings.
31. Cotter.
32. Swivel axle pin.
33. Dust excluder (bottom).
34. Spring.
35. Dust excluder (top).
36. Swivel axle.
37. Swivel axle bush (bottom).
38. Cork sealing ring.

FRONT SUSPENSION AND FRONT HUBS K

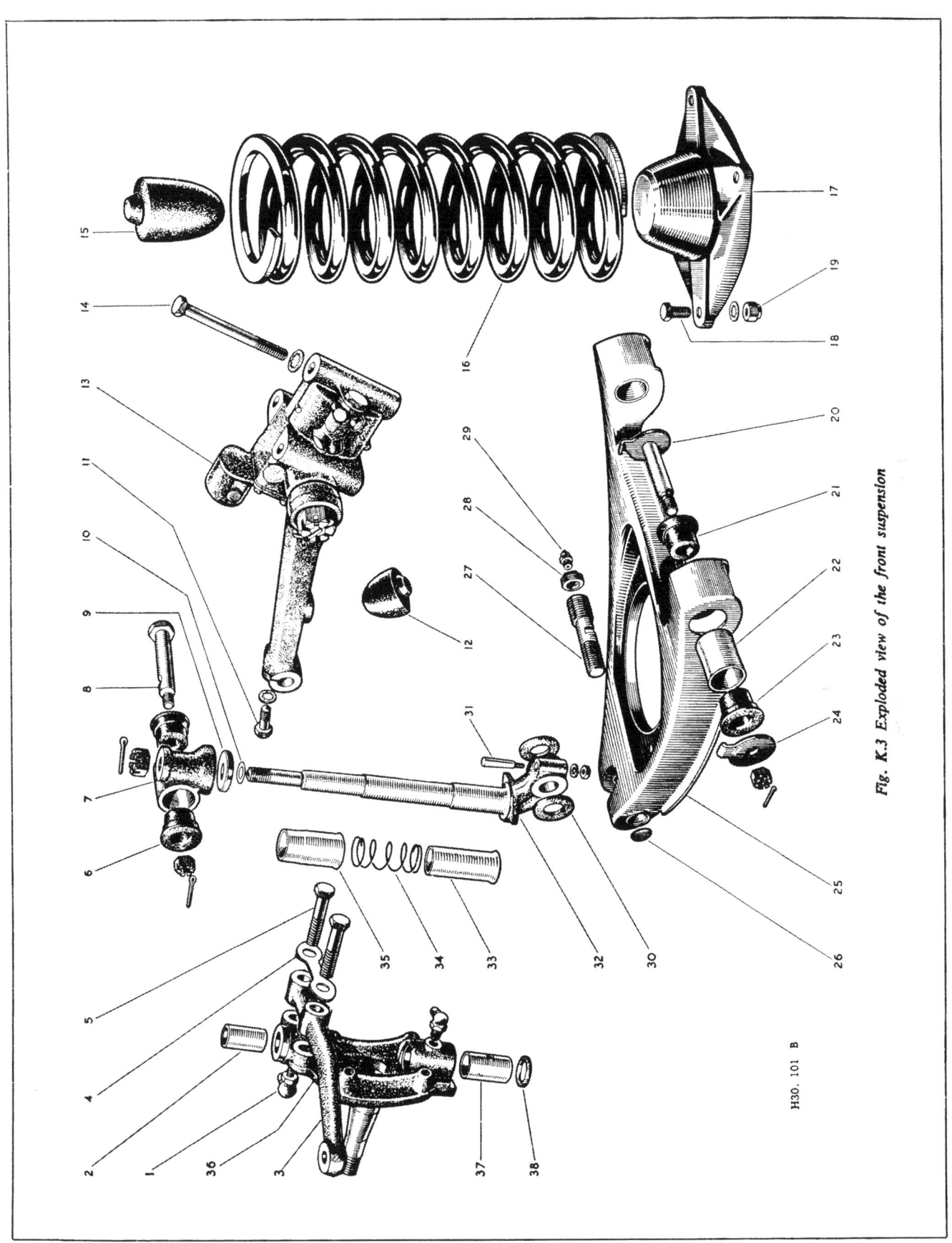

Fig. K.3 Exploded view of the front suspension

K FRONT SUSPENSION AND FRONT HUBS

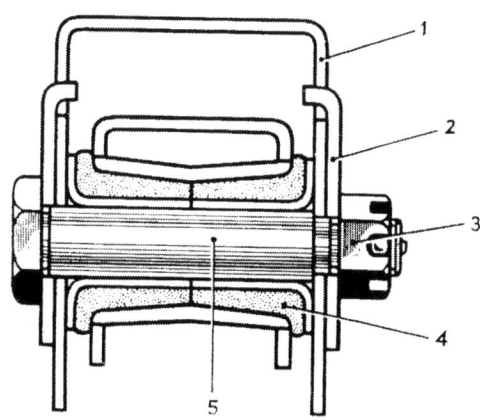

Fig. K.4. Lower link mounting (inner end).
1. Mounting bracket.   3. Castellated nut.
2. Special washer   4. Rubber bush (bearing).
                        5. Fulcrum pin.

(7) Slacken the nut on the cotter which is in the swivel pin lower trunnion and knock the cotter loose. Unscrew the nut, then remove the spring washer and cotter. Screw out the swivel pin lower trunnion oil nipple and its housing which also serves to plug the lower trunnion.

(8) Unscrew the swivel pin lower trunnion fulcrum pin, remove the swivel pin and cork sealing washers, and knock out the welch plug.

Section K.4
EXAMINATION FOR WEAR

Swivel Pin

(1) Carefully examine the swivel pin for wear by checking for ovality with a micrometer.

(2) If the pin does not show any appreciable wear renewal of the swivel bushes may effect a satisfactory cure.
The top bush should be flush with the top, and the lower bush flush with the bottom of their respective housings reamer the bushes with Service Tool 18G 155.
The two dust excluder tubes can easily be removed by telescoping them and lifting them out.

Lower Link Bushes

(1) If it is found that the fulcrum pin can be moved backwards or forwards in the lower links threads, they should be renewed.

(2) Try a new fulcrum pin and if excessive wear is still evident renew the bushes. The bushes are not renewable by themselves but only by fitting new lower links.

Damper

(1) The cross shaft bearings of the double acting hydraulic damper may have worn sufficiently to permit vertical or horizontal movement of the cross shaft. If such wear is apparent, renew the damper complete.

(2) The damper should also be carefully examined for any leaks and tested for effective damping. Damping can be tested by moving the damper arm up and down to the extremes of its stroke. Resistance should be felt throughout each stroke.

(3) If the resistance is erratic it may mean either that the fluid level is low or that there are air locks. To rectify, remove the filler plug and restore the fluid level to just below the filler plug opening, while the arm is moved up and down through several full strokes. If this treatment does not effect a cure the damper must be renewed as a complete unit.

Removing Worn Bushes

Place the swivel axle on the anvil of tool 18G 154 (larger diameter bush at the top), insert the drift and screw the adjusting plug up to the swivel axle to give it maximum support. Position the swivel axle and anvil on the table of a press and apply even pressure to remove both bushes.

Fitting and Broaching New Bushes

As the top and bottom bushes differ in internal diameter it is necessary to fit and broach one bush at a time.

Using the anvil of 18G 154, place the smaller guide bush (Code 3) flange downwards into the adjusting plug, replace the pad on top of the anvil (recess upwards) and hold the swivel axle in position for fitting the larger diameter bush. Carefully position the bush (lining up oil holes) and pass the drift through the bush, swivel axle and anvil until it locates in the large guide bush at the bottom of the anvil. **Note:** The bushes have a lead ground off at one end to enable them to easily enter their housings.

Use a press to apply a steady pressure on the drift; the new bush will then be pressed squarely into position.

This bush must now be broached; to do this, invert the swivel axle, position the larger bush support adaptor (Code 2) on the anvil of tool 18G 155, and hold the swivel axle in position so that the bush locates on the support adaptor. Insert the larger diameter broach through the small bush housing bore until it locates in the new bush. Now slide the smaller guide bush (Code 3) over the broach and position it in the small bush housing bore.

FRONT SUSPENSION AND FRONT HUBS

Check alignment and correct positioning of components before broaching by the application of a steady pressure on top of the broach.

The small bush must now be fitted using tool 18G154. Place the smaller guide bush (Code 3) flange upwards, into the adjusting plug in the anvil and hold the swivel axle in position with the broached bush at the top. Place the new bush in position and pass the drift through the bushes and swivel axle. When it has been determined that the oil holes are in line apply a steady pressure to the drift, until the bush is in position.

This bush must now be broached. With the small support adaptor (Code 4) in position on the anvil of 18G155, rest the swivel axle on the support adaptor with the bush to be broached lowermost.

Insert the smaller diameter broach from the top, so that it locates in the smaller diameter bush (at bottom), then pass the large guide bush (Code 1) over the bush until it locates in the larger diameter bush. Check that all components are in alignment and correctly positioned and press the broach through the bush.

Section K.5

FRONT SUSPENSION

To Reassemble

(1) File the lower link inner trunnion on both sides and see that the fulcrum pin is not tight in the threaded bushes or in the lower swivel pin trunnion.

(2) Position the two new cork rings one on the inside of each lower link outer screwed bush. Cover each cork ring with a thin flexible metal disc to protect the cork rings from being damaged when the swivel pin is inserted. Now slide the swivel pin between the two metal discs with its cotter hole towards the lower link inner bushes, and draw the discs out by gripping with a pair of pliers.

(3) Screw the fulcrum pin in from the end of the lower link with the larger threaded bore, until its slot is in line with the cotter hole in the swivel pin; knock in the cotter pin and secure it with its nut and spring washer. If there is difficulty in knocking the cotter pin home, it is an indication that the slot and cotter hole are not properly lined up.

(4) Screw the threaded plug into the larger bore of the lower link outer bush and an oil nipple into it. Put a welch plug in the other end and suitably punch its centre to firmly fix it. Test the leakproof properties of this welch plug by pumping oil through the oil nipple. If oil leaks through the welch plug it should be removed and a new one fitted.

(5) Slip a new chamfered cork sealing ring over the swivel pin, chamfered end down, and smear the swivel pin with oil. Fit the two dust excluders and their spring in the order in which they are shown in fig. K.3 to the swivel axle. Screw the two oil nipples into the swivel axle. Slide the swivel axle on to the swivel pin and ensure that full lock is obtained on both sides. Place the phosphor bronze thrust washer over the swivel axle. Put an ·008-in. shim (·008-in. (·2032 mm.) and ·012-in. (·3048 mm.) shims available) on to the swivel pin, followed by the trunnion with its bore towards the hub when it is fitted. Tighten the castellated nut. Resistance should be just felt when the swivel axle is moved from lock to lock and there should be no vertical movement of the swivel axle. Increase thickness of the shims to loosen and remove to tighten, depending on whether there it too much or too little thrust.

(6) Now fit the back plate assembly to the swivel axle. The flexible brake hose is to the rear and the bleeder nipple pointing to the front. The backplate is secured by four setscrews and shakeproof washers. Finally fit the hub, as explained in Section K.7, and the brake drums.

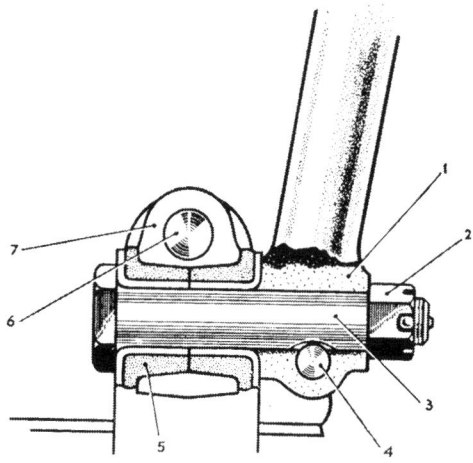

Fig. K.5. Trunnion link/damper arm assembly.

1. Damper arm.
2. Castellated nut.
3. Fulcrum pin.
4. Clamp bolt.
5. Rubber bush (bearing).
6. Swivel axle pin.
7. Trunnion link.

K FRONT SUSPENSION AND FRONT HUBS

To Replace

(1) Wet the spring rebound bumper and push it into its hole in the bottom of the damper mounting plate and the damper arm rebound buffer in the top.

(2) Wet two of the large rubber bearings and put one from inside each lower link. Lift the two arms into position, insert the fulcrum pin from the inner end so that its washer registers, position the two remaining rubber bearings from outside the lower links, locate the special washer, tighten the castellated nuts, insert and turn back the split pins.

(3) With the block still under the damper arm proceed to connect the top end.

Insert the two small rubber bearings in the upper trunnion eye, tap the fulcrum pin from the rear to go through the bearings and damper arm, and see that the notch in the fulcrum pin is to the top. Tighten the castellated nut till the notch is in line with the clamp bolt hole in the damper arm, split pin the castellated nut and tighten the clamp bolt on to its shakeproof washer.

(4) Replace the coil spring (section K.2) and wheel and lower the car.

(5) The block can now be removed from under the damper arm. Connect the flexible brake hose and bleed the brakes.

(6) Do not forget to check the caster and camber angles and swivel pin inclination. A Dunlop 'Wheel Camber, Castor and swivel pin Inclination Gauge' will be found useful.

Section K.6

CASTOR AND CAMBER ANGLES AND SWIVEL PIN INCLINATION

Description

The castor and camber angles and the swivel pin inclination are three design settings of the front suspension assembly. They have a very important bearing on the steering and general riding of the car. Each of these settings is determined by machining and assembly of the component parts during manufacture. They are not therefore adjustable.

However should the car suffer damage to the suspension affecting these settings, the various angles must be verified to ensure whether replacements are necessary.

Camber Angle

This is the outward tilt of the wheel and a rough check can be made by measuring the distance from the outside wall of the tyre immediately below the hub to a plumb line hanging from the outside wall of the tyre above the hub. The distance must be the same on both wheels. Before making this test it is very important to ensure that the tyres are in a uniform condition and at the same pressure. Also that the car is unladen and on level ground.

Damage to the upper and lower wishbone arms may well affect the camber angle.

Castor Angle

This is the tilt of the swivel pin when viewed from the side of the car. This also is only likely to be affected by damage to the upper and lower wishbone arms.

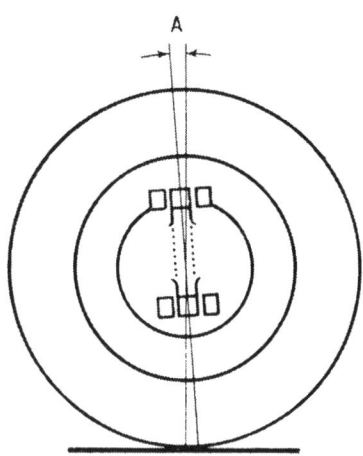 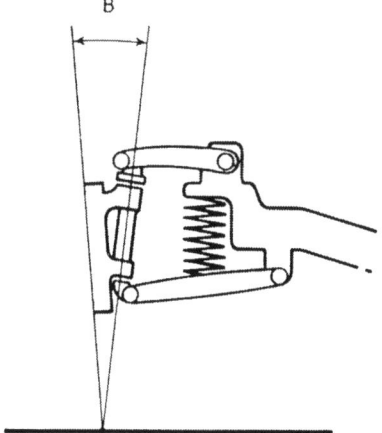 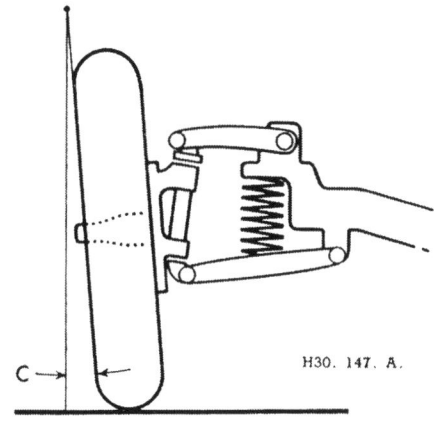

A. Castor angle—3°.
Fig. K.6.
B. Swivel pin inclination—6½°.
C. Camber angle 1°.

FRONT SUSPENSION AND FRONT HUBS   K

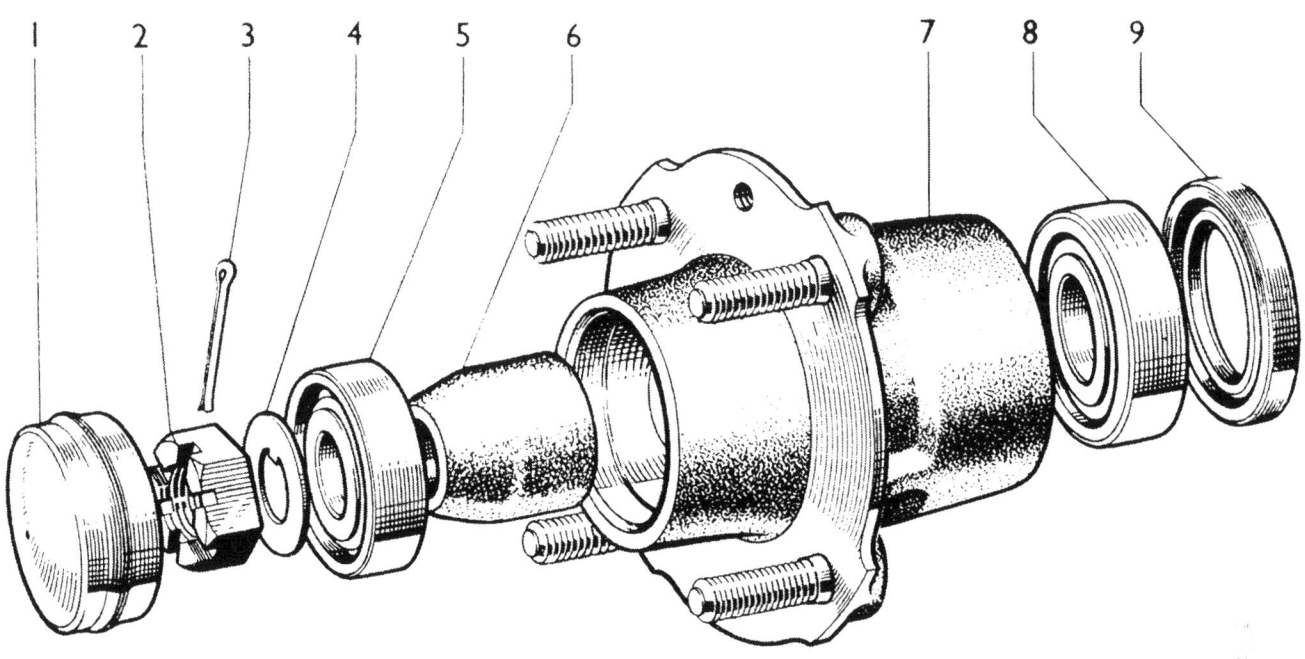

Fig. K.7. Front Hub Assembly.

1. Hub cap.
2. Castellated nut.
3. Split pin.
4. Locating washer.
5. Outer bearing.
6. Distance piece.
7. Hub.
8. Inner bearing.
9. Oil seal.

Swivel Pin Inclination

This is the tilt of the swivel pin when viewed from the front of the car and is again only likely to be affected by damage to the wishbone arms.

A useful service tool which can be used for checking these settings is the Dunlop 'Wheel Camber, Castor and Swivel Pin inclination Gauge'. Full details of this gauge can be obtained from the Dunlop Rubber Co. Ltd., Fort Dunlop, Erdington, Birmingham, England.

Section K.7

FRONT HUBS

To Check Wear

The inner and outer ball bearings of the front hub are non-adjustable, the amount of thrust on the bearings being determined by a distance piece. Wear in the bearings can be checked by jacking up the front of the car until the wheel on the hub in question is off the ground. Remove the wheel cap and hub cap, and rock the wheel in a horizontal plane. Movement between the wheel and hub as one unit and the swivel axle nut at the centre of the hub indicates wear in the hub bearings. A very positive movement indicates bearing renewal.

To Remove and Dismantle

(1) Jack up the car, remove the wheel cap and wheel. Release the screw in the counter-sunk hole and draw off the brake drum.

(2) Wipe away any excess grease, extract the split pin and release the castellated nut and washer Employ extractor 18G 146 to draw the complete hub assembly off the swivel axle.

(3) Should the inner bearing remain on the swivel axle it may be extracted by using Service Tool 18G 8P.

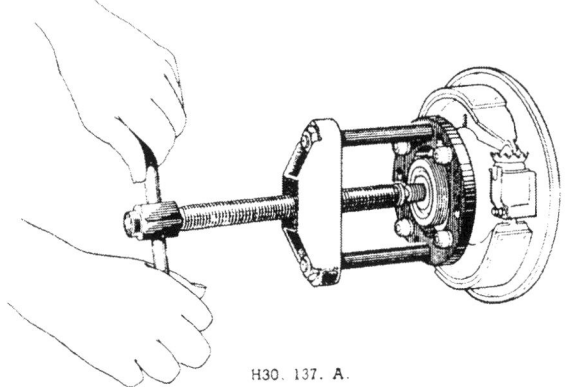

Fig. K.8.
Using Service Tool 18G 146 to extract a front hub.

K FRONT SUSPENSION AND FRONT HUBS

(4) With the hub removed, the outer bearing and distance piece can be taken out by inserting a drift through the inner bearing and carefully knocking the bearing clear of the hub. Similarly the inner bearing and oil seal can be detached by drifting them off from the other side of the hub.

To Assemble and Replace

(1) Press or drift in the outer bearing with the side marked 'thrust' towards the centre of the hub, using adaptor 18G 134B with Service Tool 18G 134.

(2) Turn the hub over, pack it with recommended grease and place the distance piece in position with its domed end towards the outer bearing.

(3) As before press or drift in the inner bearing with side marked 'thrust' towards the distance piece, using adaptor 18G 134C with Service Tool 18G 134. Then press in the oil seal with its lipped end towards the inner bearing. The oil seal should be renewed if damaged in any way.

(4) Replace the hub on the swivel axle; place the drift (Service Tool 18G 7) over the outer bearing so that the pressure is evenly distributed over the face of the bearing. Drift the hub into position until the inner race bears against the shoulder of the swivel axle. A good way of knowing when the hub is home is by listening for the change in tone when knocking the hub on. It is a good policy to place a pilot cap over the threaded end of the swivel axle to protect the thread and also to prevent the outer bearing inner race from striking the shoulder at the end of the threads.

(5) Place the pegged washer on the swivel axle so that its peg locates in the slot. Screw the castellated nut up to the flat washer.

(6) Put the brake drum on and tighten its securing screw in the countersunk hole. Tighten a pair of wheel nuts on diametrically opposite studs and see that the brake drum is quite free of the brake shoes.

(7) Tighten the castellated nut to the torque wrench loading given in 'GENERAL DATA' and align the slots with the split pin hole in the stub axle. **Never slacken back the nut to achieve alignment.** Rock the drum to check that play in the bearings has been taken out, and rotate it to ensure that the hub is correctly preloaded. Finally, lock the nut with a split pin.

(8) Charge the hub with grease, drift on the hub cap and wipe off any grease that exudes through the little hole at its centre.
Replace the wheel, wheel nuts, lower the car, tighten the wheel nuts, and position the wheel cap.

Section K.8

DAMPERS

General Description

The dampers are of the hydraulic double acting piston type. All the working parts are submerged in oil. They are carefully set before dispatch and cannot be adjusted without special equipment. Any attempt to dismantle them will seriously affect their operation and performance. Should adjustment or repair be necessary, they must be returned to their makers.

Maintenance

The maintenance of the hydraulic dampers should include a periodical examination of their anchorages to the body frame. The fixing bolts must be tightened as necessary (25 to 30 lb./ft.).

The cheese-headed screws securing the cover-plates must be kept fully tightened to prevent leakage of the fluid.

When checking the fluid level every 6,000 miles (10000 km.) all road dirt must be carefully cleared away from the vicinity of the filler plugs before the plugs are removed. This is most important as it is absolutely vital that no dirt or foreign matter should enter the operating chamber.

The correct fluid level is just below the filler plug threads.

The use of Armstrong Super (thin) Shock Absorber Oil is recommended. When this is not available any good quality mineral oil to Specification S.A.E. 20/20 W is acceptable. This alternative is not suitable for low temperature operation and is deficient in various other ways.

To Remove

Jack up the car and place stands under the body in safe positions. Remove the road wheel and place a jack beneath the outer end of the lower wishbone arm and raise it until the damper arm is clear of its rebound rubber.

Remove the damper arm clamp bolt and its shakeproof washer. Withdraw the split pin and release the castellated nut on the fulcrum pin (see Fig. K.5). Withdraw the fulcrum pin and retrieve the trunnion link rubber bushes.

Once the three securing bolts and their shakeproof washers have been removed the damper may be taken from the car.

NOTE.—The jack must be left in position under the suspension wishbone while the top link remains disconnected in order to keep the coil spring securely in position and to avoid straining the steering connections.

FRONT SUSPENSION AND FRONT HUBS **K**

To Replace

Replacement is a reversal of the above procedure, but attention must be given to the following points:

(1) The damper mounting bolts should not be tightened beyond a torque wrench loading of 30 lb. ft. Overtightening beyond this point will be detrimental to the performance of the damper.

(2) Before fitting the upper trunnion fulcrum pin, work the damper arm three or four times through its full travel to expel any air which may have found its way into the operating chamber.

(3) The metalastic fulcrum pin bushes **must** be renewed if softening of the rubber or side movement is evident.

Section K.9
LOWER LINK MOUNTINGS

On later chassis, from Car No. 11126, the lower link inner fulcrum pins are secured by Nyloc (self-locking) nuts which replace the castellated nuts and split pins formerly used. In the event of the lower links being removed from the frame, NEW Nyloc nuts must be used to secure the inner fulcrum pins upon re-assembly.

Section K.10 FAULT DIAGNOSIS

Symptom	No.	Possible Fault
(a) Wheel Wobble	1 2 3 4 5 6 7	Unbalanced wheels and tyres Slack steering connections Incorrect steering geometry Excessive play in steering gear Broken or weak front springs Worn hub bearings Loose or broken shackles
(b) Wander	1 2 3 4	Check 2, 3 and 4 in (a) Front suspension and rear axle mounting points out of alignment Uneven tyre pressures Uneven tyre wear Weak dampers or springs
(c) Heavy Steering	1 2 3 4 5 6	Check 3 in (a) Excessively low tyre pressures Insufficient lubricant in steering rack "Dry" steering connections Out of track Incorrectly adjusted steering gear Misaligned steering column
(d) Tyre Squeal		Check 3 in (a) Check 1 in (c)

Austin-Healey Sprite Mk. 1. Issue 5. 35471.

K FRONT SUSPENSION AND FRONT HUBS

SERVICE TOOLS

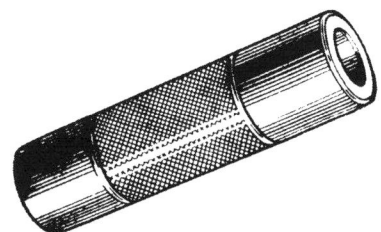

18G7

18G7. Front Hub Outer Bearing Remover

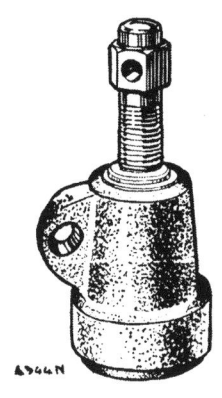

18G8

18G8. Hub Assembly Remover (basic tool)

Internally threaded for attachment to the hub and the end of the centre screw provided with a hardened steel ball to reduce friction when engaging the stub axle. Provision is also made for the use of a tommy bar to prevent the tool turning in operation.

Used on the Healey Sprite only in conjunction with adaptor 18G8P.

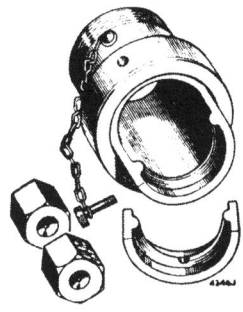

18G8P

18G8P. Front Hub Bearing Inner Race Remover Adaptor

Used with hub remover 18G8: a peg and chain is included to retain the locking ring and half-ring when not in use.

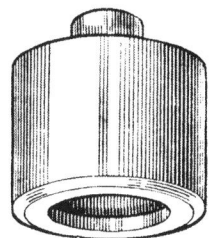

18G134B

18G134B. Front Hub Outer Bearing Replacer Adaptor

For use with 18G134.

FRONT SUSPENSION AND FRONT HUBS — K

SERVICE TOOLS

18G134. Bearing and Oil Seal Remover and Replacer (basic tool)

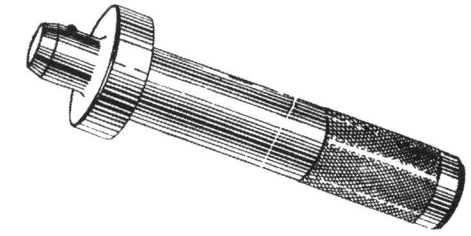

18G134

18G134C. Front Hub Inner Bearing Replacer Adaptor

For use with 18G134.

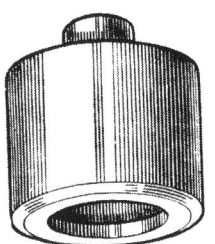

18G134C

18G146. Front and Rear Hub Remover

The thrust pad supplied with the tool is for use only when removing the rear hubs.

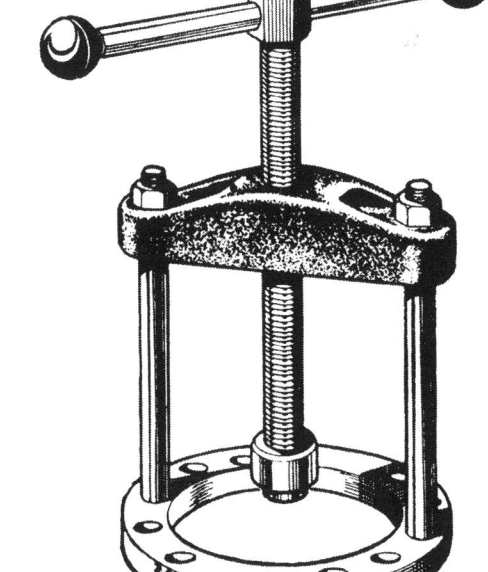

18G146

K — FRONT SUSPENSION AND FRONT HUBS

SERVICE TOOLS

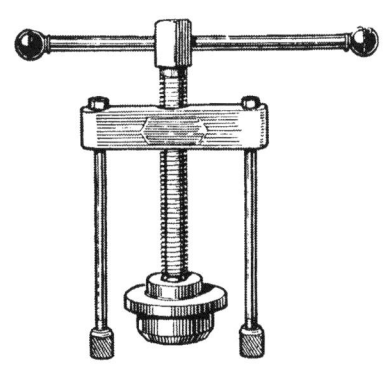

18G153

18G153. Front Suspension Spring Compressor

The spring compressor thrust pad is ball-mounted to assist in lining up the spring and spring seat.

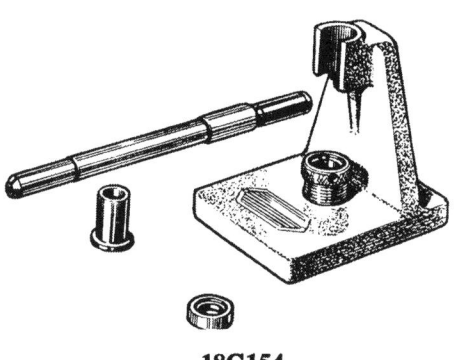

18G154

18G154. Swivel Axle Bush Remover and Replacer

This tool enables the swivel axle bushes to be removed and fitted without the distortion which would occur if an improvised drift were used. The shoulder of the driver is recessed to prevent the split bushes from opening when being pressed into position. The tool is designed for use with a press.

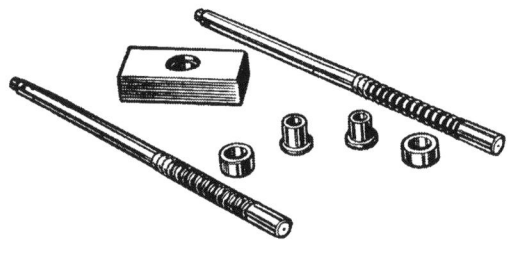

18G155

18G155. Swivel Axle Bush Broaching Equipment

Consisting of an anvil, two broaches, two guide bushes, and two support adaptors. They are for use with a light press, and will ensure highly finished bores. The worn bushes can be removed, and new bushes fitted with tool No. 18G154.

18G155A

18G155A. Swivel Axle Bush Broach Guide

For use with 18G155.

FRONT SUSPENSION AND FRONT HUBS **K**

SERVICE TOOLS

18G253. Front Suspension Assembly Fixture

Designed to serve the dual purpose of accurately assembling a front suspension unit for fitting as a replacement to a vehicle, and also as a means of checking a unit suspected of damage or misalignment.

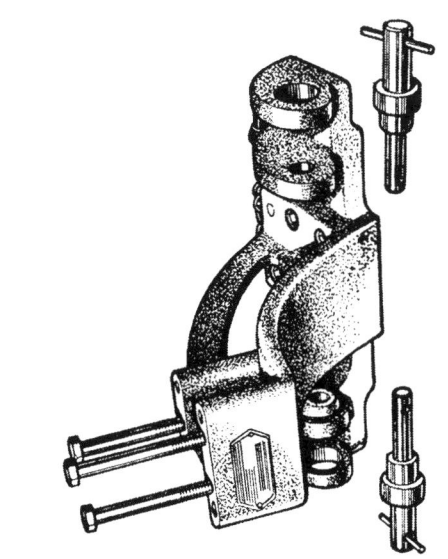

18G253

18G260. Front Hub Outer Race Remover (basic tool)

The outer race of a front hub bearing often remains inside the hub when dismantling. This remover with the appropriate adaptor will ensure easy extraction from the hub.

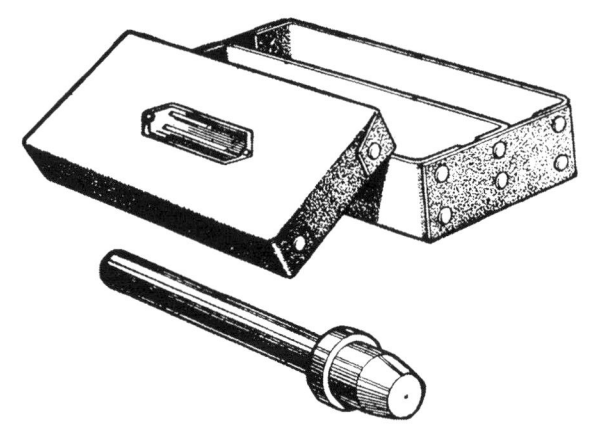

18G260

18G260A. Front-hub Outer Race Remover Adaptor

For use with 18G260 to remove the outer race of the outer bearing.

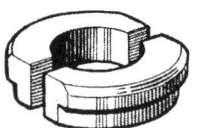

18G260A

18G260B. Front-hub Bearing Outer Race Remover Adaptor

For use with 18G260 to remove the outer race of the inner bearing

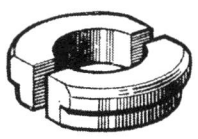

18G260B

Austin-Healey Sprite. Issue 1. 28894.

SECTION L

BRAKES

Section No. L.1.   Description.

Section No. L.2.   Front brake assemblies

Section No. L.3.   Rear brake assemblies

Section No. L.4.   Brake pedal

Section No. L.5.   Master cylinder

Section No. L.6.   Handbrake

Section No. L.7.   Maintenance

Section No. L.8.   Fault diagnosis

BRAKES

Section L.1

DESCRIPTION

The brakes on all four wheels are hydraulically operated by foot pedal application, directly coupled to a master cylinder in which the hydraulic pressure of the brake operating fluid is originated. A supply tank cast integrally with the master cylinder provides a reservoir by which the fluid is replenished, and a pipe line consisting of tube, flexible hose and unions, interconnect the master cylinder and the wheel cylinders.

The pressure generated in the master cylinder by application with the foot pedal is transmitted with equal and undiminished force to all wheel cylinders simultaneously. This moves the pistons outwards, which in turn expand the brake shoes thus producing automatic equalisation, and efficiency in direct proportion to the effort applied at the pedal.

When the pedal is released the brake shoe springs return the shoes which then return the wheel cylinder pistons, and therefore the fluid back into the pipe lines and master cylinder.

An independent mechanical linkage actuated by a handbrake, mounted alongside the propeller shaft tunnel, operates the rear wheels by mechanical expanders attached to the rear wheel cylinder bodies.

The front brakes are of the two leading shoe types with sliding shoes which ensure automatic centralisation of the brake shoe in operation.

The rear brakes are also fitted with sliding shoes, and incorporate the handbrake mechanism.

Front Brakes

The front brakes are operated by two wheel cylinders situated diametrically opposite each other on the inside of the backplate and interconnected by a bridge pipe on the outside.

Each cylinder operates one shoe only. A single piston in each cylinder acts on the leading tip of its respective shoe, while the trailing tip of the shoe finds a floating anchor by utilizing the closed end of the actuating cylinder of the other shoe as its abutment. Between the piston the leading tip of each shoe is a 'Micram' adjuster which is located in a slot in the shoe.

Each wheel cylinder (Fig. L.3.) consists of a casting containing a piston fitted with a cover and backed by a rubber cup. The space in front of the rubber cup is partially occupied by a cup filler which is loaded by a spring.

The brake shoes are held in position by two return springs.

The bleed screw is incorporated in the farthest brake cylinder from the master cylinder, being on a banjo connection at the back of the backplate. When the bleed screw is turned in an anti-clockwise direction a steel valve ball is released from its seat and hydraulic fluid escapes.

Rear Brakes

The rear brake shoes are not fixed but are allowed to slide and centralise with the same effect as in the front brakes. They are hydraulically operated by a single

Fig. L.2. The rear brake assembly.

acting wheel cylinder. The cylinder which is fitted in a slot in the rear backplate is free to slide in the slot between the tips of the brake shoes (which are of the leading and trailing type). The cylinder has a single piston operating on the tip of the leading shoe and this shoe butts against the fixed anchor block on the backplate, the web of the shoe being free to slide in a slot in the block. The trailing shoe is located in a similar way between the anchor block and the closed end of the hydraulic cylinder, and is free to slide and therefore self-centring, this shoe is operated by movement of the cylinder assembly as a result of the reaction of the leading shoe against the brake drum.

A 'Micram' adjuster is located in a slot in the tip of the leading shoe.

The wheel cylinder contains two pistons, the inner being hydraulically operated while the outer is

Fig. L.1. The front brake assembly.

BRAKES

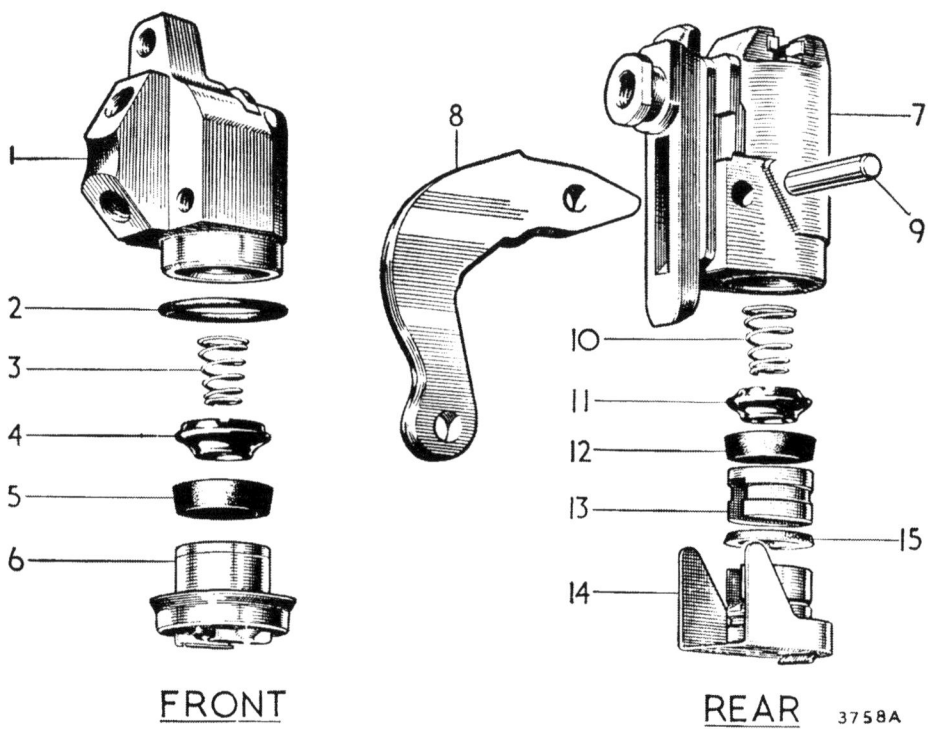

Fig. L.3. Components of the front and rear wheel cylinders.

1. Cylinder.
2. Sealing ring.
3. Spring.
4. Cup filler.
5. Piston cup.
6. Piston and dust cover.
7. Cylinder.
8. Hand-brake lever.
9. Pivot pin.
10. Spring.
11. Cup filler.
12. Piston cup.
13. Hydraulic piston.
14. Piston and dust cover.
15. Sealing ring.

manually operated by the handbrake lever. The inner piston is backed by a rubber cup and the space in front of the cup partially occupied by a cup filler which is loaded by a spring. When operated hydraulically, the inner piston butts against the outer piston leaving the handbrake lever undisturbed, and applies a thrust to the tip of the leading shoe through the dustcover, 'Micram' adjuster and mask. When operated manually, an inwards movement of the handbrake lever brings the heel of the lever into contact with the outer piston, thrusting it outwards against the leading shoe without disturbing the inner piston. A rubber boot is fitted to exclude foreign matter.

The brake shoes are held in position by two return springs.

Note: When refitting brake shoes the springs must lie between the brake shoes and the backplate, this also applies to the front brake shoes.

The rear brake shoes are located relative to the backplate by two steady springs.

Section L.2

FRONT BRAKE ASSEMBLIES

To Remove
(1) Disconnect the hydraulic pipe from the master cylinder at the backplate.
(2) Remove the front brake backplate from the front suspension as described in Section K.

To Dismantle
(1) Pull one of the brake shoes against the load of the return springs, away from the abutment on the closed end of the adjacent cylinder and slide the 'Micram' mask off the piston cover of the operating cylinder; on releasing the tension of the return springs the opposite brake shoe will fall away.
(2) Disconnect the bridge pipe between the two brake cylinders complete with the banjo adaptors.
(3) Unscrew the nuts and withdraw the brake cylinders from the backplate.
(4) To dismantle a brake cylinder withdraw the piston complete with the piston cover from the cylinder

BRAKES

and apply a gentle air pressure to the fluid connection to blow out the rubber cup, and cup filler.

Examination for Wear

Examine the rubber cups for wear perishing and swelling, and renew were necessary.

Any rust on the cylinder bore or piston must be removed or this will eventually cause a seizure of the piston. If the cup filler is fractured it must be renewed. Clean all the components with Lockheed brake fluid.

To Reassemble

(1) Fit the smaller end of the coil spring over the projection in the cup filler.
(2) Place the assembly in the cylinder, spring foremost, followed by the cup, lip foremost, and the piston. Take care not to damage or turn back the lip of the cup when entering the cylinder bore.

To Replace

The replacement is a reversal of the procedure 'To Remove'.

Before replacing the brake shoes examine them for excessive wearing or glazing. Brake linings may be removed, or complete exchange brake shoes are available.

Section L.3
REAR BRAKE ASSEMBLIES

To Remove

(1) Disconnect the hydraulic pipe from the master cylinder at the backplate.
(2) Disconnect the rod from the hand brake lever at the backplate.
(3) Remove the rear brake backplate from the back axle.

To Dismantle

(1) Pull the trailing shoe against the load of the return springs and away from its abutment at either end. On releasing the tension of the return springs the leading shoe will fall away. Collect the 'Micram' adjuster and mask.
(2) Unscrew the banjo bolt securing the banjo adaptor to the wheel cylinder and remove the rubber boot.

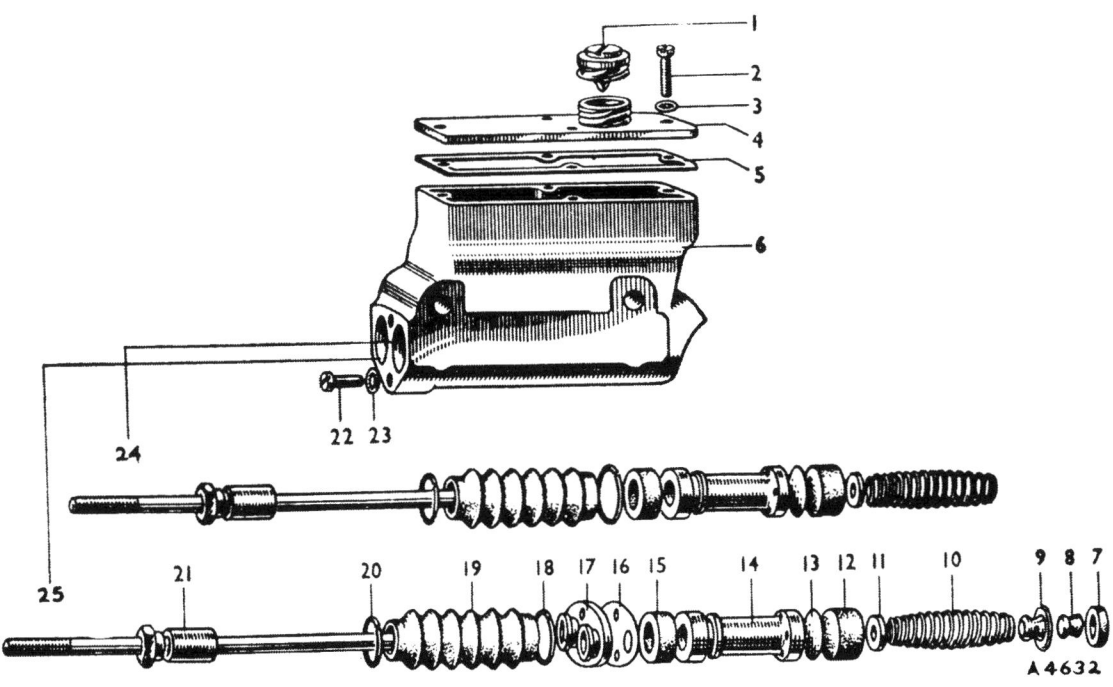

Fig. L.4. The master cylinder exploded.

1. Filler cap.
2. Fixing screw.
3. Shakeproof washer.
4. Tank cover.
5. Tank cover gasket.
6. Cylinder barrel and tank.
7. Valve washer.
8. Valve cup.
9. Valve body.
10. Return spring.
11. Spring retainer.
12. Main cup.
13. Piston washer.
14. Piston.
15. Secondary cup.
16. Gasket.
17. Boot fixing plate.
18. Boot clip.
19. Boot.
20. Boot clip.
21. Push rod.
22. Fixing screw.
23. Shakeproof washer.
24. Clutch bore.
25. Brake bore.

L BRAKES

(3) Remove the wheel cylinder piston, swing the handbrake lever until the shoulder is clear of the backplate and slide the cylinder casting forward Pivot the cylinder about its forward end and withdraw the rear end from the slot in the backplate, a rearward movement of the cylinder will now bring its forward end clear of the backplate.

(4) Withdraw the piston complete with cover from the cylinder. Remove the handbrake pivot pin and lever. Apply a gentle air pressure to the fluid connection and blow out the hydraulic piston, rubber cup, and cup filler.

To Reassemble

(1) Fit the spring in the cup filler and insert the parts, spring leading, into the bore followed by the rubber cup, lip foremost, taking care not to damage or turn back the lip of the cup.

(2) Insert the hydraulic piston ensuring that the slot in the piston coincides with the lever slot in the cylinder casting.

(3) Place the handbrake lever in position and fit the pivot pin. Insert the handbrake piston complete with dust cover, ensuring that the lever is engaged in the slot in the piston.

(4) Offer up the wheel cylinder to the backplate with the handbrake lever through the slot, and the piston pointing in the direction of forward rotation of the wheel. Engage the forward end of the cylinder in the slot and slide it well forward, taking care to position the lever so that its shoulder clears the backplate. Engage the rear end of the cylinder in the slot and slide it back to hold it in position.

(5) Fit the rubber boot. Mount the banjo connection on the cylinder and, using a new copper washer fit the banjo bolt.

(6) Assemble the brake shoes, ensuring that the 'Micram' adjuster is in the slot in the leading shoe with the mask in position, and that the return springs lie between the brake shoes and the backplate. It should be noted that the unlined end of the leading shoe is to be nearest to the brake cylinder, whilst the unlined end of the trailing shoe is to be nearest the abutment block.

(7) Reassemble the backplate to the back axle. Ensure that all the adjustment is backed-off, fit the brake drum and the road wheel, connect the handbrake pull-rod and hydraulic pipe, 'bleed' and adjust the brakes.

Section L.4
BRAKE PEDAL

To Remove

(1) Working under the bonnet disconnect the pedal from the master cylinder by removing the clevis pin anchoring the master cylinder push-rod to the brake pedal.

(2) Working within the car unscrew the nut securing the brake and clutch pedal shaft, and withdraw the shaft to release the brake and clutch pedals and their distance piece.

(3) Withdraw the brake pedal downwards out of the car.

(4) Inspect the lever bush for wear and renew if necessary.

To Adjust

The correct amount of free movement between the master cylinder push-rod and the piston is set during erection of the vehicle and should never need alteration.

In the event of the adjustment having been disturbed, reset the effective length of the rod connecting the piston to the pedal until the pedal pad can be depressed approximately $\frac{5}{32}$ in. (4 mm.) before the piston begins to move. The clearance can be felt if the pedal is depressed by hand. It is very important that the push-rod should have a minimum free movement of $\frac{1}{32}$ in. (·8 mm.) before the piston starts to move.

Section L.5
MASTER CYLINDER

Description

The master cylinder caters for operation of both brake and clutch. It has two bores which are side by side and, except for the fact that one has no check valve, each bore accommodates normal master cylinder parts. The bore with the check valve serves the brakes, the other serves the clutch slave cylinder.

Dismantling the Brake Cylinder

(1) Unscrew the set screws securing the boot fixing plate to the master cylinder body.

(2) Detach the fixing plate from the master cylinder leaving the boots and push rods attached to the clutch and brake pedals.

(3) Unscrew the common filler cap and drain the fluid into a clean container.

(4) Withdraw the piston (14) Fig. L.4, piston washer (13), main cup (12) and return spring (10), valve body (9) complete with rubber cup (8) and rubber washer (7).

(5) Using only the fingers to prevent damage, remove the secondary cup (15) by stretching it over the end flange of the piston.

BRAKES

(6) Examine all parts, especially the washers, for wear or distortion, and replace with new parts where necessary.

Assembling the Brake Cylinder

(1) Fit the secondary cup (15) on the piston (14), so that the lip of the cup faces the piston head and gently work the cup round the groove with the fingers to ensure that it is properly seated.

(2) Place the rubber washer (7) in position in the bottom of the cylinder bore. Fit the rubber cup (8) in the valve body (9) and assemble the body on the larger end of the return spring (10).

(3) Assemble the retainer (11) on the smaller end of the return spring and insert the assembly into the cylinder.

(4) Install the main cup (12) into the cylinder, lip foremost, taking care not to damage or turn back the lip of the cup.

(5) Follow up with the piston washer, pay particular attention to the illustration showing method of assembly.

(6) Press the piston (14) into the cylinder taking care not to damage or turn back the lip of the secondary cup (15).

(7) Insert the push rod in the piston and manoeuvre the boot fixing plate into position. Secure the plate by its two set screws and then ascertain that the rubber boots are seating correctly. The vent holes in each boot should be at the bottom where the cylinder is mounted on the vehicle.

If the boots are damaged or perished, new ones should be fitted.

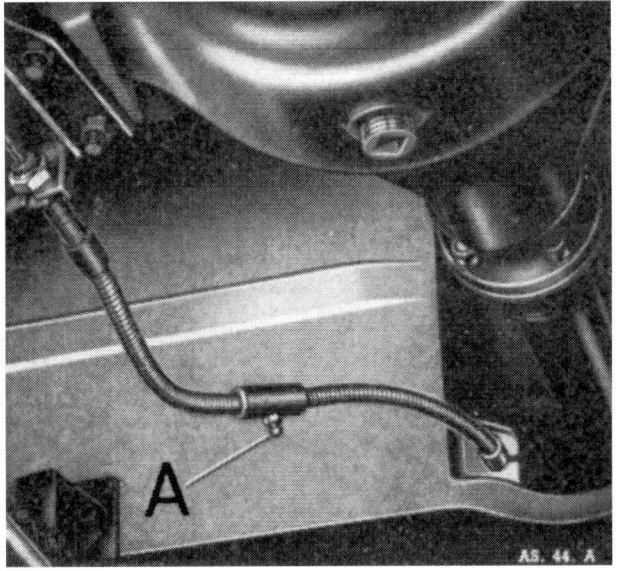

Fig. L.6. The handbrake rear cable lubricator (A).

(8) Fill the reservoir with clean Lockheed brake fluid and test the brake cylinder by pushing the piston inwards and allowing it to return unassisted. After a few applications, fluid should flow from the outlet connection in the cylinder barrel.

Replacement.

The installation of the master cylinder is the reversal of the removal procedure.

If no further maintenance of the brake is necessary remember to bleed the system.

Section L.6

HANDBRAKE

The handbrake operates on the rear wheels only and is applied by a pull-up type of lever situated on the side of the propeller shaft tunnel. The Bowden cable from the control is attached to the compensator mounted on the rear axle. From compensator to the brake levers are transverse rods which are non-adjustable.

The handbrake linkage is set when leaving the works and should not require any attention. Only when a complete overhaul is necessary should the handbrake linkage require re-setting.

To adjust the handbrake, the rear shoes should be locked to the drums, the handbrake control just slightly applied, and the cable slackness just removed, by means of adjusting the sleeve nut at the rear of the Bowden cable (Fig. L.5).

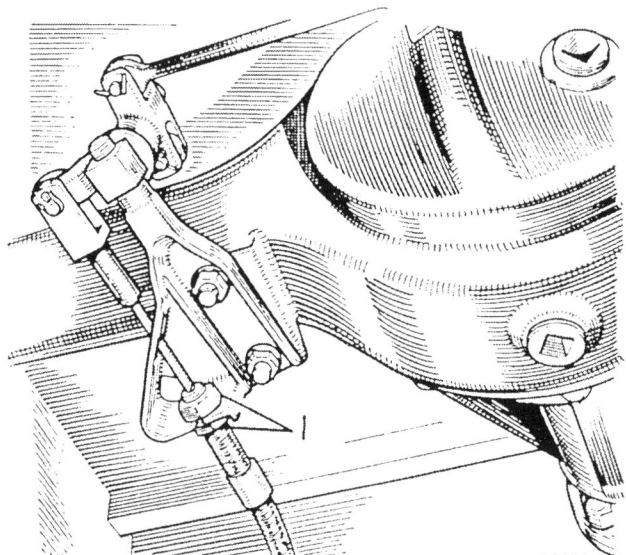

Fig. L.5. Shows location of handbrake cable adjustment (1) on the rear axle.

Austin-Healey Sprite Mk. 1. Issue 4. 50312

L

BRAKES

Fig. L.7. *Illustrating a rear brake bleed nipple.*

The handbrake mechanism is lubricated by two grease nipples, one on the compensating mechanism and the other on the Bowden cable.

Section L.7

MAINTENANCE

Replenishment of Hydraulic Fluid

Inspect the supply tank at regular intervals and ascertain that the fluid level is ¼ in. (6·35 mm.) below the bottom of the filler plug threads.

Fig. L.8. *Showing front brake drum with one of the brake shoe adjusters 'A'.*

Great care should be exercised when adding brake fluid, to prevent dirt or foreign matter entering the system.

Important: Serious consequences may result from the use of incorrect fluids, and **Lockheed Super Heavy Duty Brake Fluid** or a fluid conforming to specification S.A.E. 70 R.3 must be used. This fluid has been specially prepared and unaffected by high temperature or freezing.

Bleeding the Hydraulic System

Bleeding is necessary any time a portion of the hydraulic system has been disconnected, or if the level of the brake fluid has been allowed to fall so low that air has entered the master cylinder.

Fig. L.9. *Showing rear brake shoe adjusters 'A'.*

With all the hydraulic connections secure and the supply tank topped up with the fluid, remove the rubber cap from the rear bleed nipple which is farthest away from the master cylinder and fit the bleed tube over the bleed nipple, immersing the free end of the tube in a clean jar containing a little brake fluid.

Unscrew the bleed nipple about three-quarters of a turn and then operate the brake pedal with a slow full stroke until the fluid entering the jar is completely free of air bubbles. Then, during a down stroke of the brake pedal, tighten the bleed screw sufficiently to seat the ball, remove bleed tube and replace the bleed nipple dust cap. **Under no circumstances must excessive force be used when tightening the bleed screws.**

This process must now be repeated for each bleed screw at each of the three remaining backplates, finishing at the wheel nearest the master cylinder. Always keep a careful check on the supply tank during bleeding,

BRAKES

since it is most important that a full level is maintained. Should air reach the master cylinder from the supply tank, the whole of the bleeding operation must be repeated.

After bleeding, top up the supply tank to its correct level.

Never use fluid that has just been bled from a brake system for topping up the supply tank, as this brake fluid may be to some extent aerated. Such fluid must be allowed to stand for at **least** twenty-four hours before it is used again. This will allow the air bubbles in the fluid time to disperse.

Great cleanliness is essential when dealing with any part of the hydraulic system, and especially so where the brake fluid is concerned. Dirty fluid must never be added to the system

Note: It is advisable to turn all the brake shoe adjusters to their full 'off' position before bleeding. After bleeding adjust brakes as described below.

Adjusting the Brake Shoes

The brakes are adjusted for lining wear, **only** at the brakes themselves, and on no account should any alteration be made to the handbrake cable.

Front Brakes. A separate 'Micram' adjuster is provided for each shoe. Jack up the car until the wheel concerned is clear of the ground. Remove the wheel disc, and rubber dust plug from the adjusting hole. Rotate the wheel until the adjusting hole comes opposite one of the adjusters (located at 8 and 2 o'clock). Using a screwdriver turn the adjuster in a clockwise direction until the brake shoe is in contact with the brake drum, then turn the adjuster back one notch, this should provide correct clearance between the shoe and the drum. If closer adjustment is required spin the drum and apply the brakes hard, this will correctly position the shoe after which a further adjustment check should be made. Repeat these operations on the second adjuster. Adjust the other wheel cylinders in similar manner.

Rear Brakes. Place chocks under one of the front wheels and release the handbrake. Proceed as for the front brake adjustment but noting that there is only one wheel adjuster to adjust each rear wheel, and that it may be necessary to back off two notches to provide adequate clearance for the two shoes.

Section L.8   FAULT DIAGNOSIS

Symptom	No.	Possible Fault
(a) Spongy Pedal (loss of fluid pressure)	1 2 3 4 5	Leak in system Master cylinder plunger worn Wheel cylinder leaking Air in system Lining not "down" on shoe
(b) Excessive Pedal Depression	1 2 3	In (a) check 1 and 4 Excessive lining wear Extremely low brake fluid level Too much pedal free movement
(c) Brakes Grab or Pull to Side	1 2 3 4 5 6 7 8 9 10	Brake backplate loose on axle Scored, cracked or distorted drum High spots on drum Incorrect shoe adjustment Oily or wet linings Rear axle or front suspension anchorage loose Worn or loose rear spring anchorage Worn steering connections Different grade or types of lining fitted Uneven tyre pressures

Austin-Healey Sprite Mk. 1. Issue 2. 35471.

BRAKES

Symptom	No.	Possible Fault
(d) Dragging Brakes	1 2 3 4 5 6 7	In (c), check 3 Wheel cylinder piston seized Weak or broken brake shoe return springs Master cylinder by-pass port restricted Too little pedal free movement Handbrake mechanism seized Supply tank overfilled Filler cap air vent choked
(e) Springy Pedal	1 2 3	Lining not 'bedded-in' Brake drums weak or cracked Master cylinder fixing loose
(f) Brakes Inefficient	1	In (c), check 4 In (d), check 7 Incorrect type of linings fitted

SECTION M

ELECTRICAL SYSTEM

Section No. M.1	General description
Section No. M.2	Battery
Section No. M.3	Preparing 'dry charged' batteries for service
Section No. M.4	Preparing new unfilled, uncharged batteries for service
Section No. M.5	Generator
Section No. M.6	Maintenance
Section No. M.7	Testing in position to locate fault in charging circuit
Section No. M.8	Generator assembly
Section No. M.9	Inspection and overhaul
Section No. M.10	Assembling and replacing
Section No. M.11	The starter
Section No. M.12	Servicing the starter
Section No. M.13	Control box
Section No. M.14	Fuse unit
Section No. M.15	Flasher unit
Section No. M.16	Windscreen wipers
Section No. M.17	Ignition switch
Section No. M.18	Direction indicator warning lamp
Section No. M.19	Panel light bulbs
Section No. M.20	Headlamp main beam warning light bulb
Section No. M.21	Ignition warning light bulb
Section No. M.22	Fuel gauge
Section No. M.23	Panel lamps switch
Section No. M.24	Windscreen wiper switch
Section No. M.25	Starter switch
Section No. M.26	Horn-push
Section No. M.27	Horn
Section No. M.28	Headlamp dipping switch
Section No. M.29	Headlamp bulbs
Section No. M.30	Modified European light unit
Section No. M.31	Sealed beam light units
Section No. M.32	Headlamp beam setting
Section No. M.33	Replacing a light unit
Section No. M.34	Modified sealed beam light units
Section No. M.35	Combined side and flasher lights bulb
Section No. M.36	Rear flasher light bulb
Section No. M.37	Combined stop and tail light bulb
Section No. M.38	Rear number plate light bulb
Section No. M.39	Fault diagnosis

ELECTRICAL SYSTEM M

Section M.1

GENERAL DESCRIPTION

The 12-volt electrical equipment incorporates compensated voltage control for the charging circuit. The positive earth system of wiring is employed.

Battery details may be found in **'General Data'**.

The generator is mounted on the right of the cylinder block and driven by an endless belt from the crankshaft pulley. A rotatable mounting enables the belt tension to be adjusted.

The voltage control unit adjustment is sealed and should not normally require attention. The fuses are carried in external holders mounted in an accessible position on the right-hand side of the engine compartment together with spare fuses.

The starter motor is mounted on the flywheel housing on the right-hand side of the engine unit and operates on the flywheel through the usual sliding pinion device.

The headlamps employ the double-filament dipping system. Both lamps are fitted with double-filament bulbs, both dipping according to the regulations existing in the countries concerned.

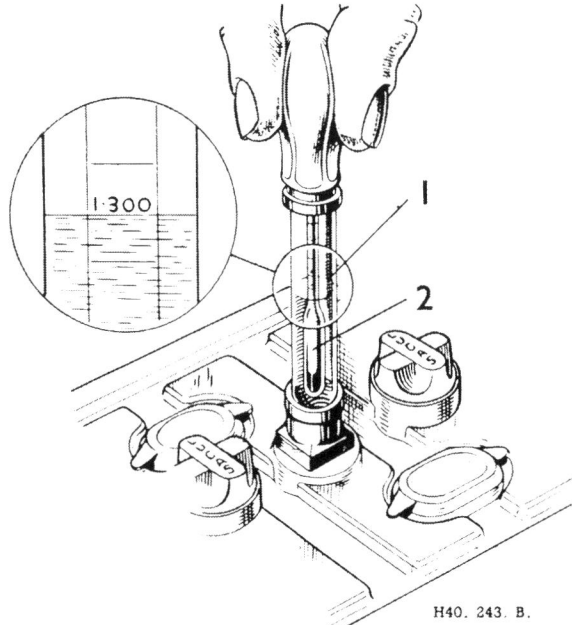

Fig. M.1. Using a hydrometer to test the specific gravity of the battery acid.
1. Reading.   2. Float.

Section M.2

BATTERY

Description

The battery is a 12-volt lead-acid type, having six cells, each cell consisting of a group of positive and negative plates immersed is a solution of sulphuric acid (electrolyte).

The battery has three functions:
(1) To supply current for starting, ignition and lighting.
(2) To provide a constant supply of current to the electrical equipment under normal operating conditions and when the consumption of the electrical equipment exceeds the output of the generator.
(3) To control the voltage of the electrical supply system.

Adjustments in the Vehicle

The purpose of the following operations is to maintain the performance of the battery at its maximum.
(1) The battery and its surrounding parts should be kept dry and clean, particularly the tops of the cells as any dampness could cause a leakage between the securing strap and the battery negative terminal, resulting in a partially discharged battery. Clean off any corrosion from the battery bolts, strap and tray with diluted ammonia, afterwards painting the affected parts with anti-sulphuric paint.
(2) Remove the vent plugs and check they are not perished or cracked, otherwise leakage of electrolyte will occur. Clean out the vent holes if necessary with a piece of wire.
(3) The electrolyte levels should be maintained just above the tops of the separators by adding distilled water. Never add acid.
(4) Check the terminal posts. If they are corroded remove the cables and clean with diluted ammonia. Smear the posts with petroleum jelly before remaking the connections and ensure that the cable terminal clamp screws are secure.
(5) Test the condition of the battery cells by using a hydrometer (see Fig. M.1.).

The specific gravity readings and their indications are as follows:

Climates below 90° F. (32° C.)
1·270 to 1·290   Cell fully charged.
1·190 to 1·210   Cell about half discharged.
1·110 to 1·130   Cell fully discharged.

Climates frequently above 90° F. (32° C.)
1·210 to 1·230   Cell fully charged.
1·130 to 1·150   Cell about half discharged.
1·050 to 1·070   Cell fully discharged.

These figures are given assuming an electrolyte temperature of 60° F. (16° C.). If the temperature of the electrolyte exceeds this, ·002 must be added to hydro-

Austin-Healey Sprite. Issue 2. 21424.

M ELECTRICAL SYSTEM

meter readings for each 5° F. rise to give the true specific gravity. Similarly ·002 must be subtracted from hydrometer readings for every 5° F. below 60° F.

To Remove

(1) Raise the bonnet to gain access to the battery.
(2) Disconnect both cables from the battery.
(3) Release the battery clamp and lift out the battery.

To View

(1) Place the battery on a lead-covered bench or on a wooden bench treated with anti-sulphuric paint.
(2) Check the electrolyte levels.
(3) Inspect the container for cracks which may be indicated by external corrosion or extreme variation in the electrolyte levels. A cracked container must be renewed.
(4) Test the condition of the battery cells by using a hydrometer (see Fig. M.1).
All readings should be uniform. The hydrometer values given indicate the state of charge of the battery.
(5) If the electolyte level is below the tops of the separators, it will not be possible to withdraw a sufficient amount to raise the hydrometer float. In such circumstances a high-rate discharge tester should be used.
Note: The use of a discharge tester is not recommended for normal testing, but only where a hydrometer reading cannot be obtained due to an excessively low electrolyte level.

Charging from an External Source

The length of time for a used battery to remain on charge before it can be accepted as fully charged depends entirely on the specific gravity before charging commences and the charging rate. The charging should continue until all cells are gassing freely and evenly and the specific gravity in each of the six cells has reached a maximum, i.e. has shown no further rise in four hours. The specific gravity at the end of charging should be within the limits given and should not vary more than ·005 from these values.

Do not allow the temperature of the electrolyte to exceed the maximum permissible temperature, i.e. 100°F (38°C) in climates ordinarily below 90°F (32°C), 120°F (49°C) in climates frequently above 90°F (32°C). If this temperature is reached the charge should be suspended to allow the temperature to fall at least 10° otherwise the life of the battery will tend to be shortened.

To Install

The installation of the battery is a reversal of the procedure 'To remove'. Smear the terminal posts and cable connections with petroleum jelly and tighten the terminal screws sufficiently to prevent the cables from moving on the terminal posts when tested by hand.

Section M.3

PREPARING 'DRY-CHARGED' BATTERIES FOR SERVICE

'Dry-charged' batteries are supplied without electrolyte but with the plates in a charged condition. When they are required for service it is only necessary to fill each cell with sulphuric acid of the correct specific gravity. No initial charging is required. This procedure ensures that there is no deterioration of the efficiency of the battery during the storage period before the battery is required for use.

In these batteries porous rubber is used for the separators between the plates.

Preparation of Electrolyte

Electrolyte is prepared by mixing distilled water and concentrated acid, usually of 1·835 S.G. The mixing must be carried out either in a lead lined tank or in suitable glass or earthenware vessels. Slowly add the acid to the water, stirring with a glass rod. **Never add the water to the acid,** as the resulting chemical reaction causes violent and dangerous spurting of the concentrated acid.

The specific gravity of the filling electrolyte depends on the climate in which the battery is to be used.

The approximate proportions of acid and water are indicated in the following table:

To obtain specific gravity (corrected to 60°F) of	Add 1 vol. of acid 1·835 S.G (corrected to 60°F) to
Climates below 90°F 1·27	2·8 volumes of water
Climates above 90°F 1·21	4·0 volumes of water

Heat is produced by mixing acid and water, and the electrolyte should be allowed to cool before taking hydrometer readings—unless a thermometer is used to measure the actual temperature, and a correction applied to the readings as described in Section M.2. To avoid damage to the battery the electrolyte must be cool before filling-in is commenced.

The total volume of electrolyte required can be estimated from the figures quoted under **'General Data'**.

Filling the Battery

Carefully break the seals in the cell filling holes and fill each cell with electrolyte to the top of the separators, **in one operation.** The temperature of the filling room,

ELECTRICAL SYSTEM

M

battery and electrolyte, should be maintained between 60° and 100°F (15·6° and 37·8°C). If the battery has been stored in a cool place it should be allowed to warm up to room temperature before filling.

Putting into Use

Batteries filled in this way are 90 per cent charged and capable of giving a starting discharge **one hour after filling**. When time permits, however, a freshening charge will ensure the battery is fully charged. Such a freshening charge should last for no more than 4 hours, at the normal recharge rate of the battery (see '**General Data**').

During the charge the electrolyte must be kept level with the top edge of the separators by addition of distilled water. Check the specific gravity of the acid at the the end of the charge; if 1·27 acid was used to fill the battery, the specific gravity should now be between 1·27 and 1·29; if 1·21, between 1·21 and 1·23. After filling, a dry-charged battery needs only the attention normally given to a lead-acid battery.

Section M.4

PREPARING NEW UNFILLED, UNCHARGED BATTERIES FOR SERVICE

Preparation of Electrolyte

Batteries having dry separators are used. The specific gravity of the filling-in solution should, therefore, be the same as that required at the end of the charge (i.e. their electrolyte requirements are the same as those of 'dry-charged' batteries).

For the precautions to be taken when preparing the electrolyte, the quantity of electrolyte required, and the proportions of acid and water necessary for different ranges of climatic temperature see 'Preparation of Electrolyte' in Section M.3.

Batteries should not be filled with acid until required for initial charging.

Filling the Battery

The temperature of the acid, battery and filling room must not be below 32°F (0°C).

Carefully break the seals in the filling holes and **half-fill** each cell with electrolyte of the appropriate specific gravity. Allow the battery to stand for at least six hours, in order to dissipate the heat generated by the chemical action of the acid on the plates and separators, and then add sufficient electrolyte to fill each cell to the top of the separators. Allow to stand for a further two hours and then proceed with the initial charge.

Initial Charge

The initial charging rate is given under '**General Data**'. Charged at this rate until the voltage and specific gravity readings show no increase over five successive hourly readings. This will take from 40 to 80 hours, depending on the length of time the battery has been stored before charging.

Keep the current constant by varying the series resistance of the circuit or the generator output. **This charge should not be broken by long rest periods.** If however the temperature of any cell rises above the permissible maximum quoted in Section M.2 the charge must be interrupted until the temperature has fallen at least 10°F (5·5°C) below that figure. Throughout the charge, the electrolyte must be kept level with the top of the separators by addition of acid solution of the same specific gravity as the original filling-in acid, until specific gravity and charge readings have remained constant for five successive hourly readings. If the charge is continued beyond that point, top-up with distilled water.

At the end of the charge carefully check the specific gravity in each cell to ensure that, when corrected to 60°F (15·6°C) it lies between the specified limits. If any cell requires adjustment some of the electrolyte must be siphoned off and replaced either by distilled water or by acid of strength originally used for filling-in, depending on whether the specific gravity is too high or too low. Continue the charge for an hour or so to ensure adequate mixing of the electrolyte and again check the specific gravity readings. If necessary repeat the adjustment process until the desired reading is obtained in each cell. Finally allow the battery to cool, and siphon off any electrolyte over the tops of the separators.

Section M.5

GENERATOR

Description

The generator is a shunt wound two-pole, two-brush machine, arranged to work in conjunction with a compensated voltage control regulator unit. A fan integral with the driving pulley draws cooling air through the generator, inlet and outlet holes being provided in the end brackets of the unit.

The output of the generator is controlled by the regulator and is dependent on the state of charge of the battery and the loading of the electrical equipment in use. When the battery is in a low state of charge the generator gives a high output, whereas if the battery is fully charged, the generator gives only sufficient output to keep the battery in good condition without any possibility of overcharging. In addition an increase in output is given

M
ELECTRICAL SYSTEM

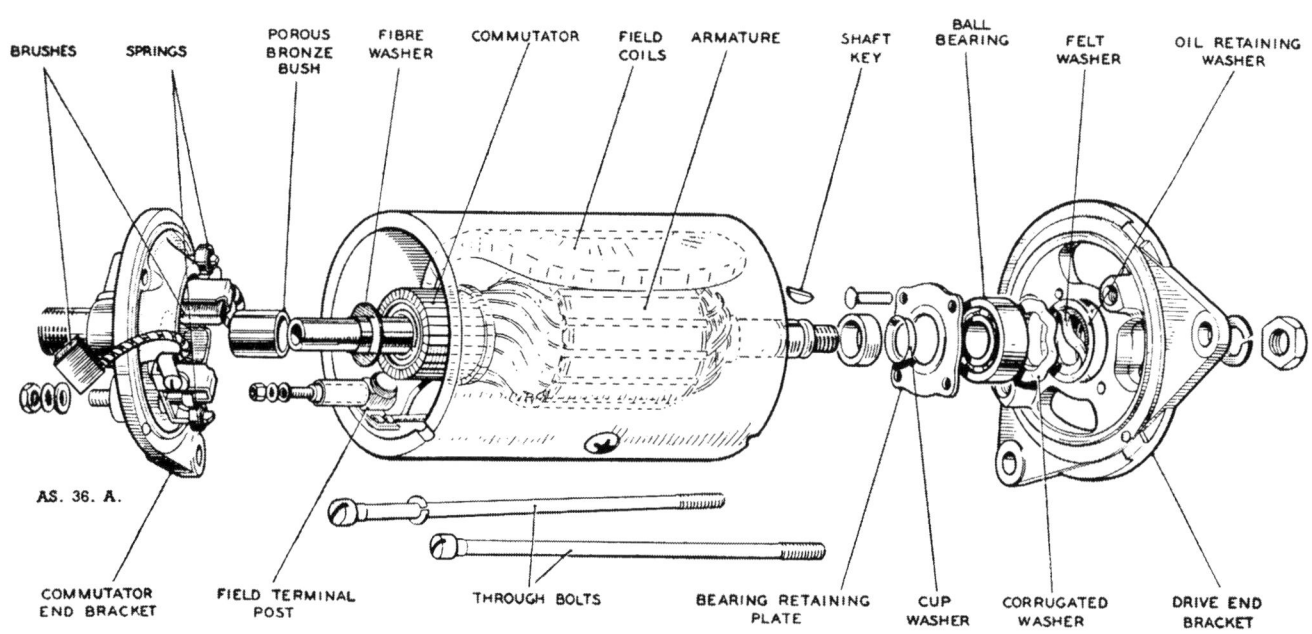

Fig. M.2. The generator exploded.

to balance the current taken by lamps and other accessories when in use. Further, a high boosting charge is given for a few minutes immediately after starting up, thus quickly restoring to the battery the energy taken from it by the electric starting motor.

Section M.6

MAINTENANCE

Lubrication

Every 12,000 miles (20000 km.) unscrew the cap of the lubricator on the side of the bearing housing, lift out the felt pad and spring and about half-fill the lubricator cap with high melting point grease. Replace the spring and felt pad and screw the lubricator cap back into position.

Belt Adjustment

Every 3,000 miles (5000 km.) inspect the generator drive belt and adjust if necessary to take up any undue slackness by turning the generator on its mounting. Care should be taken to avoid overtightening the belt which should have sufficient tension to drive without slipping.

See that the generator is properly aligned, otherwise undue strain will be thrown on the bearings.

Section M.7

TESTING IN POSITION TO LOCATE FAULT IN CHARGING CIRCUIT

In the event of a fault in the charging circuit, adopt the following procedure to locate the cause of the trouble:

(1) Inspect the driving belt and adjust if necessary.

(2) Check that the generator and control box are connected correctly. The larger generator terminal must be connected to the control box 'D' terminal, and the smaller generator terminal to control box 'F' terminal. Check the control box terminal 'E' and associated earthing cable for tightness.

(3) Switch off all lights and accessories, disconnect the cables from the generator terminals and connect the two terminals with a short length of wire.

(4) Start the engine and set to run at normal idling speed.

(5) Clip the negative lead of a moving coil voltmeter, calibrated 0 to 20 volts, to one generator terminal, and the other lead to a good earthing point on the yoke.

(6) Gradually increase the engine speed, when the voltmeter reading should rise rapidly without fluctuation. Do not allow the voltmeter reading to reach 20 volts, and do not race the engine in an attempt to increase the voltage. It is sufficient to run the generator up to a speed of 1,000 r.p.m. If there is no reading check the brushgear as described in (7) below.

If there is a low reading of approximately $\frac{1}{2}$ to 1 volt, the field winding may be at fault (see 'Field Coils'). If there is a reading of 4 to 5 volts, the armature winding may be at fault (see 'Armature').

ELECTRICAL SYSTEM

(7) If the generator is in good order, remove the link from between the terminals and restore the original connections, taking care to connect the larger generator terminal to control box terminal 'D', and the smaller terminal to control box terminal 'F'.

(8) Remove the lead from the (D) terminal on the control box and connect the voltmeter between this cable and a good earthing point on the vehicle. Run the engine as before. The reading should be the same as that measured directly at the generator. No reading on the voltmeter indicates a break in the cable to the generator. Carry out the same procedure for the (F) terminal, connecting the voltmeter between cable and earth. Finally remove the link from the generator. If the reading is correct test the control box (Section M.13).

Section M.8

GENERATOR ASSEMBLY

To Remove

(1) Disconnect the two leads to the generator.
(2) Disconnect the high tension lead and the two low tension leads to the coil.
(3) Slacken the nut securing the sliding link and the two hinge bolts holding the generator to the crankcase and water pump.
(4) Push the generator downwards to slacken the fan belt so that the latter can then be removed.
(5) Remove the set pin from the upper end of the sliding link, and take out the two generator hinge bolts, and lift the generator clear of the engine.
(6) Unscrew the nut securing the coil to its bracket on the generator and remove the coil.

To Dismantle

(1) Take off the driving pulley.
(2) Remove the nut, spring washer and flat washer from the smaller terminal (i.e. field terminal).
(3) Unscrew the two through bolts at the commutator end and remove the bracket from the generator yoke. The driving end bracket together with the armature can now be removed from the generator yoke.
(4) The driving end bracket need not be separated from the shaft unless the bearing is suspect and requires examination, or the armature is to be replaced, in this event the armature should be removed from the end bracket by means of a hand press.

Section M.9

INSPECTION AND OVERHAUL

Brushgear

Lift the brushes up into the brush boxes and secure them in that position by positioning the brush spring at the side of the brush. Fit the commutator end bracket over the commutator and release the brushes. Hold back each of the brush springs and move the brush by pulling gently on its flexible connector. If the movement is sluggish, remove the brush from its holder and ease the sides by lightly polishing it on a smooth file. Always refit the brushes in their original positions. If the brushes are badly worn, new brushes must be fitted and bedded to the commutator. The minimum permissible length of brush is $\frac{11}{32}$ in.

Test the brush spring tension using a spring scale. The tension of the springs when new is 22 to 25 oz. In service it is permissible for this value to fall to 15 oz. before performance may be affected. Fit new springs if the tension is low.

Commutator

A commutator in good condition will be smooth and free from pits or burnt spots. Clean the commutator with a petrol-moistened cloth. If this is ineffective carefully polish with a strip of fine glass paper while rotating the armature.

To remedy a badly worn commutator mount the armature, with or without the drive end bracket, in a lathe, rotate at high speed, then take a light cut with a very sharp tool. Do not remove more metal than is necessary. Polish the commutator with very fine glass

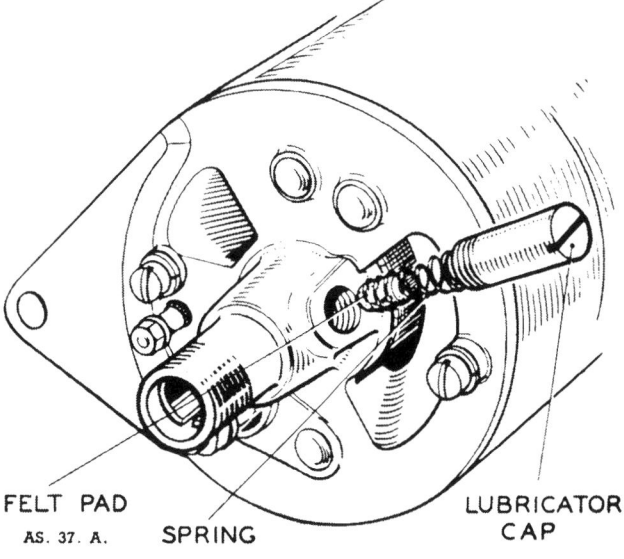

Fig. M.3. *Generator lubrication.*

M ELECTRICAL SYSTEM

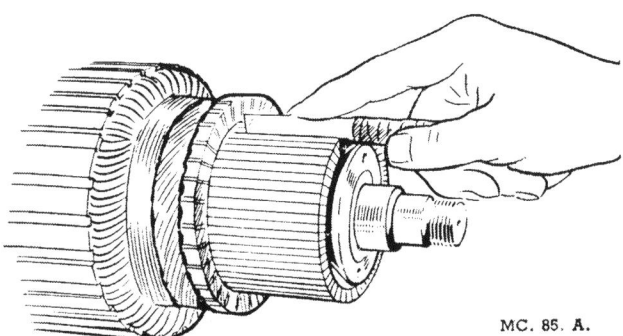

Fig. M.4. Illustrating the operation of undercutting the commutator.

paper. Undercut the insulators between the segments to a depth of $\frac{1}{32}$ in. (·8 mm.) with a hacksaw blade ground to the thickness of the insulator.

The most common armature faults are usually confined to open- or short-circuited windings. Indications of an open-circuited armature winding is given by burnt commutator segments. A short-circuited armature winding is easily identified by discolouration of the overheated windings and badly burnt commutator segments.

If armature testing facilities are not available, an armature can be tested by substitution.

To remove the armature shaft from the drive end bracket and bearing, support the bearing retaining plate firmly and press the shaft out of the drive end bracket. When fitting the new armature, support the inner journal of the ball bearing, using a mild steel tube of suitable diameter while pressing the armature shaft firmly home.

Do not use the drive end bracket as a support for the bearing whilst fitting an armature.

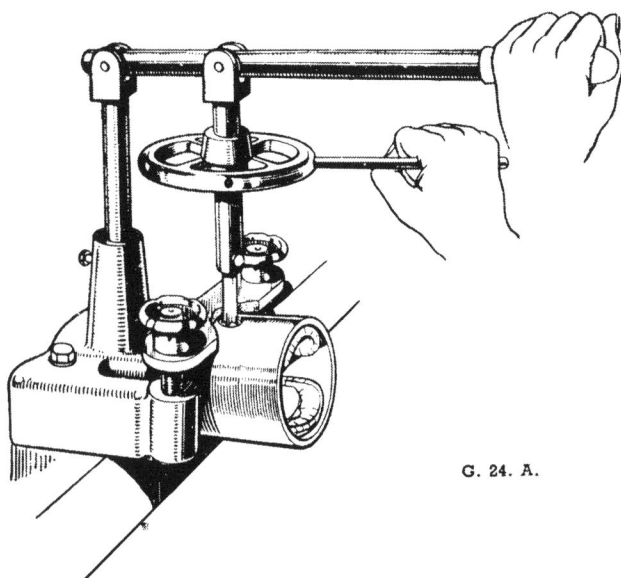

Fig. M.5. Using the wheel operated screwdriver.

Field Coils

Measure the resistance of the field coils, without removing them from the generator yoke, by means of an ohmmeter connected between the field terminal and the yoke.

The ohmmeter should read 6 ohms approximately.

If an ohmmeter is not available connect a 12-volt D.C. supply with an ammeter in series between the field terminal and generator yoke. The ammeter reading should be approximately 2 amperes. Zero on the ammeter or 'Infinity' ohmmeter reading indicates an open-circuit in the field winding.

If the current reading is much more than 2 amperes or the ohmmeter reading much below 6 ohms it is an indication that the insulation of one of the field coils has broken down.

In either case, unless a substitute generator is available, the field coils must be replaced. To do this carry out the procedure outlined below:

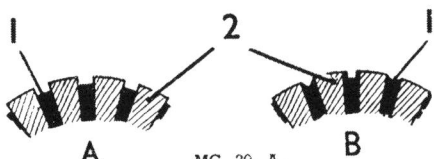

Fig. M.6. Undercutting the commutator.
'A' is the correct and 'B' the incorrect method.
1. *Insulation.*   2. *Segments.*

(1) Drill out the rivet securing the field coil terminal assembly to the yoke and unsolder the field coil connections.
(2) Remove the insulation piece which is provided to prevent the junction of the field coils from contacting with the yoke.
(3) Mark the yoke and pole shoes in order that they can be refitted in their original positions.
(4) Unscrew the two pole shoe retaining screws by means of a wheel-operated screwdriver.
(5) Draw the pole shoes and coils out of the yoke and lift off the coils.
(6) Fit the new field coils over the pole shoes and place them in position inside the yoke. Take care to ensure that the taping of the field coils is not trapped between the pole shoes and the yoke.
(7) Locate the pole shoes and field coils by lightly tightening the fixing screw.
(8) Fully tighten the screws by means of a wheel-operated screwdriver and lock them by caulking.
(9) Replace the insulation piece between the field coil connections and the yoke.
(10) Re-solder the field coil connections to the field coil terminal tags and re-rivet the terminal assembly to the yoke.

ELECTRICAL SYSTEM

Bearings

Bearings which have been worn to such an extent that they will allow side movement of the armature shaft must be replaced.

To replace the bearing bush in a commutator end bracket proceed as follows:

(1) Remove the old bearing bush from the end bracket. The bearing can be withdrawn with a suitable extractor or by screwing a ⅜ in. tap into the bush for a few turns and pulling out the bush with the tap. Screw the tap squarely into the bush to avoid damaging the bracket.

(2) Press the new bearing bush into the end bracket, using a shouldered highly polished mandrel of the same diameter as the shaft which is to be fitted in the bearing, until the visible end of the bearing is flush with the inner face of the bracket. Porous bronze bushes should not be opened out after fitting or the porosity of the bush may be impaired.

Note: Before fitting the new bearing bush it should be allowed to stand for 24 hours completely immersed in thin (S.A.E. 20) engine oil, this will allow the pores of the bush to be filled with lubricant. In cases of extreme urgency this period may be shortened by heating the oil to 100°C (212°F) for two hours then allowing to cool before removing the bearing bush.

The ball bearing at the driving end is replaced as follows:

(1) Drill out the rivets which secure the bearing retaining plate to the end bracket and remove the plate.

(2) Press the bearing out of the end bracket and remove the corrugated washer, felt washer, and oil retaining washer.

(3) Before fitting the replacement bearing see that it is clean and pack it with high melting point grease.

(4) Place the oil retaining washer, felt washer and corrugated washer in the bearing housing in the end bracket.

(5) Locate the bearing in the housing and press it home. The outer bearing journal is a light push-fit in the bearing housing.

(6) Refit the bearing retaining plate using rivets having the same dimensions as those originally fitted.

Note: When fitting a drive end bracket to the armature shaft, the inner journal of the bearing must be supported by a mild steel tube. Do not use the drive end bracket as support for the bearing when fitting an armature.

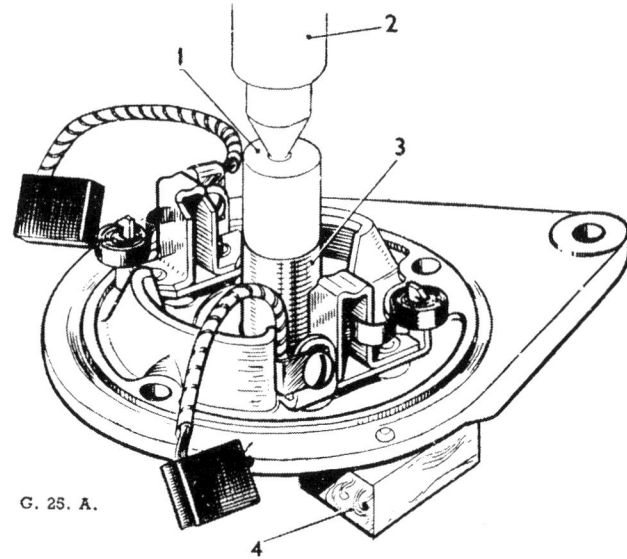

Fig. M.7. Fitting a new bush to the commutator end bracket.
1. Shouldered mandrel. 3. Bearing Bush.
2. Hand press. 4. Supporting block.

Section M.10

ASSEMBLING AND REPLACING

In the main the reassembly of the generator is a reversal of the dismantling procedure. Before refitting the generator, however, inject S.A.E. 30 oil into the commutator end bracket as previously described. The replacement is the reverse of the procedure 'To Remove' in Section M.8. Check the fan belt adjustment as described in Section C.

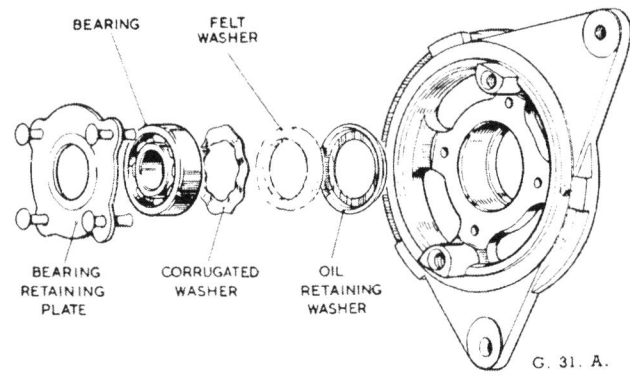

Fig. M.8. Generator drive end bracket.

ELECTRICAL SYSTEM

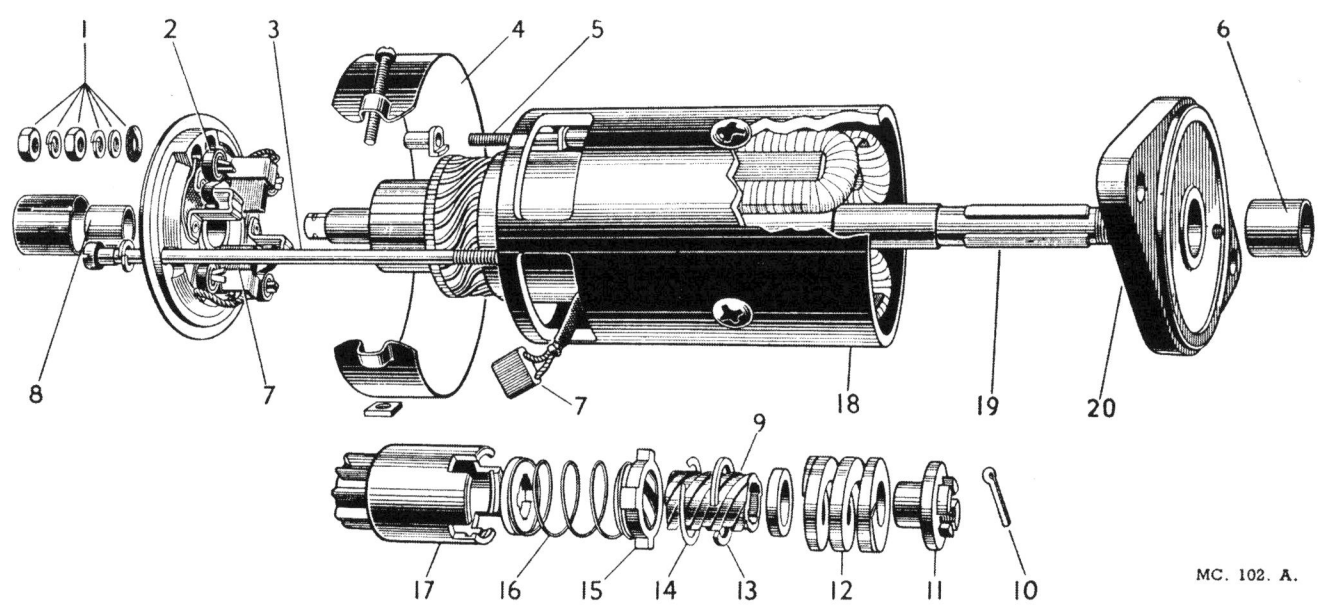

Fig. M.9. *The starter in exploded form.*

1. Terminal nuts and washers.
2. Brush spring.
3. Through bolt.
4. Cover band.
5. Terminal post.
6. Bearing bush.
7. Brushes.
8. Bearing bush.
9. Sleeve.
10. Split pin.
11. Shaft nut.
12. Main spring.
13. Retaining ring.
14. Corrugated washer.
15. Control nut.
16. Restraining spring.
17. Pinion and barrel.
18. Yoke.
19. Armature shaft.
20. Driving end bracket.

Section M.11

THE STARTER

Testing on the Vehicle

In the following test it is assumed that the battery is in a charged condition:

(1) Switch on the lamps and operate the starter control. If the lights go dim, but the starter is not heard to operate, an indication is given that the current is flowing through the starter motor windings but that for some reason the armature is not rotating; possibly the starter pinion is meshed permanently with the geared ring on the flywheel. This could be caused by the starter being operated while the engine is still moving. In this case, the starter motor must be removed from the engine for examination.

(2) Should the lamps retain their full brilliance when the starter switch is operated, check that the switch is functioning. Next if the switch is in order, examine the connections at the battery, starter switch, and also examine the wiring joining these units. Continued failure of the starter to operate indicates an internal fault in the starter which must be removed for examination.

Sluggish or slow action of the starter is usually caused by a poor connection in the wiring which causes a high resistance in the starter circuit. Check the wiring as described above.

Section M.12

SERVICING THE STARTER

To Remove and Replace

(1) Remove the distributor as described in Section B.
(2) Release the starter cable from the terminal and unscrew the top starter securing bolt.
(3) Working beneath the vehicle release and withdraw the dirt deflector situated under the starter motor and unscrew the bottom starter securing bolt.
(4) Manoeuvre the starter forward and lift clear of the engine.
(5) Installation is the reversal of the removal procedure.

ELECTRICAL SYSTEM

Examination of Commutator and Brush Gear

(1) Remove the starter cover band and examine the brushes and commutator.

(2) Hold back each of the brush springs and move the brush by pulling gently on its flexible connector. If the movement is sluggish remove the brush from its holder and ease the sides by lightly polishing with a smooth file. Always replace brushes in their original positions. If the brushes are worn so they no longer bear on the commutator, or if the brush flexible lead has become exposed on the running face, they must be renewed.

(3) If the commutator is blackened or dirty, clean it by holding a petrol-moistened cloth against it while the armature is rotated.

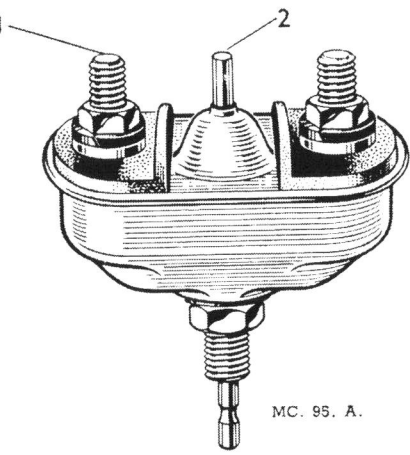

Fig. M.11. The starter switch.
1. Terminal   2. Emergency actuator.

(3) Unscrew the nut (R.H. thread) and take off the main spring. The complete drive can now be removed from the splined shaft by withdrawing it with a rotary movement.

(4) Remove the terminal nuts and washers from the terminal post on the commutator end bracket. Unscrew and withdraw the two through-bolts and

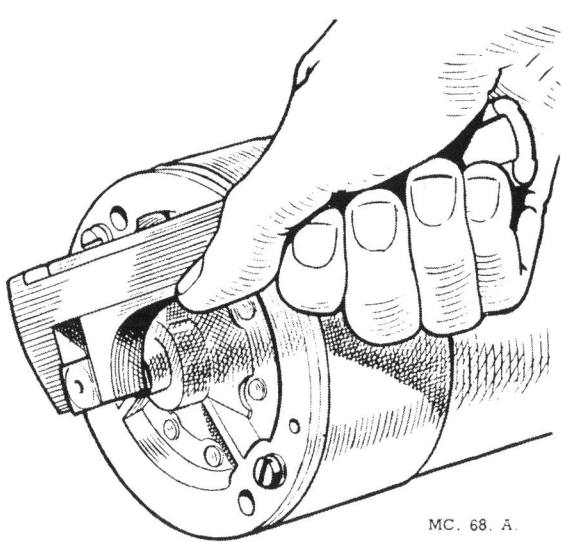

Fig. M.10. Turning the squared end of the armature shaft extension to free a jammed starter.

(4) Secure the body of the starter in a vice and test by connecting it with heavy-gauge cables to a 12-volt battery. One cable must be connected to the starter terminal the other held against the starter body or end bracket. Under these light load conditions the starter should run at a very high speed.

If the operation of the starter is still unsatisfactory, it should be dismantled for detail inspection and testing.

To Dismantle

(1) Take off the cover band at the commutator end, hold back the brush springs and take out the brushes.

(2) Extract the split pin at the driving end.

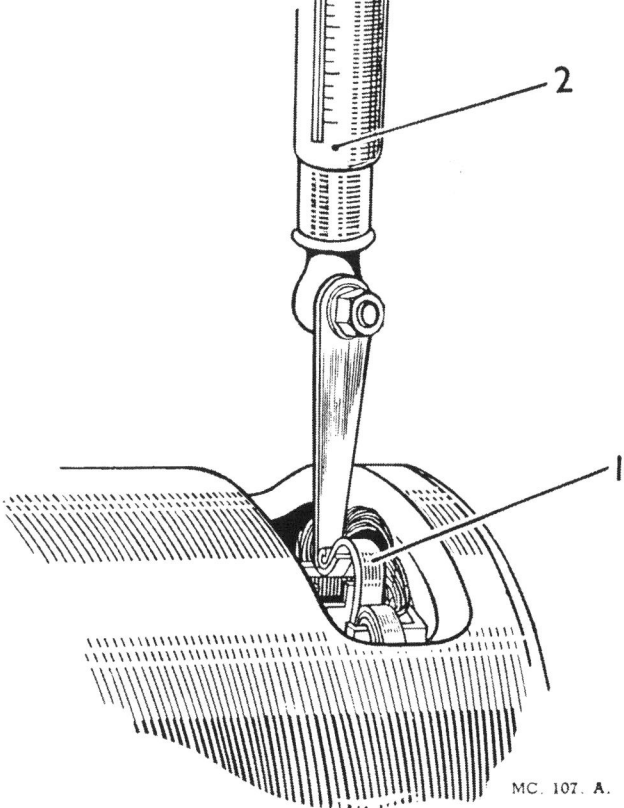

Fig. M.12. Checking the brush spring tension.
1. Brush spring.   2. Spring scale.

M.9

ELECTRICAL SYSTEM

take off the commutator end bracket.

(5) Remove the driving end bracket complete with armature end bracket.

Brushes

(1) Test the brush springs with a spring balance. The Correct tension is 25 to 15 ozs. (·7087 to ·4252 kg.). Fit a new spring if the tension is low.

(2) If the brushes are worn so that they no longer bear on the commutator, or if the flexible connector has become exposed on the running face, they must be renewed. Two of the brushes are connected to terminal eyelets attached to the brush boxes on the commutator end bracket. The other two brushes are connected to tappings on the field coils.

The flexible connectors must be removed by unsoldering and the connectors of the new brushes secured in their place by soldering. The brushes are pre-formed so that bedding of the working face to the commutator is unnecessary.

Drive

(1) If the pinion is tight on the screwed sleeve, wash away any dirt with paraffin (kerosene).

(2) If any parts are worn or damaged they must be replaced.

(3) Unscrew the nut (R.H. thread) and take off the main spring.

(4) The complete drive can now be removed for the splined shaft by pulling it off with a rotary movement. Unscrew the screwed sleeve from the barrel assembly.

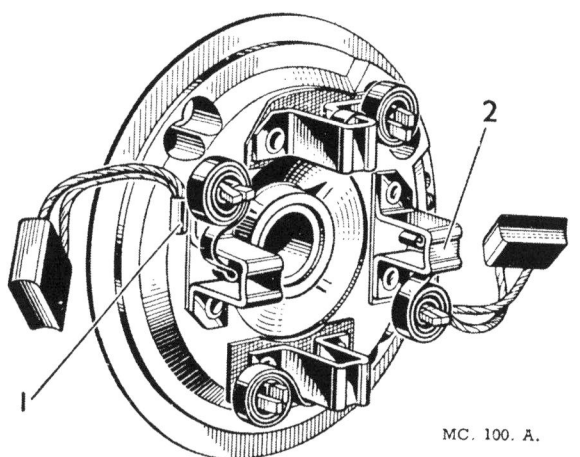

Fig. M.13. Commutator end bracket.
1. *Terminal eyelet.* 2. *Brush holder.*

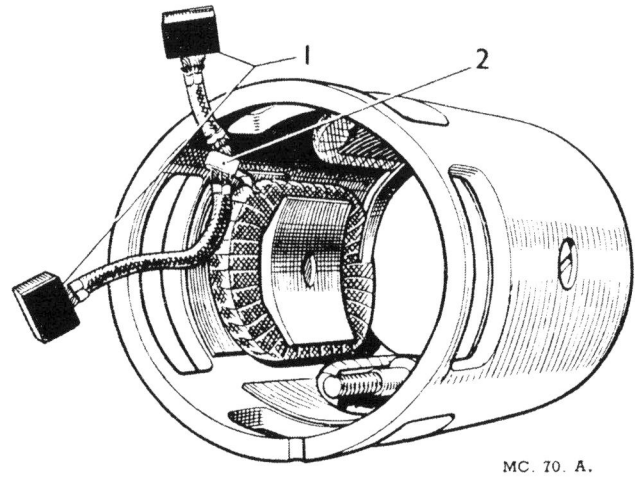

Fig. M.14. Starter yoke.
1. *Brushes.* 2. *Tapping on field coil.*

(5) Further dismantling of the barrel assembly is carried out by removing the large retaining ring.
Note: If the screwed sleeve is worn or damaged it is essential that it is replaced together with the control nut.

Reassemble by reversing the above procedure.

Commutator

A commutator in good condition will be smooth and free from pits and burnt spots. Clean the commutator with a cloth moistened with petrol (gasoline). If this is ineffective, carefully polish with a strip of fine glasspaper while rotating the armature. To remedy a badly worn commutator, dismantle the starter drive as described above and remove the armature from the end bracket. Now mount the armature in a lathe, rotate it at high speed and take a light cut with a very sharp tool. Do not remove any more metal than is absolutely necessary, and finally polish with very fine glass-paper.

The mica on the starter commutator **must not be undercut.**

Field Coils

The field coils can be tested for an open circuit by connecting a 12-volt battery having a 12-volt bulb in one of the leads to the tapping point of the field coils to which the brushes are connected and the field terminal post. If the bulb does not light there is an open circuit in the wiring of the field coils.

Lighting of the bulb does not necessarily mean that the field coils are in order, as it is possible that one of them may be earthed to a pole shoe on to the yoke. This may be checked by removing the lead from the brush connector and holding it on a clean part of the

ELECTRICAL SYSTEM

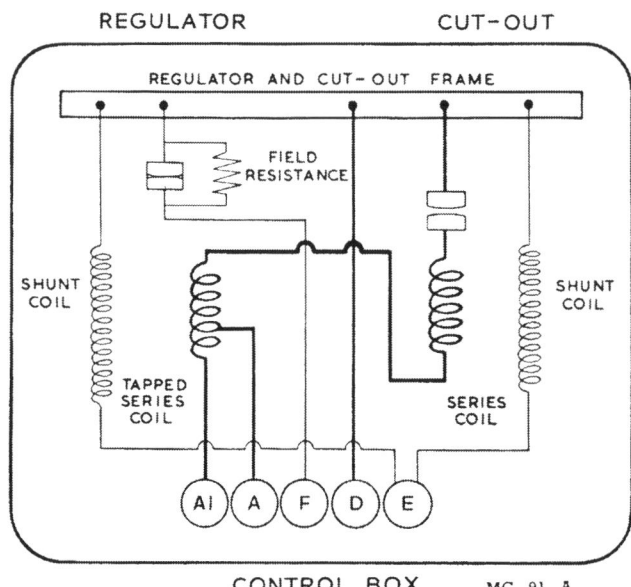

Fig. M.15 *Internal connections of control box.*

starter yoke. Should the bulb now light it indicates that the field coils are earthed.

Should the above tests indicate that the fault lies in the field coils they must be renewed. When renewing the field coils carry out the procedure detailed in the Generator Section.

Armature

Examination of the armature will in many cases reveal the cause of failure, e.g. conductors lifted from the commutator due to the starter being engaged while the engine is running and causing the armature to be rotated at an excessive speed. A damaged armature must in all cases be renewed—no attempt should be made to machine the armature core or to true a distorted armature shaft.

Bearings (Commutator End)

Bearing which are worn to such an extent that they will allow excessive sideplay of the armature shaft must be renewed. To renew the bearing bush proceed as follows:

Press the new bearing bush into the end bracket, using a shouldered mandrel of the same diameter as the shaft which is to fit into the bearing.

Note: The bearing bush is of the porous phosphor-bronze type, and before fitting, new bushes should be allowed to stand completely immersed for twenty-four hours in thin engine oil in order to fill the pores of the bush with lubricant.

Reassembly

The reassembly of the starter is a reversal of the operations described in this section.

Section M.13

THE CONTROL BOX

This unit contains the cut-out and voltage regulator. The regulator controls the generator output in accordance with the load on the battery and its state of charge. When the battery is discharged, the generator gives a high output, so that the battery receives a quick recharge which brings it back to its normal state in the minimum time.

On the other hand, if the battery is fully charged the generator is arranged to give only a trickle charge, which is sufficient to keep it in good condition without any possibility of causing damage to the battery by overcharging.

The regulator also causes the generator to give a controlled boosting charge immediately after starting up, which quickly restores to the battery the energy taken from it when starting. After about 30 minutes running, the output of the generator has fallen to a steady rate best suited to the particular state of charge of the battery.

The cut-out is an automatic switch for connecting and disconnecting the battery with the generator. This is necessary because the battery would otherwise discharge through the generator when the engine is stopped or running at a low speed.

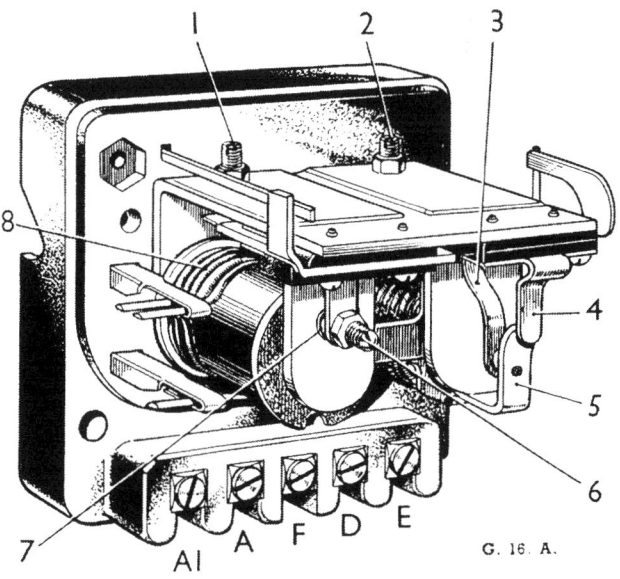

Fig. M.16. *Control box.*

1. *Regulator adjusting screw.*
2. *Cut-out adjusting screw.*
3. *Fixed contact blade.*
4. *Stop arm.*
5. *Armature tongue and moving contact.*
6. *Regulator moving contact.*
7. *Fixed contact.*
8. *Regulator series windings.*

ELECTRICAL SYSTEM

Regulator Adjustment

The regulator is carefully set before leaving the works to suit the normal requirements of the standard equipment, and in general it should not be necessary to alter it. If, however, the battery does not keep in a charged condition, or if the generator output does not fall when the battery is fully charged, it may be advisable to check the setting and if necessary to readjust.

It is important, before altering the regulator setting when the battery is in a low state of charge, to check that its condition is not due to a battery defect or to the generator belt slipping.

Checking and Adjusting the Electrical Setting

The regulator setting can be checked without removing the cover of the control box.

(1) Withdraw the cables from the terminals marked 'A' and 'A1' at the control box and join them together. Connect the negative lead of a moving coil voltmeter (0 to 20 volts full scale reading) to be 'D' terminal on the generator and connect the other lead from the meter to a convenient chassis earth.

(2) Slowly increase the speed of the engine until the voltmeter needle 'flicks' and then steadies; this should occur at a voltmeter reading between the limits given for the appropriate temperature of the regulator.

If the voltage at which the reading becomes steady occurs outside these limits, the regulator must be adjusted.

(3) Shut off the engine, remove the control box cover, release the locknut holding the adjusting screw (1, Fig. M.16) and turn the screw in a clockwise direction to raise the setting or in an anti-clockwise direction to lower the setting. Turn the adjustment screw a fraction of a turn

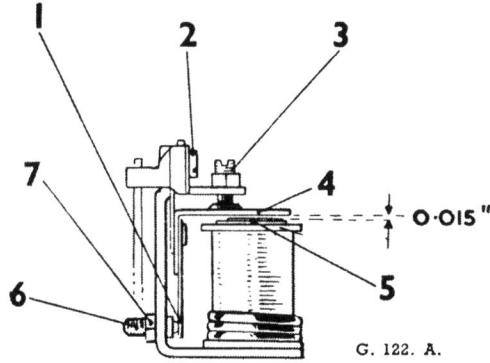

Fig. M.18. Regulator mechanical settings.
1. Armature tension spring
2. Armature securing screws.
3. Fixed contact adjustment screw.
4. Armature.
5. Core face and shim.
6. Voltage adjusting screw.
7. Locknut.

and then tighten the locknut.

When adjusting, do not run the engine up to more than half throttle because, while the generator is on open circuit, it will build up to a high voltage if run at a high speed and in consequence a false voltmeter reading would be obtained.

Mechanical Setting

The mechanical settings of the regulator are accurately adjusted before leaving the factory and provided that the armature carrying the moving contact is not removed these settings should not be tampered with. If however, the armature has been removed, the regulator will have to be reset. To do this proceed as follows:

(1) Slacken the fixed contact locking nut and unscrew the contact until it is well clear of the armature moving contact. Slacken the two armature assembly securing screws.
Slacken the voltage adjusting screw locking nut and unscrew the adjuster until it is well clear of the armature tension spring. Slacken the two armature assembly securing screws.

(2) Insert a ·015 in. (·381 mm.) feeler gauge between the armature and core shim. Take care not to turn up or damage the edge of the shim. Press the armature squarely down against the gauge and re-tighten the two armature assembly securing screws.

(3) With the gauge still in position, screw the adjustable contact down until it just touches the armature contact. Tighten the locknut and remove the feeler gauge. Reset the voltage adjusting screw as described under 'Electrical Setting'

Cleaning Regulator Contacts

After periods of long service it may be found necessary to clean the regulator contacts. Fine carborundum stone or fine emery cloth may be used. Carefully wipe away all traces of dust or other foreign matter, using a clean fluffless cloth moistened with methylated spirits.

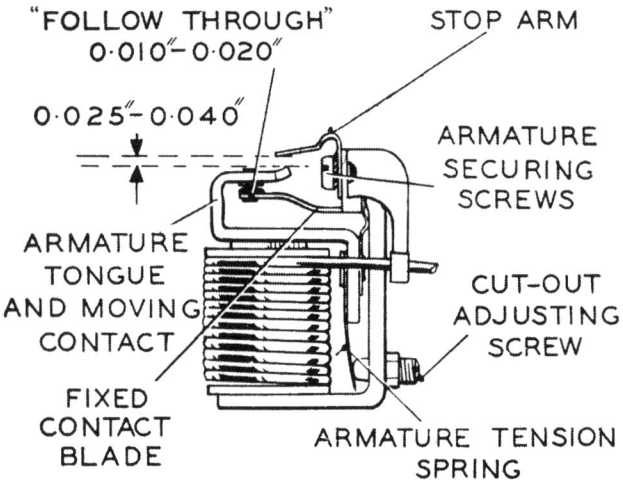

Fig. M.17. Cut-out mechanical settings.

ELECTRICAL SYSTEM

Cut-Out Electrical Setting

If the regulator is correctly set but the battery is still not being charged, the cut-out may be out of adjustment. To check the voltage at which the cut-out operates remove the control box cover and connect the voltmeter between the terminals 'D' and 'E'. Start the engine and slowly increase its speed until the cut-out contacts are seen to close, noting the voltage at which this occurs. This should be 12·7 to 13·3 volts.

If operation of the cut-out takes place outside these limits, it will be necessary to adjust. To do this, slacken the locknut of (2), Fig. M.16, securing the cut-out adjusting screw and turn the screw in a clockwise direction to raise the voltage setting, or in an anti-clockwise direction to reduce the setting. Turn the screw a fraction at a time and then tighten the locknut. Test after each adjustment by increasing the engine speed and noting the voltmeter readings at the instant of contact closure. Electrical settings of the cut-out, like the regulator, must be made as quickly as possible because of temperature rise effects. Tighten the locknut after making the adjustment.

Adjustment of the drop-off voltage is effected by carefully bending the fixed contact blade. If the cut-out does not operate there may be an open circuit in the wiring of the cut-out and regulator unit, in which case the unit should be removed for examination or renewal.

Cut-out Mechanical Setting

If for any reason the cut-out armature has to be removed from the frame, care must be taken to obtain the correct air gap settings on reassembly. These can be obtained as follows:

(1) Slacken the adjusting screw locking nut and unscrew the adjusting screw until it is well clear of the armature tension spring. Slacken the two armature assembly securing screws. (Fig. M.17).

(2) Press the armature firmly down against the copper sprayed core face and re-tighten the two armature assembly securing screws.

(3) Using a pair of round-nosed pliers, adjust the gap between the armature stop-arm and armature tongue by bending the stop-arm. The gap must be ·025 to ·040 in. (·635 to 1·016 mm.) when the armature is pressed squarely down on the core face.

(4) Similarly the insulated contact blade must be bent so that when the armature is pressed squarely down against the core face there is a 'follow through' or contact deflection of ·010 to ·020 in. (·254 to ·508 mm.). Reset the cut-out adjusting screw as described under 'Cut-out Electrical Setting'.

Cleaning Cut-out Contacts

If the contacts appear rough or burnt place a strip of fine glass paper between, and with them closed by hand draw the paper through. This should be done two or three times with the rough side towards each contact. Wipe away all dust or other foreign matter, using a clean flufless cloth moistened with methylated spirits.

Do not use emery cloth or carborundum stone for cleaning the cut-out contacts.

Section M.14

FUSE UNIT

Description

The fuse unit which is located on the right-hand side of the engine compartment, is an open insulated moulding carrying two single-pole 35-amp. cartridge-type fuses which are held in spring clips between the grub-screw-type terminal blocks. Two spare fuses are carried in recesses in the fuse unit box and are positioned by retaining springs. The fuse which bridges the terminal blocks (A1—A2) is to protect general auxiliary circuits, e.g. the horn which is independent of the ignition switch. The other fuse, bridging terminal blocks (A3—A4) is to protect the ignition and auxiliary circuits, e.g. the fuel gauge, windscreen wiper motor and flasher indicators which only operate when the ignition is switched on.

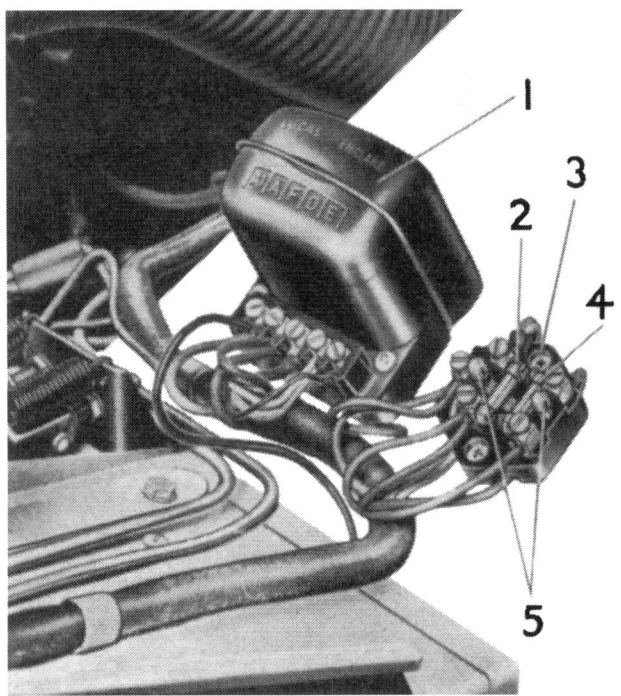

Fig. M.19. Fuse unit and control box.
1. Control box.
2. Auxiliary ignition fuse (35 amps.)
3. Fuse unit.
4. Auxiliary fuse (50 amps.)
5. Spare fuses.

ELECTRICAL SYSTEM

Section M.15

THE FLASHER UNIT

Description

The Lucas flasher unit is situated in the engine compartment on the right-hand side, and is operated by a switch centrally mounted on the facia panel, a warning light being provided on the right side of the facia.

The unit is contained in a small cylindrical metal container, one end of which is rolled over on to an insulated plate carrying the mechanism and three terminals. The unit depends for its operation on the linear expansion of a length of wire which becomes heated by an electric current flowing through it. This actuating wire controls the movement of a spring loaded armature attached to a central steel core and carrying a moving contact—the sequence of operation being as follows:

When the direction-indicator switch is turned either to the left or right, current flows through the actuating wire, ballast resistor and coil wound on the central core and hence to earth via the flasher lamp filaments. This current is limited by the ballast resistor to a valve which will ensure that the flasher lamp filaments do not light at this stage. The actuating wire grows in length under the heating influence of the current and allows the armature to move inwards to its alternative position, thereby closing a pair of contacts in the supply circuit to the flasher lamps, and at the same time, short circuiting the actuating wire. The increased electro-magnetic attraction of the armature to the core, due to the full lamp current now flowing through the coils, serves to hold the closed contacts firmly together. At the same time a secondary spring loaded armature is attracted to the core and closes a pilot warning lamp circuit so that now both flasher lamps and warning lamp are illuminated.

Since, however, heating current no longer flows through the short-circuited actuating wire, the latter cools and consequently contracts in length. The main armature is therefore pulled away from the core, the contacts opened and the light signals extinguished. The consequent reduction of electro-magnetism in the core allows the secondary armature to return to its original position and so extinguish the pilot warning light. The above sequence of operations continues to be repeated until the indicator switch is returned to the off position. A symbolic representation of the flasher unit is shown in Fig. M.20.

Functions of Warning Lamp

The warning lamp not only serves to indicate that the flasher unit is functioning correctly but also gives a warning of any bulb failure occuring in the external direction-indicator lamps—since a reduction in bulb current flowing through the coil reduces the electro-magnetic effect acting on the secondary armature and so prevents closure of the pilot light contacts.

Checking Faulty Operation

In the event of trouble occurring with a flashing light direction-indicator system, the following procedure should be followed:
(1) Check the bulbs for broken filaments.
(2) Refer to the vehicle wiring diagram and check all flasher circuit connections.
(3) Switch on the ignition.
(4) Check with the voltmeter that the flasher unit terminal 'B' is a battery voltage with respect to earth.
(5) Connect together flasher unit terminals 'B' (or 'X') and 'L' and operate the direction-indicator switch. If the flasher lamps now light, the flasher unit is defective and must be replaced.

Maintenance

Flasher units cannot be dismantled for subsequent reassembly. A defective unit must therefore be replaced, care being taken to connect as the original.

Replacement of Flasher Unit

When replacing a flasher unit or installing a flashing light system, it is advisable to test the circuits before connections to flasher terminals are made. When testing join the cables normally connected to those terminals (green, green with brown, and light green) together and operate the direction indicator switch. In the event of a

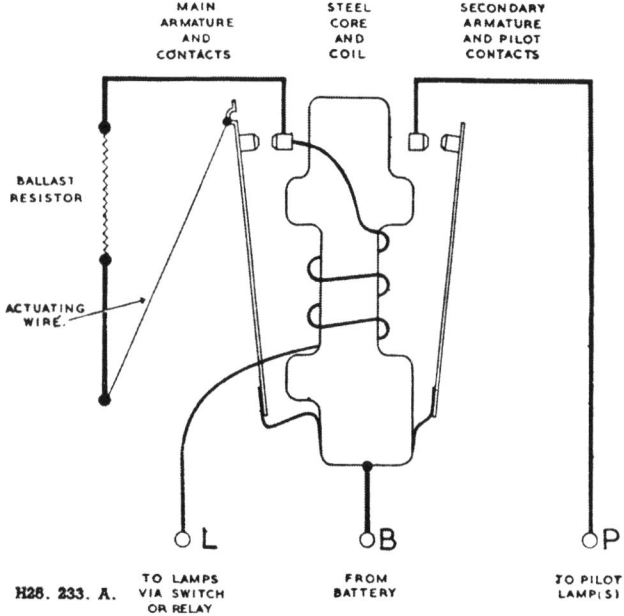

Fig. M.20. Symbolic representation of flasher unit model FL.5

ELECTRICAL SYSTEM

wrong connection having been made, the ignition auxiliaries fuse will blow but no damage will be done to the flasher unit.

Section M.16

WINDSCREEN WIPERS

Maintenance

(1) Inspection should be made of the rubber wiping elements which after long service become worn and should be renewed.

(3) The rubber grommet or washer around the wheel box spindle should be lubricated with a few drops of glycerine.

(3) Methylated spirits (de-natured alcohol) should be used to remove oil, tar spots and other stains from the windscreen. It has been founded that the use of some silicone and wax-based polishes for this purpose can be detrimental to the rubber wiping elements.

(4) The gearbox and cable rack are packed with grease during manufacture and need no further lubrication.

Checking Switching Mechanism

If the wiper fails to park or parks unsatisfactorily, the limit switch in the gearbox cover should be checked. Unless the limit switch is correctly set, it is possible for the wiper motor to overrun the open circuit position and continue to draw current.

Resetting the Limit Switch

Slacken the four screws securing the gearbox cover and observe the projection near the rim of the limit switch. Position the projection in line with the groove in the gearbox cover. Turn the limit switch 25° in an anti-clockwise direction and tighten the four securing screws. if the wiping blades are required to park on the opposition side of the screen, the limit switch should be turned back 180° in a clockwise direction.

Checking Current Consumption

If the wiper fails to operate, or operates unsatisfactorily, switch on the wiper and note the current being supplied to the motor. The normal running current should be 2·3 to 3·1 amps. Use a 0 to 15 amp. moving coil ammeter connected in the wiper circuit, then proceed as follows:

Wiper takes no Current. Examine the fuse protecting the wiper circuit. If the fuse has 'blown', examine the wiring of the motor circuit and of all other circuits protected by that fuse. Replace any cables which are badly worn or chafed, if necessary fitting protective sleeving over the cables to prevent a recurrence of the fault.

If the external wiring is found to be in order, replace the fuse with one of the recommended size. Then proceed as for wiper taking an abnormally high current.

If the fuse is intact, examine the wiring of the motor circuit for breaks and ensure that the wiper control switch is operating correctly.

When a current-operated thermostat is fitted, test it by connecting an ohmmeter across its terminals in place of the two cables. If closed circuit is indicated, the thermostat is in order, and the cables must be refitted. An open circuit means that the thermostat has operated but not reset. Check the thermostat by substitution. Adjustment of the thermostat must not be attempted.

If the thermostat is in order, proceed as for the wiper taking an abnormally high current.

Wiper takes Abnormally Low Current. Check that the battery is fully charged. The performance of the motor is dependent on the condition of the battery.

Remove the commutator end bracket and examine the brush gear, ensuring that it bears firmly on the commutator. The tension spring must be renewed if the brushes do not bear firmly on the commutator. Brush levers must move freely on the pivots. If these levers are stiff they should be freed by working them backwards and forwards by hand.

Examine the commutator and, if necessary, clean with a petrol-moistened cloth. A suspected armature should be checked by substitution.

Wiper takes Abnormally High Current. If an abnormally high current is shown on the ammeter, this may be due to excessive load on the driving shaft. The stall current of the motor cold is 14 amp., and hot is 8 amp.

If there is no obvious reason for this, such as a sticking wiper blade, a check should be made at the gearbox.

Remove the gearbox cover and examine the gear assembly, checking that a blow on the gearbox end bracket has not reduced the armature end float. The armature end float adjusting screw must be set to give an armature end play of 0·008 in. (·20 mm.) to 0·012 in. (·30 mm.).

Sluggish operation with excessive current consumption may be caused through frictional losses in badly positioned or defective connecting tubes. The connecting tubes can be checked, using a cable gauge. (Details of this gauge can be obtained from any Lucas Agent.) The

ELECTRICAL SYSTEM

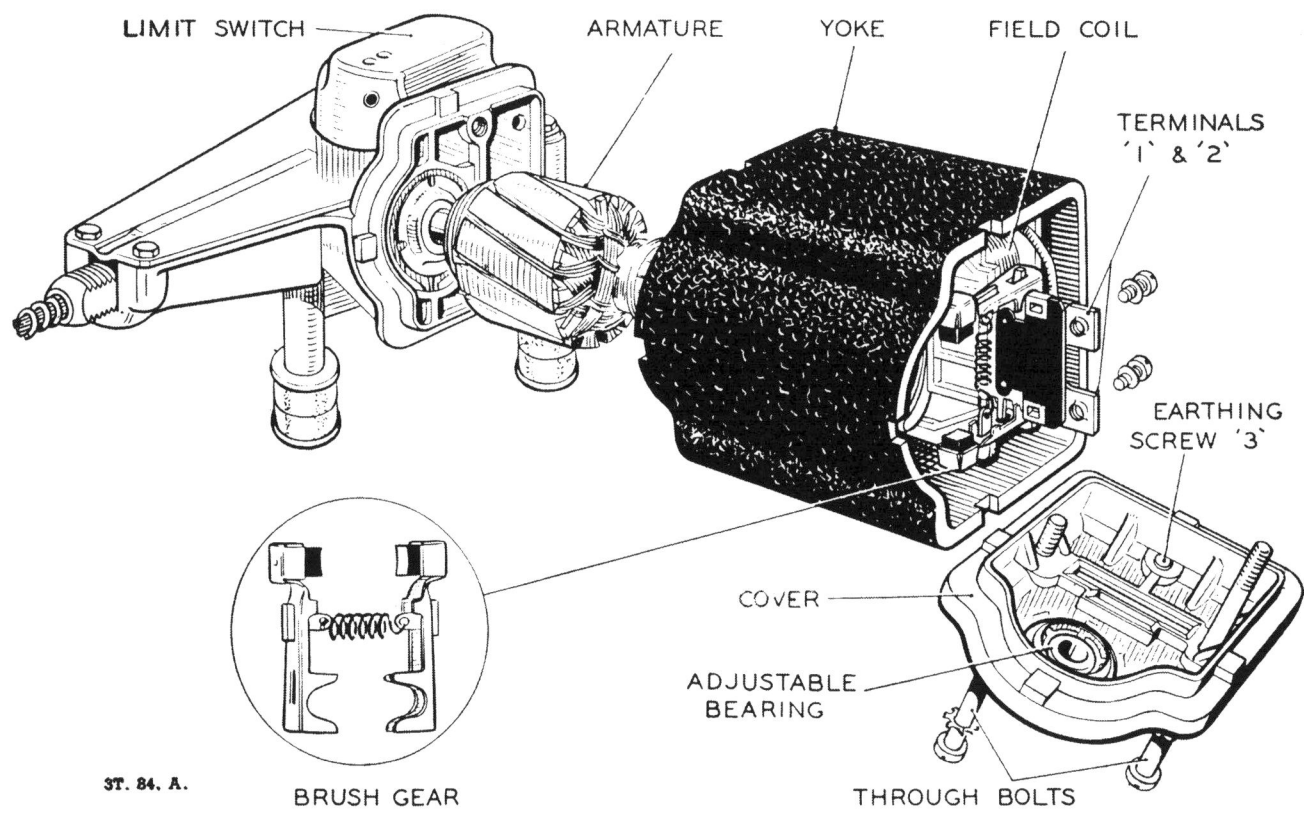

Fig. M.21. Wiper motor exploded.

gauge cable is similar in appearance to the driving rack but is 0·010 in. (·25 mm.) larger in diameter and is less flexible. The gauge will not easily pass through connecting tubes having less than the minimum permissible curvature.

To check the tubing using the gauge, it is necessary to remove the inner rack. Insert the gauge into the connecting tube as far as the first wheel box and then withdraw it. Remove the tubing connecting the wheelboxes. Insert and withdraw the gauge. If the gauge moves freely the tubing is correctly installed. If the gauge does not move freely, the tubing must be checked for sharp bends and obstructions. Check the wheel boxes for alignment and then re-assemble.

Pieces of carbon short-circuiting adjacent segments of the commutator will also cause excessive current consumption. The resistance between adjacent commutator segments should be 0·34 to 0·41 ohms. Cleaning the commutator and brushgear removes this fault. When dismantling, check the internal wiring of the motor for evidence of short-circuiting due to chafed or charred insulation. Slip a new piece of sleeving over any charred connections, and arrange them so that they do not rub against sharp edges.

While the motor is dismantled check the valve of the field resistance. If it is found to be lower than 12·8 to 14 ohms, a short-circuit in the windings is indicated and a new field coil must be fitted. Other evidence of a short-circuit will be given by charred leads from the field coil.

To Remove the Rack and Motor Unit

Release the wiping arms from the spindles, see Fig. M.22, disconnect the union on the Bundy tube at the gearbox, and remove the nuts from the motor mounting bolts. Withdraw the motor and cable rack clear of the Bundy tube.

To Dismantle the Motor

(1) Withdraw the four screws securing the gearbox cover and remove the cover.
(2) Withdraw the terminal screws and through bolts at the commutator end bracket.
(3) Remove the commutator end bracket clear of the yoke.
(4) The brush gear can be removed by lifting it clear of the commutator and withdrawing it as a unit. Care should be taken at this point to note the particular side occupied by each brush so that each may be replaced in its original setting on the commutator.

ELECTRICAL SYSTEM

(5) Access to the armature and field coils can be gained by withdrawing the yoke.

(6) If it is necessary to remove the field coil, unscrew the two screws securing the pole piece to the yoke. These screws should be marked so that they can be returned to their original holes.

(7) Press out the pole pieces complete with field coil, marking the pole piece so that it can be replaced in its correct position inside the yoke. The pole piece can now be pressed out of the field coil.

To Dismantle the Gearbox Unit

Remove the circlip and washer from the crosshead connecting link pin and lift off the crosshead and cable rack assembly. Then remove the circlip and washer from the final gear shaft located underneath the gearbox unit. Remove any burr from the circlip groove before lifting out the final gear. The armature and worm drive can now be withdrawn from the gearbox. All gear teeth should be examined for signs of damage or wear and, if necessary, new gears fitted.

Reassembly

Reassembly is a reversal of the above procedures. When reassembling, the following components should be lubricated, using the lubricants recommended:

(1) **Armature bearings.** These should be lubricated with S.A.E.20 engine oil—the self-aligning bearing being immersed in this for 24 hours before assembly.

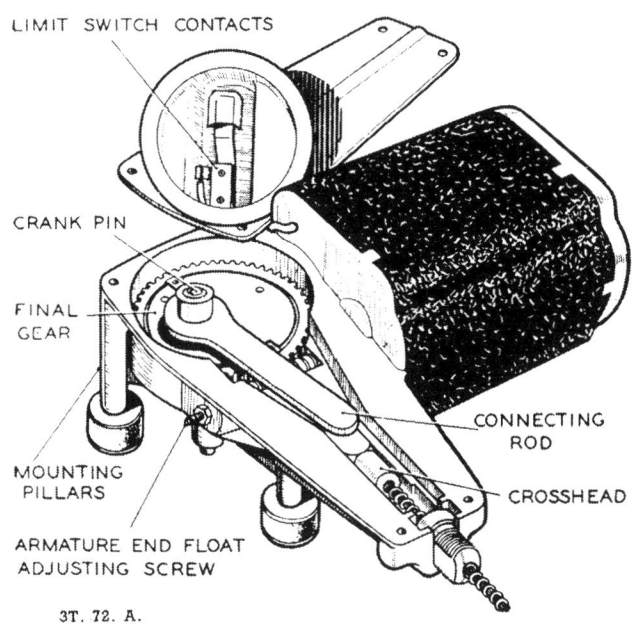

Fig. M.22. *Wiper motor gearbox cover removed.*

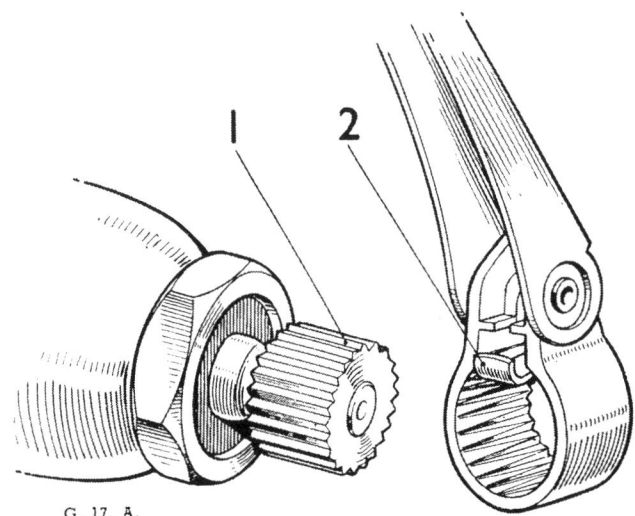

Fig. M.23. *Windscreen wiper arm assembly.*
1. *Splined driving drum.*   2. *Retaining clip.*

(2) **Armature shaft (commutator end).** Apply S.A.E.20 engine oil sparingly.

(3) **Felt lubricator in gearbox.** Apply S.A.E.20 engine oil carefully.

(4) **Worm wheel bearings, crosshead, guide channel, connecting rod, crank pin, eccentric coupling assembly, worm and final gear shaft.** Grease liberally as for front hubs.

(5) **Cable rack and wheelboxes.** Grease liberally as for front hubs.

Testing

Switch on the ignition and the wiper control. The two wiper areas should be approximately symmetrical on the windscreen.

Fitting a Blade to a Wiper Arm

Pull the wiper arm away from the windscreen and insert the curved 'wrist' of the arm into slotted spring fastening of the blade. Swivel the two components into engagement.

Fitting a Wiper Arm to Driving Spindle

(1) First ensure that the wiper spindles are in the correct parking position by switching on the ignition and turning the wiper control on and then off.

(2) To fit the arms, press the headpieces on to the spindles at the correct parking angle until the retaining clip is heard to snap over the end of the spindle drum.

(3) Switch off the wiper control. The arms should come to rest in the correct parking position.

M ELECTRICAL SYSTEM

Adjusting

Correct operation can be obtained by adjusting the position of the arms relative to the spindles. If necessary the position of the arms may be adjusted by removing and re-engaging them with the splined driving spindles, the angular pitch of the splines being 5°.

Do not attempt to turn the arms whilst in position, but press back the retaining clip (Fig. M.23) in the headpieces and withdraw the arms from the driving spindles. Refit in the desired position. The above adjustment may affect the self-parking position. If so, it may be corrected by adjustment of the limit switch position, as described above.

If the arms and blades are required to come to rest on the opposite side, the limit switch should be turned through 180°. It should be noted that the switch cover is designed for turning through a sector only and not through 360°. This feature prevents unnecessary twisting of the external flexible connections.

Section M.17

IGNITION SWITCH

Description

The ignition switch is of the rotary barrel-type Yale lock located centrally on the facia panel. Operation of the switch is carried out by inserting the ignition key into the lock and turning it in a clockwise direction. In addition to controlling the primary circuit of the ignition coil the switch also operates as a master switch for the ignition, fuel gauge and flashing indicators.

To Test in the Vehicle

Test the ignition switch in the manner described in Section B.

To Remove

(1) Remove the earth lead from the battery.
(2) Disconnect the clip surrounding the switch body behind the facia.
(3) Disconnect the cables from the switch terminals.
(4) Withdraw the switch from the facia.

Section M.18

DIRECTION INDICATOR WARNING LAMP

To Remove and Dismantle

(1) Pull out the bulb holder and bulb from the rear of the warning lamp.
(2) Unscrew the bulb.
(3) To release the red lens unscrew the chrome retaining ring situated on the front of the facia panel.

To Reassemble and Install

The reassembly and installation is the reversal of the procedure 'To Remove and Dismantle'.

Section M.19

PANEL LIGHT BULBS

To Remove

(1) Pull out the bulb holder and bulb from the rear of the facia.
(2) Unscrew the bulb.

To Replace

The replacement of the panel light bulb is a reversal of removal procedure.

Section M.20

HEADLAMP MAIN BEAM WARNING LIGHT BULB

For details see Section M.19.

Section M.21

IGNITION WARNING LIGHT BULB

For details see Section M.19.

Section M.22

FUEL GAUGE SYSTEM

Description

The fuel gauge circuit consists of an instrument panel gauge, a tank unit, and the necessary cables. Its operating current is controlled by the ignition switch.

The gauge is mounted on the facia panel and consists of a metal case and bezel with a dial calibrated to indicate the contents of the fuel tank. Two coils wound on bakelite bobbins with soft iron cores, and shaped pole-pieces, exert a magnetic force on a pivoted soft iron armature, to which is attached the pointer. The magnetic effect of the two coils causes the armature (and therefore the pointer) to be deflected in relation to the amount of fuel in the tank. The voltage across each coil is varied according to the position of the tank unit float arm. The instrument is practically independent of normal variation of battery voltage.

The tank unit is attached by six screws to a flange in the top of the fuel tank, and consists of a float and float arm mounted to a zinc-base die-casting enclosing a

ELECTRICAL SYSTEM

M

wound resistance. The float arm carries a contact arm which travels over the resistance taking up a position which corresponds to the quantity of fuel in the tank, and this varies the current flowing through the meter.

To Test in the Vehicle

If the gauge fails to register or registers incorrectly, with current available at the (B) terminal of the gauge the fault should be diagnosed by tests as follows:

(1) Disconnect the green with black cable from the fuel gauge terminal marked (T). If the gauge does not register 'FULL' or over with the ignition switched on, then the gauge is faulty. If the gauge registers 'FULL' or over, proceed with test (2) as follows:

(2) With the green with black cable still disconnected, connect a temporary cable between the fuel gauge terminal marked (T) and earth. If the gauge does not register 'EMPTY' or lower with the ignition switched on, then the gauge is faulty. If the gauge registers 'EMPTY' or lower proceed with test (3) as follows:

(3) Disconnect the green with black cable from the fuel tank unit and connect a temporary cable from the fuel gauge terminal marked (T) to the tank unit terminal. If the gauge does not register according to the position of the float in the tank, or registers 'FULL' irrespective of the float position, with the ignition switched on then the tank unit is at fault.

If the contents of the tank are registered correctly with the test cable, but registers 'EMPTY' when in normal circuit, then the cable between the gauge and the tank unit is earthed.

Important: In no circumstances should the battery supply be connected directly to the terminal of the tank unit.

FUEL GAUGE

To Remove

(1) Release the (T) and (B) terminals from behind the gauge.
(2) Free the fuel gauge from the facia by unscrewing the two knurled nuts at the back of the gauge.
(3) Withdraw the gauge forward from the facia panel.

To Replace

The replacement is the reversal of the procedure 'To Remove' noting the following point:
Connect the cables in accordance with the colour code given in the wiring diagram.

TANK UNIT

To Remove

(1) Lower the fuel tank as described in Section D.1.
(2) Remove the six screws securing the tank unit to the fuel tank and withdraw the unit from the tank.

To Replace

The installation of the tank unit is a reversal of the procedure 'To Remove'. Renew the gasket between the unit and the fuel tank flange and tighten the securing screws evenly.

Section M.23

PANEL LAMPS SWITCH

To Remove

(1) Remove the two screws securing the panel lamps switch to the underside of the instrument panel.
(2) Disconnect the cables (red and red with white) from the switch terminals.
(3) Withdraw the switch from the instrument panel.

To Replace

The replacement of the panel lamps switch is the reversal of the procedure 'To Remove', reconnect the cables in accordance with the colour code given in the wiring diagram.

Section M.24

WINDSCREEN WIPER SWITCH

Description

The windscreen wiper switch is located on the left-hand side of the facia panel, and consists of a perspex body with two terminal contacts secured at the base. A spring bridge connector attached to the spindle completes the circuit when the switch knob is pulled outwards. The current supply is via the ignition switch and fuse unit to the wiper motor and then to earth at the switch.

To Test in the Vehicle

If the windscreen wiper fails to operate and it is suspected that the switch is at fault check whether the fault lies in the switch in the following manner:

(1) Disconnect the fuse from the terminal (A4) on the fuse unit.
(2) Disconnect the two cables from the switch terminals.
(3) Connect a test lamp in series with a 12-volt battery and the switch. Operate the switch. If the test lamp fails to light then the switch is faulty.

Austin-Healey Sprite. Issue 3. 24975.

M.19

M

WIRING DIAGRAM

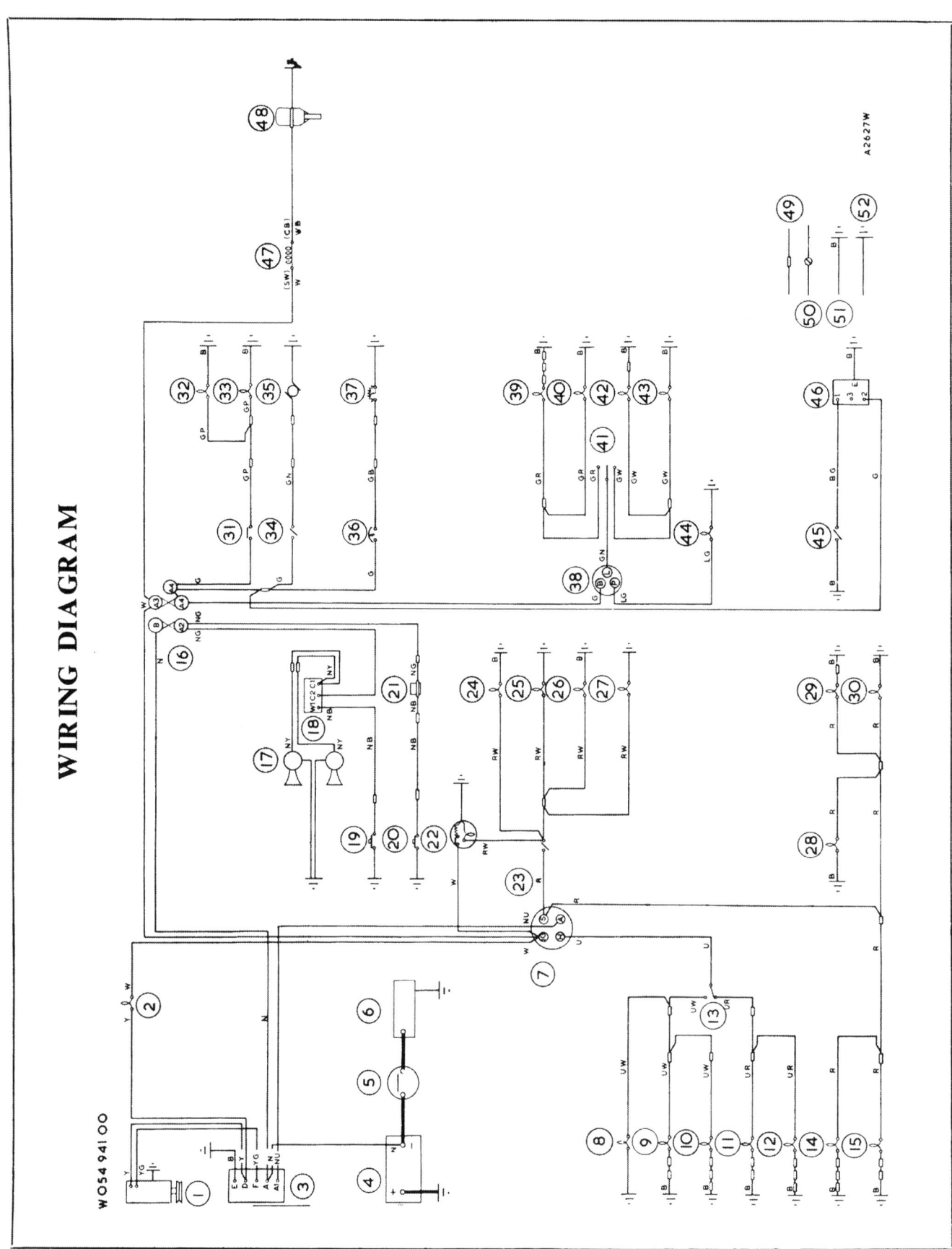

M.20

Austin-Healey Sprite. Issue 3   24975.

KEY TO WIRING DIAGRAM (R.H.D. AND L.H.D.)

1. Generator.
2. Ignition Warning Light.
3. Control Box.
4. 12-volt Battery.
5. Starter Switch.
6. Starter Motor.
7. Lighting and Ignition Switch.
8. Main Beam Warning Light.
9. R/H Headlamp Main Beam.
10. L/H Headlamp Main Beam.
11. L/H Headlamp Dip Beam.
12. R/H Headlamp Dip Beam.
13. Dipper Switch.
14. L/H Sidelamp.
15. R/H Sidelamp.
16. Fuse Unit.
17. Connections for Twin Windtone Horns (when fitted)
18. Horn Relay.
19. Horn Push.
20. Horn Push.
21. Horn.
22. Cigar Lighter & Illumination.
23. Panel Light Switch.
24. Panel Light.
25. Speedometer Light.
26. Panel Light.
27. Tachometer Light (when fitted)
28. R/H Tail Lamp.
29. Number Plate Lamp.
30. L/H Tail Lamp.
31. Stop Lamp Switch.
32. R/H Stop Lamp.
33. L/H Stop Lamp.
34. Heater Switch ⎫ when fitted
35. Heater Motor ⎭
36. Fuel Gauge.
37. Fuel Gauge Tank Unit.
38. Flasher Unit.
39. L/H Front Flasher.
40. L/H Rear Flasher.
41. Flasher Switch.
42. R/H Rear Flasher.
43. R/H Front Flasher.
44. Flasher Warning Light.
45. Windshield Switch.
46. Windshield Wipers.
47. Ignition Coil.
48. Distributor.
49. Snap Connectors.
50. Terminal Blocks or Junction Box.
51. Earth Connections made via Cable or
52. Via Fixing Bolts.

B Black
U Blue
N Brown
G Green

CABLE COLOUR CODE

P Purple
R Red
S Slate
W White

Y Yellow
L Light
D Dark
M Medium

When a cable has two colour code letters the first denotes the main colour and the second denotes the tracer colour.

ELECTRICAL SYSTEM

To Remove

(1) Disconnect the fuse from the terminal (A4) on the fuse unit.
(2) Remove the knob from the switch spindle by unscrewing the grubscrew on the underside of the knob and pulling it off.
(3) Unscrew the front bezel securing the switch to the facia panel.
(4) Disconnect the two cables from the back of the switch, and withdraw the switch through the back of the facia panel.

To Install

The installation is a reversal of the procedure 'To Remove'. Reconnect the cables in accordance with the colour code given in the wiring diagram.

Section M.25

STARTER SWITCH

Description

The starter switch is mounted on the right-hand side of the scuttle within the engine compartment and is operated by a flexible cable attached to a pull knob on the right-hand side of the facia panel. One terminal of the switch is connected to the negative terminal of the battery by a heavy duty cable, and the other terminal is connected by a similar cable to the starter motor.

To Test in the Vehicle

To determine whether the switch will pass current to the starter motor, connect a voltmeter (0 to 20 volts) across the switch terminals, when the voltmeter should register the battery voltage (assuming the starter motor is not defective). Operate the starter switch and note the voltmeter reading: it should fall back to approximately zero. No maintenance is required other than keeping the switch terminals clean and the connections tight. If the switch is found to be faulty it must be renewed as a complete unit.

To Remove

(1) Disconnect the cables from the battery.
(2) Disconnect the switch cable by slackening the locknut on the connecting sleeve, and pulling the wire out of the sleeve.
(3) Remove the locknut from the threaded sleeve of the switch, thus releasing the switch from its mounting bracket.

To Replace

The installation of the switch is the reversal of the procedure 'To Remove'.

Section M.26

HORN-PUSH

Description

The horn-push is located on the steering wheel hub, and comprises an aluminium alloy body containing a brass ring mounted behind an insulating disc in which there are three equally displaced holes. The push-button consists of a steel disc faced with perspex, and is held clear of the cross ring by a helical spring. Current is conducted from the horn via a brown with black wire to an insulated contact ring mounted in the steering column surround. A spring loaded contact plunger mounted in the steering wheel hub connects the contact ring with the brass ring in the horn-push body by passing through one of the holes in the insulating ring.

On pressing the horn-push button the brass ring is connected to earth via the steel disc of the push-button and the helical spring, thus energising the horn circuit.

To Test in the Vehicle

If the horn will not sound when the push-button is depressed remove the horn push, and short the contact plunger direct to earth. If the horn now sounds, the push-button is faulty.

To Remove

The horn-push is held in position by three spring clips, and may be removed by pulling it off the steering wheel hub.

To Replace

When replacing the horn-push align the three spring clips with the depressions in the steering wheel hub so that the contact plunger will pass through one of the holes in the insulating disc.

Section M.27

HORN

Description

The operation of the horn is based on a simple trembler principle. When the horn push is pressed, current flows through the closed contacts of the contact breaker and energises the coil. The coil core is thus magnetised and attracts a leafspring-suspended armature towards an adjustable push rod attached to the diaphragm and tone disc. Movement of the armature opens the contact breaker each time the armature is drawn into the coil, de-energising the magnet system and causing the cycle to be repeated at a frequency determined by the characteristics of the diaphragm and spring leaves.

ELECTRICAL SYSTEM

The diaphragm and tone disc are coupled by an adjustable push rod. The vibrating armature impinging on this push rod sets the diaphragm and tone disc into vibration, the diaphragm at a relatively low frequency and the tone disc at a higher frequency. These two sets of vibrations combine together with their various harmonics to give the horn a characteristic note.

To Remove

The horn is located at the front of the vehicle being mounted on the right-hand radiator support bracket.
(1) Disconnect the wires (brown with green and brown with black) at their two snap fasteners.
(2) Unscrew the two cross head bolts and nuts, and remove the horn.

To Replace

Replacement is a reversal of 'To Remove'. Reconnect the wires according to the colour code given in the wiring diagram.

Maintenance

No internal maintenance is required, externally all that is required is an occasional inspection of the horn circuit cables and the fixing bolts.

If the horn fails to operate, or operates unsatisfactorily, first carry out the following external checks.
(1) Examine the cables of the horn circuit, renewing any that are badly worn or chafed. Ensure that all connections are clean and tight and that the connecting nipples are firmly soldered to the cables.
(2) Check that the bolts securing the horn bracket are tight and that the horn body does not foul any other fixture.
(3) Check the current consumption which should be 3 to 3½ amps. when the horn is operating correctly.

After making a thorough external check remove the horn cover, secured by a single screw, and examine the cable connections inside the horn. Examine the contact breaker contacts. If they are burnt or blackened clean them with a fine file, then wipe with a petrol moistened cloth.

Section M.28

HEADLAMP DIPPING SWITCH

To Remove

The switch is foot-operated and is mounted on a bracket welded to the floor assembly.
(1) Remove the two screws securing the switch to the bracket and withdraw the switch.
(2) Disconnect the three cables from the connectors.

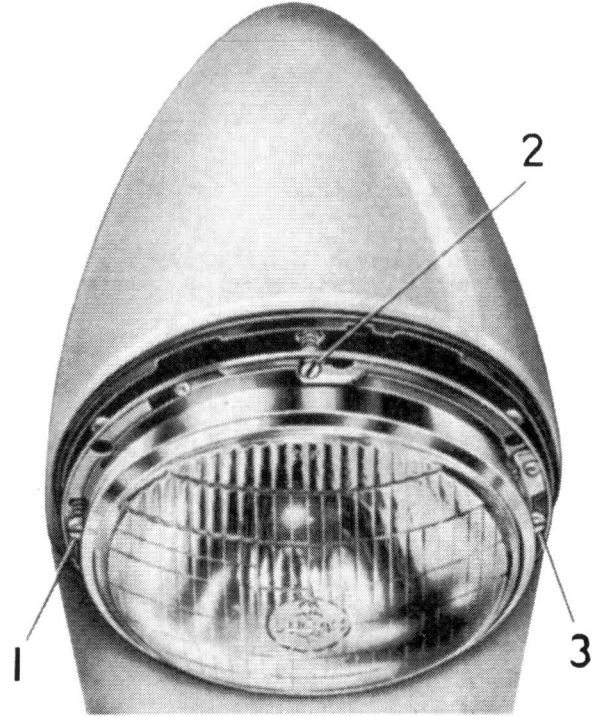

Fig. M.24. Headlamp adjustment.
1. *Horizontal adjustment screw.* 2. *Vertical adjustment screw.*
3. *Horizontal adjustment screw.*

(3) Check the operation of the dip switch. Lightly smear the mechanism with petroleum jelly.
A faulty switch must be renewed as a complete unit.

To Replace

The installation of the switch is a reversal of the procedure 'To Remove'. Reconnect the cables in accordance with the colour code in the wiring diagram.

Section M.29

HEADLAMP BULBS

To Remove

(1) Remove the screw securing the front rim to the headlamp unit. This screw is accessible through a hole in the underside of the bonnet.
(2) Remove the dust excluding cover to expose the three-spring-loaded adjustment screws.
(3) Press the light unit inwards against the tension of the adjusting spring and turn it in an anti-clockwise direction until the heads of the screws can be disengaged through the slotted holes in the light unit rim.
Note: Do not disturb the screws as this will alter the lamp setting.

Austin-Healey Sprite. Issue 3. 24975.

ELECTRICAL SYSTEM

(4) Twist the adaptor in an anti-clockwise direction and pull it off.

(5) Remove the bulb.

To Replace

(1) Install the replacement bulb in the holder, taking care to locate it correctly.

(2) Engage the projections on the inside of the adaptor with the slots in the holder, press on and secure by twisting in a clockwise direction.

(3) Position the light unit so that the heads of the adjustment screws protrude through the slotted holes in the flange, press the unit in and turn in a clockwise direction.

(4) Replace the dust-excluding cover and refit the front rim.

Section M.30

MODIFIED EUROPEAN LIGHT UNIT

Cars exported to Europe are now fitted with the new European-type headlamps. These lamp units are fitted with special bulbs, and front lenses giving an assymetrical beam to the right-or left-hand side to meet the requirements in the Country to which the car is exported. This modification was introduced on the following cars:

from Car No. 10489 (Europe except France).
from Car No. 7782 (France).
from Car No. 21118 (Sweden).

Access to the bulb is gained in the same way as described in Section M.29. The bulb, however, is released from the reflector by withdrawing the three-pin socket and pinching the two ends of the wire retaining clip to clear the bulb flange (see Fig. M.25).

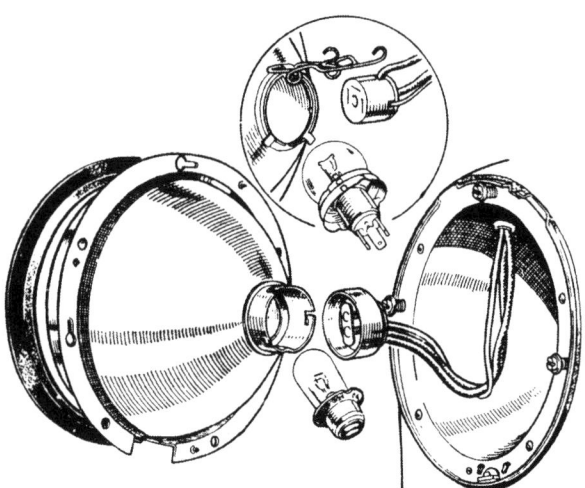

Fig. M.25. The headlamp light unit, with the European-type lamp bulb arrangement inset.

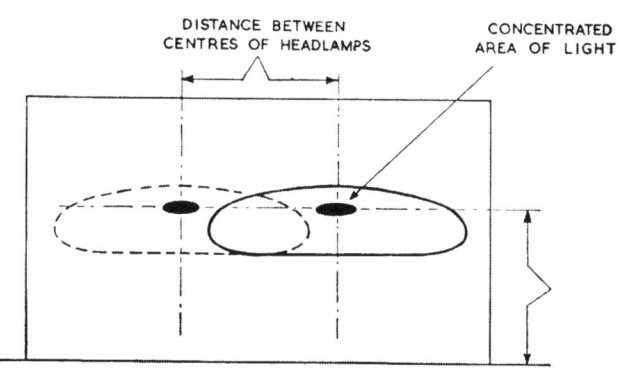

Fig. M.26. Headlamp beam setting.

(a) *Front of the vehicle to be square with the wall.*
(b) *Vehicle to be loaded and on level ground.*
(c) *Recommended distance for setting is at least 25 feet. (7·6 m.).*

When replacing the bulb care must be taken to see that the rectangular pip on the bulb flange engages the slot in the reflector seating for the bulb.

Replace the spring clip with its coils resting in the base of the bulb flange and engaging in the two retaining lugs on the reflector seating.

The appropriate replacement bulbs are listed in 'GENERAL DATA'. They are not interchangeable with those used in conjunction with the Continental-type headlamps previously fitted.

Section M.31

SEALED BEAM LIGHT UNITS

Cars exported to the U.S.A. are now fitted at the Works with headlamps incorporating sealed beam light units.

To change a sealed beam light unit, remove the headlamp rim and slacken the three retaining screws securing the light unit rim. Rotate the rim anti-clockwise to disengage the slotted holes from the heads of the retaining screws. Pull the light unit forward and disconnect the three-pin socket to release from the backshell.

Section M.32

HEADLAMP BEAM SETTING

The lamps should be set so that the main driving beams are straight ahead and parallel to one another, and parallel to the road surface. If adjustment to the setting is required, first remove the front rim and rubber as previously described. Set each lamp to the correct position in the vertical plane by means of the vertical adjustment screw at the top of the reflector unit. Turn

ELECTRICAL SYSTEM

the screw in a clockwise direction to raise the beam and in an anti-clockwise direction to lower it. Horizontal adjustment can be altered by turning the adjustment screws on each side of the light unit.

The setting of the lamps can best be carried out by placing the car in front of a blank wall at a distance of not less than 25 feet taking care that the surface on which the car is standing is level and not sloping relative to the wall.

It will be found an advantage to cover one lamp while setting the other.

Section M.33

REPLACING A LIGHT UNIT

In the event of damage to either the front lens or reflector, a replacement light unit must be fitted as follows:

(1) Remove the light unit as already described.

(2) Withdraw the three screws from the unit rim and remove the seating rim and unit rim from the light unit.

(3) Position the replacement light unit between the unit rim and setting rim, taking care to see that the die cast projection at the edge of the light unit fits into the slot in the seating rim, and also check that the seating rim is correctly positioned. Finally secure in position by means of the three fixing screws.

Fig. M.28. Rear number plate light.
1. Bulbs.   2. Glass.   3. Cover.

Section M.34

MODIFIED SEALED BEAM LIGHT UNITS

An improved type of sealed beam light unit is now being fitted to all cars exported to the U.S.A. Headlamps that embody the improved light unit can be identified by a figure '2' moulded into the lens at the twelve o'clock position.

When setting these headlamps they must be aimed and set in the dip position in accordance with the regulations of the State in which the vehicle is operating.

Section M.35

COMBINED SIDE AND FLASHER LIGHTS BULB

To Remove

(1) Prise back the rubber lip and insert a screwdriver blade under the glass retaining collar.

(2) Lever the collar out from the lamp body.

(3) Remove the lamp glass and unscrew the bulb.

To Replace

The installation of a side lamp bulb is a reversal of the procedure 'To Remove'.

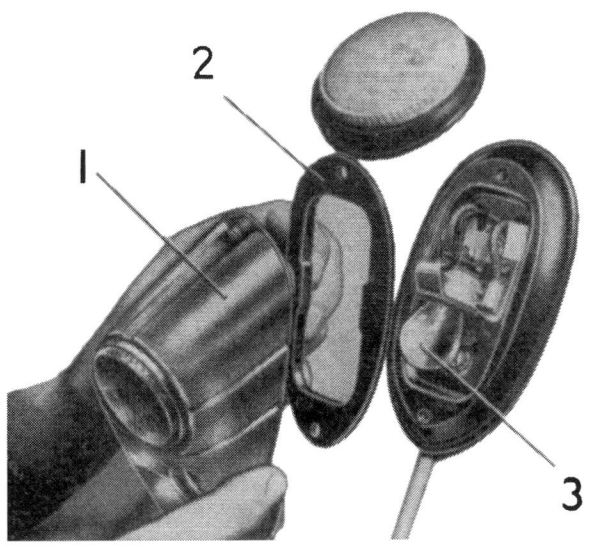

Fig. M.27. Combined stop and tail lamp.
1. Stop/tail glass.   2. Rubber sealing ring.
3. Stop/tail bulb.

Section M.36

REAR FLASHER LIGHT BULB

For details see Section M.35.

Austin-Healey Sprite Mk. 1. Issue 3. 35471.

M — ELECTRICAL SYSTEM

Section M.37

COMBINED STOP AND TAIL LIGHT BULBS

To Remove
(1) Unscrew the two screws securing the lamp cover glass.
(2) Remove the cover glass.
(3) Unscrew the bulb.

To Replace
The installation of a stop/tail light bulb is a reversal of the procedure 'To Remove'.

Section M.38

REAR NUMBER PLATE LIGHT BULB

To Remove
(1) Unscrew the screw securing the lamp cover and lift off the cover.
(2) Remove the bulb.

To Replace
The installation of the number plate light bulb is a reversal of the procedure 'To Remove'.

Section M.39   FAULT DIAGNOSIS

Symptom	No.	Possible Fault
(a) Battery discharge	1 2 3 4 5	Terminals loose or dirty Lighting circuit shorted Generator not charging Regulator unit not operating properly Battery internally defective
(b) Insufficient current flow to battery	1 2	Loose or corroded terminal connections Generator belt slipping
(c) Battery fails to retain charge	1 2 3 4	Electrolyte levels low Battery plates badly sulphated Electrolyte leakage due to cracked cell or sealing compound Plate separators not effective
(d) Battery overcharged	1	Voltage regulator out of adjustment

ELECTRICAL SYSTEM

Symptom	No.	Possible Fault
(e) Generator not charging properly or inoperative	1	Driving belt slipping or broken
	2	Regulator unit not operating properly
	3	Badly worn bearings or pole pieces loose
	4	Short between commutator bars
	5	Armature worn or shaft bent
	6	Commutator out of round
	7	Insulation high between commutator bars
	8	Commutator greasy, glazed or burned
	9	Brush springs weak or broken
	10	Brushes sticking
	11	Field coils shorted, open or burned
(f) Starter motor lacks power or fails to turn the engine	1	Battery in need of attention
	2	Loose or broken connection in starter circuit
	3	Starter motor pinion jammed in mesh with flywheel gear
	4	Starter switch faulty
	5	Brushes worn, sticking or not bedded
	6	Engine abnormally stiff
	7	Commutator dirty or worn
	8	Starter shaft bent
(g) Starter motor operates but does not turn the engine	1	Pinion sticking on the screwed sleeve
	2	Broken pinion or flywheel gear teeth
(h) Noise from starter pinion when engine is running	1	Restraining spring weak or broken
(j) Starter motor inoperative	1	Battery needs attention
	2	Loose or broken connection in starter circuit or switch
	3	Armature faulty
	4	Field coils earthed
(k) Starter motor rough or noisy engagement	1	Starter motor loose on mounting bolts
	2	Damaged pinion and/or flywheel gear teeth
	3	Main spring broken

M ELECTRICAL SYSTEM

Symptom	No.	Possible Fault
(l) Lamps inoperative	1 2 3 4	Battery discharged Lamp bulbs burned out Loose or broken connections Lighting switch faulty
(m) Lamps operate when switched on but gradually fade out	1	Battery discharged
(n) Lamps give insufficient illumination	1 2 3 4	Battery in low state of charge Headlamps out of alignment Bulbs discoloured through use Reflector surface deteriorated
(o) Lamps erratic	1 2 3	Lights switch contacts faulty Battery to earth connections faulty Lamp earth faulty
(p) Flashing indicator warning lamp or direction indicator lamp inoperative	1	Check the bulbs and renew if necessary Also see 'Section M.15'
(q) Horn inoperative	1 2 3	Fuse blown Faulty connection Horn faulty internally
(r) Horn operates continuously	1 2	Horn-push stuck or earthed Horn cable (brown with black) to horn-push earthed
(s) Horn note unsatisfactory	1 2	Loose cable connection Horn out of adjustment
(t) Wiper motor inoperative or takes no current	1 2 3 4 5	Fuse blown Battery needs attention Loose or broken connection in the motor circuit Armature faulty Field coils earthed
(u) Wiper motor takes abnormally low current	1 2 3 4	Battery needs attention Armature faulty Commutator dirty Brushes worn or not bedded

ELECTRICAL SYSTEM

Symptom	No.	Possible Fault
(v) Wiper motor sluggish and takes abnormally high current	1 2 3 4	Armature faulty Armature bearings out of alignment Commutator dirty or short-circuited Wheelbox spindle binding or bent
(w) Wiper motor operates but does not drive the wiper arms	1 2 3	Wheelbox gear and spindle worn Driving cable rack faulty Gearbox components worn
(x) Fuel gauge fails to register	1 2 3	Gauge supply interrupted Gauge case not earthed Cable between gauge and tank unit earthed
(y) Fuel gauge registers full	1	Cable between gauge and tank unit broken or disconnected

SECTION N

WHEELS AND TYRES

Section No. N.1   Description

Section No. N.2   Adjustments

Section No. N.3   Wheel and tyre assemblies

Section No. N.4   Tyre life

Section No. N.5   Balance

Section No. N.6   Jack

WHEELS AND TYRES

Section N.1

DESCRIPTION

The Austin-Healey Sprite is fitted with 5.20—13 tubeless tyres upon 15 × 4J ventilated steel disc wheels. each wheel being secured by four nuts.

Section N.2

ADJUSTMENTS IN THE VEHICLE

The purpose of the following adjustments is to obtain the best performance from the wheels and tyres. Proceed as detailed below. Other faults should be diagnosed after consulting Section N.4.

(1) Tighten the road wheel nuts to a torque wrench reading of 37 to 39 lb. ft. (5·02 to 5·4 kg. m.). **Do not overtighten.**
(2) Check the tyre pressures regularly with a gauge and inflate them to the recommended pressures.
(3) Change the positions of the wheel and tyre assemblies, bringing the spare into use, at the recommended intervals.
(4) Remove any oil, grease or foreign objects from the tyres.

Section N.3

WHEEL AND TYRE ASSEMBLIES

To Remove
(1) Apply the handbrake and scotch one of the wheels.
(2) Jack up the vehicle sufficiently to ensure that the wheel with a fully inflated tyre can be removed or installed.
(3) Remove the hub cover.
(4) Remove the four wheel nuts, which have right-hand threads, *i.e.* turn anti-clockwise to loosen. Lift off the wheel.

Fig. N.1. Tyre Repair Kit.

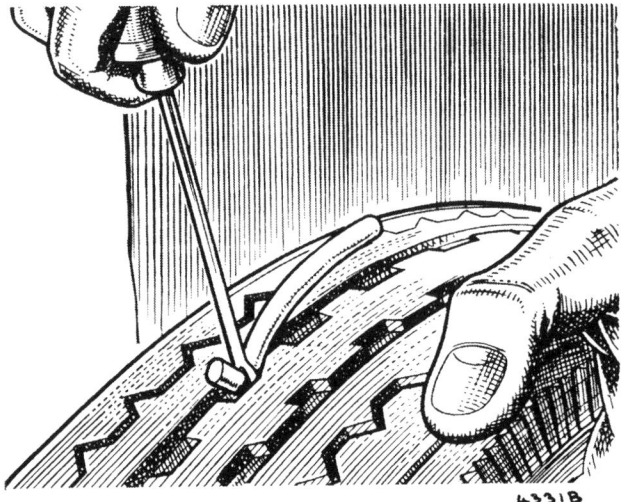

Fig. N.2. Inserting the plug and needle through the hole in the tyre

To Repair Simple Tyre Penetrations

Normally a tubeless tyre will not leak as the result of penetration by a nail or other normal puncturing objects provided that it is left in the tyre, but repair should be effected at the earliest convenient time.

In the case of a nail penetrating the tyre, a repair can be carried out externally without removing the tyre from the rim, providing the special repair kit is available. If the hole fails to seal, mark the spot and extract the nail, taking note of the direction of penetration. If the tyre is leaking and the puncturing object cannot be located by sight, immerse the wheel and tyre in water.

Repair the tyre as follows:

(1) Insert the needle of the repair kit through the hole in the tyre in the same direction as the penetration to free it from road grit. Dip the needle into the rubber solution and re-insert it through the hole, repeating this operation until the hole is well lubricated with the solution.
(2) Select a repair plug of about twice the diameter of the puncturing object, stretch and roll it into the eye of the needle, about ¼ in. (6 mm.) from its end. Dip the plug into the rubber solution and insert the needle through the hole in the tyre so that the end of the rubber plug passes through the hole into the interior of the tyre. Withdraw the needle, leaving the plug in the tyre, and cut off the plug about ⅛ in. (3 mm.) from the surface of the tread.
(3) Inflate the tyre (see "To inflate the tyre").

To Dismantle
(1) Lay the wheel on the ground, with the valve uppermost. Deflate the tyre by removing the valve cap and interior.

Austin-Healey Sprite Mk. 1. Issue 3. 35471.

WHEELS AND TYRES

(2) Using tyre levers, which must be in good condition, separate the beads from the rim flange in the manner shown in Fig. N.6 until both beads are in the base of the rim. As inextensible wires are incorporated in the edges of the tyres, no attempt should be made to stretch the edges over the rim as the beads must in **NO WAY BE DAMAGED**. Keep the levers moistened with water.

(3) With the bead of the tyre held in the base of the rim at a point diametrically opposite the valve, insert a lever close to the valve and carefully lift the tyre over the rim. Using two levers at intervals of about 6 in. (15 cm.) apart, continue to lift the tyre bead over the rim until this bead is entirely free.

(4) Stand the tyre and wheel upright, keeping the bead in the base of the rim. Lever the bead over the rim flange, and at the same time push the wheel away from the tyre with the other hand to completely remove the tyre off the wheel.

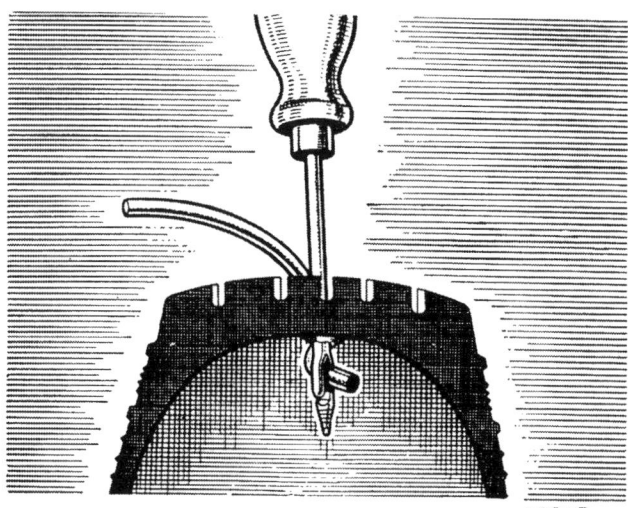

Fig. N.4. The inserted plug prior to withdrawing the needle.

fix" patch, or preferably use an uncured rubber patch and vulcanise it in position.

(3) In the event of more serious damage, the tubeless tyre can undergo a major vulcanised repair in the same way as a normal tyre. The tubeless tyre can also be re-treaded.

To Prepare the rim before Fitting the Tyre

(1) Examine the condition of the wheel and renew if cracked, or if the attachment holes are elongated.

(2) Check for loose rivets in the base of the wheel rim and fit oversize rivets if necessary, ensuring that they do not protrude the beyond height of the original rivets. An airtight seat must be maintained.

(3) Clean off all rust, rubber, etc., from the wheel flange and rim seat, using steel wool, emery or similar cleaning medium. In extreme cases of rusty rims it may be necessary to use a wire brush or even a file.

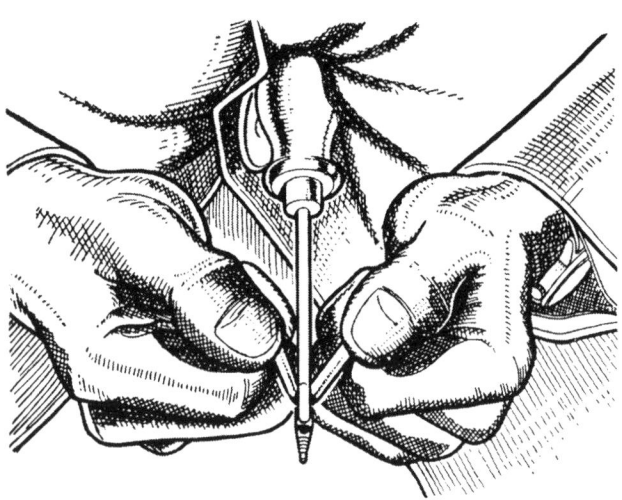

Fig. N.3. Rolling the plug into the needle eye.

To Repair Severe Tyre Penetrations

Severe penetrations which are outside the scope of the small repair kit can be repaired in a similar manner to conventional covers which will necessitate the removal of the tyre (see above).

Repair the tyre as follows:

(1) Inspect the tyre for damage and remove any puncturing objects.

(2) Clean the area around the hole on the inside of the tyre, roughen with a scratchbrush and apply a rubber solution to the surface to receive an ordinary tube patch such as the Dunlop "Vulca-

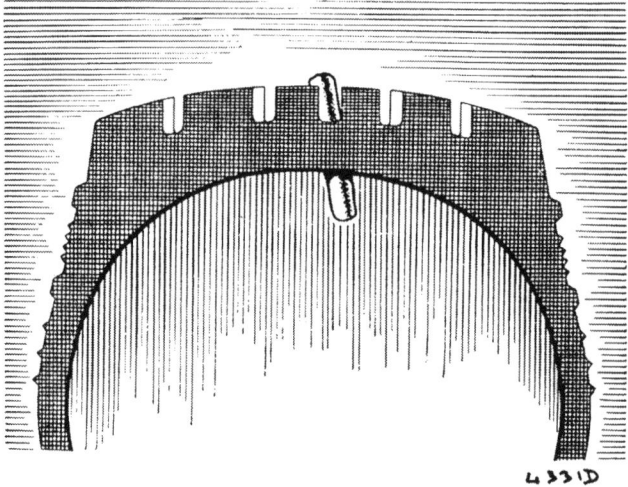

Fig. N.5. Plug inserted in the tyre and cut-off.

WHEELS AND TYRES

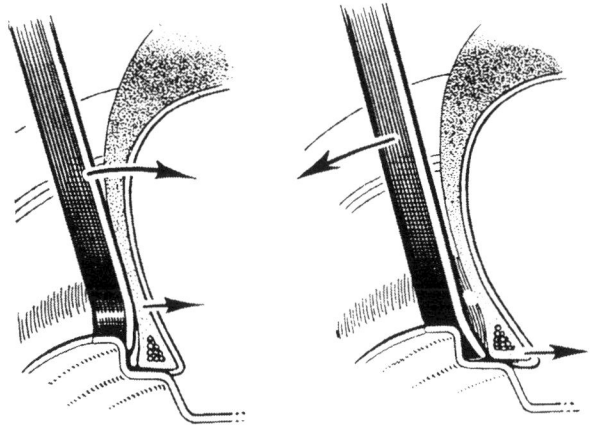

Fig. N.6. *Removing a tyre bead off the rim*

(4) Remove any dents in the flange by hammering out carefully to maintain an airtight seat.
(5) High spots in the welded joint of the rim must be filed or buffed away.

To Renew a Valve

A valve should never be refitted once it has been removed from the rim, and it should be renewed every time a new tyre is fitted.

Cut out or pull outwardly the old valve from the rim. Lubricate a new valve with soap solution and pull it through the rim hole from the inside. The valve should be pulled until the flange on the rubber base of the valve is in full contact with the inner rim surface. If the valve is pulled too far, the base will be damaged and another new valve will have to be fitted.

The use of the Schrader valve mounting Tool No. 553 is recommended, so as to avoid damage.

To Reassemble

When replacing the tubeless tyre a similar technique has to be employed to that used for removal, first fitting the tyre into the base of the rim at a point opposite the valve. Make sure the valve interior is removed and that the balance spots near the tyre bead are at the valve position. Wipe clean and moisten the beads of the tyre, rim flanges and tyre levers with clean water. Do not use petrol. Carry out the final fitting of the tyre, using levers which are in good condition and free from burrs. Take small "bites" with the levers.

To Inflate the Tyre

(1) Before inflating the tyre, bounce the crown of the tyre on the ground at various points round its circumference, to snap the beads home against the rim. This will provide a partial seal.

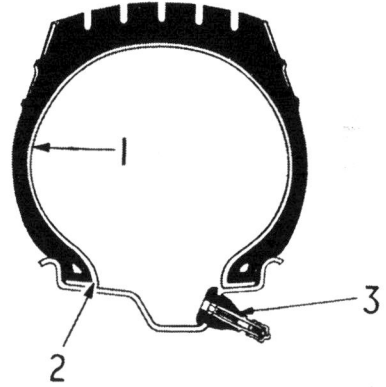

Fig. N.8. *A section through the rim, tyre and valve.*
1. *Air retainer liner.*
2. *Rubber air seal.*
3. *Rubber-sealed valve.*

(2) Connect an air line to the valve, with its interior plunger omitted, and inflate the tyre with the wheel in an upright position. If a seal cannot be effected by the first rush of air, bounce the tyre on its crown at various points round the circumference with the air line still attached. In cases of difficulty apply the special tourniquet consisting of a strap incorporating a lever, but a suitably strong cord or rope around the circumference of the tread and a twisting bar or stick will also serve. If no air line is available and the tyre has to be inflated by a foot- or hand-pump, then the use of a tourniquet is essential to force the beads outwards against the rim flanges to effect a seal. Remove the air line, insert the valve interior and re-inflate, for test purposes, to 50 lb./sq. in. (3·5 kg./cm.²).

(3) Allow the tyre to stand for a few minutes so that any free air trapped between the flange and the bead clinch can escape. Test the complete assembly in a water tank to check for leaks, special attention being paid to the areas at the beads, valve and wheel rivets. Should leakage occur

Fig. N.7. *The use of a tourniquet to seal the beads.*

Austin Healey-Sprite. Issue 2. 21424.

at the valve base, this can only be rectified by renewing the valve. Loss of air around the bead seat and flange is generally due to a high spot on the rim (foreign matter, rust, weld, etc.) and in most cases this can be cured by holding the tyre bead away from the rim, with the tyre deflated, in order to effect further cleaning of the rim bead seat with emery, steel wool, etc. Air leakage at the rivets can be remedied by peening over the rivet head with a ball-pane hammer. The rivet should be backed up with another, and preferably larger, hammer. In extreme cases where major leaks occur at the flanges or rivets, mark off the position of the leaks on the tyre and the rim before removing the tyre for inspection and rectification.

(4) When satisfied that there are no air leaks, and that the tyre is correctly fitted, adjust the tyre to the recommended working pressure.

To Replace

(1) Install the wheel and tyre assembly on the hub.
(2) Screw on the wheel nuts, which have right-hand threads, *i.e.* turn in a clockwise direction, and tighten them in diagonal sequence.

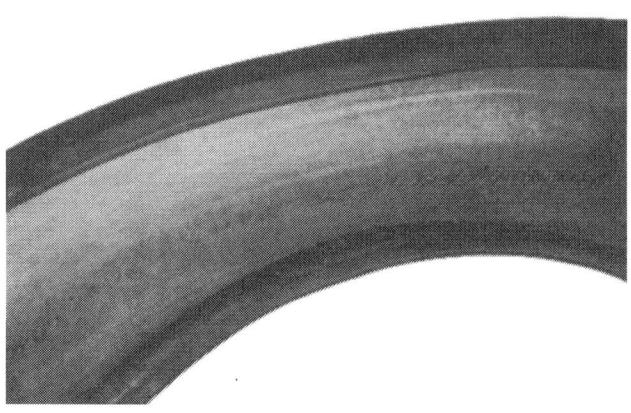

Fig. N.10. This casing is breaking up due to over-flexing and heat generation.

(3) Release the jack and scotch; check the wheel nuts again, using a torque wrench such as Service Tool 18G 372, to a tightness of 37 to 39 lb. ft. (5·02 to 5·4 kg. m.). **Do not overtighten.**
(4) Place the rim of the hub cover over two of the buttons on the wheel centre and give the outer face a sharp blow of the fist over the third button.

Section N.4

FACTORS AFFECTING TYRE LIFE AND PERFORMANCE

Inflation Pressures

All other conditions being favourable there is an average loss of 13% tread mileage for every 10% reduction in inflation pressure below the recommended figure.

A tyre is designed so that there is a minimum pattern shuffle on the road surface and a suitable distribution of load over the tyres contact area when deflection is correct.

Moderate underinflation causes an increased rate of tread wear although the tyre's appearance may remain normal. Severe and persistent underinflation produces unmistakable evidence on the tread, see Fig. N.9. It also causes structural failure due to excessive friction and temperature within the casing, Figs. N.10 and N.11.

Pressures which are higher than those recommended for the car reduce comfort. They may also reduce tread life due to a concentration of the load and wear on a smaller area of tread, aggravated by increased wheel bounce on uneven road surfaces. Excessive pressures overstrain the casing cords, in addition to causing rapid wear, and the tyres are more susceptible to impact fractures and cuts.

Fig. N.9. Excessive tyre distortion from persistent underinflation causes rapid wear on the shoulders and leaves the centres standing proud. If the effects of underinflation are aggravated by other factors, such as camber and excessive braking, the irregular and rapid wear is more pronounced.

WHEELS AND TYRES

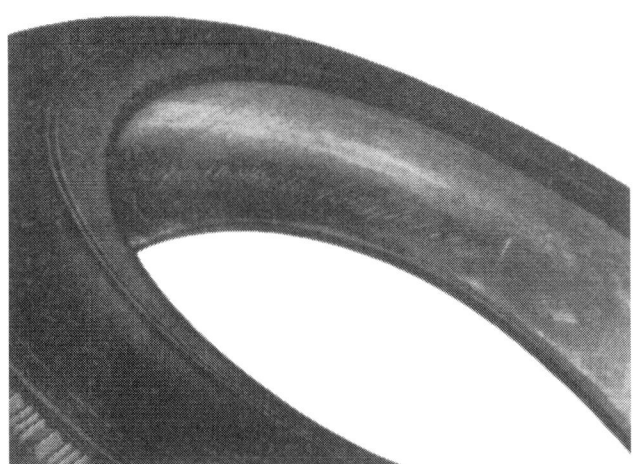

Fig. N.11. Running deflated has destroyed this tyre.

Effect of Temperature

Air expands with heating and tyre pressures increase as the tyres warm up. Pressures increase more in hot weather than in cold weather and as a result of high speed. These factors are taken into account when designing the tyre and in preparing Load Pressure schedules.

Pressures in warm tyres should not be reduced to standard pressure for cold tyres. "Bleeding" the tyres increases their deflections and causes their temperatures to climb still higher. The tyres will also be underinflated when they have cooled.

Speed

High speed is expensive and the rate of tread wear may be twice as fast at 50 m.p.h. as at 30 m.p.h.

High speed involves:
(1) Increased tyre temperatures due to more deflections per minute and a faster rate of deflection and recovery. The resistance of the tread to abrasion decreases with increase of temperature.
(2) Fierce acceleration and braking.
(3) More tyre distortion and slip when negotiating bends and corners.
(4) More "thrash" and "scuffing" from road surface irregularities.

Braking

"Driving on the brakes" increases the rate of tyre wear, apart from being generally undesirable. It is not necessary for wheels to be locked for an abnormal amount of tread rubber to be worn away.

Other braking factors not directly connected with the method of driving can affect tyre wear, for instance correct balance and lining clearances, and freedom from binding, are very important. Braking may vary between one wheel position and another due to oil or foreign matter on the shoes even when the brake mechanism is free and correctly balanced.

Brakes should be relined and drums reconditioned in complete sets. Tyre wear may be affected if shoes are relined with non-standard material having suitable characteristics or dimensions, especially if the linings differ between one wheel position and another in such a way as to upset the brake balance. Front tyres, and particularly near front tyres, are very sensitive to any condition which adds to the severity of front braking in relation to the rear.

"Picking-up" of shoe lining leading edges can cause grab and reduce tyre life. Local "pulling-up" or flats on the tread pattern can often be traced to brake drum eccentricity, Fig. N.12. The braking varies during each wheel revolution as the minor and major axis of the eccentric drum pass alternately over the shoes. Drums should be free from excessive scoring and be true when mounted on their hubs with the road wheels attached.

Climatic Conditions

The fate of tread wear during a reasonably dry and warm summer can be twice as great as during an average winter.

Water is a rubber lubricant and tread abrasion is much less on wet roads than on dry roads. In addition resistance of the tread to abrasion decreases with increase in temperature.

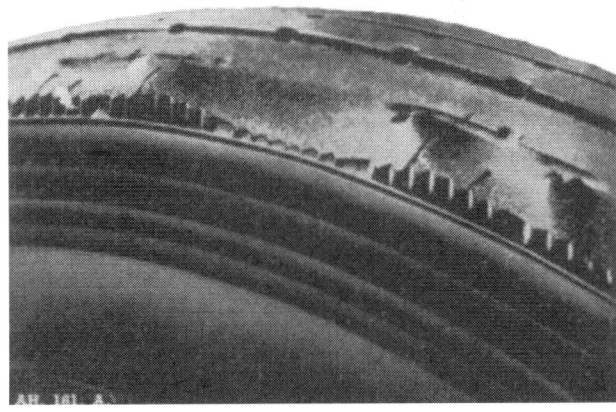

Fig. N.12. Local excessive wear due to brake drum eccentricity.

When a tyre is new its thickness and pattern depth are at their greatest. It follows that heat generation and pattern distortion due to flexing, cornering, driving and braking are greater than when the tyre is part worn.

Higher tread mileages will usually be obtained if new tyres are fitted in the autumn or winter rather than in the spring or summer. This practice also tends to

WHEELS AND TYRES

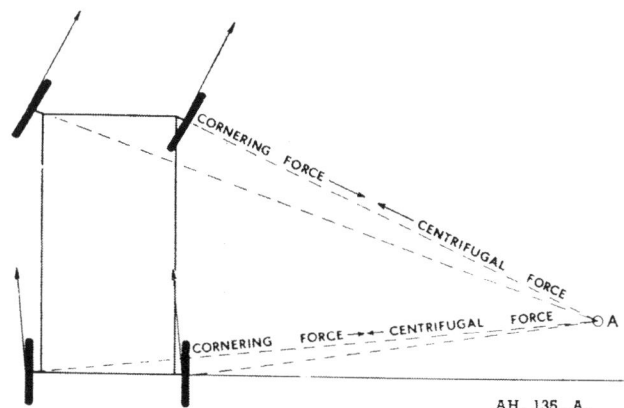

Fig. N.13. *Slip when cornering causes increased tyre wear.*

reduce the risk of road delays because tyres are more easily cut and penetrated when they are wet than when they are dry. It is, therefore, advantageous to have maximum tread thickness during wet seasons of the year.

Road Surface

Present day roads generally have better non-skid surfaces than formerly. This factor, combined with improved car performance, has tended to cause faster tyre wear, although developments in tread compounds and patterns have done much to offset the full effects.

Road surfaces vary widely between one part of the country and another, often due to surfacing with local material. In some area the surface dressing is coarser than others; the material may be comparatively harmless rounded gravel, or more abrasive crushed granite, or knife-edged flint. Examples of surfaces producing very slow tyre wear are smooth stone setts and wood blocks, but their non-skid properties are poor.

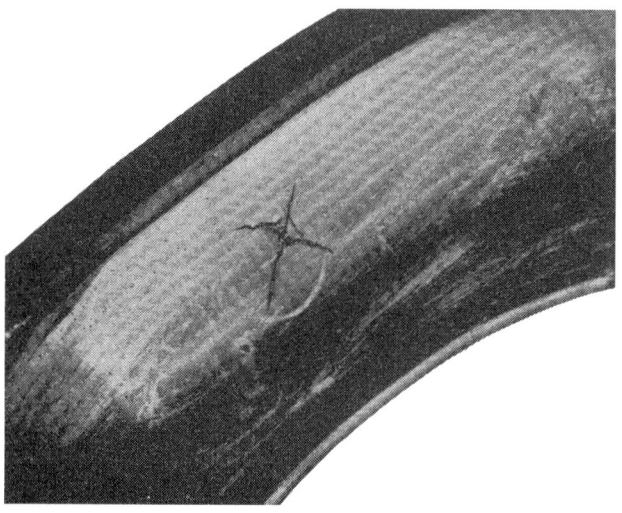

Fig. N.14. *Severe impact has fractured the casing.*

Bends and corners are severe on tyres because a car can be steered only by misaligning its wheels relative to the direction of the car. This condition applies to the rear tyres as well as the front tyres. The resulting tyre slip and distortion increase the rate of wear according to speed, load, road camber and other factors, Fig. N.13.

The effect of hills, causing increased driving and braking torques with which the tyres must cope, needs no elaboration.

Impact Fractures

In order to provide adequate strength, resistance to wear, stability, road grip and other necessary qualities, a tyre has a certain thickness and stiffness. Excessive and sudden local distortion, such as may result from striking a kerb, a large stone or brick, an upstanding manhole cover, or deep pothole may fracture the casing cords; Figs. N.14 and N.15.

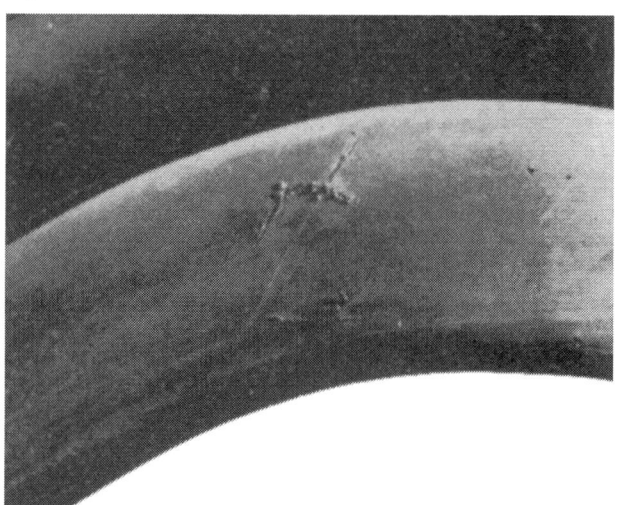

Fig. N.15. *A double fracture caused by the tyre being crushed between the rim and an obstacle, such as the edge of a kerb.*

Impact fractures often puzzle the car owner because the tyre and road spring may have absorbed the impact without his being aware of anything unusual. Only one or two casing cords may be fractured by the blow and the weakened tyre fails some time later. Generally there is no clear evidence on the outside of the tyre unless the object has been sufficiently sharp to cut it.

This damage is not associated solely with speed, and care should be exercised at all times, particularly when drawing up to a kerb.

"Spotty Wear"

Fig. N.16 shows a type of irregular wear which sometimes develops on front tyres and particularly on near-side front tyres.

The nature of "spotty" wear—the pattern being much worn and little worn at irregular spacings round the circumference—indicates an alternating "slip grip" phenomenon, but it is seldom possible to associate its origin and development with any single cause. There is evidence of camber wear, misalignment, underinflation, or braking troubles.

It is preferable to check all points which may be contributory factors. The front tyres and wheel assemblies may then be interchanged, which will also reverse their direction of rotation, or better still the front tyres may be interchanged with the rear tyres.

Points for checking are:
(1) Inflation pressures and the consistency with which the pressures are maintained.
(2) Brake freedom and balance, shoe settings, lining condition, drum condition and truth.
(3) Wheel alignment.

Fig. N.16. Irregular 'Spotty' wear, to which a variety of causes may contribute.

(4) Camber and similarity of camber of the front wheels.
(5) Play in hub bearings, swivel pin bearings, suspension bearings, and steering joints.
(6) Wheel concentricity at the tyre bead seats.
(7) Balance of the wheel and tyre assemblies.
(8) Conditions of road springs and shock absorbers.

Corrections which may follow a check of these points will not always effect a complete cure and it may be necessary to continue to interchange wheel positions and reverse directions of rotation at suitable intervals.

Fig. N.17. Fins or feathers caused by severe misalignment. With minor misalignment, probably aggravated by road camber, the ribs may have sharp edges instead of upstanding fins. The conditions will usually be accompanied by heel and toe wear across the tread due to its being distorted and worn away laterally instead of in a true rolling direction.

Irregular wear may be inherent in the local road conditions such as from a combination of steep camber, abrasive surfaces, and frequent hills and bends. Driving methods may also be involved. Irregular wear is likely to be more prevalent in summer than in winter, particularly on new or little worn tyres.

Wheel Alignment and Road Camber

It is very important that correct wheel alignment should be maintained. Misalignment causes a tyre tread to be scrubbed off laterally because the natural direction of the wheel differs from that of the car.

An upstanding fin on the edge of each pattern rib is a sure sign of misalignment and it is possible to determine from the position of the "fins" whether the wheels are toed in or toed out, see Fig. N.17. Fins on the inside edges of the pattern ribs—nearest to the car—and particularly on the off-side tyre, indicate toe-out.

With minor misalignment the evidence is less noticeable and the sharp pattern edges may be caused by road camber even when wheel alignment is correct. In such cases it is better to make sure by checking with an alignment gauge.

Road camber affects the direction of the car by imposing a side thrust and if left to follow its natural course the car will drift to the near side. This is instinctively corrected by steering towards the road centre. As a result the car runs crab-wise. Fig. N.18 shows, in exaggerated form, the effect this has upon the tyres.

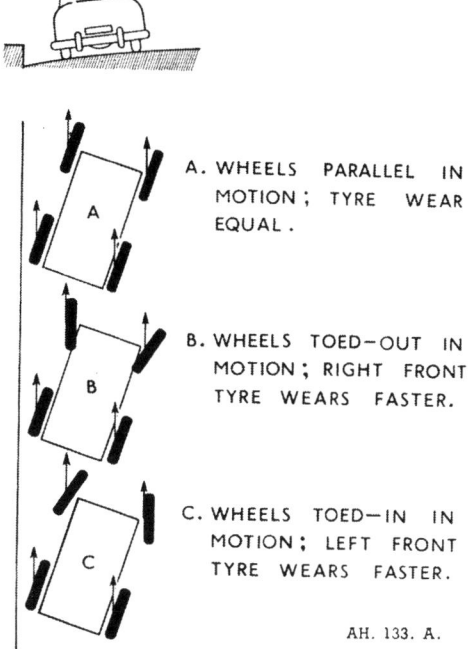

Fig. N.18. *Exaggerated diagram of the way in which road camber affects a car's progress.*

The near front tyre sometimes persists in wearing faster and more unevenly than the other tyres even when the mechanical condition of the car and tyre maintenance are satisfactory. The more severe the average road camber the more marked will this tendency be. This is an additional reason for the regular interchange of tyres.

Camber Angle

This angle normally requires no attention unless disturbed by a severe impact, however, it is always advisable to check this angle if steering irregularities develop, see K6.

Wheel camber usually combined with road camber, causes a wheel to try to turn in the direction of lean, due to one side of the tread attempting to make more revolutions per mile than the other side. The resulting increased tread shuffle on the road and the off centre tyre loading tend to cause rapid and one sided wear. If wheel camber is excessive for any reason the rapid and one sided tyre wear will be correspondingly greater. Unequal cambers introduce unbalanced forces which try to steer the car one way or the other. This must be countered by steering in the opposite direction which results in faster tread wear.

Section N.5

TYRE AND WHEEL BALANCE

Static Balance

In the interests of smooth riding, precise steering and the avoidance of high speed "tramp" or "wheel hop," all tyres are balance checked to predetermined limits.

To ensure the best degree of tyre balance the covers are marked with white spots on one bead and these indicate the lightest part of the cover. The white balance spots near the tyre bead should be at the valve position.

Some tyres are slightly outside standard balance limits and are corrected before issue by attaching special loaded patches to the inside of the covers at the crown. These patches contain no fabric, they do not affect the local stiffness of the tyre and should not be mistaken for repair patches—they are embossed "Balance Adjustment Rubber".

The original degree of balance is not necessarily maintained and it may be affected by uneven tread wear, by cover and tube repairs, by tyre removal and refitting or by wheel damage and eccentricity. The car may also become more sensitive to unbalance due to normal wear of moving parts.

Should roughness or high speed steering troubles develop, and mechanical investigation fails to disclose a possible cause, wheel and tyre balance should be suspected.

A tyre balancing machine is marketed by the Dunlop Company to enable service stations to deal with such cases.

Dynamic Balance

Static unbalance, as its name implies, can be measured when the tyre and wheel assembly is stationary. There is, however, another form known as dynamic unbalance which can be detected only when the assembly is revolving.

WHEELS AND TYRES

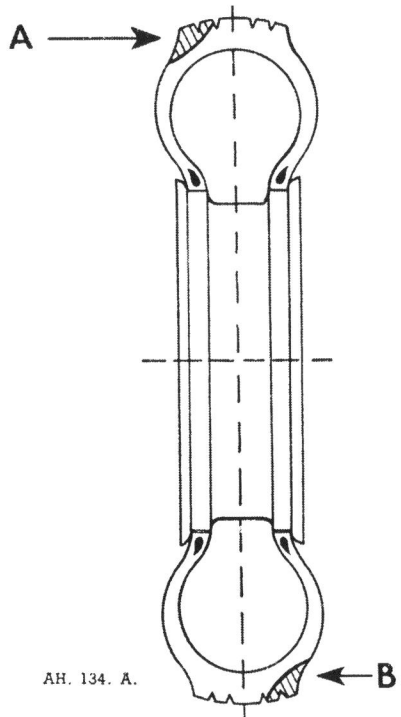

Fig. N.19. Dynamic or couple unbalance, produces wear at 'A' and 'B'.

There may be no heavy spot—that is, there may be no natural tendency for the assembly to rotate about its centre due to gravity—but the weight may be unevenly distributed each side of the tyre centre line, see Fig. N.19.

Laterally eccentric wheels give the same effect. During rotation the offset weight distribution sets up a rotating couple which tends to steer the wheel to right and left alternately.

Dynamic unbalance of tyre and wheel assemblies can be measured on the Dunlop tyre balancing machine and suitable corrections made when a car shows sensitivity to this form of unbalance. Where it is clear that a damaged wheel is the primary cause of severe unbalance it is advisable for the wheel to be replaced.

Changing Position of Tyres

Reference has already been made to irregular tread wear which is confined almost entirely to front tyres and there may be different rates of wear between one tyre and another.

It is, therefore, recommended that front tyres be interchanged with rear tyres at least every 3,000 miles (5000 km.). Diagonal interchanging between near-side front and off-side rear and between off-side front and near-side rear provides the most satisfactory first change because it reverses the direction of rotation.

Subsequent interchanging of front and rear tyres should be as indicated by the appearance of the tyres, with the object of keeping the wear of all tyres even and uniform.

Wheel Wobble: The lateral variation measured on the vertical inside face of a flange should not exceed $\frac{3}{32}$ in. (2·3812 mm.).

Wheel Lift: On a truly mounted and revolving wheel the difference between the high and low points, measured at any location on either tyre bead seat, should not exceed $\frac{3}{32}$ in. (2·3812 mm.).

Radial and lateral eccentricity outside these limits contribute to static and dynamic unbalance respectively. Severe radial eccentricity also imposes intermittent loading on the tyre. Static balancing does not correct this condition which can be an aggravating factor in the development of irregular wear.

A wheel which is eccentric laterally will cause the tyre to snake on the road, but this in itself has no effect on the rate of tread wear.

At the same time undue lateral eccentricity is undesirable and it affects dynamic balance.

Rim seatings and flanges in contact with the tyre beads should be free from rust and dirt.

Section N.6

JACK

The jack (Fig. N.20) supplied with the car, can be operated from either side, thus enabling either the right or left side to be raised completely.

Before jacking up the car first apply the handbrake and if necessary (car on a gradient) chock one of the

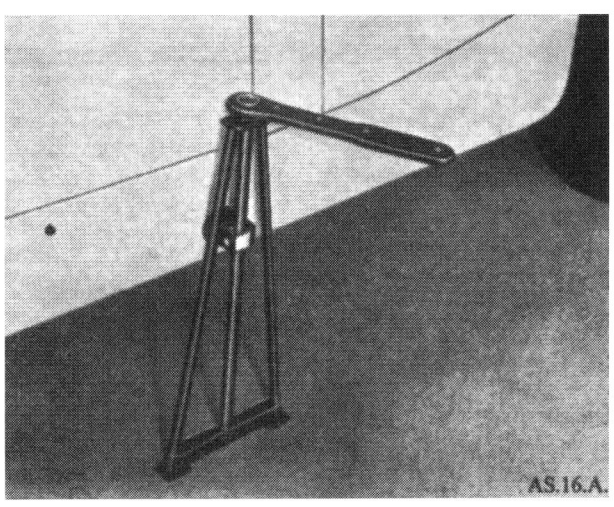

Fig. N.20 The jack.

WHEELS AND TYRES

wheels on the opposite side to that requiring attention. Insert the jack lug into the socket provided under the car.

Ensure that the lug is fully engaged in the socket and that the base has a firm footing on the ground, before commencing to wind the screw clockwise with the aid of the ratchet spanner.

Immediately the car is felt to lift, recheck that the lug is correctly located within its socket.

Naturally, to lower the car the jack screw must be turned in an anti-clockwise direction.

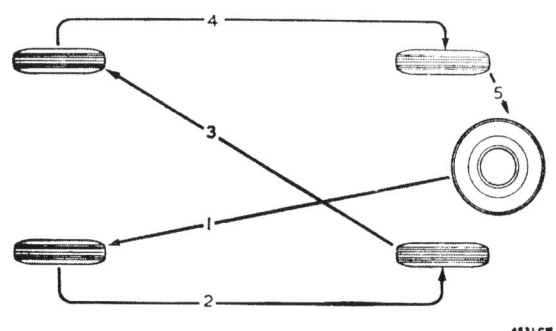

Fig. N.21
Interchange the road wheels diagonally in the order shown above, bringing the spare wheel into use.

SECTION O

BODYWORK

Section No. O.1.   Maintenance and adjustments

Section No. O.2.   Dismantling

Section No. O.3.   Repair procedure

Section No. O.4.   Welding methods

Section No. O.5.   Welding technique

Section No. O.6.   Torch-soldering

Section No. O.7   Body alignment checking jig.

Section No. O.8   Luggage grid.

Section No. O.9   Seat belts

BODYWORK — O

Section O.1

MAINTENANCE AND ADJUSTMENTS

Synthetic Enamel

A synthetic enamel requires frequent washing to retain the high degree of finish and a good emulsion polish, occasionally applied, is sufficient to preserve the paintwork. Never use a liquid wax polish on synthetic enamel.

Bright Trim

Metal polish must not be used to clean chromium, plastic, stainless steel or anodised aluminium bright parts. Wash them frequently with soap and water and when the dirt has been removed, polish the surface with a clean dry cloth or chamois leather until bright.

Never use an abrasive.

A slight tarnish may be found on stainless steel that has not been washed regularly and this can be removed with impregnated wadding such as is used on silverware.

Surface deposits on chromium parts may be removed with a chromium cleaner.

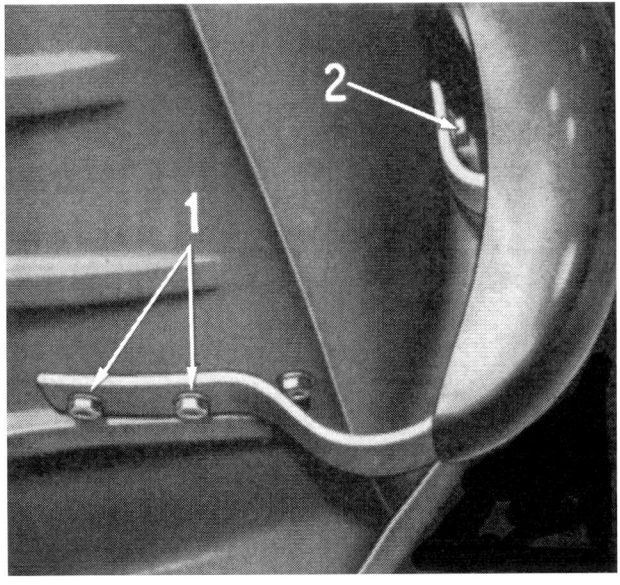

Fig. O.2. Rear bumper securing points (1 and 2).

An occasional application of wax polish or light oil to metal trim will help to preserve the finish particularly during winter when salt has been applied to the roads, but these protectives should not be applied to plastic finishers.

Door Locks and Hinges

Occasionally apply a few drops of oil on the moving parts of all door locks and hinges. A light touch of grease should be smeared on the lock striker plates to ensure free movement and reduce wear of the locks.

In addition, the security of door hinges, locks, dovetails and striker plate should be checked periodically with a screwdriver.

Windows

Windscreen, sidescreens, rear window and driving mirror should be cleaned with a damp leather.

Section O.2

DISMANTLING

Bonnet Top

Removal of the bonnet top entails disconnection of the wiring harness which feeds the headlamps, side lamps and flashing indicators, all mounted on the bonnet.

Fig. O.1. The bonnet to hinge setpins are shown at (1).

BODYWORK

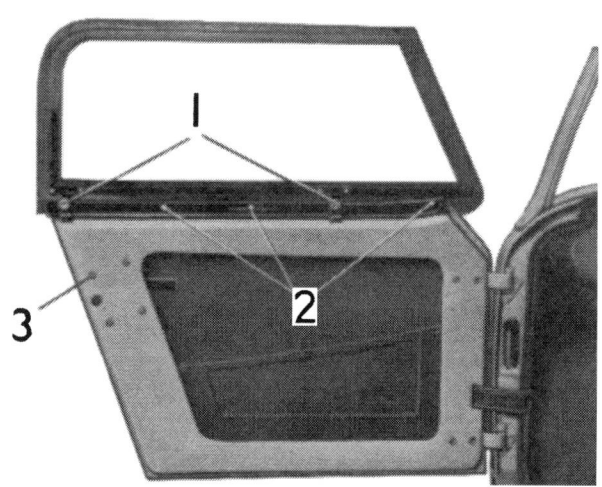

Fig. O.3. The sidescreen, top moulding and door lock fixings are shown at 1, 2, and 3 respectively.

Remove the earth terminal of the battery and disconnect the harness at the snap connectors (four double and two single) situated alongside the right-hand bonnet hinge.

The harness should also be released at its connection with the hinge itself. Unscrew the setpin at the top of each telescopic stay.

Withdraw the four setpins securing each hinge to the underside of the bonnet (Fig. O.1) when the bonnet can be lifted clear of the car.

Note: The two inside setpins on each bonnet hinge are longer than the outside pair.

Grille

The grille is secured by thirteen spring clips each easily accessible when the bonnet is raised.

Bonnet Lock

Raise the bonnet and detach the lock handle by unscrewing its securing pin situated on the opposite side of the lock.

Withdraw the four lock mounting setscrews and remove the lock together with its two locking rods.

Bumpers

Rear: Each rear bumper is secured at the points 1 and 2 shown in Fig. O.2.

Front: The front bumper is released by unscrewing the two setpins mounted on each box section end of the body reinforcement.

Sidescreens

Each sidescreen has two clamping brackets at its base which are held by two large headed screws (1, Fig. O.3) at the door top moulding.

Doors

Hinges and Door Removal: Both the upper and lower hinge of each door is secured to the door pillar by three cross-head screws. At the door frame each hinge is fixed by two cross-head screws (Fig. O.4).

There is a check strap fitted to each door which must be released when dismantling a door from the bodywork. This check strap can be released by withdrawing the two setpins from the coupling bracket in the inside of the door pillar. Thus with the door wide open, the hinges can readily be uncoupled from the door pillar and the door and hinges removed.

Door Top Moulding: The aluminium moulding at each top edge is held in place by three cross-head screws, Fig. O.3.

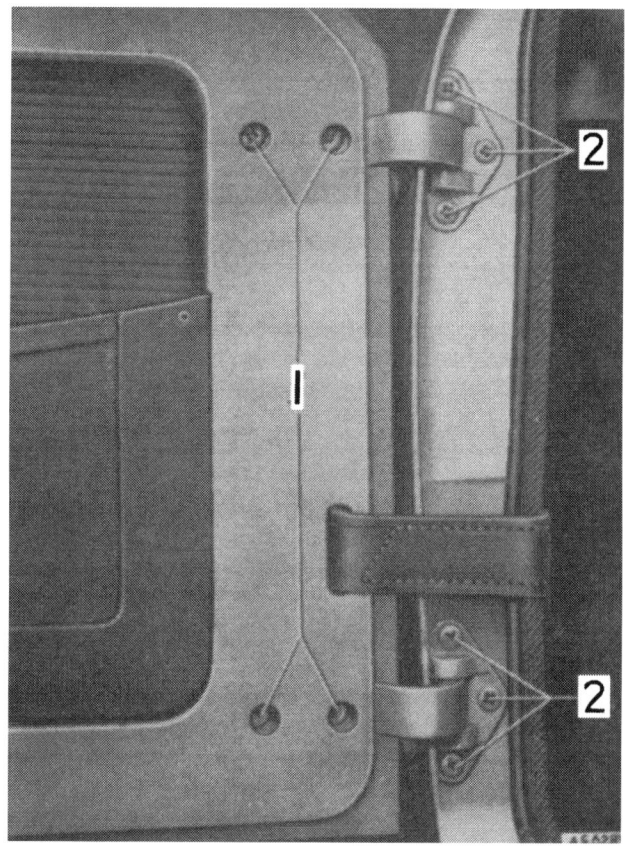

Fig. O.4. Door hinges.
1. *Door to hinge screws.*   2. *Hinge to pillar screws.*

BODYWORK

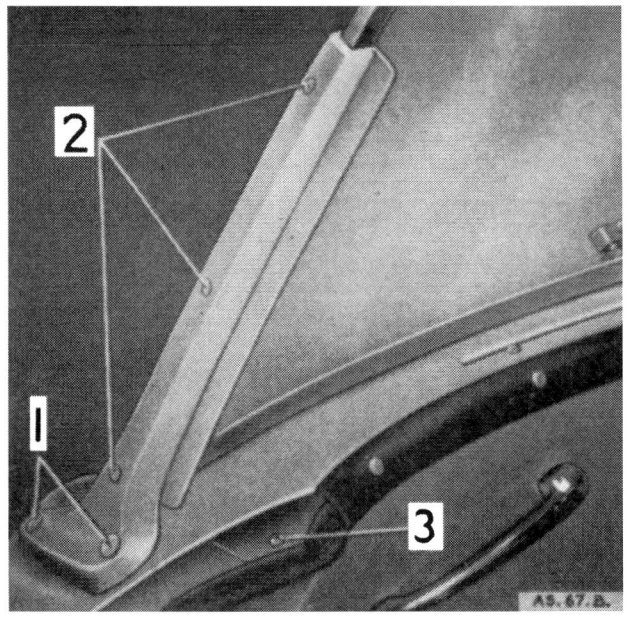

Fig. O.5. Windscreen pillar and fascia.
1. Pillar to body screws.   2. Windscreen to pillar screws
3. A fascia screw.

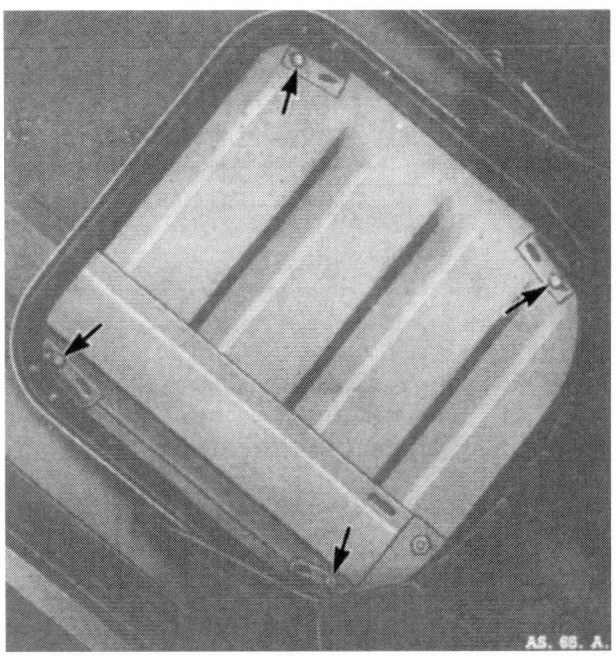

Fig. O.6. Seat frame securing points.

Door Catch: The catch and operating handle complete may be withdrawn by unscrewing the four setscrews positioned inside the door, Fig. O.3.

Windscreen

The windscreen is secured at each side pillar by three cross-head screws (Fig. O.5). The pillars themselves are attached to the scuttle by one cross-head setpin and one bolt, the nut for which is accessible when the door is open.

Cockpit Mouldings

The front and rear cockpit mouldings are secured by nine and eleven cross-head screws respectively.

Fascia Panel

Remove the steering wheel as described in Section J.

Along the top edge of the fascia are three securing points, one nut and bolt in each corner and one nut at the centre.

Two cross-head screws secure the fascia at its bottom edge together with the three setscrews behind the steering column surround.

Unscrew the speedometer and tachometer drives at their instrument unions and disconnect the oil pressure pipe from behind the combined oil pressure and water temperature gauge. It is advisable to withdraw the water thermal element at its connection with the radiator.

Release the starter and choke cables when the fascia can be brought forward into the cockpit thus giving access to the rear of each instrument.

Grab Handle

The passenger grab handle is fixed to the fascia panel by two studs. The securing nuts being situated behind the panel.

Seats

To remove the passenger's seat the cushion must be lifted whereupon eight nuts are accessible. These nuts must be unscrewed to release the seat frame, Fig. O.6.

The adjustment of the seat can be carried out after slackening the four floor setpins.

For the driver an adjustable driving seat is provided for forward or rearward positioning by pushing the lever beneath the seat, toward the runner then moving the seat to the required setting and releasing the lever.

Lift out the seat cushion to gain access to the four nuts securing the seat to the runners.

The seat runners, with their packing pieces, are bolted to the floor, each runner having two bolts with nuts accessible beneath the floor.

Section O.3

REPAIR PROCEDURE

Body jack

The specially designed body jack, obtainable under

Austin-Healey Sprite Mk. I. Issue 3. 35471.

BODYWORK

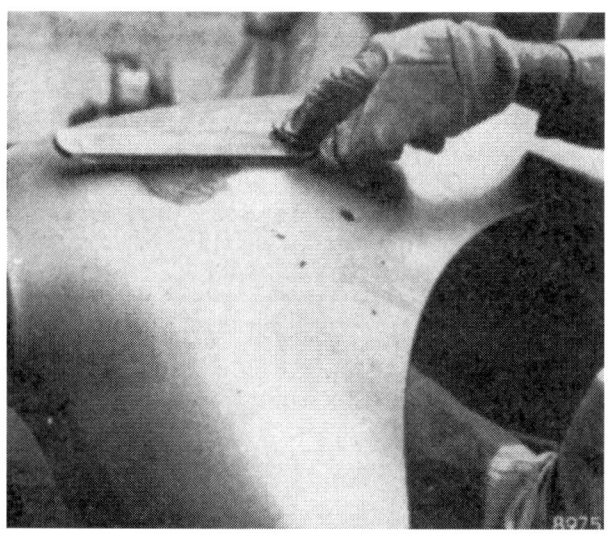

Fig. O.7. Removing a dent by tapping with a spoon; a dolly is held below the dent.

18G 308B, is an absolutely essential item when rectifying any misalignment of the body construction. The jack is provided with a ratchet turnscrew, and the pitch of the centre spindle thread is such that considerable force (either pulling or pushing) can be exerted. The extension pieces are made from solid drawn steel tubes and their lengths are such that the effective length of the jack can be made to vary between 21 and 94 in. (533 and 2388 mm.).

Considerable thought has been given to their construction and design, and careful study of the equipment will be amply repaid.

The body jack is supplied by the B.M.C. Service Department at current prices. A metal box in which the jack and its components can be neatly stored is supplied with the jack.

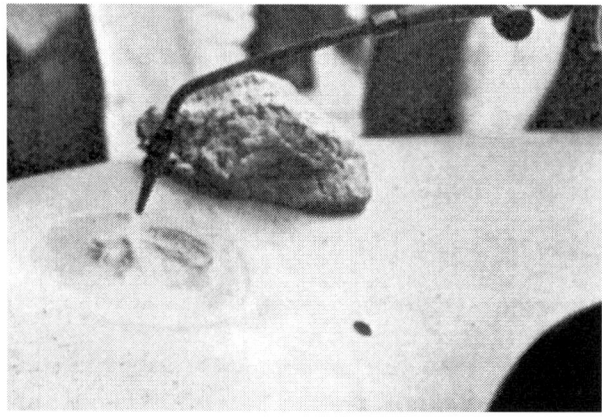

Fig. O.8. Application of heat prior to tapping with a mallet; a dolly is held below the dent while tapping.

Fig. O.9. A dolly block and mallet.

With the addition of a suitable oxy-acetylene outfit (Section O.5) any type of mono-construction repair can be effected. The initial outlay need only be small, and, considering the wide range of operations covered, there should be no hesitation in deciding that the kit must figure as part of the equipment of your repair shop.

Rectification of buckled panels or underframe

Experience will prove that parts of the body which at first sight would be considered beyond repair can be rectified easily by straightening.

It is of paramount importance to return the damaged portion of the body to its original position before deciding whether replacement panels are necessary or not.

With the use of the special jack this method enables a buckled or damaged structure to be returned to its original relative position without straining the surrounding metal, which would be the inevitable result

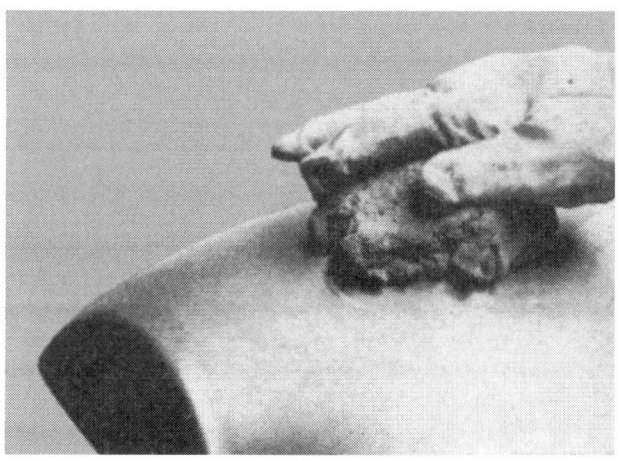

Fig. O.10. Cooling the damaged area with wet asbestos.

BODYWORK

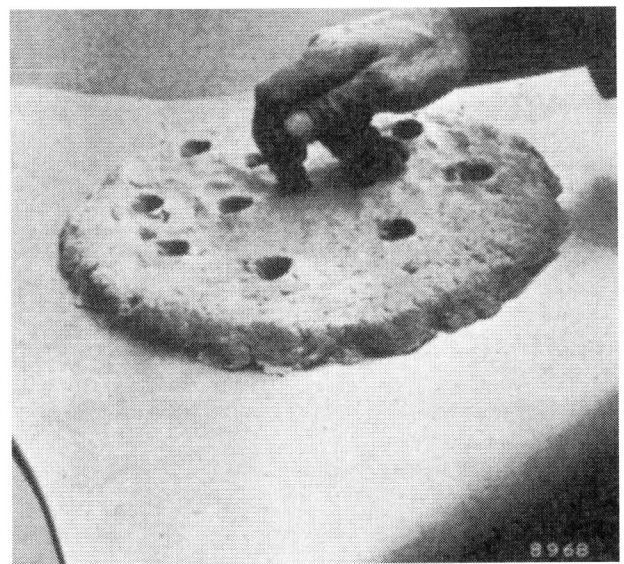

Fig. O.11. Piercing a series of holes in wet asbestos prior to the application of heat.

if the damaged portion were pounded by means of a hammer. At this stage a decision can be reached as to whether any damaged panel is to be repaired or renewed.

Spoon for removal of small dents

To remove small dents a spoon which is made from a coarse-cut file, specially shaped and having the teeth intact, is used in conjunction with a suitably shaped dolly block (Fig. O.7).

The use of a hammer to remove small dents is to be deprecated, as hammer blows tend to stretch the surrounding metal, giving rise to further complications. It is for this reason that the spoon is recommended as by its use a depression can be raised to its original level without stretching.

On panel work such as doors, or where inside reinforcements prevent the use of a dolly block, a hole can be punched or drilled through the inside panel and a suitable drift pin, about $\frac{1}{2}$ in. (13 mm.) in diameter, used in conjunction with the spoon in place of the dolly block.

Sharper dents or a dent or collection of dents covering a large area will require the use of heat, a dolly, and a spoon in the following manner (Fig. O.8).

With the welding torch heat a small area at the outside of the collection of dents, then, holding the dolly below, hammer the raised portion with a wooden

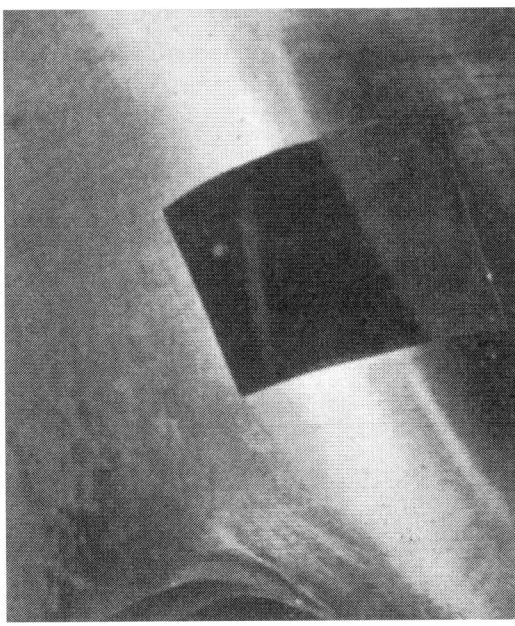

Fig. O.13. A damaged piece removed for patching.

mallet (Fig. O.9). When the metal cools remove the dolly and place a large handful of wet asbestos over the heated area to prevent the heat spreading (Fig. O.10). Continue to heat and tap, working from the outside of the damaged area, until something like the original contour and level is attained.

Lightly file the surface to show up the high-spots and remove these with the dolly and spoon without further heating.

Take care when using the file not to thin the metal more than is necessary to show up the high-spots.

Alternative checking by filing and raising with the dolly block and spoon will eventually produce a flat and clean surface without weakening the metal unduly, provided excessive filing is avoided. Care should be exercised to reduce filing to a minimum as otherwise the thickness of the panel will be seriously reduced.

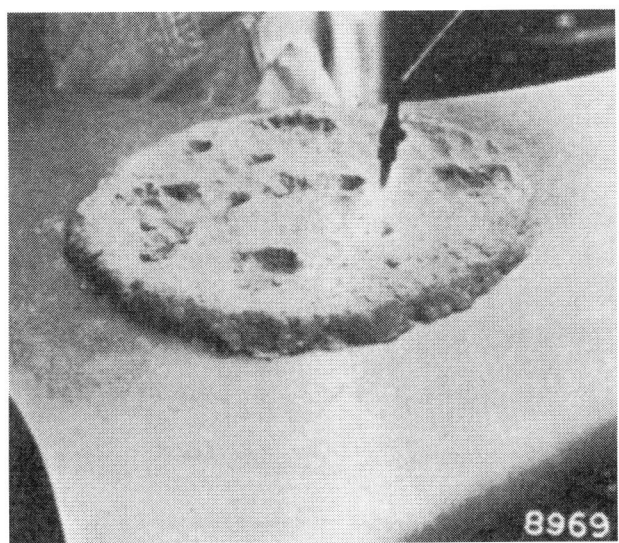

Fig. O.12. Heating the stretched panel through holes in the asbestos.

BODYWORK

On completion, the surface may be tinned and any small indentations filled with plumber's solder.

Preservation of paintwork

A special spoon, having the teeth removed and its surface planished and polished, is required to enable small dents to be removed without damage to paintwork. Where it is possible to preserve paintwork when rectifying comparatively large dents a sandbag should be placed against the painted surface of the panel and the dent removed from the underside by the use of a wooden mallet. A suitable sandbag for this operation may be made from a leather oval bag 8 in. (203 mm.) long, 6 in. (152 mm.) wide, and 4 in. (102 mm.) thick which is packed tightly with sand.

Stretched panels

Stretched panels which are liable to cause drumming can be rectified by local shrinking. A liberal heap of wet asbestos is placed over the stretched panel at the point of greatest resiliency, and a hole just large enough to apply the flame of the oxy-acetylene torch is made with a finger through the centre of the asbestos. The portion of the panel which is visible is heated to a cherry-red colour and is afterwards cooled off by the wet asbestos which surrounds it. For large panels it may be necessary to repeat this operation several times at different locations over the area.

Where a panel is stretched over a fairly extensive area and produces what is known as an 'oilcan' effect the following shrinking method should be used to restore the original contour.

Mix a quantity of wet asbestos sufficient to cover the damaged area with a thickness as shown in Fig. O.11. Press the asbestos down firmly to ensure that no air

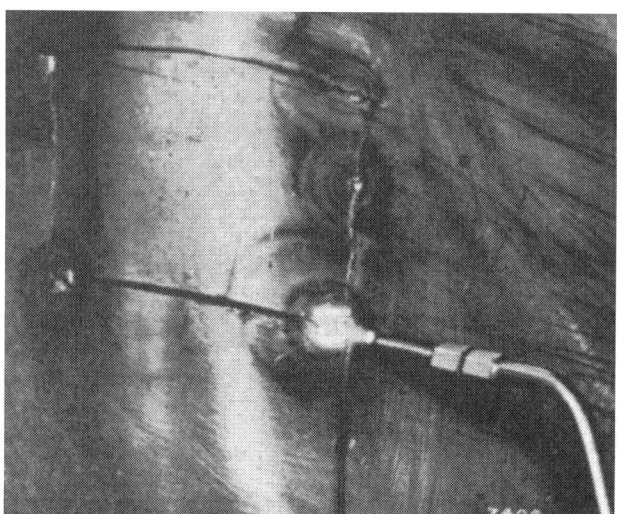

Fig. O.14. After the patch is formed it is held in position by gas-weld tacks.

Fig. O.15. To prevent buckling of the surrounding metal during welding surround the joint with wet asbestos.

is trapped below, as it is important to confine the applied heat to the points of application.

With a finger pierce a series of holes in the asbestos extending to the surface of the metal. Direct the flame of the welding torch to one of the holes near the perimeter of the asbestos and heat the metal to cherry red, remove the torch, and immediately press the surrounding asbestos into the hole (Fig. O.12).

Carry out the same procedure with the remaining holes, working around the asbestos and inwards towards the centre. When the asbestos is removed the surface is cleaned up in the usual manner.

Patching

An extensively damaged panel can frequently be repaired quite satisfactorily and more economically by patching rather than by renewing the entire assembly. This type of repair does not in the least weaken the surrounding structure, as a patch which is correctly gas-welded in position is equal in strength to the original structure. A patch can be introduced so efficiently that it is impossible to trace its presence.

The damaged portion of the panel should be cut out with a cold chisel or, if possible, by means of a hacksaw. The edges of the opening should then be filed until an even contour is obtained (Fig. O.13).

The patch to be fitted should preferably be cut from sheet metal of similar gauge and specification to that being repaired. First, it is rough-shaped to the contour

BODYWORK

of the panel, after which it is fitted to the opening to allow a clearance on all sides equal to the gauge of the metal.

In all probability, particularly during welding operations, difficulty will be experienced in holding the patch in place. This can be overcome satisfactorily by welding one or two short pieces of welding wire to act as convenient handles.

The patch is now fastened at intervals of 2 to 3 in. (51 to 76 mm.) to the panel by means of gas-weld tacks (Fig. O.14). During the tacking operation it should be reshaped to the panel to ensure that the contour is correct.

To prevent expansion and possible buckling of the surrounding panel during the welding operation a liberal quantity of wet asbestos must be placed on the panel round the patch, approximately ¼ in. (6 mm.) away from the joint (Fig. O.15). The joint is now gas-welded between the tacks, whilst precautions are taken to keep the patch to the correct contour by using a suitable dolly block and bumping hammer. On completion, any excrescences in the welding are removed by filing and, after straightening with the dolly block and bumping hammer, the patching is finally finished by tinning and solder-filling as described in Section O.6.

Patch forming

Where it is necessary to 'form' a patch from the flat sheet to any particular contour a wooden or lead raising block is generally employed. The raising block should have several elliptical depressions of varying depths and diameters.

The patch is placed over the selected depression and is raised by hammering with the ball-pane end of a hammer, starting from the outer edges and gradually working towards the centre. A mistake frequently made is to strike too hard whilst raising the centre, with the result that the curve is of greater depth than that required.

Repair of beadings and mouldings

Where difficulty is experienced in straightening or renewing a beading, moulding, or corner the original contour may be obtained by careful tinning and filling with plumber's solder. The finished work will be equal in appearance and equal in strength, whilst the substitution of soldering for straightening, or renewing, will save the necessity for removing inside trimmings, etc.

Filing

It should be understood that in every case filing must be reduced to a minimum owing to the thinness of the material. Wrinkles or ridges should be removed by the spoon or dolly block, as explained on page O.4, and finished finally by tinning and solder-filling.

Replacing panels

In cases of extreme damage it will be found more economical to remove the damaged portions and replace them with new panels, which are obtainable from B.M.C. Service Ltd. The panels and assemblies which are available are illustrated on pages O.12, O.14 and O.16 and the part numbers are given in the current Service Parts List.

The illustrations show clearly the location and types of joints used in the construction of the body, and, following the instructions already given and the instructions to follow on welding, any portion of the body can be removed, either by a hacksaw or cold chisel, and a suitable replacement fitted in position.

Owing to the fact that damage is usually localized, it will only infrequently be found necessary to remove a complete panel or unit. In the great majority of cases the damaged portion can be removed and a corresponding part cut from a replacement unit and located in position by gas-welding.

Section O.4

WELDING METHODS

Spot-welds

This form of welding is used extensively throughout the assembly of the mono-construction body.

The units to be joined are pressed together between two copper electrodes through which an electric current of low voltage and high amperage is passed. The resistance of the steel to the electric current raises the metal to welding temperature and the pressure between the electrodes produces complete fusion. The resulting joint is as strong as the surrounding structure, and a correctly made spot-weld will not break or become loose by vibration.

Spot-welds cannot be broken satisfactorily by inserting a cold chisel or lever between the two panels. Each weld must be carefully drilled in the centre, using a drill approximately $\frac{3}{16}$ in. in diameter. There is no necessity to drill through both panels as it is sufficient if the point of the drill merely penetrates the second panel. The weld is finally broken by inserting a thin, sharp, cold chisel between the joint and tapping it lightly with a hammer.

On panels where the spot-welds are covered by paint it is necessary to use a suitable paint remover to clean the paint from the joints. The spot-welds will easily be located by the discolouration of the metal. Reference to the body build-up illustrations will facilitate tracing the various joints.

BODYWORK

Gas-welds

A gas-weld may be broken either by cutting with a hacksaw or, alternatively, with a sharp cold chisel. Place a suitable support at the back of the panel to act as an anvil whenever possible.

Lap-welds

Most lap-welds used in the mono-construction body are hidden from view by solder-filling. Reference should be made to the illustrations showing the build-up of the body in order to obtain the location of the various lap joints. This will enable the operator to direct the flame of the oxy-acetylene blowpipe onto the joint so that the solder filling can be melted and removed by the use of a duster. A lap-weld is broken by drilling out the spot-welds as previously explained.

Butt-welds

A butt-weld can be broken by the use of a hammer and chisel, the blows being directed against the panel which is to be renewed. If this method does not quickly break the weld heat applied from the oxy-acetylene torch will soften the fused edges, thus assisting the operation. Alternatively, the joint may be cut by a hacksaw.

Remaking welds

The special section of this Manual devoted to welding should be studied carefully before any attempt is made to reweld a joint on the body by an operator who has not had the necessary experience in this class of work.

When a joint is remade it is necessary, prior to paint-

Fig. O.17. Type B.A.R.9 two-stage acetylene regulator.

ing, to clean the surface of the weld. During this operation, as previously mentioned, care should be taken to see that the structure is not unnecessarily weakened by excessive grinding or filing. It is preferable to hammer the joint so that it lies slightly lower than the surrounding metal and to flow solder into the depression. No amount of filing on the surface of the solder can reduce the strength of the joint below (See Section O.6).

When placing a new panel in position it should be joined where possible by gas-welding through the holes drilled in breaking the original spot-welds. During the welding operations a liberal heap of wet asbestos should be placed over the surrounding panels to prevent buckling and distortion due to heat.

Section O.5

WELDING TECHNIQUE

The following applies to equipment supplied by the British Oxygen Co. Ltd., although it also applies, in the main, to other similar equipment.

Welding equipment

High-pressure oxy-acetylene welding equipment using dissolved acetylene is recommended. This consists of:
    (1) Supply of acetylene in cylinders.
    (2) Supply of oxygen in cylinders.
    (3) Blowpipe with necessary nozzles.
    (4) Acetylene pressure regulator.

Fig. O.16. Type B.O.R.12A two-stage oxygen regulator.

BODYWORK O

(5) Oxygen pressure regulator.
(6) Two lengths of rubber-canvas hose.
(7) Set of spanners and spindle key.
(8) Welding goggles and spark lighter.
(9) Welding rods.
(10) Welding fluxes.
(11) Trolley for accommodating complete equipment and cylinders.

Assembly

(1) Stand both cylinders vertically on the ground or on a trolley. Oxygen cylinders are painted BLACK. Acetylene cylinders are painted MAROON. **Never** attempt to interfere with the colour of cylinders or to repaint them.
(2) See that jointing surfaces in cylinder valves and regulators are free from oil and grease.
(3) Open the valve on the oxygen cylinder momentarily in order to dislodge dirt or other obstruction in the cylinder valve, then close.

Fig. O.19. The welding blowpipe.

(4) Screw the oxygen regulator (painted BLACK) (Fig. O.16) into the oxygen cylinder valve. The oxygen cylinder valve outlet and oxygen regulator connection have **right-hand** screw threads.
(5) Screw the acetylene regulator (painted MAROON) (Fig. O.17) into the acetylene cylinder valve. The acetylene cylinder valve outlet and acetylene regulator connection have **left-hand** screw threads.
(6) Tighten the regulator in the cylinder valve. Do not use excessive force, but make certain that the joints are gastight.
(7) Connect the hose (acetylene RED, oxygen BLACK) to the screwed outlets of the regulators by means of the screwed connections secured in the ends of the hose. Blow the hose through before attaching to the regulator or blowpipe in order to remove dust and dirt and to remove chalk when the hose is new.
(8) Connect the other end of the hose, that fitted with a hose protector, to the blowpipe—the acetylene hose to the connection marked 'A', the oxygen to the connection marked 'O'. Keep the blowpipe control valves closed. (A high- or low-pressure blowpipe can be used with the dissolved acetylene. If a low-pressure blowpipe is used the acetylene pressure should never exceed 2 lb./sq. in. [·14 kg./cm.^{2}].)
(9) Fix the appropriate nozzle to the blowpipe. (See the table, page O.10.)
(10) Open the cylinder valves very slowly by means of the cylinder key. Do not open suddenly, or there may be serious damage to the regulator and the possibility of an accident. Open the cylinder valve spindle one turn only.
(11) Set the regulators at the correct working pressures. (See the table, page O.10.)
(12) Open the acetylene control valve on the blowpipe, wait a few seconds until air is blown out and pure acetylene is coming from the blowpipe nozzle, then light, preferably by means of a spark lighter, type S.L.I.

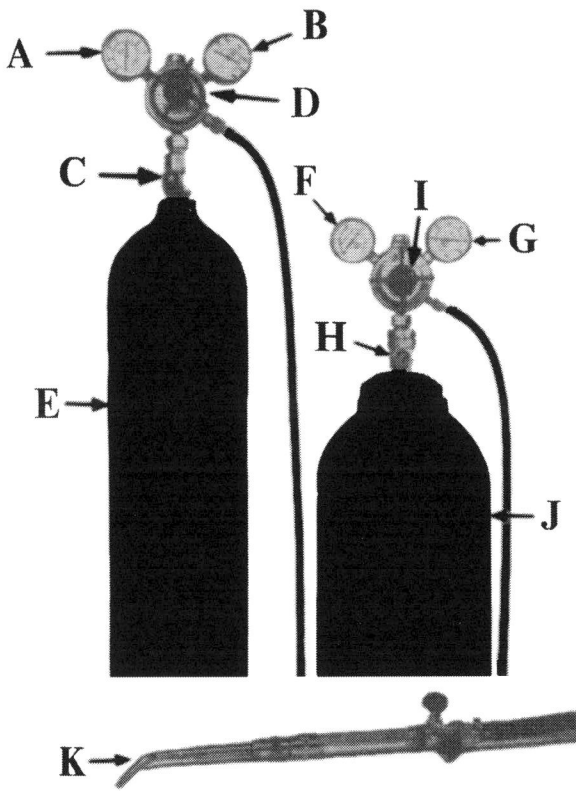

Fig. O.18. High-pressure oxy-acetylene welding outfit.

A. Outlet pressure gauge (O).
B. Cylinder contents gauge (O).
C. Valve.
D. Pressure regulating screw.
E. Oxygen cylinder (BLACK).
F. Outlet pressure gauge (A).
G. Cylinder contents gauge (A).
H. Valve.
I. Pressure regulating screw.
J. Acetylene cylinder (MAROON).
K. Blowpipe (interchangeable nozzles).

WELDING
HIGH-PRESSURE BLOWPIPES
Nozzle Sizes, Working Pressures, and Gas Consumptions for Various Metal Thicknesses

M.S. plate thickness		Nozzle size	Regulator pressures, oxygen and acetylene Saffire equipment		Approximate consumption of each gas	
in.	mm.		lb./sq. in.	kg./cm.²	cu. ft./hr.	m.³/hr.
$\frac{1}{32}$	·79	1	2	·141	1	·028
$\frac{3}{64}$	1·19	2	2	·141	2	·056
$\frac{1}{16}$	1·58	3	2	·141	3	·084
$\frac{3}{32}$	2·38	5	2	·141	5	·140
$\frac{1}{8}$	3·17	7	2	·141	7	·196
$\frac{5}{32}$	3·96	10	3	·211	10	·283
$\frac{3}{16}$	4·76	13	3	·211	13	·367
$\frac{1}{4}$	6·35	18	3	·211	18	·504
$\frac{5}{16}$	7·93	25	4	·281	25	·700

(13) Reduce or increase the acetylene supply by the blowpipe valve until the flame just ceases to smoke.

(14) Turn on the oxygen by the blowpipe control valve until the white inner cone in the flame is sharply defined, with the merest trace of an acetylene haze.

The blowpipe is now adjusted for welding steel, and work may be commenced.

The size of nozzle given for a particular thickness of steel is for general guidance only and will vary according to the skill of the welder, mass of metal, etc. The capacity of each nozzle overlaps the capacities of those next in size to it. The values given are for down-hand butt-welds in mild steel. For other techniques nozzle size and pressure may have to be varied slightly, e.g. for copper select a larger nozzle, for aluminium a smaller nozzle.

On thin-gauge steel up to and including $\frac{1}{16}$ in. thickness tacks should be slightly closer together—say, 1 to 1½ in. (25 to 38 mm.) apart—to keep the edges in alignment and minimize distortion.

For the same reason patches should, wherever possible, be oval or circular. Before welding, these should be slightly 'dished' below the level of the surface to be patched, since welding—even by the correct 'sequence'—will cause them to expand and rise.

Fig. O.20. Painting the hollow area with flux.

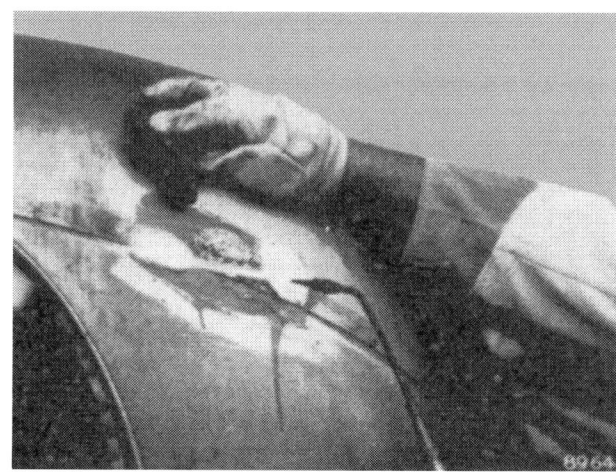

Fig. O.21. Tinning by heating the flux-painted area.

BODYWORK

Do not light the blowpipe until everything else has been prepared for welding in accordance with the instructions given above. On completion of the job proceed as follows:

(1) Turn off the acetylene first by the blowpipe control valve, and then the oxygen.
(2) Close the cylinder valves.
(3) Open the blowpipe valves one at a time to release the pressure in the hose—open the oxygen valve and shut it open the acetylene valve and shut it.
(4) Unscrew the pressure regulating screws on the oxygen and acetylene regulators.
(5) In the case of backfire turn of the oxygen first.

Section O.6
TORCH-SOLDERING

Torch-soldering is the method employed to obtain the desired contour of a panel without weakening the structure and with the minimum amount of straightening, filing, and polishing.

The solder used is an alloy of lead and tin. Lead melts at a temperature of 621° F. (327° C.) and tin at 450° F. (232° C.). Alloys of the two metals change from a solid to a liquid state over this range of temperature within which they are in a plastic condition. The alloys used for torch-soldering are known as tinman's solder (which contains 60 per cent. lead and 40 per cent. tin) and plumber's solder (which contains 70 per cent. lead and 30 per cent. tin). Tinman's solder, as a result of its higher tin content, alloys more readily with the surface of the sheet steel and is applied as a 'base' to which the plumber's solder adheres firmly. Plumber's solder remains plastic over a wide range of temperature (from 509 to 358° F. [265 to 181° C.]), and within this range can be moulded to any desired shape. For this reason it is used to obtain the required contours.

Where it is desired to build up a contour with solder the surface of the steel must first of all be cleaned thoroughly. Rust, scale, welding oxide, or any other impurity must be removed by means of a wire brush, file, and emery-cloth. A polishing wheel, if available, is useful for this operation.

The surface of the metal is heated gently with a blowlamp or gas-torch, and soldering flux applied with a brush. (See Fig. O.20.)

The flux will melt and act upon the heated surface so that when tinman's solder is applied and rubbed with a wad of hemp the metal will become evenly coated with a thin layer of solder, or 'tinned' (Fig. O.21). The secret of successful torch-soldering lies in the thoroughness with which the tinning operation is carried out as it is the foundation on which the plumber's solder is to be built up.

A second application of flux should be made and gently heated by means of the torch. When wiped by the wad of hemp the entire surface of the metal should have a spotlessly clean and bright appearance.

Plumber's solder is now melted onto the surface (Fig. O.22) and maintained by careful use of the torch in the plastic condition whilst it is moulded to the desired contour with a hardwood paddle coated with palm oil (Fig. O.23). During the moulding operation frequent immersion of the paddle in palm oil assists in the manipulation of the solder. If palm oil is not available boiled linseed, lard, or machine oil will be found satisfactory.

The final contour is obtained by filing or, if available, by the use of a polishing wheel. If the work is carefully carried out it should be impossible to trace the presence of the filling.

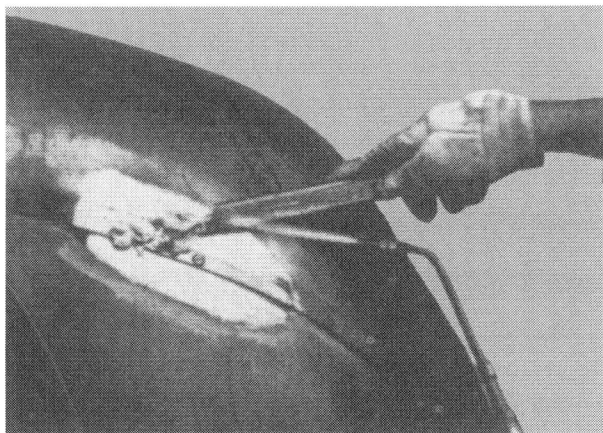

Fig. O.22. Applying the solder.

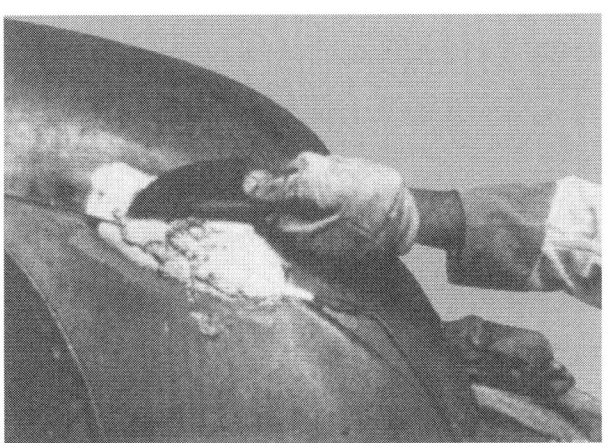

Fig. O.23. Spreading the solder.

BODYWORK

THE BODY SHELL

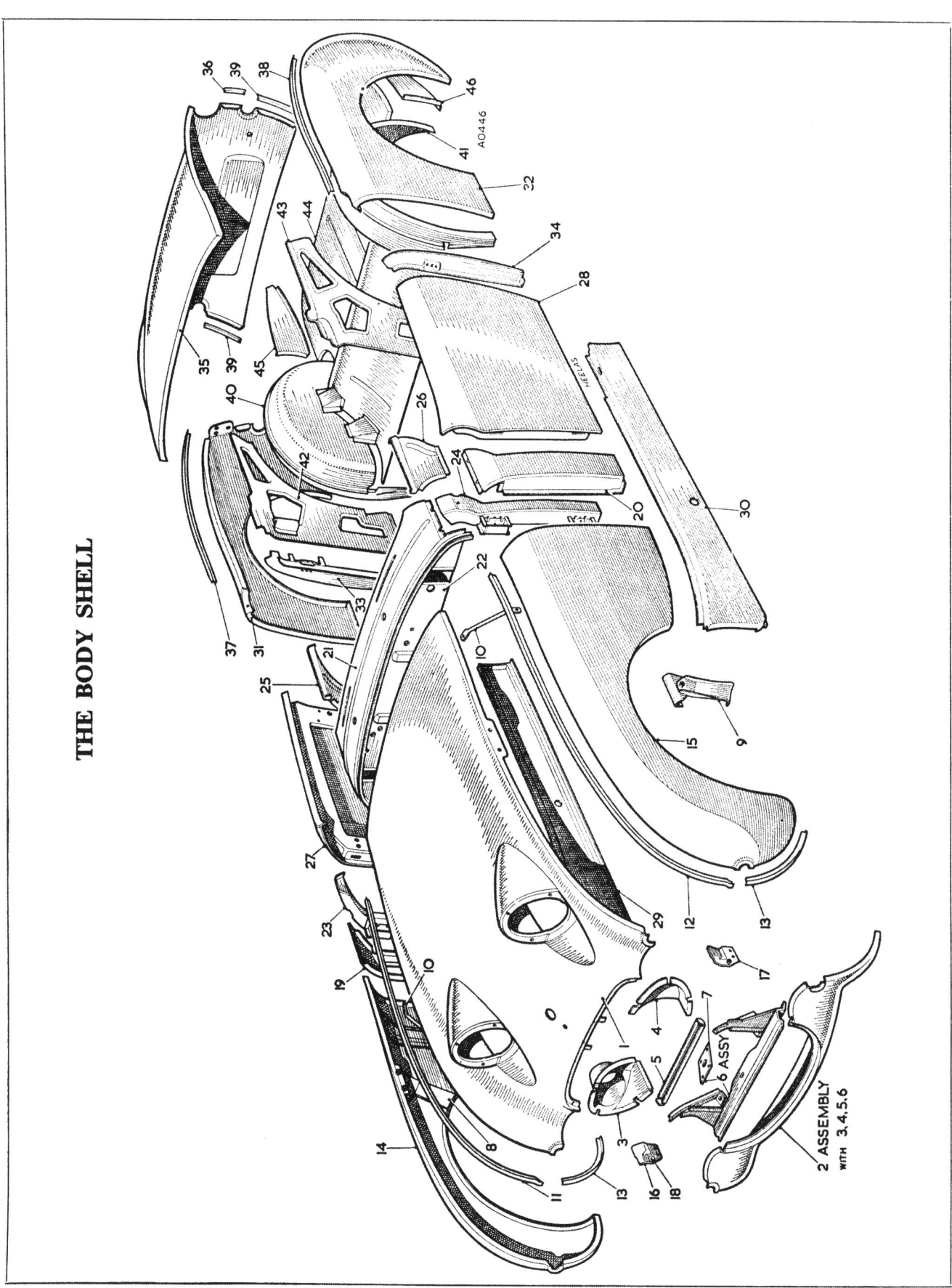

KEY TO THE BODY SHELL

No. Description
1. Panel assembly—bonnet top.
2. Panel assembly—bonnet front (bottom).
3. Baffle assembly—grille (R/H).
4. Baffle—grille (L/H).
5. Channel—support—grille baffle.
6. Reinforcement assembly—bonnet front (bottom).
7. Plate assembly—bonnet lock.
8. Bracket assembly—bonnet stay (R/H).
9. Bracket assembly—bonnet stay (L/H).
10. Strut—bonnet.
11. Moulding—bonnet top (R/H).
12. Moulding—bonnet top (L/H).
13. Moulding—bonnet—lower.
14. Wing assembly—front (R/H).
15. Wing assembly—front (L/H).
16. Bracket assembly—bonnet lock striker (R/H).

No. Description
17. Bracket assembly—bonnet lock striker (L/H).
18. Bush—striker plate.
19. Panel assembly—shroud side (R/H).
20. Panel assembly—shroud side (L/H).
21. Panel assembly—shroud and dash top.
22. Panel assembly—dash front top.
23. 'A' post assembly (R/H).
24. 'A' post assembly (L/H).
25. Extension—'A' post to scuttle (R/H).
26. Extension—'A' post to scuttle (L/H).
27. Door assembly—less lock (R/H).
28. Door assembly—less lock (L/H).
29. Panel—sill outer (R/H).
30. Panel—sill outer (L/H).
31. Wing assembly—rear (R/H).
32. Wing assembly—rear (L/H).

No. Description
33. 'B' post assembly (R/H).
34. 'B' post assembly (L/H).
35. Panel—body rear.
36. Moulding—rear wing to panel (intermediate).
37. Moulding—rear wing to panel—top (R/H).
38. Moulding—rear wing to panel—top (L/H).
39. Moulding—lower (rear).
40. Panel assembly—rear wheel arch (R/H).
41. Panel assembly—rear wheel arch (L/H).
42. Reinforcement assembly—'B' post to wheel arch (R/H).
43. Reinforcement assembly—'B' post to wheel arch (L/H).
44. Panel assembly—luggage floor.
45. Panel assembly—luggage floor to wing (R/H).
46. Panel assembly—luggage floor to wing (L/H).

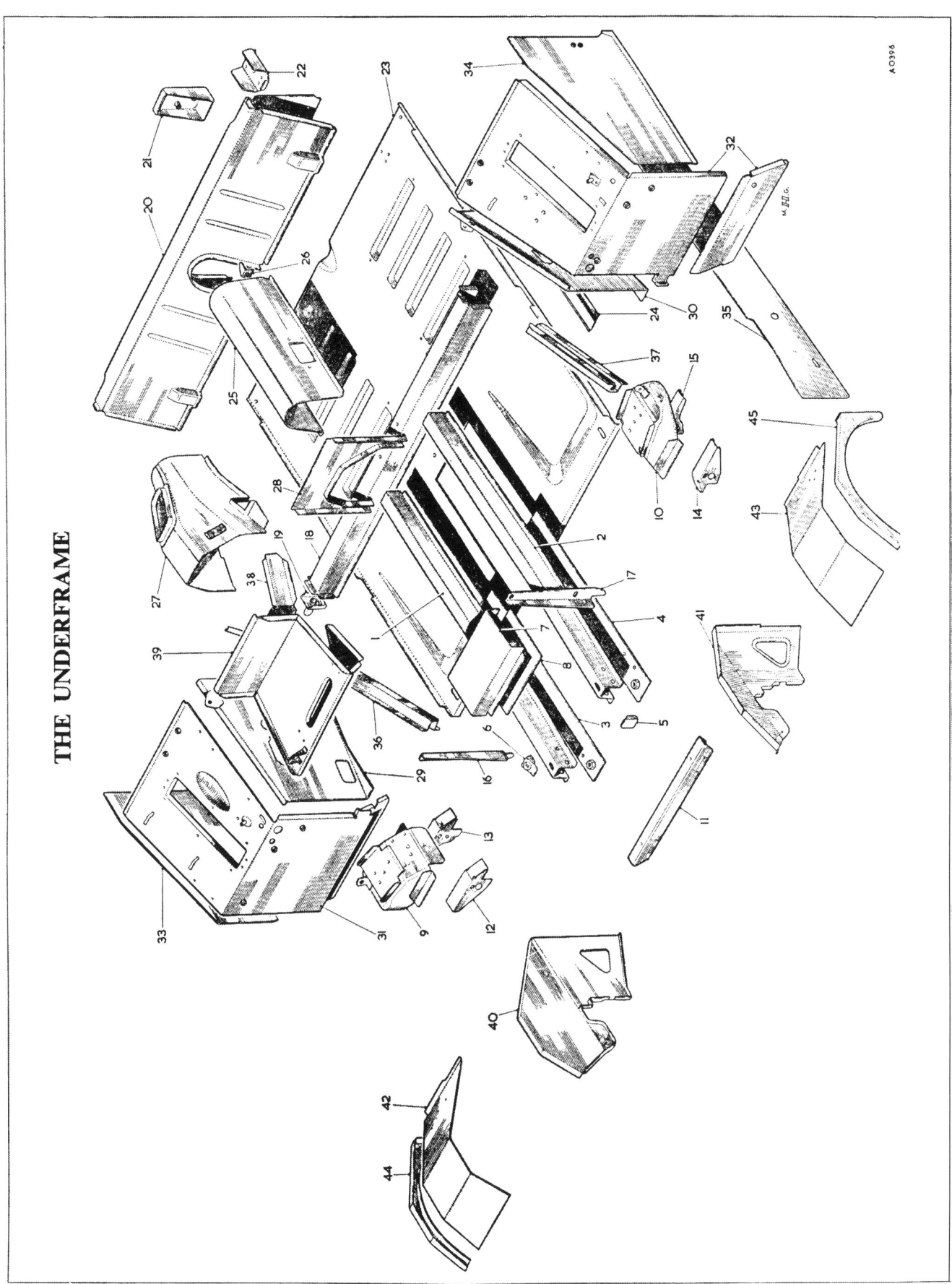

THE UNDERFRAME

KEY TO THE UNDERFRAME

No.	Description
1.	Member assembly—frame side (R/H).
2.	Member assembly—frame side (L/H).
3.	Plate assembly—closing—side member (R/H).
4.	Plate assembly—closing—side member (L/H).
5.	Plate—end closing—side member.
6.	Bracket—bonnet locating.
7.	Cross member—front.
8.	Plate—closing—front cross member.
9.	Spring bracket assembly—front suspension (R/H).
10.	Spring bracket assembly—front suspension (L/H).
11.	Support assembly—suspension housing.
12.	Bracket—front—front suspension link (R/H).
13.	Bracket—rear—front suspension link (R/H).
14.	Bracket—front—front suspension link (L/H).
15.	Bracket—rear—front suspension link (L/H).
16.	Bracket assembly—radiator mounting (R/H).
17.	Bracket assembly—radiator mounting (L/H).
18.	Cross member assembly—centre.
19.	Support assembly—jack tube.
20.	Cross member assembly—rear.
21.	Bracket assembly—shock absorber mounting (L/H).
22.	Plate—spring mounting.
23.	Floor assembly—main.
24.	Channel assembly—stiffening—main floor.
25.	Tunnel assembly.
26.	Bracket—hand brake abutment.
27.	Cover assembly—gearbox.
28.	Panel—tunnel front.
29.	Panel assembly—inner side—foot well (R/H).
30.	Panel assembly—inner side—foot well (L/H).
31.	Panel assembly—foot well front and roof (R/H).
32.	Panel assembly—foot well front and roof (L/H).
33.	Panel assembly—outer—foot well (R/H).
34.	Panel assembly—outer—foot well (L/H).
35.	Plate—side—sill (L/H).
36.	Strut—front suspension (R/H).
37.	Strut—front suspension (L/H).
38.	Support—heater platform.
39.	Platform assembly—heater.
40.	Wheel arch assembly—inner (front R/H).
41.	Wheel arch assembly—inner (front L/H).
42.	Wheel arch assembly—top (front R/H).
43.	Wheel arch assembly—top (front L/H).
44.	Wheel arch—outer (front R/H).
45.	Wheel arch—outer (front L/H).

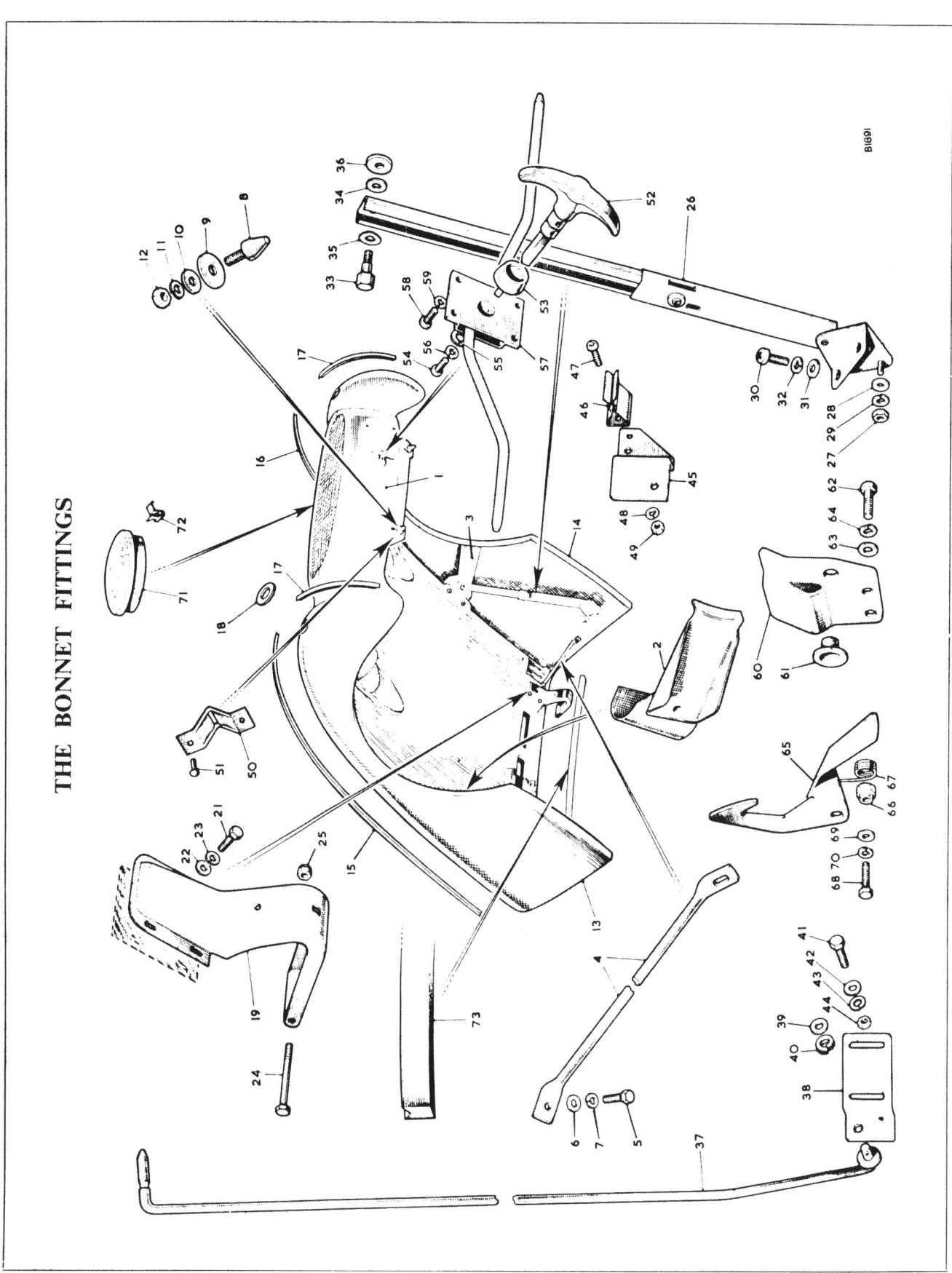

KEY TO THE BONNET FITTINGS

No.	Description
1.	Bonnet assembly.
2.	Bracket assembly—bonnet stay (R/H).
3.	Bracket assembly—bonnet stay (L/H).
4.	Strut—bonnet.
5.	Screw—strut to bonnet.
6.	Washer—screw (plain).
7.	Washer—screw (spring).
8.	Peg—bonnet locating.
9.	Washer—locating peg (plain).
10.	Washer—locating peg (plain).
11.	Washer—locating (spring).
12.	Nut—locating peg.
13.	Wing assembly—front (R/H).
14.	Wing assembly—front (L/H).
15.	Moulding—bonnet top (R/H).
16.	Moulding—bonnet top (L/H).
17.	Moulding—bonnet lower.
18.	Filler—lamp.
19.	Hinge assembly—bonnet.
21.	Screw—hinge to bonnet.
22.	Washer—hinge screw (plain).
23.	Washer—hinge screw (spring).
24.	Bolt—hinge to bulkhead.
25.	Nut—bolt.
26.	Stay assembly—telescopic—bonnet.
27.	Nut—pivot bracket to pedal box side.
28.	Washer—nut (plain).
29.	Washer—nut (spring).
30.	Screw—stay bracket to pedal box.
31.	Washer—stay bracket screw (plain).
32.	Washer—stay bracket screw (spring).
33.	Bolt—special—bonnet stay.
34.	Washer—stay bolt (plain).
35.	Washer—stay bolt (curved).
36.	Washer—stay bolt—brass (plain).
37.	Stay—bonnet—auxiliary.
38.	Bracket—pivot—bonnet stay.
39.	Washer—stay to bracket (plain).
40.	Washer—stay to bracket (spring).
41.	Screw—bracket to radiator support (R/H).
42.	Washer—screw (plain).
43.	Washer—screw (spring).
44.	Nut—screw.
45.	Bracket—clip—bonnet stay.
46.	Clip—bonnet stay.
47.	Screw—clip to bracket.
48.	Washer—screw (spring).
49.	Nut—screw.
50.	Clip—spring.
51.	Rivet—clip to bonnet reinforcement.
52.	Handle—bonnet.
53.	Escutcheon—handle.
54.	Screw—handle to lock.
55.	Washer—screw (plain).
56.	Washer—screw (spring).
57.	Lock assembly—bonnet.
58.	Screw—lock to bonnet.
59.	Washer—screw (spring).
60.	Bracket assembly—bonnet lock striker (R/H).
61.	Bush—striker plate.
62.	Screw—bracket to side-member.
63.	Washer—screw (plain).
64.	Washer—screw (spring).
65.	Catch—safety—bonnet.
66.	Bush—safety catch.
67.	Spring—safety catch.
68.	Bolt—safety catch to side-member.
69.	Washer—screw (plain).
70.	Washer—bolt (spring).
71.	Badge—bonnet top.
72.	Clip—badge to bonnet top.
73.	Seal—bonnet sealing.

BODYWORK

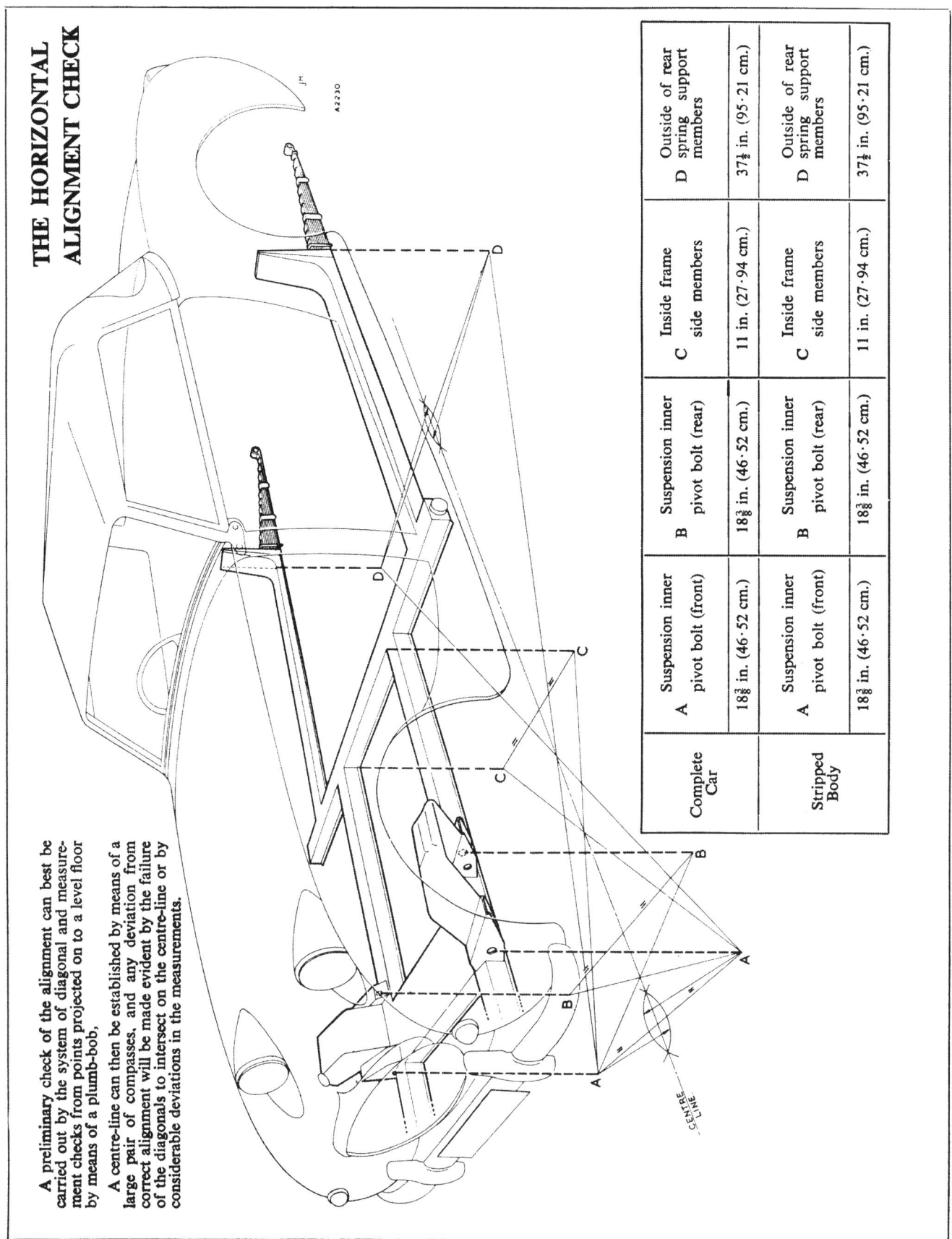

THE HORIZONTAL ALIGNMENT CHECK

A preliminary check of the alignment can best be carried out by the system of diagonal and measurement checks from points projected on to a level floor by means of a plumb-bob.

A centre-line can then be established by means of a large pair of compasses, and any deviation from correct alignment will be made evident by the failure of the diagonals to intersect on the centre-line or by considerable deviations in the measurements.

	A Suspension inner pivot bolt (front)	B Suspension inner pivot bolt (rear)	C Inside frame side members	D Outside of rear spring support members
Complete Car	$18\frac{3}{8}$ in. (46·52 cm.)	$18\frac{3}{8}$ in. (46·52 cm.)	11 in. (27·94 cm.)	$37\frac{1}{2}$ in. (95·21 cm.)
Stripped Body	$18\frac{3}{8}$ in. (46·52 cm.)	$18\frac{3}{8}$ in. (46·52 cm.)	11 in. (27·94 cm.)	$37\frac{1}{2}$ in. (95·21 cm.)

Austin-Healey Sprite. Issue 3. 58110.

BODYWORK

O

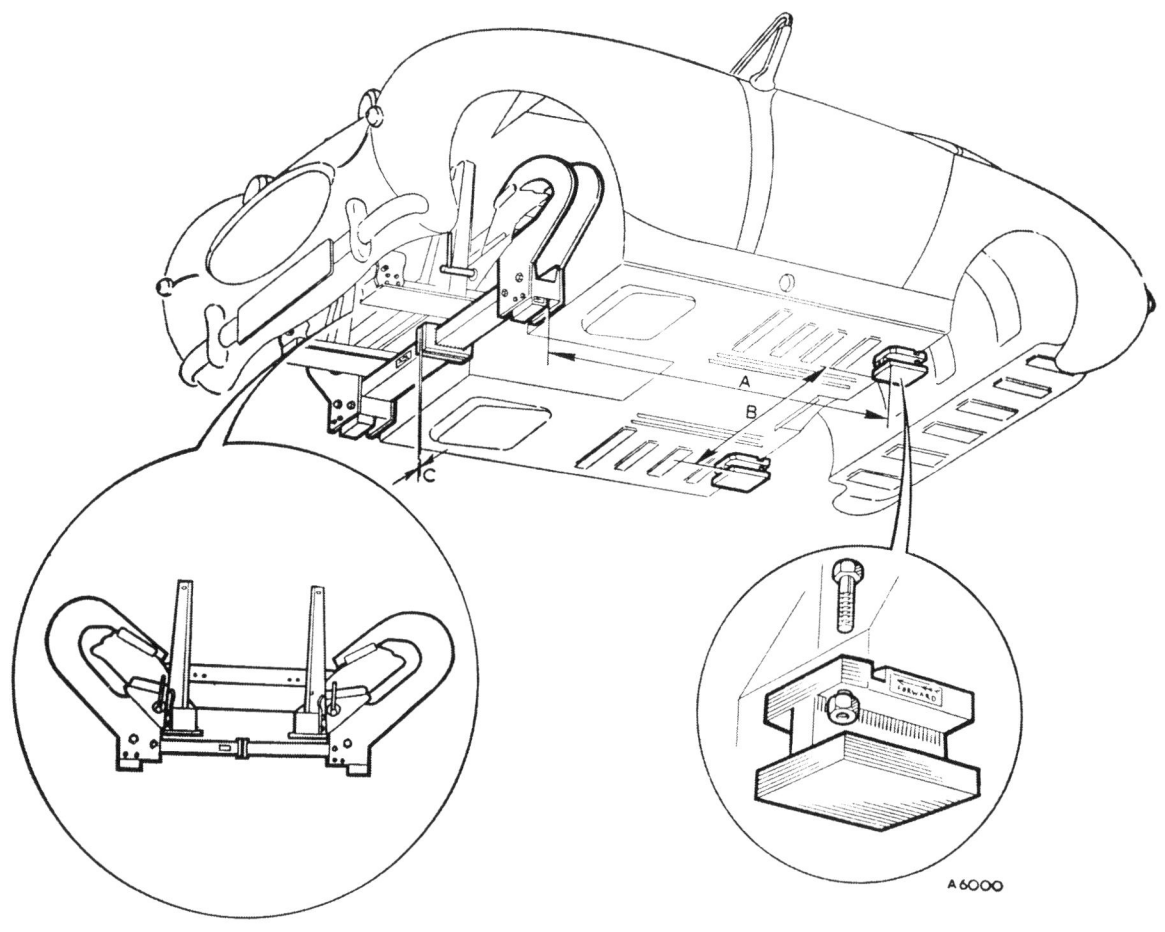

Fig. O.24.

A. 63·25 *in.* (1606 *mm.*).   B. 31·75 *in.* (806·5 *mm.*)   C. ·25 *in.* ± ·0625 (6·35 *mm.* ±1·59).

Section O.7

BODY ALIGNMENT CHECKING JIG

Before checking the body alignment it is most important that the body is raised to a workable height on a level plane. This is done to facilitate body jig checking with the aid of a straight edge or a stout cord stretched from one point to another, to obtain measurements between jig components. These measurements should then be checked against the correct dimensions provided in Fig. O.24.

This tool is intended to be used solely as a checking fixture and not as a welding jig. No welding whatsoever must be undertaken with the body jig in position.

The left-hand inset in the above illustration shows the front section of the jig mounted in position. While the right-hand inset shows the correct method of fitting the rear section to the rear spring mountings.

NOTE.—All jig sections are marked 'FORWARD' for correct positioning.

O BODYWORK

Section O.8

LUGGAGE GRID

This luggage grid can be supplied as an optional extra, but can only be fitted to cars after car No. 4333, with the exception of car Nos. 4471, 4622, 4680 and 4684.

Fitting instructions are as follows: Using the luggage grid placed centrally on the car as a guide to give the correct hole centres, drill 4 holes $\frac{11}{32}$ in. dia. in the body panel at the positions shown in the sketch.

Remove the trim pads behind the rear wheel-arch when the support brackets Pt. Nos. AHA5473-4 and AHA5475-6 can be located on the underside of the main tonneau panel and 4 $\frac{11}{32}$ in. dia. holes drilled in the floor to wheel-arch gusset panel. Care must be taken when drilling to ensure that the wiring harness is well clear.

Using the tapping plates (AHA5477), drill 8 holes, $\frac{7}{32}$ in. dia., and screw the tapping plates to the outside of the gusset panel.

Replace the trim pads, after cutting two holes in each to clear the support brackets.

Section O.9

SEAT BELTS

Fitting Instructions

Rear Wheel Arch

Mark off and drill two $\frac{11}{32}$ in. (8·73 mm.) diameter holes in the wheel arch from the under side and forward of the centre line as shown in the illustration.

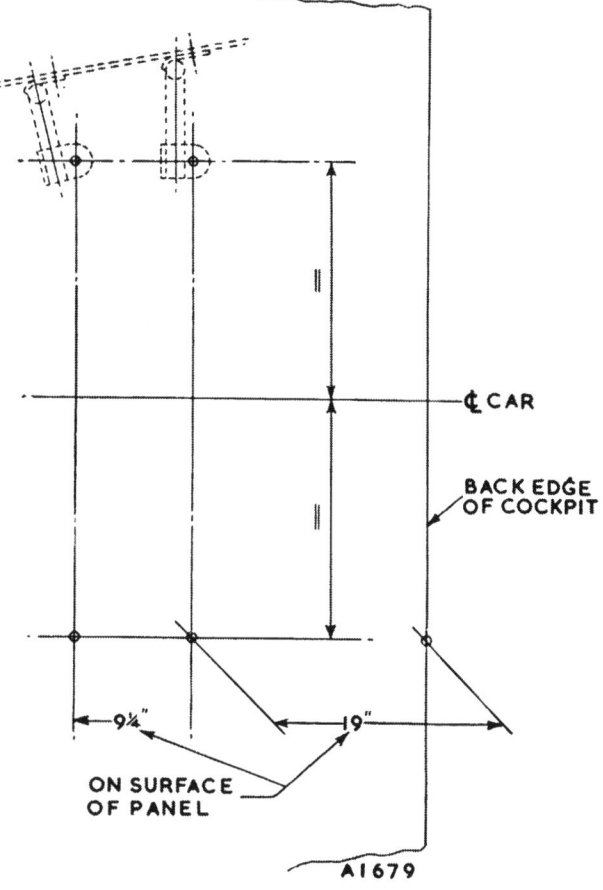

Fig. O.26
Fitting diagram for luggage grid

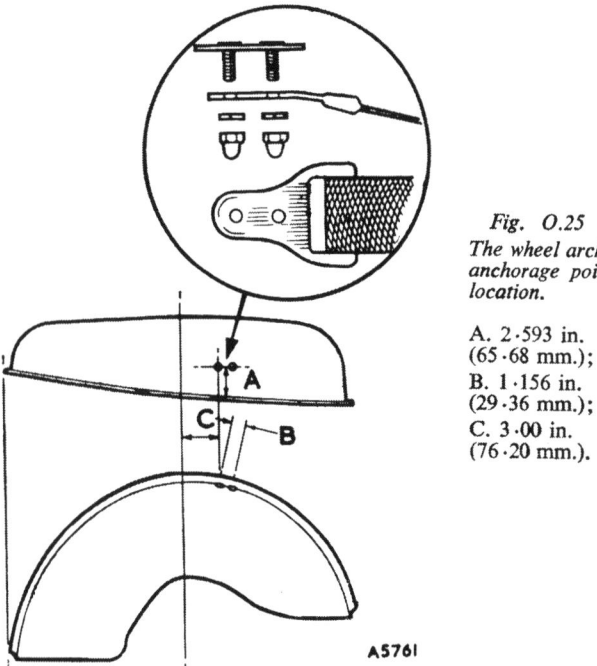

Fig. O.25
The wheel arch anchorage point location.

A. 2·593 in. (65·68 mm.);
B. 1·156 in. (29·36 mm.);
C. 3·00 in. (76·20 mm.).

Pass the two bolts attached to the reinforcement plate through the $\frac{11}{32}$ in. (8·73 mm.) diameter holes and secure the belt bracket with the plain washer, spring washers, and dome nuts.

Sill

Cut a $1\frac{3}{8}$ in. (34·92 mm.) diameter hole in the sill panel forward of the heel board 'Y' and $1\frac{1}{2}$ in. (38·1 mm.) from the floor 'X' also cut two $\frac{11}{32}$ in. (8·73 mm.) as shown in the illustration.

Insert the sill tapping plate through the $1\frac{3}{8}$ in. (34·92 mm.) diameter hole using the $\frac{7}{16}$ in. (11·11 mm.) diameter screw to lift the plate into position. Place a spring washer on a $\frac{5}{16}$ in. (7·94 mm.) diameter hexagon head screw and pass it through the cover plate with the register away from the head of the screw and attach it to the sill and tapping plate. Remove the $\frac{7}{16}$ in. (11·11 mm.) diameter screw and finally secure the cover plate with the second $\frac{5}{16}$ in. (7·94 mm.) diameter hexagon head screw and spring washer.

Cut a 1 in. (25·4 mm.) diameter hole in the sill board trim as to clear the projection of the mounting bracket, and

BODYWORK

circle diameter, as illustrated, using the mounting bracket as a template. From inside the tunnel place the mounting bracket into position and secure it with the six No. 10 U.N.F. pan head screws. The heads of which must be inside the nuts and spring washers inside the car.

Cut a 1 in. (25·4 mm.) diameter hole in the carpet on the same side of the tunnel as the seat for which the belt is being fitted. Place the bracket, a waved washer and shouldered distance piece (the smaller diameter of which will slot into the bracket) in the $\frac{7}{16}$ in. (11·11 mm.) bolt provided and secure inside the tunnel with the spring washer and nut.

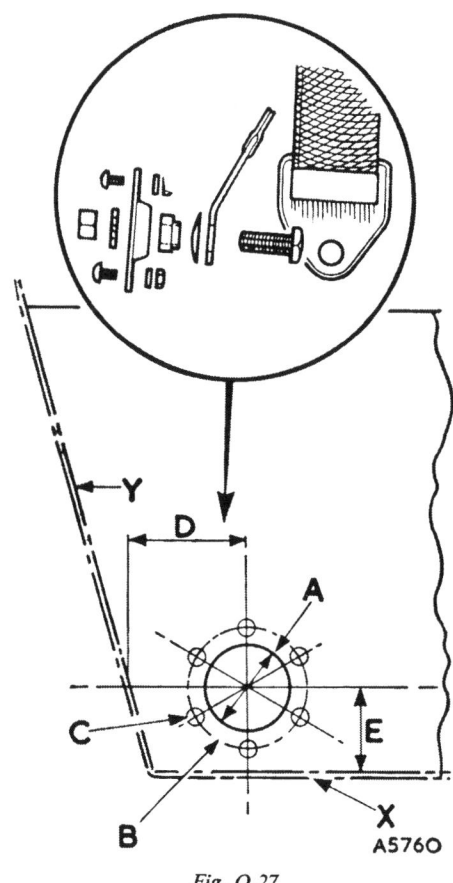

Fig. O.27
The propeller shaft tunnel anchorage point location.
A. 1·500 in. (38·10 mm.); B. 2·000 in. (50·80 mm.); C. ·203 in. (5·16 mm.); D. 2·000 in. (5·80 mm.); E. 1·500 in. (38·10 mm.).

so coincide with that of the hole drilled in sill panel.

Place the bracket and waved washer, the shouldered distance piece (the smaller diameter of which will slot into the bracket) and plain washer on the $\frac{7}{16}$ in. (11·11 mm.) screw provided and screw the assembly into the hole in the sill.

Propeller Shaft Tunnel

Cut a $1\frac{1}{2}$ in. (38·1 mm.) diameter hole $1\frac{1}{2}$ in. (8·1 mm.) from the floor 'X' and forward of the heel board 'Y'. Drill six $\frac{13}{64}$ in. (5·16 mm.) diameter holes round this hole, equally spaced or a 2 in. (50·8 mm.) pitch

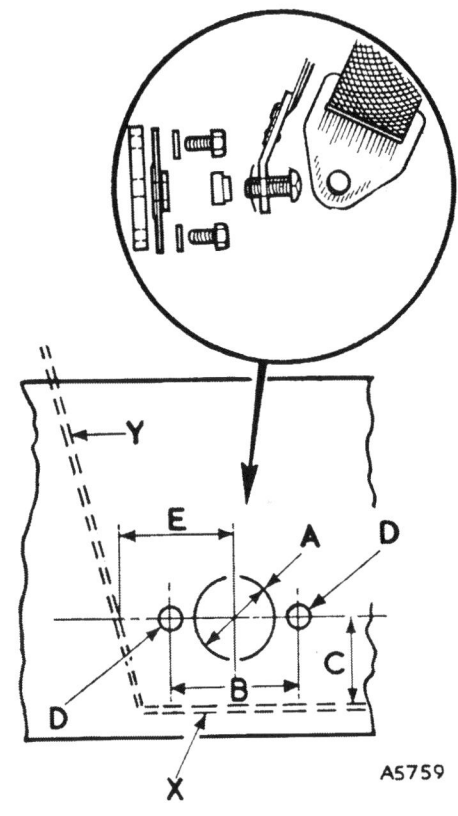

Fig. O.28
The sill panel anchorage point location.
A. 1·375 in. (34·92 mm.); B. 2·250 in. (57·15 mm.); C. 1·500 in. (38·10 mm.); D. ·343 in. (8·73 mm.); E. 2·250 in. (57·15 mm.).

SECTION P

LUBRICATION

Recommended lubricants

Section No. P.1   **Daily Attention**
    Engine

Section No. P.2.   **3,000 miles (5000 km.) service**
    Engine oil change
    Steering gear
    Propeller shaft
    Hand brake compensator
    Hand brake cable
    Gearbox
    Rear axle
    Air cleaners
    Carburetter dampers
    Carburetter controls
    Clutch and brake pedal linkage
    Miscellaneous items

Section No. P.3.   **6,000 miles (10000 km.) service**
    Gearbox oil change
    Rear axle oil change
    Engine oil filter
    Dynamo
    Distributor

Section No. P.4.   **12,000 miles (20000 km.) service**
    Engine flushing
    Steering rack
    Water pump

Correct lubrication of any piece of mechanism is of paramount importance, and in no instance is it of greater importance than in the correct choice of lubricant for a motor car engine. Automobile engines have different characteristics, such as operating temperatures, oiling systems, size of oilways, clearances and similiar technicalities, and the use of the correct oil is therefore essential.

LUBRICATION **P**

The following is a list of lubricants recommended:

A ENGINE

Climatic conditions	Duckham's	Castrol	Esso	Mobil	Shell	BP	Filtrate	Sternol
Tropical and temperate down to 32° F. (0° C.)	Duckham's NOL Thirty	Castrol X.L.	Esso Extra Motor Oil 20W/30	Mobiloil A	Shell X—100 30	Energol S.A.E. 30	Filtrate Medium 30	Sternol W.W. 30
Extreme cold down to 10° F. (—12° C.)	Duckham's NOL Twenty	Castrolite	Esso Extra Motor Oil 20W/30	Mobiloil Arctic	Shell X—100 20W	Energol S.A.E. 20W	Filtrate Zero 20/20W	Sternol W.W. 20
Arctic consistently below 10°F. (—12°C.)	Duckham's NOL Ten	Castrol Z	Esso Motor Oil 10	Mobiloil 10W	Shell X—100 10W or Rotella 10W	Energol S.A.E. 10W	Filtrate Sub-Zero 10W	Sternol W.W. 10

GEARBOX

	Duckham's	Castrol	Esso	Mobil	Shell	BP	Filtrate	Sternol
All conditions	Duckham's NOL Thirty	Castrol X.L.	Esso Extra Motor Oil 20W/30	Mobiloil A	Shell X—100 30	Energol S.A.E. 30	Filtrate Medium 30	Sternol W.W. 30

B REAR AXLE (HYPOID), STEERING RACK

	Duckham's	Castrol	Esso	Mobil	Shell	BP	Filtrate	Sternol
All conditions down to 10° F. (—12° C.)	Duckham's Hypoid 90	Castrol Hypoy	Esso Gear Oil G.P. 90	Mobilube G.X. 90	Shell Spirax 90 E.P.	Energol S.A.E. 90 E.P.	Filtrate Hypoid Gear 90	Ambroleum E.P. 90
Arctic consistently below 10°F. (—12°C.)	Duckham's Hypoid 80	Castrol Hypoy Light	Esso Gear Oil G.P. 80	Mobilube G.X. 80	Shell Spirax 80 E.P.	Energol S.A.E. 80 E.P.	Filtrate Hypoid Gear 80	Ambroleum E.P. 80

C LUBRICATION NIPPLES AND WHEEL HUBS.

	Duckham's	Castrol	Esso	Mobil	Shell	BP	Filtrate	Sternol
Wheel hubs, handbrake cable and lubrication nipples.	Duckham's L.B. 10 Grease	Castrolease L.M.	Esso Multi-purpose Grease H.	Mobilgrease M.P.	Shell Retinax A	Energrease L.2.	Filtrate Super Lithium Grease	Ambroline L.H.T.

D UTILITY LUBRICANT, S.U. CARBURETTER DAMPER, OILCAN POINTS, ETC.

	Duckham's	Castrol	Esso	Mobil	Shell	BP	Filtrate	Sternol
All conditions	Duckham's NOL Twenty	Castrolite	Esso Extra Motor Oil 20W/30	Mobiloil Arctic	Shell X—100 20W	Energol S.A.E. 20W	Filtrate Zero 20/20W	Sternol W.W. 20

E UPPER CYLINDER LUBRICANT

	Duckham's	Castrol	Esso	Mobil	Shell	BP	Filtrate	Sternol
All conditions	Duckham's Adcoid Liquid	Castrollo	Esso Upper Cylinder Lubricant	Mobil Upperlube	Shell Upper Cylinder Lubricant	Energol U.C.L.	Filtrate Petroyle	Sternol Magikoyl

Austin-Healey Sprite Mk. 1. Issue 5. 50312

P LUBRICATION

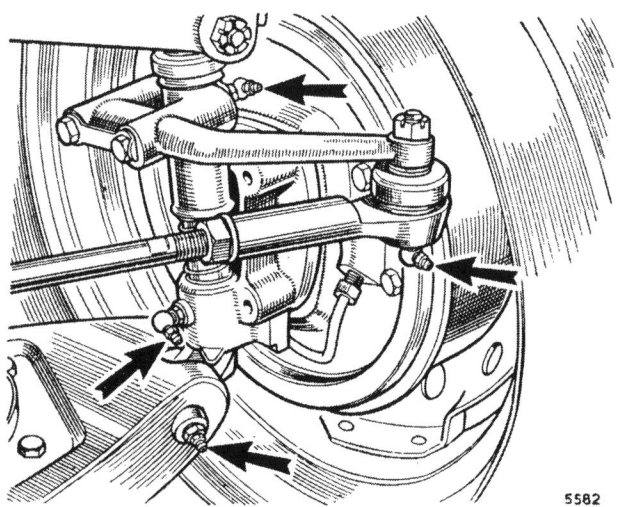

Fig. P.1. The four steering gear nipples on the left-hand wheel assembly.

Section P.1

DAILY ATTENTION

ENGINE

Inspect the oil level in the engine and refill if necessary to the 'FULL' mark on the dipstick. The oil filler cap is on top of the engine valve cover and is released by turning it anti-clockwise.

Section P.2

3000 MILES (5000 km.) SERVICE

Carry out the instruction detailed in Section P.1 and then continue with the following:

STEERING GEAR

A lubricating gun filled with grease to Ref. C (page P.1)

Fig. P.2. The arrow indicates the brake compensator lubricating nipple.

should be applied to each of the eight steering gear nipples and three or four strokes given. Nipples are provided on both lower arm joints where they meet the swivel axle housings and on the two tie rod ball joints. There are two nipples on each swivel axle pin which are best lubricated when the weight of the car has been taken off the suspension with a jack or sling. This will allow the lubricant to penetrate around the bushes more effectively.

PROPELLER SHAFT

The two needle type universal joints at each end of the propeller shaft are provided with nipples which should receive two or three strokes with a gun filled with oil or grease to Ref. C (page P.1). Access to the front universal joint is gained by lifting the floor covering and removing the rubber plug on the left-hand side of the propeller shaft tunnel. If necessary move the car to bring the nipple in line with the tunnel hole.

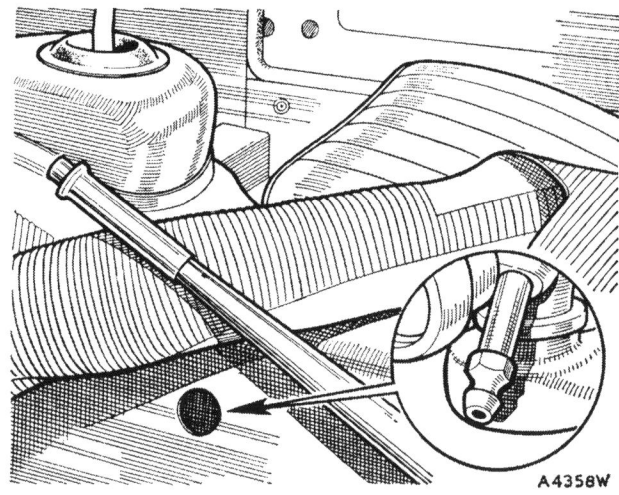

Fig. P.3. The lubricating nipple for the front universal joint. The sliding joint is lubricated from the gearbox.

HAND BRAKE COMPENSATOR

There is one lubricating nipple on the top of the hand brake compensating lever, and this is accessible from underneath the rear of the car. Wipe away all the dirt from the nipple and give one or two strokes with a gun filled with oil or grease to Ref. C (page P.1).

HAND BRAKE CABLE

The hand brake cable nipple located just forward of the rear axle must receive three or four strokes with a grease gun filled with grease to Ref. C (page P.1).

LUBRICATION

P

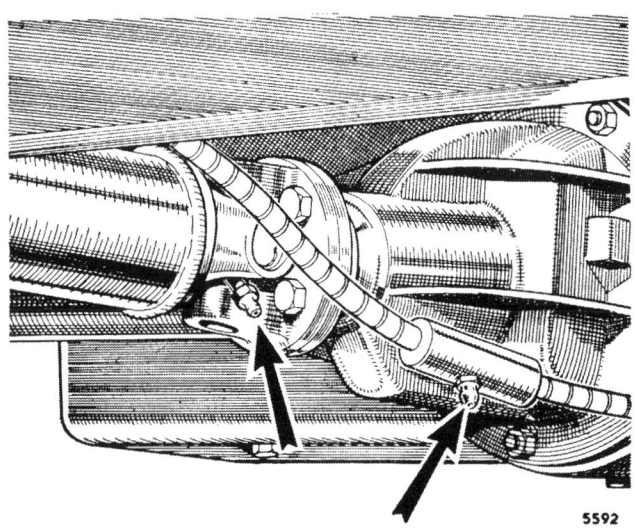

Fig. P.4. The arrows indicate the rear universal joint and hand brake cable lubricating nipples.

ENGINE OIL CHANGE

Drain the oil from the engine by removing the drain plug on the right-hand side of the engine sump after a journey when the oil is still warm. The sump capacity is 7 pints (8·5 U.S. pints, 4 litres), including the oil filter.

GEARBOX

Remove the combined filler and level plug on the gearbox extension and top up the oil level to the bottom of the filler hole with oil to Ref. A (page P.1). Access to the plug is gained by lifting the floor covering and removing the rubber plug on the left-hand side of the gearbox cover.

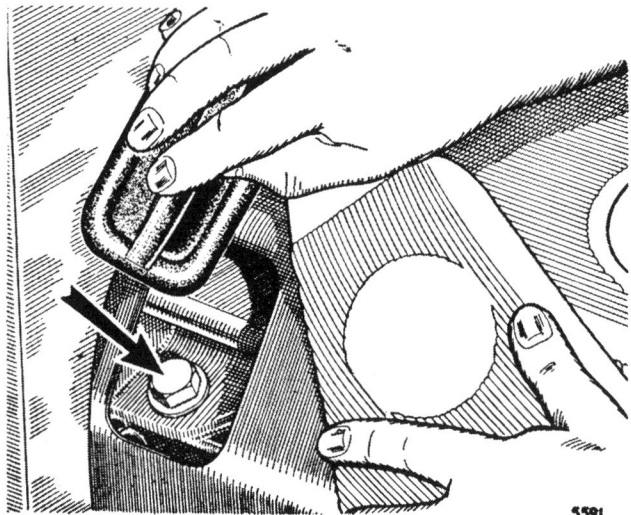

Fig. P. 5. The gearbox oil level and filler plug.

REAR AXLE

The combined filler and level plug situated on the rear of the axle casing is reached from underneath the rear of the car. Use the special key (Part No. 1G 7372). The oil level should be replenished if necessary to the level of the filler plug hole.

NOTE:— **It is essential that only hypoid oil be used in the rear axle.**

AIR CLEANERS

Remove, clean in petrol, drain and wet the air cleaners with oil to Ref. A (page P.1).

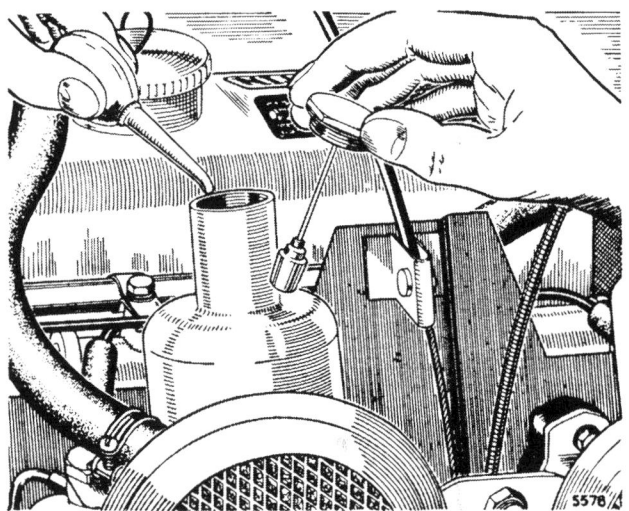

Fig. P.6. Use S.A.E. 20 engine oil to lubricate the carburetter piston dampers.

CARBURETTER DAMPERS

Unscrew the caps from the tops of the suction chambers, pour in a small quantity of oil to Ref. D (page P.1) and replace the caps. In no circumstances should a heavy-bodied lubricant be used. Failure to lubricate the piston dampers will cause the pistons to flutter and reduce acceleration.

CARBURETTER CONTROLS

Using an oil to Ref. D (page P.1), lubricate lightly all carburetter linkages.

MISCELLANEOUS ITEMS

With an oilcan filled with oil to Ref. D (page P.1) lubricate lightly the door locks, hinges, and bonnet lock mechanism.

Austin-Healey Sprite. Mk. 1. Issue 4 50312

P

LUBRICATION

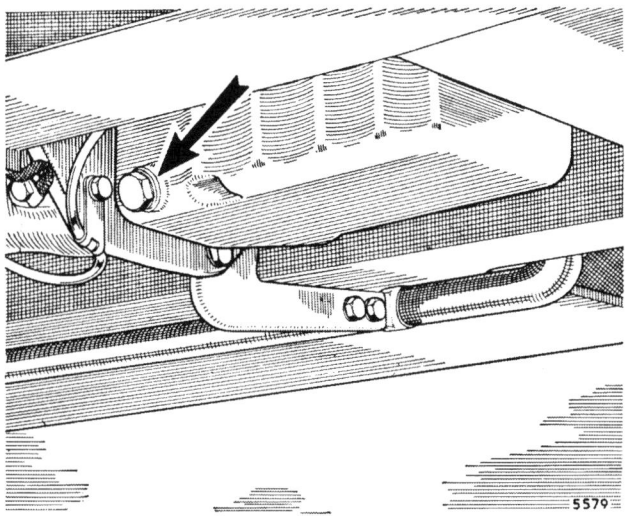

Fig. P.7. The engine sump drain plug.

Section P.3

6,000 MILES (10000 km.) SERVICE

Carry out the instructions detailed in Section P.2 except those under 'GEARBOX' and 'REAR AXLE' and continue with the following.

DISTRIBUTOR

Cam bearing

Lift the rotor off the top of the spindle by pulling it squarely and add a few drops of oil to Ref. D. (page P.1) to the cam bearing. Do not remove the screw which is exposed. There is a clearance between the screw and the inner face of the spindle for the oil to pass.

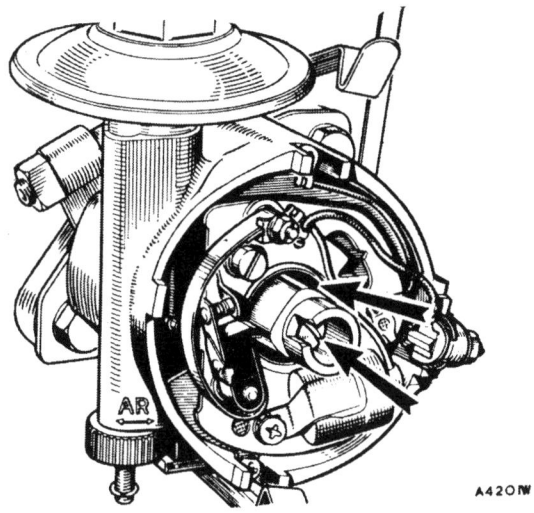

Fig. P.8. Add a few drops only of thin engine oil as indicated by the lower arrow to lubricate the cam bearing. Apply a smear of grease to the cam as indicated by the upper arrow.

Replace the rotor with its drive lug correctly engaging the spindle slot and push it on to the shaft as far as it will go.

Cam

Lightly smear the cam with a very small amount of grease to Ref. C (page P.1), or, if this is not available, clean engine oil may be used.

Automatic timing control

Carefully add a few drops of oil to Ref. D (page P.1) through the hole in the contact breaker base through which the cam passes. Do not allow the oil to get on or near the contacts. Do not over-oil.

Contact breaker pivot

Add a spot of oil to Ref. D (page P.1) to the moving contact pivot pin.

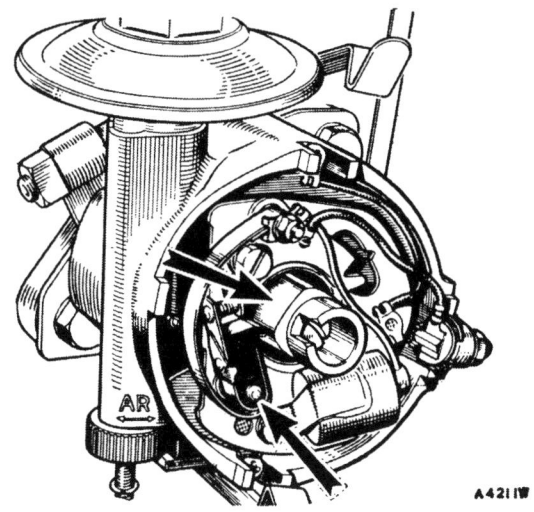

Fig. P.9. The moving contact pivot pin and the automatic timing control mechanism should receive a few spots only of thin engine oil.

ENGINE OIL FILTER

Fit a new external engine oil filter element.

The oil filter is of the full-flow type and the bowl should be washed in petrol. The filter is released by unscrewing the central bolt securing the filter to the filter head. When refitting ensure that the seating washer for the filter body is correctly positioned, clean, and serviceable. Care must also be taken to ensure that the washers below the element inside the bowl are fitted correctly. The small felt washer must be positioned between the element pressure plate and the metal washer above the pressure spring. It is essential for correct oil filtration that the felt washer should be in good condition and be a snug fit on the centre-securing bolt.

LUBRICATION

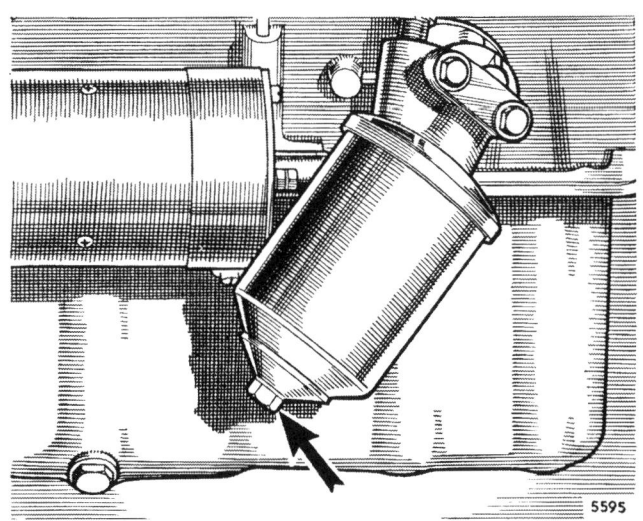

Fig. P.10. Indicated by the arrow is the centre securing bolt for the engine oil filter.

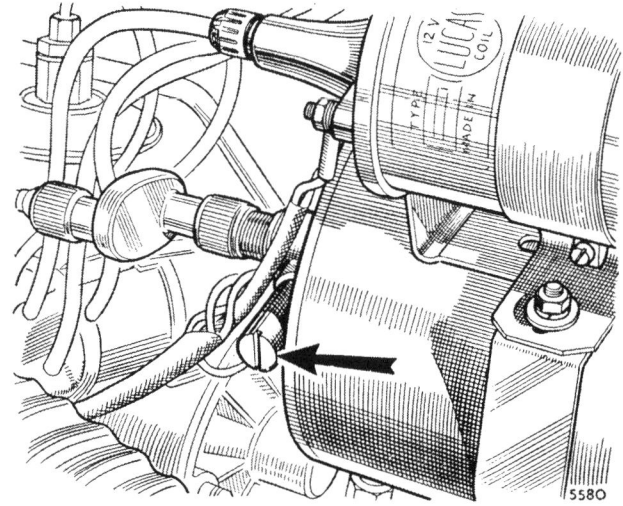

Fig. P.12. The dynamo lubricator cap.

GEARBOX OIL CHANGE

Drain the gearbox oil when the oil is warm by removing the hexagon headed plug from the base of the gearbox. Ensure that the hollow centre of the drain plug is kept clean. The capacity of the gearbox is $2\frac{1}{3}$ pints (2·807 U.S. pints, 1·325 litres).

REAR AXLE OIL CHANGE

Remove the drain plug with the special key (Part No. 1G 7372) and drain out the oil while it is warm. Refill with **Hypoid** oil to Ref. B (page P.1) to the level of the filler plug hole.

Approximately $1\frac{3}{4}$ pints (1 litre, 2·1 U.S. pints) of oil are required to refill the axle.

DYNAMO

Unscrew the lubricator cap, remove the felt pad and spring, and half-fill the cup with grease to Ref. C (page P.1).

Section P.4

12,000 MILES (20000 km.) SERVICE

Carry out the instructions detailed in Sections P.2, and P.3 and proceed with the following:

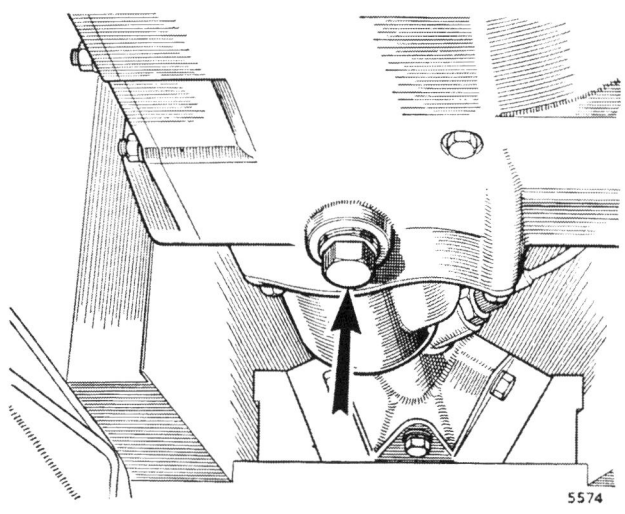

Fig. P.11. The gearbox drain plug.

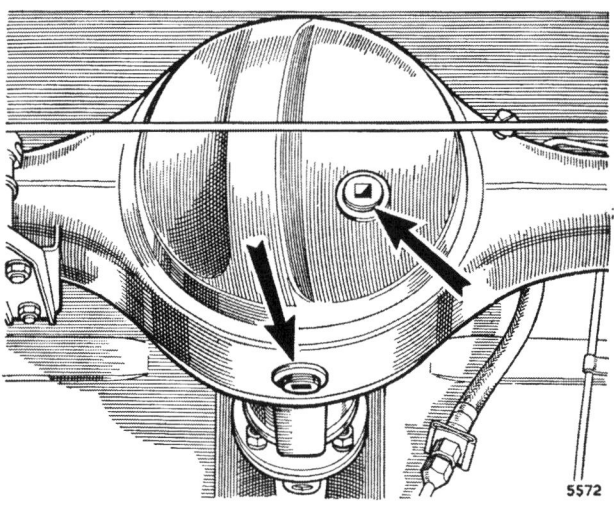

Fig. P.13. The rear axle oil filler and drain plugs.

Austin-Healey Sprite Mk. 1. Issue 5. 50312

LUBRICATION

Fig. P.14. *The water pump oiling plug.*

Fig. P.15. *The arrow indicates the position of the steering rack oil nipple.*

ENGINE FLUSHING

Flush the engine with a flushing oil supplied by one of the recommended manufacturers (page P.1). This operation must be carried out prior to oil filter changing. Use approximately half the normal sump capacity and run the engine for $2\frac{1}{2}$ to 3 minutes at a fast tickover, after which special care must be taken to ensure complete draining of the flushing oil.

It is recommended that at 24,000 miles (40000 km.) the sump and oil pump pick-up strainer should be removed for cleaning.

WATER PUMP

Remove the water pump greasing plug on the water pump casing and add a small quantity of grease to Ref. C. The greasing of the pump must be done very sparingly, otherwise grease will flow past the bearings on to the face of the carbon sealing ring and impair its efficiency.

STEERING RACK

The oil nipple provided at the left-hand side of the rack housing (right-hand side on L.H.D. cars) is accessible when the bonnet is raised. Apply the gun filled with oil to Ref. B (page P.1) and give 10 strokes **only**.

LUBRICATION DIAGRAM

LUBRICATION DIAGRAM

DAILY

(1) ENGINE. Inspect the oil level by the dipstick, and top up if necessary with oil to Ref. A.

EVERY 3,000 MILES (5000 km.)

(2) ENGINE. Drain off the old oil and refill with fresh oil to Ref. A.

(3) GEARBOX. Remove the filler plug, and top up if necessary to the filler plug level with oil to Ref. A.

(4) REAR AXLE. Remove the filler plug, and top up if necessary to the filler plug level with oil to Ref. B.

(5) STEERING TIE ROD BALL JOINTS.

(6) SWIVEL AXLES AND SUSPENSION LOWER JOINTS.

(7) PROPELLER SHAFT UNIVERSAL JOINTS.

(8) HAND BRAKE CABLE.

(9) HAND BRAKE COMPENSATOR LEVER.

Lubricate with the gun filled to Ref. C.

(10) HAND BRAKE LINKAGE JOINTS. Lubricate with an oil can filled with oil to Ref. D.

(11) CARBURETTERS. Top up damper assembly reservoirs with oil to Ref. D.

EVERY 6,000 MILES (10000 km.)

(12) AIR CLEANERS. Remove, clean in fuel, drain and wet the air cleaners with oil to Ref. A.

(13) DISTRIBUTOR. Withdraw the rotor arm and add a few drops of oil to Ref. D to the cam bearing and to the advance mechanism through the gap around the cam spindle. Lightly smear the cam with grease to Ref. C.

(14) OIL FILTER. Wash the bowl in fuel and fit a new element.

(15) GEARBOX. Drain off the old oil and refill with fresh oil to Ref. A.

(16) REAR AXLE. Drain off the old oil and refill with fresh oil to Ref. B.

(17) DYNAMO. Unscrew the lubricator cap, remove the felt pad and spring, and half fill the cup with grease to Ref. C.

EVERY 12,000 MILES (20000 km.)

(18) STEERING RACK. Apply the grease gun filled with oil to Ref. B to the nipple on the steering rack and give 10 strokes only.

(19) WATER PUMP. Lubricate sparingly with grease to Ref. C.

MULTIGRADE MOTOR OILS

In addition to the recommended lubricants listed on page P.1. we approve the use of these new motor oils as produced by the companies there indicated, for all climatic temperatures unless the engine is in poor mechanical condition.

NOTE—Oil and grease references are to be found on page P.1.

LUBRICATION DIAGRAM

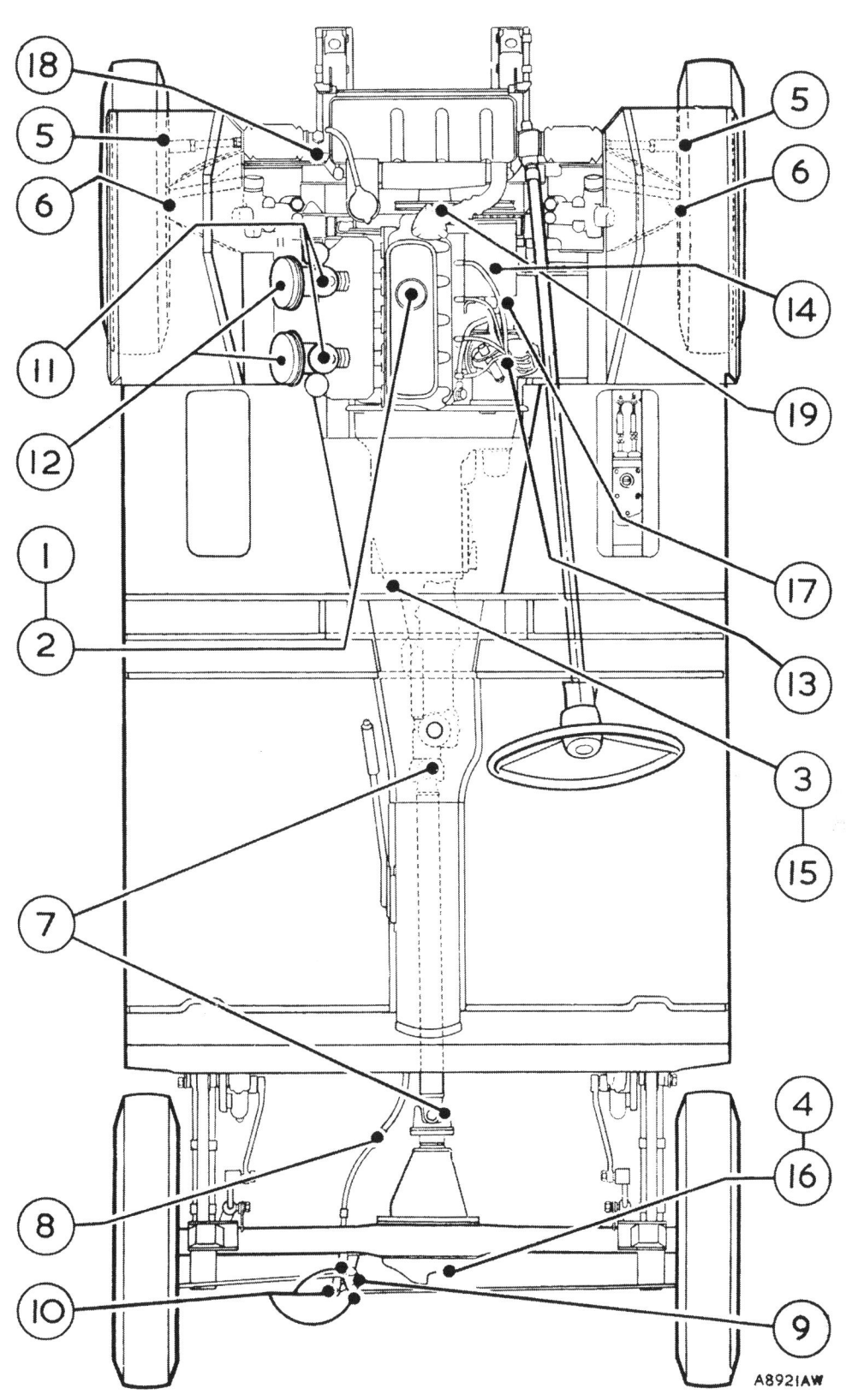

Austin-Healey Sprite Mk. 1. Issue 4. 50312

© **Copyright British Motor Corporation Limited 1960
and Brooklands Books Limited 1984 and 2007**

This book is published by Brooklands Books Limited and based upon text
and illustrations protected by copyright and first published in 1960 by
The British Motor Corporation Limited and may not be
reproduced transmitted or copied by any means without the
prior written permission of Rover Group Limited and
Brooklands Books Limited.

Printed and distributed by Brooklands Books Ltd., PO Box 146, Cobham,
Surrey KT11 1LG, England Phone: 01932 865051 Fax: 01932 868803
E-mail: sales@brooklands-books.com   www.brooklands-books.com

Part Number: AKD 4884

ISBN: 9781855201262   Ref: A13WH   2241/11T3

Printed in Great Britain
by Amazon